# JOSEPH KOOT

# EUROPE, ONE STEP AT A TIME

Clifftop
Sackville
New Brunswick
Canada

Third Printing, 2020

Joseph Koot
101 – 15 York Street
Sackville NB
E4L 4R3
Canada

koot.joseph@gmail.com

ISBN 978-0-9936085-1-3

**Dedication**

With thanks to

My late brother Bill who helped prepare me for this trek

My wife Joanne who supported it unconditionally

# Acknowledgements

I am grateful to Joanne for her encouragement and for suggestions as the narrative unfolded. Friends and family were concerned for Joanne while I travelled, and I appreciate their thoughtfulness.

Thank you to the people at the National Post newspaper for publishing my reports during the first two hikes. This provided the push to document my adventure.

Ed Colquhoun, Gene Goodrich and Liz Hulsman read a rough draft of the first few chapters and gave me direction that helped set the flow of this book. Gerry Bartlett reviewed a final draft, giving me the confidence to send it to the printer.

I recognize librarians throughout Europe who helped me access computers for my blog entries. Many individuals went out of their way so I could type my anecdotes, sometimes letting me use their own laptops.

The people of Europe were helpful, considerate and patient with me. After all, I was a stranger walking through their lives.

# Contents

Foreword

# Foreword

In my book "Looking for Bill, Finding Myself," I told the story of my childhood – my early years in the Netherlands, my boyhood on an Ontario farm and my teen years in a minor seminary. My childhood ended with the death of my brother Bill under a tractor when we were alone in a back field. That memoir came out of analyzing my youth while struggling to face up to my relationship with Bill.

My search intensified during the journey that took me across Europe on foot. The rhythm of walking forced my mind to explore old feelings – powerlessness as the youngest of a dozen children, confusion about my seven-year path toward the priesthood and bitterness toward the aggressiveness of my brother Bill. "Europe, One Step at a Time" is the account of that quest.

The material for this book is based on the blog "oldkootwalking" that was my chronicle of the journey. I have not provided pictures in this book, but a computer search engine can give the reader photos of the buildings, scenery and trails I describe.

In crossing Europe, I passed through a number of languages, all of which – except Dutch and French – were unfamiliar. I have given the highlights of conversations as direct quotations in clear English although they might have been said in another language or in more hesitant English.

Though I covered every step from Portugal to Estonia, I didn't always go in a northeasterly direction. On the main

Camino pilgrimage route in northern Spain, for example, I joined in the flow of hikers heading west.

At the end of the journey, I was a different person than I had been at its beginning. Over the six years and 6,000 kilometres, I changed, and this change is reflected in my writing style. Each of my six trips held a unique set of experiences; each country presented its challenges and delights.

# Trip 1: Dream to Nightmare

*September 13 to September 28, 2007 – 176 kilometres*
*Cabo de São Vicente northeast to Aljustrel, Portugal*

**Innocence**
"I'd like to go for a walk. Across Europe."

My dream had started as a fantasy of hiking through Canada when I read of people walking the tracks from Atlantic to Pacific in the early days of our national railway. But crossing Canada was out of the question: in sparsely populated areas, distances between towns would leave me short of food and water.

How about Europe? The map showed few empty spaces, so it looked feasible. Cabo de São Vicente in Portugal's southwest could be the starting point; Narva-Jõesuu in Estonia's northeast would be my goal. I simply needed to stroll from one to the other.

When I retired, I had the time to fulfill this fantasy. Joanne believes in making dreams reality and commented: "You've often talked about walking across Europe. Why not try it?"

And I thought to myself, "Why not? It could be fun." And it would be – for the first 176 kilometres.

I take my new hiking socks from the shopping bag and feel their soft texture: it should help prevent blisters. I place them on the bed and take another look at my list. Our five children have left home, and their bedrooms have become guest rooms. Now a bed is the gathering spot for my "stuff" – a backpack, hip pack, tent and sleeping bag. In visualizing my hike, I have seen myself pulling a cart across Canada, not carrying a knapsack across Europe. My choice of land mass has changed and so has the means of transport: using a cart would be less weighty but more awkward, and I opt for the freedom that comes with carrying necessities on my back.

Now a pedometer, first aid kit, aluminum hiking poles, toiletries and map of southern Portugal go in the backpack. At the local Canadian Tire store, I have purchased a plastic compass, complete with whistle and magnifying glass. I realize my hike will become a search – looking for roads that head in the right direction, finding my way through cities, locating a place to spend the night – and the compass can help guide me through this.

The search will also be an exploration of my life while free to ramble without responsibility for others, whether at home as a parent or at work as a supervisor. Without the constraints of daily life, my mind will be open; it will be limited only by the expectations of the trail.

Whether in my childhood, adolescence or adult years, I have felt alone within a group. People seem surprised that I am travelling by myself, but it's how I feel most comfortable. I have not been one to show spontaneity, and now I can stop worrying about reacting with enough enthusiasm over the delightful moments of my hike. Instead, on my own, I can turn my energy toward perseverance while completely dependent on myself. This hike will meet my needs on many levels – a chance to be alone, to think, to work on my memoir, to appreciate Europe and to live a teenage freedom I missed in my life at the seminary. In that sense, my goal is not Estonia but the hike itself.

I pack two t-shirts, two pairs of shorts, long trousers, a light jacket as well as three pairs of socks and underwear. Each item is carefully chosen, not for style or colour but by weight and usefulness. How often will I need it? Should I buy it overseas? Can it be washed by hand? I have placed items on the bed and removed others till I'm sure of a compact load.

I add Canada lapel pins, key tags and bookmarks – souvenirs to dispense in my travels. I'll leave the iPod behind in favour of local sounds and the fall breeze. I take a digital camera but no books as they add weight and I'll be busy composing my own narrative. Instead of taking a laptop, I'll use libraries or Internet cafés for entries into my "oldkootwalking" blog and for weekly updates to the National Post newspaper.

My life will be reduced to the 15 kilograms I carry on my back. My work as a nurse manager in Canada's prisons has given me a reasonable income. Now house, car and furniture will be left behind. Signs of success will mean nothing in my struggle with the trail. A routine of walking, swimming and yoga – as well as medical and dental appointments – should help ensure a worry-free trip.

During the summer months, Moncton is favoured with a direct flight to Paris. From there I'll count on one of those dependable European trains to get me to southwest Portugal. A campground or hostel will give me time to acclimatize and to chat with other walkers. Then I can start my dream of hiking across Europe in instalments over the next few years. I'm not booking a return flight as this amble could continue for a month and a half, taking me through Portugal and most of Spain. Or I might come to my senses and fly home next week. Eventually I could get to Estonia. At that point I would need to decide on a southeasterly crossing from Denmark to Greece, but that's 10 million steps in the future.

Joanne and I share a final kiss at Moncton Airport as she proceeds to her job as schoolteacher. Her work life continues; my travels begin. Sixty years ago my family took the immigrant ship Sibajak from Europe to find hope in Canada. Now I shall miss my life in Canada as I look for myself in Europe, as I look through old memories that continue to haunt me.

When I land, an information desk advises me that no long-distance trains run from Orly airport, so I need to go into Paris to see a travel agent. I question this and approach a travel kiosk a few desks over. As quickly as you can say, *"Croque-monsieur,"* I am provided with train tickets to Lagos, Portugal. I shake my head at this first mystery on my European adventure.

After a disruptive passenger is escorted from the train, we speed through France without incident and switch to an overnight train upon entering Spain. In the lethargy of travel, we are directed to lug our bags to a security scanner in response to Basque separatist threats. Our sleeping car holds six bunks, three stacked against each wall. My cot is a top one, placing me two metres in the air. In a lower bed across from me, a German engineering student is heading for Portugal's shores in a break from his studies. He says little and busies himself with his phone.

An English-speaking group of four young men arrive to occupy the remaining beds in our car. Unfortunately, their tickets show the wrong date, and the conductor says he needs to hold the bunks for others who may have booked them. They moan: "Our travel agent didn't know what he was doing." Now they are doomed to spend the night upright in a regular train seat when they had paid the extra for a bunk. By bedtime no one else has shown up, and I am tempted to find this group and have them sneak into our compartment. But it could lead to questions that would be tough to answer in this foreign language, so I think better of it.

At a stop through the night, I rush past the passengers out for a smoke so I can catch a photo of the town's sign, "Fatima." Our Catholic mythology told us the Blessed Virgin Mary had appeared to three Portuguese children from this area. As an adult I think more critically, but childhood religious fervour is not easily dismissed. So begins a series of connections between my Catholic upbringing and the Catholic traditions of Europe. And each time I squirm as I dig through memories of childhood's magical beliefs that would lead us to heaven.

Up in my bunk, I close my eyes, and the rhythm and rumble of this slow overnight train carry us through the darkness. Squeezed under the ceiling, my happy reveries become: "Don't fall out of bed! Don't fall out of bed!" I make it to morning intact and drink in the new day from the platform at the end of the train. Woods, streams and farms zip by and slide into a vanishing point as I anticipate hiking northeastward through this countryside.

Lagos, Portugal is bustling with students, and I am sent to an overflow hostel. Our building backs onto Rising Cock Hostel whose music and beer make it the centre of the party scene. I learn nothing from fellow travellers to help in my endless trek. They are a friendly international group but have other pastimes in mind: hiking is not their priority.

I take the bus to a campground in Salema where the staff's ease with five or six languages puts Canadian bilingualism issues to shame. In a British accent, a fellow camper says, "The hike will make you the healthiest person in the churchyard," and I hope he's talking about my death in old age. Another bus delivers me to a campground in Sagres, six kilometres from the starting point of my trek.

The intense sunshine, brief twilight and subtropical scenery indicate how far south I've gone, and it's northeast from here. As I type my blog entry at an Internet café, the keyboard is a tangle of accent options, and ants scurry across the keys. They have also invaded my tent and think nothing of disrupting my sleep.

I phone home to let Joanne know I'm about to start my hike across the continent. I'll leave my things in the tent and walk six kilometres southward to my starting point at Cabo de São Vicente. I ponder whether it's cheating to begin without the burden of a backpack, but Joanne assures me, "It's the walking you're after, not the carrying."

This becomes the first of many decisions that lead me to concentrate on the hiking and ignore other details. For example, it will be okay to take the train to a further point and walk back – west or south – for a section even though my journey is taking me northeast through Europe. This leaves me with only two rules: I need to walk each step across the continent; I need to take notes along the way.

## Beginnings

On September 18, 2007, I feel giddy in sauntering down the country road from Sagres to Cabo de São Vicente where my hike across Europe is about to start. I find it difficult to make my way through the crowds gathered to wish me well, or so I imagine. Actually, no one is there for me. Instead, they are tourist groups visiting tacky stands for souvenirs and food. One of these advertises, "The last bratwurst before America," while I'm about to tackle Europe.

The cape lighthouse is perched on a sheer cliff. A security fence limits access to Europe's southwesternmost point, so I lean against the barrier and get a tourist to take my picture. And I think: "So this is it! Here it begins." I discover a secluded beach nearby and remove hiking boots and socks to dunk my feet in the ocean as the tangible start of my journey.

The area between Cabo de São Vicente and Sagres mirrors the barren roughness of Iqaluit on Baffin Island in Canada's Arctic. I stop at the Sagres campground to retrieve my tent and gear, and I'm on my way. As I veer away from the coast, the desert hills become an Arizona cowboy movie set. Then, over the next rise, a tractor is cultivating a field. I'm astonished at how quickly the land changes from barren to lush, from desolate to arable. Even at a walking pace, I pass through one microclimate after the other.

I arrive in Vila do Bispo and stop at its café for supper. The owner has no suggestions as to where I might camp for the night. In gestures sprinkled with a few English words, she mentions a field she owns at the edge of town. It's a few blocks away, and she interrupts her adult son's supper so he can walk me there. With its Canada-flag design, my tent is far from camouflaged, but a growth of bamboo gives me privacy from the road. I settle in for the night and wonder how I'm going to be lucky enough to find a spot like this every evening. By five in the morning, roosters crow from all directions, and that's the end of my slumber.

Along the Atlantic shore near Carrapateira, I make my way down to the beach. Jagged tan-coloured cliffs look impressive on camera, and they serve as backdrop to powdery sand. The waves churn constantly, and I admire the prowess of the surfers among the breakers. I camp next to a Spanish group who leave me the rest of a bottle of rum and armfuls of canned food: "Our mothers won't want this at home."

Two German medical students ask me to watch their surfboard as they head into town for dinner. I perch on a log to gaze at a Portuguese sunset, watch a German surfboard and get bleary-eyed on Spanish rum. When alone, I spend hours reviewing the course of my life as grist for my memoir, but I've had only momentary glimpses on this hike. Instead, I've been consumed with practical issues – which road to follow, what to eat and where to spend the night. Now the rum works its magic, and I sink into reveries; but they are not productive since they are about nothing in particular. I realize I'm falling asleep on that log, so I unzip my tent and slide into my sleeping bag as I sink into oblivion.

The rising sun lights my tent, and I check on the German surfers. They are still asleep, so I leave two Canada lapel pins on the surfboard. On my way out of the campground, I take the extra food to the colony of young families housed in vans in the parking lot. A sleepy-eyed father stoops to answer my knock while his unkempt daughter plays on the floor. He seems more confused than grateful at this offer of a dozen cans of food so early in the morning. It's a bright day; I feel invigorated and take off at a trot.

Portuguese houses and businesses are tidy, and I take several pictures. White stucco houses with red tile roofs are accented with bright doorways and windows: each community has its own colour palette. However, public spaces are cluttered with debris, and I explore the reason I find this unsettling. My reaction stems from my parents' diligence as they were both fussy – Dad in the barn, Mom in the house.

They would have appreciated the attention paid to Portuguese homes but would have expressed Dutch disdain for public areas, *"Die zijn echt slordig"* ("They are really untidy").

Many of these busy roads have no shoulders, and I am forced into the ditch, which is a receptacle for used water bottles flung from passing cars. Meanwhile drivers respond to this lone hiker with pleasant waves or irritating long honks. Barking is constant, but dogs are always on a leash or behind a gate, whether that of a modest house or an extravagant wine estate. Though annoying, dogs have not been a threat. The edge of the roadway is a graveyard for birds, and I realize the roadside has become my life.

Despite uphill climbs, it's not the walking that gets to you – it's the stopping. Each afternoon I search out a place to spend the night. Real campgrounds are few and far between, so I look for seashores, churches and parks. The people are supportive but reluctant to offer their yard for the night. In the mornings I sweep sand out of my tent, do a yoga session and repack my load.

I live on bread, cheese, fruit and water but find treasures like a sparkling bakery in Rogil where the rolls and coffee are delicious. A truck stop features scraps of pork cooked in oil and tasting better than they look as this dish is reminiscent of the Dutch *kaantjes* (cracklings) of my youth.

As I leave the truck stop, I meet a young couple along the road with right arm extended and thumb up. They have knapsacks and tell me they are hitchhiking through Portugal, "We're going to Lisbon next." For a moment I think they may be right: that's the way to travel through Europe. Before I clear the next hill, I look behind me, and they are statues in the distance while I march on.

My impressions so far – the people are friendly, I'm adapting to sweaty clothes and I've never drunk so much water in my life. I've reorganized my load to make life on the trail simpler, and my hip pack now holds camera, note booklet with pen, panic alarm, and Canada lapel pins but most precious is the water bottle in its netting on the front of this satchel. I carry an extra bottle of water in my backpack, estimating that I need one litre for every 10 kilometres of hiking. As well, in the quest to slake my thirst, I recognize the Delta Cafés and their draft beer as my new golden arches.

I enjoy the attention of entering an eatery and being the new stranger in town. In a café in São Teotónio, an elderly man, driving a black sports car, arrives for his afternoon cup of tea. In perfect English he asks about my hike and says he may have joined me if he were 20 years younger.

Greeting older people – *"Boa tarde"* ("Good afternoon") – ensures a warm reply. Other than the simple pleasantries, I am unsure of the rules of conduct, and it's challenging never to be in the same place twice. I'm always passing through, always the stranger, always looking for a place to stop for the night.

At the same time, I'm learning how to walk through Europe, a series of lessons with no curriculum. In the first country of my journey, I try things like walking certain distances, choosing food in grocery stores, using gestures in restaurants and managing a heavy knapsack. And I hope these things work and that nothing will go wrong – and, so far, it hasn't.

Near Odemira I notice a roadside park next to a farm field. A young man bikes up and tells me, "Put up your tent when it's dark, and no one will know you are here." I set my tent out of view behind a barbecue and appreciate the lush grass – the first I've seen in Portugal. I'm falling asleep when I hear a car pull in. Thinking I've been "busted," I get ready to face the police. Instead, I hear the voices of a young couple talking about whatever young couples talk about.

My dozing is again disturbed at 2:00 a.m. when irrigation channels start filling nearby cisterns. The park's sprinkler system starts up, and my tent becomes its target. It's wet for the first time. I feel the spray through the nylon, but it withstands the assault.

The next morning I snap a picture of a carpet of green stretching across a valley. These are the irrigated fields of watercress, arugula and spinach of the Vitacress Company. It's my first view of such abundance in Portugal, but a kilometre later I am back to a dry landscape.

I had not predicted the stretches between towns. In much of Europe, one community runs into the next, but the towns of southern Portugal have definite boundaries. With few houses out in the country, it proves to be a solitary walk. My companions become the newts scurrying through the ditches and the frogs in the odd puddle.

At Santa Luzia I pitch my tent beside the church, shielded from view by a board fence. I can be seen only by those taking their garbage to the container at the corner of the churchyard. In the quiet evening, the garbage bin clatters shut, and an elderly woman saunters back to her house. She says not a word and looks straight ahead as though I'm not there. She doesn't report me for trespassing, and I have a restful sleep. In the morning I join those stopping at a bar for coffee on their way to work, and I set off refreshed.

**Threat**

I stop to talk to a farmer struggling with an irrigation pipe. We cannot understand each other's words, but his gestures are clear in refusing to join me on this venture. He mounts his big blue tractor and hurries on his way. I look back at his modern machine and realize this trek will keep reminding me of my past, including the grey Ford-Ferguson tractor that haunts my thoughts. Once again, I run through the script I have reviewed so often.

*"We had an immense yellow and orange Case tractor and a mid-sized red Massey-Harris, but Bill chose one of our two smaller Ford-Ferguson tractors for us to ride to a back field. I was a 14-year-old with a childhood of being teased and beaten up by this 16-year-old brother. At other times we had a close bond, and now he needed my help to get our pick-up truck that was stuck in a muddy spot. Bill attached a chain from the front of the truck to a bolt just under the tractor seat. He climbed onto the tractor, and I got into the truck. The*

*tractor was to pull the truck forward slowly, but the chain was attached too high on the tractor, and its front wheels rose into the air. The front wheels bounced, the machine reared and Bill fell backward to the ground. The tractor flipped and landed on him, and he was gone."*

My brother had decided not to return to school after Grade Ten: "That's enough education for me. I want to stay home on the farm." He was learning what to feed a cow so it gave more milk. He knew how to fix the hay baler when it broke. He was sure of wanting to be a farmer while I had dreams of becoming a priest. Suddenly he was gone forever, and I am here to walk through the memories. I'm awakening to the truth that this is not just an adventure; it's become a tussle with my past.

Suddenly new beatings join old ones when, halfway across southern Portugal, I stop in the town of Aljustrel for the evening. A park in front of a seniors' home is a convenient place to spend the night. Older people are enjoying the flowers and shrubbery. As dusk arrives, they leave, and I set up my tent behind a hedge. As I doze off, voices disturb my slumber. Then a group in their late teens and early twenties start asking harassing questions. They want to know how much money I have and whether I have drugs with me. Their tone of voice is threatening. The air and their behaviour smell of drug use.

Soon the dozen people also include a few women and children. In recounting this incident, I have been asked repeatedly whether these were Roma ("Gypsy") people. I have no reason to think they were. Other than the stylish clothes of their leader, they looked like a bunch of local thugs. I could become their victim as an obvious minority – a lone hiker who looked different and didn't speak their language, much as Bill had picked on me as a "loner" who sounded studious and was different from other farm boys. I had survived Bill's assaults and could survive this as well.

I realize I must have invaded this group's "turf" and prepare to leave. In the twilight of a distant street lamp, I pack up while trying to maintain a cool composure. One of the women asks me in clear English: "Where are you going to sleep? You don't have a place to go, and it's late at night."

I reply: "I'll just keep walking. I have to get out of here."

I put on my knapsack and head for the steps leading up to the street. The group leader takes one of my hiking poles from me and starts discussing it with others. In his foreign chatter, he uses the word, "Weapon," as he feels its point. I fear I am being chosen as the victim for their drug-addled brains, so I grab the stick, but he holds on. My defiance is a challenge, and one of them jumps me from behind.

Wearing a heavy backpack does not allow me to run, and I fall forward at the bottom of the cement steps. I have the presence of mind to pull the pin on my alarm and throw it as it screeches into the night, but no one comes to my aid from the nearby houses. Four or five thugs punch the back of my head and kick my ribs, arms and legs. I yell, "Stop it." Then, "Help! Help! Help!" I scream till I'm hoarse, but no help comes. I feel them tug at my backpack and hip pack as knives slash the straps. They run off with my belongings – tent, clothes, camera and personal items. I have survived but feel so alone.

I am left with my watch, a flashlight and battered glasses. They also fail to take my money belt in which credit card and passport are hidden under my clothing. My nose is bleeding onto my shirt, and I'm a mess.

I find my way to the police station and give a statement. The presence of those thugs is news to the police: "Nothing like that ever happens here." An ambulance team drives me to the hospital in Castro Verde for a check-up and x-rays of my ribs. I have no broken bones but lots of pain, scratches and bruising. I welcome the staff's support as I cry tears of grief at having been robbed of my adventure.

The ambulance people say they have a cot where I can spend the night. They change their minds and say they have no room, but I can stay at the police station. However, the police say they have no authorization for me to stay with them. An officer takes me to the two guest houses in town, but neither has a vacancy. One look at me, and they hesitate in taking me in for the night.

I'm desperate to be on the 8:50 bus to Lisbon Airport the next morning. The police officer suggests I seek shelter in an unfinished apartment building across from the bus depot. It's a useful suggestion but hardly the stuff of a caring community. The officer drops me off at a pay phone near the bus station so I can let Joanne know what has happened. Then I am alone and worried that the group will see me and continue its pummelling.

In the unfinished building, I get progressively colder in my shorts and t-shirt as I lie on bags of cement and try to fall asleep: my dream has become a nightmare. An unfinished closet gives some shelter from the cool breeze, and I doze fitfully. It's a tough night, and – thankfully – the bus depot opens early. When the clerk arrives at 6:30, I clean up in the washroom. The bus to Lisbon pulls in, and I board without luggage.

At Lisbon Airport I wander among the hive of airline desks to search out a route home, but no one can get me there. I phone our Canadian Automobile Association office in Moncton. Twenty minutes later they have a route for me, and I board a plane for Heathrow immediately. My seatmate is a London businessman who takes a look at my blood-spattered shirt and asks: "Do you need money?" I appreciate his concern but assure him I still have my credit card.

We land at Heathrow Airport, and I have just enough time to buy a new shirt and to board for Toronto. I'm beginning to tremble, and a compassionate Air Canada employee brings me coffee and a blanket. On the plane they move other passengers so I can stretch out on a row of seats.

With a lack of phone information, British pounds and time between flights – and considering time zone differences with home – I did not follow my phone call from Aljustrel with another while on my way back. This lack of a second call caused Joanne needless worry and served as a tough lesson:

either follow up with a second call or delay the first call till close to home.

I spend a second uncomfortable night – this one at Toronto Airport. Sprawled across an unforgiving bench, I catch a nap alongside a few stranded passengers. The monorail that runs between terminals is being upgraded, and at two in the morning the technician is eager to take a break and tell me how the system works. I catch a bit more sleep and, in the early morning hours, board a flight home to Moncton. On seeing Joanne at the airport, I feel a surge of wishing things had gone differently while grateful to be home and safe.

When I left home two weeks ago, I was in sound shape. Now I return with pain in a right rib, a swollen left arm and scrapes on my arms and legs. My nose is tender: it must have hit the cement steps as they punched the back of my head. I am surprised at my calmness in discussing the incident. The opportunity to talk, cry and write about it has been helpful.

A visit to our hospital's outpatient department ensures I am mending, and I seek out a counsellor to help me review my response and deal with the grief. He consoles me: "You used your alarm and called for help. That shows you stayed in control and didn't become their victim." His advice helps me resolve the distress. It seems common to have a nighttime dream about being unable to move or call for help when under attack. I have also had those dreams and was now relieved to know that, when required, I could take action. I was outnumbered but not defeated.

That group may have taken my possessions, but they couldn't rob me of my resolve. In fact, they strengthened motivation that had lain dormant. When I started, I lacked both confidence and determination as the hike was a dream, a lark. I wanted to walk across Europe but wasn't sure if I could. It would be a trial marriage of the path and me: I'd attempt it; if I didn't like it, I'd go home. After Aljustrel I became motivated and knew I had a claim to this, just as everyone else has rights. Now I had to find a safer way to travel, but nothing could stop me.

The incident lifted the scab off childhood wounds that had never healed. The walk would be a pilgrimage, a search for meaning: hiking across Europe was to become a walk through my life. When Bill died, I lost my focus; I regained it after my beating in Aljustrel. Continuing after the assault was as purposeful as anything I've done in my adult life. Nothing pushed me forward like my walk across Europe, but I would have to dig deep into myself for the resources to continue day after day. I had had negative experience in my life, and now I was driven to make this undertaking a positive. It would become an athletic drive of Olympic proportions.

On two counts I have to thank my brother Bill: our life together taught me I could survive aggression, and his death showed me I could overcome grief. Fifty years earlier Bill prepared me for the group in Aljustrel, Portugal. In that distant mirror, I'm a sensitive lad, so easily hurt. Now I'm a toughened adult, determined to succeed.

# Trip 2: Dare to Continue

*May 18 to June 20, 2008 – 392 kilometres*
*Aljustrel, Portugal northeast to Badajoz, Spain (256 km)*
*Mérida north to Cáceres, Spain (77 km)*
*Mérida west to Badajoz, Spain (59 km)*

**Grit**

In the first 176 kilometres through Portugal I was like a player in a travel film: every day brought new scenery, new experiences. Unfortunately, they were overshadowed by my exposure to the criminal element and my use of Portugal's police and health services. Leaving all that in the past, I'm starting over.

I'm determined to continue the trek, Joanne is supportive of my return and people are encouraging: "You have to get right back on that horse" and "If you don't continue, you'll always wonder." But they must find my notions baffling, and I wish I had a simple explanation. At times persistence takes over where good judgment leaves off. If only I could simply climb a mountain: that's a dream people seem to understand.

Normally, travel involves plans, hopes and wishes while my solitary trek is all about daydreams and nostalgia. I want to be open to the dreams and face the memories, to come to terms with the past. The energy I put into the repetitive action of walking leaves my mind free to review old hurts and to resolve old anxieties.

17

I look forward to discovering how this adventure unfolds. I'll have worries about food and water, disorientation around people and places, hours of loneliness and moments of self-doubt. I can't wait to get started.

What is it like going back? I feel surprisingly relaxed, but I'll be more cautious of groups that may be up to no good. More streetwise, I'll stick to tenting in people's yards or in official campgrounds. A piece of camouflage fabric will help conceal my tent, should that be required. Cellphone reception may not be constant, so a rented satellite phone with flexible solar panel will help keep Joanne informed along the way. I embarked on an Internet search for this gadget all over the USA only to find it at DownEast Communications in nearby Halifax. This was meant to be: I was meant to keep hiking.

Gone are the photos of my starting point at Cabo de São Vicente. Gone are the notes of my progress and my digital camera. The loss of those items has freed me from having to do things exactly right: now I can be more relaxed about details. My photographs don't need to become a documentary; instead, I'm taking a disposable camera to catch a few highlights.

My Aeroplan Miles are sufficient to get me to Europe and back. I'll fly to Lisbon, stay in a hostel for a day or two and take the bus to Aljustrel. Starting in the morning at the park where I was assaulted, I'll begin walking – and walking and walking. A month later I'll fly home from Madrid, Spain.

Moncton, Toronto, London-Heathrow, Lisbon – I home in on my starting point at Aljustrel, Portugal with a mixture of feelings. I'm uneasy about returning to the spot that caused me so much anguish, but I'm eager to start the hike again and reclaim what had been snatched from me. The 45-minute walk between gates at Heathrow Airport serves as my warm-up exercise. A dizzying escalator prepares me for the fear of heights I'll experience in crossing high bridges.

At the Lisbon hostel, I recognize Leslie Feist's catchy tune "1, 2, 3, 4" on the sound system and feel comfort in the familiarity of Canadian voices that break through the American music mix. I find a lounge area on the second floor and say hello to a young man writing postcards home. He is from Japan and grins at his own folly: "I went to visit South Korea and couldn't stop. I haven't been home for two years." He's explored the Orient, North America, the Middle East and now Europe. And I thought I was determined!

To confirm my drive, I need to start my wanderings at the park where I was assaulted. The Lisbon bus doesn't arrive in Aljustrel till 4:00 p.m. – too late to start a day's hike. After my last experience, I want to avoid another night in Aljustrel, so I opt to travel to Beja, a small city with frequent bus service to neighbouring towns. There I can come to terms with thoughts about returning where I left off eight months ago, and I can catch the morning bus to Aljustrel.

Arriving in Beja, I go for an evening stroll, and a well-dressed woman approaches. She helps herself to a last candy and tosses the packaging to the ground. I had wondered what was the source of all the litter; now it is clear. I appreciate towns that are clean and find troubling those that show a lack of care. Through the messy streets, I return to the hostel and prepare for bed. It could be an unsettled night: I'll be alone in my musings as to why I'm doing this; I'll be alone in facing my demons waiting in Aljustrel. Nighttimes can be long and lonely. From a fitful sleep, I awaken at dawn to come to terms with the assault of eight months ago.

With my backpack at my feet, I wait at a downtown curb for the bus to Aljustrel and observe the morning's greeting ritual. As they walk to work or school, men shake hands with friends they meet on the way. This means a brief handshake, a few words and a quick departure. It's a pleasant way to start the day, but the number of greetings is endless. No one shakes my hand: I'm a stranger in this foreign land.

From Beja I make it to Aljustrel at 10:00 a.m. The bus depot hasn't changed since that fateful night last September. Across the road is the building where I shivered through the night; it has become home to several families. I set out to look for the park, but things become confusing: all the streets seem to run in circles. I follow a roadway that twists and turns before

19

veering back toward the bus depot. "It's daring me to continue on to the park," I muse. Several people are stumped by my question about the location of the park till I realize they call it a *"jardim"* ("garden"), and they point me in the general direction.

A cluster of high school students is out chatting with their teacher. When I address the teacher in English, the students raise their eyebrows and turn toward him as though to say, "Okay, let's see how good your English really is." He gives me general instructions, but they are hard to follow. As I walk away, Sara, Anna and Miguel run up and happily offer to miss the start of their next class so they can be my guides.

What a difference – being accompanied by these delightful teens in daylight to visit that peaceful *"Jardim 25 de Abril"* ("Garden of the 25th of April"). My resentment toward a town where half a dozen men had beaten and robbed me begins to fade. From this strange traveller, they get mementos of Canada and a fascinating tale for their classmates.

I stop at an optometrist's office for a screwdriver to set my panic alarm. The amiable clerk adjusts the gadget for me, and I appreciate this twist of fate. She is setting my alarm as I prepare to leave Aljustrel – the town where I had used my alarm, but no one responded. At the edge of the community, I glimpse a gas station attendant up ahead. This woman, who had spent time in Switzerland, gives me directions in enthusiastic French, and I continue down the road, leaving Aljustrel as a memory.

**Apprehension**

As I head north toward Ferreira do Alentejo, nature lifts me out of my doldrums. The twitter of birds animates the rolling hills, and I snap pictures of roadside clumps of cacti alternating with the yellow blossoms of broom bushes. Olive groves are interspersed with fields of barley as well as acres of sunflower plants that will look spectacular when they blossom. I feel comfortable in this pleasant countryside though negative thoughts are ready to bubble to the surface.

The price for my return to walking through Europe is the burden of the satellite phone. It weighs several kilograms, and its solar panel is bulky, but only with this ready contact with Joanne can I continue my venture. I decide to make the extra load worthwhile by using it from time to time although most downtown areas feature phone booths. In my first call using the satellite phone, Joanne is busy in her classroom, so I leave a message that things are going well. A flock of sheep moves in for a closer look at this odd hiker talking into a strange contraption.

After the incident in Aljustrel, the unexpected has bothered me, and now I feel uneasy about a distant grinding sound. Ten minutes later I arrive at its source – a square metal building whose Portuguese sign indicates it is an olive oil extraction plant. It's nothing to be afraid of, and I'm pleased to see that the oil is processed here, supporting the local economy.

It is now late afternoon and time to look for a spot to tent for the night. Up a side road, I see an elderly couple in their yard and approach them to ask about camping on their property. They use animated gestures to suggest I cross the road and go down a laneway. I have no idea why I need to do this, but they seem like trustworthy people. Sometimes you just need to trust, but I do wish I'd learned more Portuguese before crossing the ocean.

As it turns out, the lane leads to a community of British expatriates. The founder of this group explains, "My wife and I happened to drive through the area, and we thought it was a perfect spot to retire." Other couples joined them to form this grouping of four neat houses. A safe night on their lawn is interrupted only by the eerie squawks of ostriches in a nearby farm field. A morning chat over coffee and toast on the front porch sends me on my way refreshed.

A store clerk tells me of a campground that is on my route, and it becomes my day's goal. An exhausting trek of 30 kilometres leads me to this haven with its Dutch owner and international clientele. The complex boasts two restaurants, laundry facilities and freshly baked bread. This is a chance to practise the language of my childhood as I was born in the Netherlands and immigrated to Canada when five years of age. My Dutch conversation quickly loses its rustiness, and I get a sense of comfort in those memorable sounds. Now, on my second day in this sanctuary, a torrent of rain against the restaurant windows tells me I've chosen wisely.

Over a bottle of wine, Hans and I chat into the evening. We relax in lawn chairs on the patio of his trailer overlooking the lake. This fellow camper – also in his retirement years – has stories to share about the recent deaths of two loved ones. I am sensitive to the hurt caused by death as I have been left as the only boy in our family. As his Dutch drones on, I muse on my endurance. I had four brothers: Wimpie drowned as a toddler; Bill died under that tractor in his teens; John and Tony died of cancer in their mid-fifties, still much too young. I had four brothers; now I have none.

As we reminisce, the bottle empties, and my Dutch improves. We start into a second bottle but won't be finishing it tonight. We need our rest, and those roosters will be up early. After our comforting chat over love and loss, I hobble back to my tent and slide into a sound sleep.

Within my little world, business realities still arise, and this campground does not accept credit card payment from non-Europeans. A Dutch friend of the owner offers a car ride back to the cash machine in Odivelas, and I joke to myself, "Now I'm really driven to walk." Then he drops me off at the entrance to the campground, and I struggle on.

In the Hospedaria A Varanda in Alvito I seek shelter from the elements and a chance to be spoiled after nights in a tent. The owner of this inn looks after every detail – registering me, cooking my meals and giving me information about the community. He takes pride in his display of artwork and in the menu that follows the local tradition. The stewed rabbit and grilled pork are delicious, and a night's stay is nowhere near the hundreds of dollars charged at the *pousada* (historical hotel) in a castle across the street. My weekly article in the

National Post newspaper is due, and I'm "stuck" at this inn for two days waiting for the town library to open so I can use its computer.

I seek comfort through the rituals of my Catholic faith in the local church that shows hints of past glory. Statues are crumbling, and paintings on the ceiling are unrecognizable – so much art, so little money. Before Sunday Mass a woman whispers that she has a sister in Sarnia, Ontario. "So do I!" comes my startled reply, and I think of my five sisters whose only surviving brother is tramping the roads of Europe. The liturgy transports me home when it is surprisingly similar to ours back in New Brunswick. The language barrier lifts, and I feel at ease in the celebration of the Mass.

When feet are the sole mode of transportation, you worry about every ache. When my evening sandals annoy my right little toe, I place them in a garbage bin along the way. Now that irritant has become a corn, and the woman at the *farmacia* (pharmacy) sells me a box of corn plasters. They have to work: I can't let anything stop me in my campaign.

As I approach Viana do Alentejo, a rainstorm forces me to take refuge in the shelter of trees. My jacket offers resistance to a drizzle but not to a downpour, so I arrive in the town cold and uncomfortable and eager for shelter. A gas station attendant suggests the *quartos* (rooms) owned by Maria de Jésus, and I set out in search of them.

I approach Maria's wooden gate, ring the bell and let out a gasp as a haggard face appears beside me at an open window. It is that of Maria's mother, and – in breakneck Portuguese and with gestures toward town – she explains that I need to see her daughter and describes where she is working.

After a search of a few blocks, I return to the *quartos* for more details from the mother. The hope of a bed for the night stays out of reach when the gate in front of me opens and I come face to face with another Dutchman. He teaches at a nearby pilot school and rents a room from Maria. He takes me to see her in the flower shop where she works, and I'm relieved to have a bed for the night.

After supper at a café, he and I relax on the balcony at our *quartos* where Scotch whiskey helps give our Dutch a hint of silliness. He remarks on a phone message from his wife in the Netherlands, *"Zij heeft een dressoir gekocht"* ("She bought a chest of drawers"). Then she managed to get it into the trunk of her car and take it home. He thinks this is terrific – that his wife buy a piece of furniture on her own and get it home without his help. She is doing fine on her own, but he wishes he were home. He had accepted the job of teaching future pilots at a nearby college so he could benefit from Portugal's hot summer. Instead, it's been cold and rainy, and he's tired of it.

I feel the hollowness of my own longing for home while yellow, white and mauve field flowers try to lift my spirits on the way to Évora. The countryside is now more active – a group of men working here, farm tractors there. A steep climb brings me to the centre of the historic walled city in search of Évora's youth hostel. To my chagrin, it is closed for renovation, and I trudge three kilometres downhill to a campground on the outskirts of town.

I have a nap and do my laundry in preparation for departure the next morning, but a nighttime downpour forms a puddle in my tent. I take a few hours in the drudgery of drying sleeping bag and gear to bring order back into my life on the road. Leaving my backpack in the tent, I spend the afternoon exploring Évora, which is built around a sixteenth century aqueduct towering above me. It carried water nine kilometres to the city; now four lanes of traffic zoom under its arches. I climb into town to see where the soaring aqueduct meets the crest of a hill and the water trough comes to an abrupt end.

Back at the campground, I chat with a British couple, and they ask: "Would you like to join us for a meal? We're having barbecued shrimp and salads." I leave these folks my box of laundry soap as it is too bulky for my knapsack. The shrimp are mouth-watering, and I seem to have gotten the better of the deal.

The number of storks around Évora does not reflect the local birth rate. Poles with platforms holding the nests are numerous; the laughter of children is rare. And, in this solo trek, I reflect on our daily walk to primary school.

*"We weren't told that storks delivered babies, and yet they did arrive – in large numbers. As we hiked the four kilometres to the one-room St. Mary's Separate School from our farm near Arkona, Ontario, groups would leave their homes to join us on the way. I was the youngest in our family and the last to take that walk. Among those Dutch immigrant families, we lived the farthest from the school. At the end of the day, schoolmates arrived at their homes and left me alone for the last stretch."*

That walk was tedious. This walk allows old feelings to find a home: it is healing.

Much of the hike has taken me through countryside where the few farms lie deserted, but now I'm invigorated by active farms and houses with lush gardens. Perhaps this area receives more rainfall and is less reliant on irrigation. Yet it continues to be dry enough that around each hayfield a five-metre swath is ploughed to control the spread of grass fires.

More taxis pass within a day than I have seen on the rest of my journey. On a long trek, such details intrude into my little world. While I'm destined to transport myself, others are carried in the comfort of a car; while I'm walking, they are seated; while I choose my starts and stops, they are reliant on the driver.

I head for São Miguel de Machede but can find no place to rest for the night. Despite my resolution to stay out of danger, no campground or guest house appears. I wish I had more information but have had the misfortune of finding every tourism centre closed. If I passed one on Monday, that would be the day it was closed; if on Saturday, it would be closed for the weekend. In every town I was the stranger who knew nothing about its long-established schedules and who would have no access to details about lodging. But – darn it! – that can't stop me. I wonder: "Why continue?" And I reflect on a drive that comes out of the family relationships of my childhood.

*"Being the youngest of a dozen children, I was treated as someone special. Brothers and sisters doted on me as a playful toddler but were irritated by my distracted nature in later childhood. As others hunched over their dinner plates, they would ignore my rambling ideas about similarities between the Dutch and English languages. Mom would come to my defence with a suffocating fondness while siblings teased me, but I stayed my own person within the cobweb of family relationships. I learned to fend for myself."*

Now I continue to fend for myself and to find comfort in my independence. At twilight I seek out people in the sparse houses to place my tent on a lawn, but they are not open to the idea. An elderly woman says she is a widow and rents the house so she can't let me camp there. She hesitates under my pleading but finally gives a firm, *"Não."*

At the decorative gates of an estate, I press the intercom button, and a voice answers but disconnects me immediately. At home I would welcome a cross-Canada hiker who asked to tent in our field. It would be both hospitable and interesting. Here I get the feeling people are afraid – iron gates, guard dogs and a look of unease. Their anxieties begin to infect my self-assurance: now I too am on edge.

I am haunted by Joanne's expectation that I not tent outside of campgrounds, but here I am, not having found a home for the night. As dark closes in, I locate a grassy hollow beside a brook. Protected from sparse traffic by a row of trees and dimly lit by nearby streetlamps, this is the perfect hideaway. At daybreak I awaken from sleeping in the open to nature chirping and shining in all its glory. I go on my way refreshed but with damp socks that lead to my first blister.

A long day of going up and down through hill country brings me to Alandroal and its *hospedaria* (inn) where I treat my blister to a day of rest. The owner takes pride in spotless guest rooms above a driving school. He leads me downstairs to the classroom and, in halting English, describes the workings of a car he built – a full-sized model powered by an electric motor. I am happy to be an audience for this tinkerer. He comments that he passed me on the road yesterday, and this draws together my daytime isolated self with my evening sociable side: suddenly we share a bond.

I am fascinated by Alandroal's mix of the old and the new. To reach the church for Sunday morning Mass, I pass through the archway of an ancient fort in the Wi-Fi enabled downtown. The congregation is fervent but elderly. Next to this complex, an outdoor bar is serving a few rowdies. I do not see them at Mass.

Throughout the day television channels cover *futbol* (soccer) championship ceremonies. We follow the players through the crowds as they travel on a bus, meet dignitaries and board a plane headed somewhere. *Futbol* is a religion: Sunday's church services have become Sunday's sports activities as they have in Canada. I reminisce on the Sundays of my childhood that eerily reflect those of today.

*"As youngsters, we served as altar boys at Sunday Mass. Dressed in cassocks and surplices, we took pride in representing the devoutness of the assembly, following a complex ritual and answering the priest in Latin."*

Now youngsters serve as athletes at Sunday games. Dressed in sports gear, they take pride in representing the dreams of the crowd, following complex tactics and using the jargon of their sport. Their heroes are sports stars; ours were Christian saints.

A hike of almost 40 kilometres along busy, narrow roads leads me to safety at the campground in the city of Elvas. This facility is starting up for the season, and some of the shower rooms are not ready, but I am welcome to stay for the night. Its clientele is Portuguese and Spanish, with not a Dutch or British person in sight. I understand little and feel ill at ease as the sole member of a minority. Then I realize that this, too, is the reason I'm crossing Europe: uncomfortable situations force me to adapt, to grow.

As I approach Portugal's border, I avoid the dangers of walking along the major highway into Spain by choosing secondary roads. These cause me hours of extra hiking as they meander through the countryside near the border. I hear of a campground near Campo Maior and hike toward it, but this home for the night refuses to appear on the horizon. I finally get there at the end of a 10-kilometre hike west of town when I'm meant to be heading east toward Spain. On foot it's a two-hour hike and another two hours back in the morning. If I were travelling by car, this would be a drive of less than ten minutes.

**Goodbye**

After Campo Maior I end up on another narrow shoulder of another narrow road. One transport truck after another forces me to hug the grassy bank of the ditch. Ten kilometres of frustration bring me to Retiro, which straddles the Spanish border. I had hoped to buy supplies in this place and maybe say, "*Adeus*" ("Goodbye"), to Portugal with a drink at its bar.

As it turns out, this is a ghost town of half a dozen buildings, long ago abandoned to their memories and the elements. In the shade of an abandoned house, I have a snack to celebrate the end of my 430 kilometres across southern Portugal. Despite being assaulted – or because of that – I have persevered through my first European country. I review the experience and recall the highlights.

I'm astonished that I saw no evidence of a car accident, given the number of vehicles racing down narrow roads. Only once did I view a flowing stream under a bridge; all other bridges crossed stagnant puddles or marshy areas. I met only two people walking outside the built-up areas – a man in a track suit power walking near a town and a German hiker headed south to Faro. Having lost 10 pounds, I feel healthy and fit. I estimate that it took a half million steps to get me to this point, and I have millions left to go. Meanwhile a lone truck driver rumbles in to wait for another vehicle, but – once again – I see no laudatory crowds cheering me on.

The abandoned border community of Retiro, with its poor roads and worn signs, suddenly open onto the quality highway and modern signage of Spain. Six kilometres beyond the border, I enter the city of Badajoz. I'm exhausted from being forced in and out of roadside grass by passing trucks: I've spent as much time struggling through Portugal's ditches as walking on the edge of the roadway.

When I prepared for this journey, no one could advise me on how to walk across Europe, so I had looked at the map and simply chosen roads heading northeast. Near the start of my walk, a German couple had mentioned the odd local trail: these might be pleasant but couldn't get me across Europe. Now I need to talk to someone so I can find a better way to hike, but Badajoz doesn't look like a tourist city.

I feel defeated, have no idea as to what to do next and head for the train station. Railway personnel deal with travellers, and they might have a suggestion for me. I stop to ask a young man at a bus stop the way to the station, and he points down a side street at a building a mere block away. This was meant to be: my next steps were intended to fall into place.

My fifty Portuguese words are now worthless. My Spanish is almost non-existent, but I gather from the ticket agent that there is no hostel in Badajoz. Instead, he seems to suggest that I take the 45-minute trip to Mérida where I would find other travellers. Initially I think he's talking about Madrid; then I realize he's referring to a nearby city. Becoming confused is easy in the mix of language barrier, fatigue and lack of personal space. This long-distance hike leaves me open to uncertainty every step of the way.

Arriving from the gloomy industrial city of Badajoz, I step off the train and recognize Mérida as a sightseer's haven and my refuge. As the old Roman capital of the Iberian Peninsula, it even boasts its own coliseum ruins. I find a room at the small family-run Hotel Lusitania, located – much to my delight – on John Lennon Street.

At breakfast in the hotel the next morning, I chat with a German guest named Henry. He makes a casual comment that will change the next few thousand kilometres for me: "You might want to take the Via de la Plata north. I hiked it a few years ago." I've never heard of the Via de la Plata pilgrimage route, but Henry says it is part of Spain's Camino de Santiago de Compostela trail system. To my surprise, the hostel for this section of the path is mere blocks away, and we go in search of it. The *hospitalero* (hostel attendant) welcomes me to the pilgrimage and provides me with a *credencial* (pilgrim passport) in which he applies the first of the stamps to be added at towns on my hike.

Then I find a laundry service a few blocks from my hotel and treat my sweaty clothes to a good cleaning. The before-and-after difference could be the scenario for a soap commercial. With the pilgrimage trail stretched out before me and with clean clothes on my back, I feel renewed.

**Pilgrim**

The Via de la Plata provides a series of hostels, so I won't need my tent. I leave it in storage at the hotel and deliver my backpack to the *albergue* (pilgrimage hostel, also known as a *refugio*). It is early afternoon, and I continue toward the tourist information office to learn which sights I should catch before leaving in the morning. I suddenly notice I am alone on the street: it has become so hot as to be dangerous. Everyone else is safely at home, and I make it to the shelter of my hotel. The air does not move.

At five o'clock the city's heat has become concentrated and swoops upward, bringing in cooling breezes from all directions as tree branches sway. I am told this weather feature is a daily occurrence during the warmer months and is already remarkable during this first week of June.

After a quick supper, I return to the *refugio* and accept my new role as pilgrim. Fifteen *peregrinos* (pilgrims) share a dorm room of bunk beds amid a chorus of snoring in various languages. At six in the morning, the Spandex bicycle crowd races off to do the track in fashion. Those of us walking – like

30

snails with packs on our backs – prod ourselves to trudge the distance.

The Via de la Plata route follows the course of a Roman road. Some of its three-metre-wide bridges of fieldstone, with half-metre high stone sides, are still in their original form as are a few granite *miliarios*, carved pillars that served as distance markers. This path winds from south to north through Spain – 700 kilometres, from Seville to Astorga, which beckons in the distance. In Astorga it meets the Camino Francés, which is the main east-to-west section of the cobweb of pilgrimage routes leading to the city of Santiago de Compostela.

I leave the hostel's closeness for the morning's freshness as well as uncertainty about my next move. I am baffled as I have no information about the route when two angels hike out of the building and I ask: "Can I join you for a few days? I don't know where to go without a guidebook?" They agree, and I become their companion.

Marie and Anna from Germany are following the path their mother and father had taken a few years back. The two young women have covered the initial section from Seville and are experts at spotting the yellow painted arrows that indicate the trail. These are marked on road sign, tree trunk or fence post, and a wrong turn can leave you lost. Best of all, they have two guidebooks. I am pleased to be their shadow for the duration.

I had been immersed in my solo hike through Portugal: as I scoured my map for roads, I searched my mind for memories. For the time being, my solo hike has become one of camaraderie while I avoid taking sides when Anna gets annoyed with Marie for her frequent pauses to take photos. Walking the roads of Portugal, I managed my own progress: I chose starts and stops as well as my speed. Now we are clusters of pilgrims that meet, part and meet again as we journey and rest for the night.

The path through fields, parks and trails is uneven; towns pass in the distance. During a morning's hike, I'm carrying no food as I have assumed we would leave the path to visit a town on the way. But my two companions don't detour to a store, and I'm forced to stay with them to avoid getting lost without a guidebook. When we stand up after a routine 20-minute trailside rest, I comment: "I don't feel well." They realize I'm getting faint and share their supply: a handful of cookies comes to my rescue, and I learn a valuable lesson about the energy reserves I require.

Each day a fatiguing hike ends with a shower, a nap and hours of socializing. Visits to cafés expose us to local culture – bowls of olives, card games and bullfights on TV. During the stop in Aljucén, I visit a Roman-style bath facility. I am alone in rotating among hot and cold pools, leaving me refreshed in body and spirit. Some of us opt for a gourmet meal at a *casa rural* (country inn). The owner serves as cook and describes her dishes in Spanish while Anna translates into English. Anna had been an exchange student in Spain, and she and her sister Marie are typical Europeans in not being affected by the limitations of language.

One evening we are spoiled with a banquet at the "Monastery of the Slaves of Mary and the Poor" in Alcuescar where men follow the example of a previous parish priest. He cared for the rural poor whom he had found to be malnourished and illiterate. Within the monastery walls, a facility for men with special needs shelters them from the world. As a pilgrim seeking a bed for the night, I feel at ease in this caring community, and each of us is assigned a cramped bedroom with cot. The springs of my bed are so flexible as to be concave, so I toss the mattress on the floor for a healthier sleep.

Then in Valdesalor we sleep on exercise mats in a village's council chamber where my feet reach under the mayor's desk. Its shower wins our first prize with lots of hot water and an intense spray. I attend evening Mass in the day chapel of the new church, a block from the village office. Other than the ten-year-old altar boy and me, the dozen worshippers are older women.

After Mass the priest shakes my hand and starts a conversation in Spanish. I signal that I don't understand and ask: "English?" He shakes his head. I try: *"Français? Nederlands?"* And finally: *"Lingua Latina?"* The priest takes off in a Latin conversation, leaving me in his dust as I think of my seminary days and Latin class.

*"Latin was the official language of the Catholic Church, and the minor seminary's high school program drilled into us vocabulary, grammar, declensions and conjugations. On the path to priesthood, we were special: we spent hours in the chapel; we were virtuous; we knew our Latin."*

Perhaps I should have studied more diligently all those years ago, but I can't change the past. Instead, I'm looking forward to tomorrow when we hike into Cáceres, the end of my pilgrimage for now.

On the way into Cáceres, we pass a church with our record of 13 storks' nests balanced on its surfaces. Then we book rooms at a three-storey hotel and make our way to a sidewalk café. Marie, Anna and I have spent evenings relaxing with two fellow pilgrims, a man from Italy and a woman from Spain. Our hiking boots come off and encircle the table at this outdoor bar as we enjoy a beer while they chat about tomorrow's hike northward. I shall miss their company as I head southward to complete an unfinished part of my path – the section I missed by taking the train. Returning by bus to Mérida, I rest up to begin a two-day 60-kilometre jaunt westward back to Badajoz. After all, I need to cross all of Europe, one step at a time.

## Jaunt

Once I have finished the section from Mérida to Badajoz, my feet will have taken me 600 kilometres into Europe. Covering those last 60 kilometres before returning to Canada will give me the satisfaction of resuming in Cáceres on my next hike. I entrust my backpack to the family at the Mérida hotel and minimize my world to a day pack – with toiletries and a change of clothes – to ensure a brisk walk.

Again, I am alone to choose my own path. With a long hike ahead of me, I set out in the early morning light. A vegetable stand is opening for the day, and it provides fresh fruit as my snack. Finding a route out of the city proves a challenge: I seek the calm of a country trail, but all signs lead to major highways. Instead, I detour through a meadow around a barrier of freeway construction, come upon a stretch of rural road and finally get on my way. Many cars are marked as "student drivers." They must be learning to ignore the distraction of this lone Canadian.

A motherly librarian in Montijo suggests: "Go to the hotel in Valdelacalzada. It is near the main road, halfway to Badajoz." As it turns out, this *hostal* (long-stay hotel) has a bar straight out of the Wild West. Balancing a tray with glasses of beer, the waitress slithers between groups of tough men staring at me in the doorway. I feel uneasy and hightail it out of there (as our cowboy comic books used to say).

The joint is located four kilometres off the main road, so I end up hiking an extra eight kilometres. The frustration of having been led so far out of my way results in a burst of energy that sees me zip down the road. After a record day's walk of 45 kilometres, I fall into a hotel at about eight in the evening. This drab red-brick building feels like the Holiday Inns of the 1970's and is located on the outskirts of a little village with a big name, Pueblonuevo del Guadiana.

At seven o'clock the next morning, traffic already competes with farm tractors – John Deere being the brand of choice. This fruit and vegetable oasis is interlaced with concrete irrigation canals. These channels fill and empty repeatedly, and fields get flooded and then drained of the excess water. The region becomes a web of moving water to produce hardy crops, and I am reminded of channels of water running in the other direction during my Dutch childhood. Here in Spain the water is guided toward the fields; in the Netherlands, it was directed from the fields and taken upward by windmills to reach the height of sea level and empty into the ocean.

I get within view of Badajoz, but I'm tested by another series of obstacles – a jumble of road construction, railway right-of-way and four-lane highway. I choose a tertiary road headed toward the city; when it veers into countryside, I guess at a meandering trail. As it turns out, this is the correct path and delivers me onto the sidewalks of Badajoz.

At the train station, I order a salad in celebration. I have now covered the 600 kilometres from Cabo de São Vicente, Portugal to Cáceres, Spain – a strong beginning to crossing all of Europe.

I take the train back to Mérida and spend one more night in the Hotel Lusitania. I have gotten to know the owner and his long-haired teenage son who take turns at the reception desk. Occasionally the young daughter plays with her toys in the lobby while waiting for her mother to come from work and pick her up on the way home. It all seems so universal: this could be a family-run hotel in Canada. They have been helpful in providing information and in storing my possessions for the hike to Cáceres and the jaunt back to Badajoz. I appreciate this sense of family when I'm so far from home.

## Madrid

I have time to visit Madrid and connect with its culture before my scheduled flight back to Canada. Arriving on the Mérida bus, I head for the Madrid *metro* (subway). After 10 minutes of confusion, the system makes sense, and I'm on my way.

The youth hostel is crowded, and my reservation has not been confirmed. Following a two-hour wait, they have a spot for me – a lower bunk in an eight-bed room. A group of Korean high school students are letting loose in the facility. The three frazzled teachers look homesick. Sometimes home is where you need to be.

In an outdoor café, the waiter acknowledges his presence by banging dirty dishes as he stacks them. At the next table, a group from US Airways is celebrating, and we strike up a conversation. I tell them I live near Moncton, New

Brunswick and – as usual – expect that no one has heard of the place. But one of the flight attendants surprises me: "I was in Moncton once. We were grounded there on '9-11.' The people were very good to us." During conversations like this, it seems to be a truly small world.

Late in the evening, the boom and crackling of fireworks awakens us in the hostel. The festivities probably have to do with *futbol* as does so much in Portugal and Spain. We give up on sleep, get dressed and find a place between office buildings where we watch the night sky come to life. The shower of colourful sparks alternates between being thunderous and hushed, and the child in each adult finds it magical. We trundle back to our bunks as I formulate a plan for two major activities the next day – watch a bullfight and meet an ambassador – though neither happens.

As it turns out, the Sunday bullfight, with ticket prices up to 3,000 Euros, is a special end-of-season Internet broadcast. This figure is far beyond the limits of my budget. I'll save that wish for next time.

Thinking the Canadian ambassador might be interested in my story, I phone the embassy. When the hostel phone has eaten four of my coins, I decide to hop on the *metro* and head to the embassy, located on the fourth floor of a concrete-and-glass office building. The consul greets me, and we have a chat in the hallway. I miss a chance to meet the ambassador as he is busy at the city's airport, officiating at the launch of Air Canada's daily service between Toronto and Madrid. Carlos suggests I call ahead next time and something can be arranged. That's another item for my list.

This world-class city boasts enough museums, parks and Starbucks to keep me running. Under an overpass I locate the area featuring a dozen modern sculptures. Then my visits to four art galleries, including the Prado, turn both my right and left brain to mush. People in cafés and shops are welcoming and helpful, as is the manager of the *locutorio* (Internet service). Back at the hostel, two young men are travelling street performers and entertain us on cello and violin. And, of course, each day ends with cheers and groans during the televised *futbol* game.

I'll soon be back home in the stillness of my retirement in Dorchester Cape, New Brunswick. I shall miss the hustle and bustle of Portugal and Spain – the barking dogs, crowing roosters, car horns, church bells, rattling dishes, blaring TV's, cellphones, scooters, traffic cop's whistle and midnight clattering garbage pick-up; those, and the quiet of a peaceful pilgrimage. I can't wait to return to my European adventure.

*JOSEPH KOOT*

# Trip 3: Pilgrimage Path

*April 19 to June 20, 2009 – 958 kilometres*
*Cáceres north to Astorga, Spain (453 km)*
*Saint-Jean-Pied-de-Port, France west to Astorga, Spain*
*(505 km)*

## Calm

Once again, I am organizing my backpack before a flight to Europe. This is my third trip as part of a campaign to cross the continent on foot. I have walked 600 kilometres of its expanse and am determined to cover another 1000 over the next two months.

This time my nephew Peter will join me for the first three weeks, so I'll have to make adjustments from my solo hiking. It will be good company on the one hand while adapting to one another's needs on the other. We will hike the Via de la Plata pilgrimage trail from Cáceres in southern Spain northward to Astorga. At that point the Via de la Plata meets the Camino Francés, the main east-to-west route through northern Spain stretching from the French border to Santiago de Compostela. When we reach Astorga, Peter will leave for work in France while I resume the hike westward from Saint-Jean-Pied-de-Port, at the French-Spanish border, back to Astorga.

I look forward to the camaraderie, and I've purchased two guidebooks to the Via de la Plata. One is from the Confraternity of Saint James in Britain, but the other – "Walking the Via de la Plata," published by Pili Pala Press of

Vancouver – proves most helpful. It describes clearly at which farm gate to turn, during which period of history a town was significant and at which hostel to seek shelter for the night.

This time I'll look for phone booths to stay in contact with Joanne. I've not had to rent a satellite phone since I won't be isolated, but in the company of Peter and other hikers. I'll be less pressured to find a computer with Internet access once a week since my weekly articles to the National Post have been terminated as a result of the newspaper's cost-cutting measures.

My boots have been reheeled since thousands of steps have left their mark. My knapsack weighs a more reasonable 10 kilograms; that's 5 kilograms lighter than during my first two treks because I shall not need a tent on the Spanish pilgrimage routes. Instead, *albergues* (also called *refugios*) will serve as shelter at night and will consist of basic accommodation – sitting area, bathroom and bunk beds. Arriving in Madrid, we'll take the bus to Cáceres, the small city I had reached on my previous excursion. There the walking will start in earnest.

People ask how I feel about continuing my trek, particularly the thought of taking two months away from home to engage in this struggle. Am I enthused about continuing? Yes. Am I aware of the intense work I am facing? Definitely. Do I realize the lonely moments and the longing for home will recur? Of course. But despite my mixed emotions – or, perhaps, because of them – on I go. The dream remains alive: I'm committed to continue the trek from southwest Portugal to northeast Estonia in the far distance.

I had thought that my preparations for this third trip would be routine. Instead, I empty and refill my backpack several times to decrease both weight and volume. Even a thick elastic clothesline gets replaced with a length of string. When I have it down to a comfortable burden, I head for Moncton Airport and the connecting flight to Toronto.

Among the hundreds of faces at the boarding gate in Toronto, I spot Peter and ask, "So, are you ready for this?" Our pilgrimage together is becoming a reality. The flight via Frankfurt, followed by a *metro* ride from the airport, brings us to the Madrid bus station. Peter stores a bag of items for retrieval at the end of this hike on his way to work in France. Then we board the bus to Cáceres for arrival at the start of our walk.

A mundane bus ride takes on a personality when our vehicle hits a tollgate that has descended too quickly. The driver stops to assess damages, and our little distracted community becomes a buzz of stranger talking to stranger. Moments later we are on our way.

In Cáceres we seek shelter in the three-storey hotel where I stayed at the end of my last walk on the Via de la Plata. It's good to be back, and I feel at home. In the year since my last visit, little has changed: I recognize the massive archways that hide its drab stucco walls. In this seclusion a night's rest will prepare us to face the journey.

As pilgrims, we have access to the *poste restante* (general delivery) of Spain's *correos* (mail service). We send parcels ahead to the post office at Astorga, our final stop on the Via de la Plata, and Peter stops to buy a rain jacket. With the purchase of bread, cheese and fruit, tomorrow's hike becomes a reality.

## Companion

On the first day, a jaunt of a mere 11 kilometres brings us to Casar de Cáceres, a sprawling town. Its hostel features a clothes dryer, so our handwashed items are repacked in short order. This is a gentle start to a demanding trek.

I've relished the peace of a solitary trek and wonder whether Peter's presence spells the end of my musings for a while and whether our continuous contact might cause friction. However, Peter spends hours walking some distance behind me: his earbuds are delivering the narration of an electronic book while I'm lost in thoughts about my past.

In the morning we check with each other: "Is anything I'm doing bothering you?" We continue this throughout the trip as a way to minimize any conflict, and we get along well. Peter, who is a Catholic priest, proves to be a pleasant travelling companion: his kindness is real. My days in the "major seminary" led me to watch for the artificial piety I met on my path to the priesthood, and the memories flow back.

*"In the mansion that served as seminary in Ottawa, I was faced with my own humanness and that of fellow seminarians as we strived for perfection. We looked so good worshipping our little God in the chapel's tabernacle, but I was uncomfortable in the seminary's social situations. I felt excluded from the group dynamics: our life of piety didn't ensure friendliness. Instead, it contributed to the stress that led me to abandon the path I had followed for seven long years. Five years before my planned ordination as a priest, I was home once again."*

Peter and I share both the trail and our thoughts, and – in the rhythm of a steady hiking pace – old wounds are healing. During the 20-kilometre hike to Linda Mar, I begin to feel renewed as I leave behind the loneliness of Portugal and that of my youth. We arrive at a guest house that is a combination of hostel for *peregrinos* and hotel for tourists. The Dutch owner and staff give me the opportunity to practise my mother tongue. They also handle English, German and Spanish with ease. Peter and I camp out on free mattresses in a common room instead of renting a room for 40 Euros. We take the pilgrim experience seriously.

At supper we are joined by a woman from Germany and Michael, a young German man now residing in Spain. The wine flows freely, and Michael and I delve into our feelings toward modern music. I am surprised at the passion with which I disparage rap songs, and I add: "There hasn't been any progress in popular music since the heroes of the fifties and sixties – people like Buddy Holly, the Beatles and Roy Orbison. I can't understand that the hip hop fad has lasted so long." Michael has a few modern favourites but generally agrees with me. One of the kitchen staff empties a leftover half-bottle of wine into our glasses as it is not worth keeping, and we keep drinking and talking.

In the morning I shake off the wine from the night before and repack my things. When hiking with Marie and Anna on my last trip, my preparations felt rushed. They must have packed their bags in the evening in preparation for a quick departure in the morning. I would wake up to hear them begin their day, but minutes later they would be heading out the door, and I would have to hurry to tie my boots, put on my back pack and chase them into the dawn. Now, Peter's preparations fit perfectly with mine: we take our time to prepare, and each morning we are ready to leave at exactly the same time.

At lunchtime Peter and I come across an oasis in the town of Cañaveral: at its Taiku Bar, the menu features a whole chicken. In the middle of a long day's hike, half a chicken for each of us, along with a hunk of bread, serves as a reward for our hard work. Over bulging plates, we discuss the most and least favoured aspects of this journey. Peter decides, "The best part is the walking itself," and I agree wholeheartedly.

I suggest, "The worst part is the constant unpacking, repacking and managing of supplies in my backpack."

Peter disagrees and finds most troubling, "A guy snoring on either side of me." The hostels do have their share of snorers, and – yes – I am one of them.

Blisters and foot-related issues are a constant concern among *peregrinos*. To my dismay, the boots that served me so well in my first 600 kilometres through Europe have now caused a blister at the back of each foot. A shoemaker in Moncton replaced the worn heels with new ones, but these are less flexible and less forgiving of step after step after step. I become fussy in changing damp socks and trust I'll prevent new blisters from forming. One can only hope.

We are making good headway on a lane cutting through fields, when a farmer stops to tell us we have veered from the route. On this portion of the trail, its direction is indicated by yellow markings on half-metre-high cubes of granite. One of these cubes was not turned correctly, and we chose the wrong path, taking us a few kilometres out of our way. An elderly man happens along in his car and drives us to a further point on the trail. People living along the Via de la Plata prove to be considerate and attentive to our needs.

As it turns out, this incident leads to a decision that would affect my itinerary across Europe. By this point I have simply decided to cross the continent from southwest to northeast and to be unconcerned about missing pieces at ferry crossings, for example. Peter suggests, "Let's go back so you can connect the dots," and we hike back a kilometre or two to the point where we went in the wrong direction. Now I shall not have missed the part where we were given a ride, and I become meticulous about taking every step across Europe.

As we round a rock-strewn curve in the trail, one of the stones rolls underfoot. This sends me off balance, and I catch myself just short of crashing to the ground under the weight of my backpack. It's a warning to stay on guard at every moment: a slip can lead to a twisted ankle and the need to return home. On this trip I did not pack hiking poles since I had used them so little on the previous laps. Now Peter is concerned whenever the trail is steep or rough: "Here, Uncle Joseph, use one of my poles." My solitary hike, with its anxieties and lonesomeness, has become a joint venture.

In a stop at a hostel, I take out my guidebooks and am dismayed by the extra weight: it's time to downsize. I become the nightmare of librarians everywhere when I tear the books apart and toss out unnecessary pages. The introductory chapter goes in the garbage; it is joined by the concluding sections and the book covers. I have tired of juggling two books and taking them out of my backpack over and over. Now I keep the next few pages in my pocket and discard them when we have completed that part of the journey. Thus, my burden is lighter, and I have the information within reach.

The length of a day's walk depends on the choice of hostel for the night, and one day the first *albergue* is so near we continue to the next one. This leads to a trek of 40 kilometres that takes us through the tall Roman arch at Caparra, part of an archaeological dig. Enjoying the view of glistening snow on a distant mountain range, we continue on to Aldeanueva del Camino. The hike proves strenuous, and we arrive at its *refugio* as darkness is setting in.

There to greet us is Roger who hails from Cornwall, England, and we recognize him as having biked past us earlier in the day. Roger mentions: "Kilometres back I met a pilgrim named Michael who said he was having trouble walking. He'd had too much wine to drink with a Canadian hiker the evening before." I recognize that Canadian hiker as myself and feel smug about my endurance. No bottle of wine is going to slow me down, especially when Peter's long legs are setting the pace. From this incident I learn that we pilgrims are a tight-knit community – one with a built-in telegraph system.

The following morning is Sunday, and we attend Mass in Aldeanueva del Camino. Then we struggle up the long, steep grade to Baños de Montemayor, a community with mineral pools serving those with arthritic conditions. On Sundays the baths are available only to people with medical prescriptions, so they are off limits to us. Instead, a visit to the local bar gives us immersion in the enthusiasm over *futbol*. I try the Brandy de Jerez and am impressed with its smoothness. I feel accepted by the locals when a fellow patron pays for the coffee I order after my drink. Mentioning our Canadian homeland always brings smiles of recognition and interest.

**Plateau**

After Baños de Montemayor, we say farewell to the southern region of Extramadura and enter the *meseta* (plateau) of the province of Salamanca. It is nearing the end of April, and we've been enjoying the hint of summer's warmth as we hiked through small acreages and stands of trees. Suddenly we are passing great fields stretching into the distance, and they come with cold wind, dampness and the unsettled conditions of a tableland environment. Peter and I miss Canada's pleasant spring, and a roaring blaze in the fireplace at the hostel in Fuenterroble de Salvatierra is a welcome sight.

The *credencial* (pilgrim passport) is stamped every day at stops along the route as proof of participation in the pilgrimage trek. When the pilgrim arrives in Santiago, these stamps indicate completion of the pilgrimage and are rewarded with a certificate, the *compostela*. One of my guidebooks advises to avoid having all the stamps originate at bars or the good folks at Santiago de Compostela will think that's how we made our way – from beer to beer.

This is certainly not true for us, although there is that occasion when we endure the gruelling climb to the Pico de la Dueña, the highest point on the Via de la Plata. This peak is decorated with one of a series of wind turbines towering over a cross of Santiago. It is shaped like a sword with its point stuck downward into a tall pole that is planted in a mound of rocks. Upon our descent I stop a car of the *guardia civil* (police) as it emerges from a side road. I am eager for a drink and ask if there is a bar in the village they just left. Unfortunately, there is not, and I remain thirsty for a beer till the next café on our route.

The cooperation of farmers in allowing us to cut through their farms on the trail is impressive. Some days we open and close up to 20 farm gates. If a *peregrino* were careless in leaving a gate unsecured, it could mean extra work for the farmer in gathering his cattle from far and wide. A few gates are padlocked: perhaps those farmers are worried we might not close the entries behind us. Then we throw our backpacks over and follow with a climb and a jump.

Having fought blisters, chilliness, hills and gates, we approach picturesque Salamanca. Road construction hinders our progress at every turn, but we finally reach an ancient Roman bridge into the city. This has become a pattern – the mix of the new with the old. The European Union has invested in modernizing its infrastructure, and highway construction is everywhere. We are enthralled at Salamanca's architecture, particularly the number of figurines carved into classical buildings.

Peter and I head to a bar for supper. A variety of *tapas* (bar snacks) is listed on the wall in Spanish. The words are unfamiliar, so I simply choose numbers 4, 8 and 12 on the list. Placed in front of me are three unusual dishes that I ask about halfway through the meal. It turns out I have been munching on cow's stomach, cow's snout and a blood-rice mixture. Despite that unwelcome information, I am determined to make my way through these "delicacies." In an aside to the waiter, Peter asks, *"Una cuchara, por favor,"* which turns out to mean, "A spoon, please," and he attacks my crème brûlée dessert with vigour. On the trail Peter is sometimes concerned about my eating habits: "Uncle Joseph, you need to eat more." Then he shares a bag of peanuts or raisins as we traverse Spain's countryside.

The Salamanca *refugio* is managed by a German retiree named Klaus. He seems overwhelmed by his duties and complains about the amount of work involved. I listen patiently, but he is so glum that I look forward to leaving the next day. On my hiking route, I enjoy passing through people's lives but avoid getting involved: my stay is too brief to worry about local issues that are beyond my control, and I need my energy for walking. In any case, Klaus seems in better spirits in the morning. At 7:00 a.m. we are awakened with the Taizé version of "Laudate Dominum" played at full volume and supported by Klaus as he chants the bass parts.

A pleasant hike becomes a challenge on the way to the wonderfully named town of El Cubo de la Tierra del Vino ("the bucket of the land of wine"). New highway construction forces us to follow a dirt roadbed over 10 kilometres. Then a sudden storm lashes us with a driving downpour and sends us scurrying for our raingear. The wind makes sport of attempts to put our arms into the sleeves as they become whipping pieces of plastic. The storm passes, but our path around this construction takes us across a boggy field, covering our boots in sticky clay. The driver of a cement truck busies himself with a high-pressure sprayer to clean his chute, and I point out the mud on our boots. He kindly agrees to give them a rinse, and that saves us intense scrubbing later.

Arriving at an *albergue*, the first agenda item is the washing of t-shirts, socks and underwear. As they hang to dry, it would be easy to forget these articles when packing for departure in the early morning hours, and hiking back to retrieve them would be wearisome. In a stroke of genius, Peter pins a clothespin to his hat brim in the evening as a reminder to get the clothes from the line before setting out. Now I follow this housekeeping tip that has worked remarkably well.

We are intrigued by "The Mystery of the Disappearing Peregrinos." In some *refugios* more than a dozen of us share tight quarters. On another evening this crowd may have shrunk to a few people – in one case, only Peter and me. We wonder: "Where would they all have gone?" Pilgrims on bicycles often travel in packs, and that partly explains the arrival and departure of crowds but doesn't seem to be the whole story. *Peregrinos* simply vanish during the hike to the next *refugio*. Perhaps they prefer taking the bus past some sections while Peter and I are resolute in walking.

Zamora looks like another city with a long history, but what catches our attention is the modern – a cafés orange juice machine. This colourful unit does all the work: it slices, squeezes and then disposes of the peelings. The complex toy is a great distraction for us, one we agree could sell itself.

Our lengthy hikes are leading to blisters, and our feet are starting to protest. We stop at a *farmacia* on the way out of town in hopes of finding help for this. By the time we finish, the clerk has filled the counter with a host of items. We settle for silicone heel cushions that give the sensation of walking on air.

Spain's *meseta* is home to hundreds of wind turbines, and we have met clusters of them along the way. The wind is cool, non-stop and consistently from the north. I don black woollen gloves as we set out on the coolest mornings, and we spend our days trudging into our shadows and the wind.

When stopping at a bar for a drink or snack, we can take a seat anywhere. However, if having a meal, we are seated in a separate *comedor* (dining area) with white tablecloth and bottle of wine. Settling into a bar with half a dozen other *peregrinos* in the village of Riego del Camino, Peter and I place our food order. As this is more food than one should consume at a bar table, we are ushered into the back room – actually a storage room holding some of the facility's outdated equipment. A few travelling companions join us there, and the conversation continues.

In Granja de Moreruela, Peter and I get to practice our skills. As a retired nurse, I bandage the feet of a fellow pilgrim named Herman and suggest this sociable Dutchman take a few days' pause in his hiking: his gaping blisters need a rest. As a Catholic priest, Peter presides at our Sunday Eucharistic Celebration. The altar – a card table with a beer ad emblazoned on its surface – is covered with a white cloth. As we gather in the entrance to the sleeping area with our six German and Dutch peers, this Mass is a truly moving experience.

Now our trail divides in two: here in the town of Granja de Moreruela, half of the group chooses the route to the left, heading westward directly toward Santiago de Compostela; the rest of us continue northward toward Astorga. There the Via de la Plata intersects with the Camino Francés, which is the main east-to-west section of the Camino de Santiago de Compostela through northern Spain. In my case, this path provides a more direct route in my northeasterly wanderings through Europe. And I review memories of a split in another trail in another life so long ago.

*"As the remaining group of seminarians, we were determined to go the distance. Forty-two of us had started the trek in Grade 9 that September of 1960. Over the five years, we would make a pastime of predicting which students would drop off along the way to return to the comfort of home. Now, at the end of Grade 13, we reached a split in the trail, and several peers were entering St. Peter's Seminary in London, Ontario to become diocesan priests. A majority was heading to a year of*

*novitiate in Ste. Marie, Illinois in the USA on the way to becoming Priests of the Sacred Heart. We half dozen crossed into a foreign land to continue our path to the priesthood."*

That now seems like a distant century. I've had such a full life since those days and couldn't have predicted the trail that now takes me across European borders in my retirement years.

## Lost

Having left our companions to proceed on their own journey, Peter and I approach Benavente. An hour before we get to the city, we pass through Castropepe where a sign indicates the services available in this village. Strangely, it lists eight services not available (such as phone booth, pharmacy and cash machine) and only three that are to be found – bakery, bar and cellphone coverage. I assume the sign is in response to pilgrims' questions about services in the community, but it does look unusual to list eleven services and only provide three of them.

The city of Benavente seems resolute in making our visit memorable but for all the wrong reasons. As we approach, buildings lie stretched out within easy reach. Yet, the path leads off to the right as we veer farther and farther from the built-up area. A narrow walkway directs us over a highway, but the rush of traffic below makes me hesitant to cross. I ask Peter to walk ahead of me, and I keep my hand on his backpack while struggling with my fear of heights. Somehow, this comforts me as we parade across. Now arrows direct us through an underpass and back to the other side. Finally, we arrive at a paved stretch serving an industrial complex and are led into Benavente itself. A long section of hot pavement past a series of boring buildings can't help but irritate visiting pilgrims.

In need of cash, I stop at a machine on the outside wall of a bank. However, at the end of the transaction, the precious bills get pulled back into the apparatus: while I'm putting away my credit card, it swallows my Euros. Arriving at the bank bright and early the next morning, I understand from my limited Spanish that the bank machine gives people only five seconds to grab their money. I am told the device is opened at 2:00 p.m. every day to balance the books. At that time they can return a customer's cash if a complaint has been filed.

In my few Spanish words – and lots of gestures – I explain that, as a *peregrino*, I need to start walking again as soon as I leave the bank. Perhaps in sensitivity to pilgrims' needs, they respond to my look of desperation by opening the apparatus immediately, finding the extra Euros and returning them to me intact. My sigh of relief requires no translation.

My four-year-old guidebook gives details of the route into Benavente that do not reflect the newer path we encountered: it mentions a railway bed that is no longer used as a trail. Consequently, we find the guidebook of no use when searching for the way out of town the next morning. Instead, we locate the rundown *albergue* that we had been advised to avoid in favour of inexpensive hotel rooms, and we follow the arrows from there. To our surprise, this trail leads us in a westerly direction through the town of Santa Christina de la Polvorosa, which isn't on our Via de la Plata map.

As we saunter down the sidewalk, we see a woman set her bags of groceries on the ground. She crosses the street to tell us where the trail leads as she seems to think we're headed the wrong way. Another woman arrives, and they have a discussion, none of which we understand. The second woman thinks we're going the right way, so we continue on. As we find out by the end of the day, we ignored valuable advice: we should have paid more attention to the concerns of the woman shopper.

A wonderful walk in the country takes us through scrubland and then provides hilltop views, and we keep on. Neither guidebook nor compass agrees with this choice of route, and we realize we are lost. We approach a worker at a gravel pit for directions back to the Via de la Plata. He points down the highway, and we follow it into a town.

51

Buildings look strangely familiar, and I ask Peter, "Didn't we pass that church this morning?" Sure enough, we are back in Santa Christina de la Polvorosa, the town we hiked through earlier in the day. We are near today's starting point in Benavente and have walked six hours to cover three kilometres! None of this makes sense, so off we go to the Benavente tourist information office. We are told that two trails lead through the city and we had chanced upon the Camino Sanabrés instead of our Via de la Plata.

On the positive side, we happen to be back in town on an evening of celebration. The bars are providing free samples of *tapas* to all customers, so we join in the festivities. Another night in the Hostal La Trucha, and we are on our way – embarrassed, but less perplexed. Peter was successful in providing a pithy statement to cover the above missteps: "The appearance of failure is just that." That says it all.

## Endings

Suddenly we leave the *meseta* scenery of sweeping vistas that reminded us of the Canadian prairies, and we enjoy a more comfortable breeze from the southwest in this first week of May. As we enter the province of León, we are greeted with rolling terrain clustered with wine storage chambers. Hillsides are decorated with heavy wooden entrances to these chambers and with chimneys serving as vents. These *bodegas* look delightfully similar to the "Hobbit Holes" of the Lord of the Rings film trilogy.

Then we arrive in Alija del Infantado and enjoy another unusual sight: signs point the way to the tourism office, police station, pilgrim hostel or the next town. After so many towns in Portugal and Spain with no signage, this one has a series of the colourful displays. All those markers give this old town a modern look.

The next day a hike of 15 kilometres takes us along a river with banks of marsh grass. Willow trees and cattails hover over a profusion of tiny flowers whose five white petals and yellow centres incongruously decorate the river sludge.

Twittering birds and flocks of ducks lighten our spirits as we pass through the fertile river valley where farm crops stretch out to the distant hills on either side. A cloudless sky makes for a wonderful morning's walk.

As frequently happens, the town of La Bañeza challenges us with finding supper when the local population takes its evening meal after 9:30 p.m. We are never defeated and always manage to locate a bar or restaurant with sufficient *tapas* to meet our needs. At this town's *refugio*, we are assigned retired hospital beds, and Peter comments, "Your previous employment as a nurse has now come full circle."

We reach Celada, the last town before Astorga, our destination on the Via de la Plata. This place boasts a restaurant that serves pork from an attached abattoir. It must be fresh and is certainly tasty as we enjoy a break before our last few kilometres into the city.

Our end point stays tantalizingly close till we make our way through a highway underpass, and there we are – in Astorga. The city is a bustling community of *peregrinos*: it is a pilgrimage hub as the junction of the Via de la Plata with the Camino Francés. We relish our accomplishment and welcome the chance to catch our breath as we settle into a massive *refugio* with 50 people sharing one room.

The following morning Peter and I scamper to the post office to claim the packages we sent through the mail from Cáceres. "What did you get?" we ask each other as we make a show of excitement over receiving these "surprise gifts" we sent ourselves to avoid carrying the items over the 400 kilometres. My package contains a pair of socks and underwear, more mementos of Canada (to distribute to helpful locals and fellow pilgrims) and a second bottle of Camp Soap. This is available at Canadian Tire and useful for anything from shampoo to shaving foam to body wash to laundry soap: I give it a superior rating – it takes up little room, works effectively and is biodegradable. And the plastic bottle never leaks.

Then we hurry to catch our bus to Madrid. Upon arrival Peter retrieves his belongings from the bus station storage area:

these are the more urbane items he will need for his work in France. Then we catch the *metro* to the youth hostel where I had stayed during last year's few days in Madrid. After some disorientation in this hectic part of the city, we find the hostel but are informed they have no vacancy. Down we go to the efficient *metro* and make our way to an alternate hostel – one that is full but will let us stay in their overflow area. In fact, this room is a luxury: it is spacious and has few other occupants. Here each of us can come to grips with our own travelling world: we spread out belongings on vacant beds and reorganize in preparation for the next steps in our two journeys.

During our brief stay in Madrid, Peter and I are exposed to two extremes of the worshipping environment. We pay a Saturday evening visit to the temporary quarters that serve as a local parish church during the construction of a new house of worship. This building consists of a few trailers joined together, and it contrasts sharply with the Basilica of San Francisco El Grande, which we attend on Sunday morning. Its dome is the third largest in Europe, its walls are covered in painted works of art and the glimmer of gold is everywhere.

Within this extravagance I find it disconcerting that 12 oversized marble apostles (including James the Greater of "Santiago de Compostela" fame) are staring down at the huddled masses. I'm troubled by the lavishness: it doesn't support the thoughts of humility that are found so easily in the neighbouring parish's temporary church.

Our wanderings through El Rastro (an endless Sunday afternoon flea market) bring us face to face with a Spanish *peregrino* we have come to name "Mime." The nickname reflects his ease in communicating with non-Spanish-speaking people, using gestures and the odd "pfft" sound. We met up with Mime on the trail, in *albergues*, on the bus to this city (where he and a friend were reluctant to move from seats reserved for Peter and me) and now – incredibly – among the immense crowds in Madrid. He kept walking into our lives like the subject of the old song, "The Cat Came Back."

We return to our hostel where a group of middle school students from France has replaced the visually impaired group of teenagers we had encountered upon our arrival. Europeans make good use of hostels, and each of these groups gives the stone structure a heart. Our overflow area is away from the hostel's activity, so we can retire in peace. However, as is common on a non-hiking day, both Peter and I have trouble falling asleep. Our bodies remind us they need less rest during this well-deserved break from daily 30-kilometre treks.

## Mending

On Monday May 11th, Peter departs for the L'Arche community in Trosly, France. This was the first in a worldwide series of homes established by Jean Vanier – Canadian Catholic philosopher turned theologian and humanitarian – for people with developmental disabilities.

I have reservations about religious systems but remain committed to a divine spark in each person. And so it is that I place my hands, palms down, over Peter's head and seek a blessing to guide him on his way. And Peter's gift of his hiking poles will guide me on my way. At the end of his term in France, Peter will return to finish his Camino from Astorga to Santiago de Compostela. He will be using a pair of poles from the assortment left behind by those going home from Astorga. And so, others will help him on his way. Peter's spark has shone brightly, and his presence will continue to be appreciated by all while my life now seems too quiet.

The next morning I awaken with a sense of disorientation. I have ideas to share with Peter, but he is absent from his bunk bed as he left through Madrid Airport yesterday. I suddenly miss Joanne and home more than I had in the previous three weeks.

For a year or two, I have spent hours at my laptop, organizing my childhood into the draft of a memoir. The repetition of walking has opened my mind to a number of hidden memories, and the hours of stillness has helped them come to life. Now I wish I were home at my laptop to put those thoughts into words.

I am also coming to terms with an event of last evening – witnessing my first bullfight. It took place in Madrid's Plaza de Toros at the Las Ventas Bullfighting Ring, the red-brick complex with its colourful ceramic inlays. The ceremony started with costumed people and horses parading through the ring. Then, during each of six rounds, I was left with a mix of enthusiasm about the techniques, disgust over the spectacle and sensitivity to the plight of the bull.

I cheered inwardly when one of the *banderilleros* – those who jab colourful sticks into the bull's upper neck – was trampled (though not seriously hurt, I should add). The incident showed that a bullfight is not completely one-sided although the bull invariably dies. My feelings were confused and fell over each other like moths in porch light. As I stretch and yawn one last time in my sleeping bag in this Madrid hostel, I think of Ernest Hemingway and wish he had been seated next to me to interpret the bullfight choreography. We could have shared in manly chatter. And I think of my developing masculinity.

*"I was the product of a childhood with a brooding father, a youth that included a dislike of competitive sports and an adolescence in seminary piety. As a young adult, I yearned for images of manliness. At a used book store in my university days, I happened upon a copy of Ernest Hemingway's "Death in the Afternoon". The author's studied prose captivated me. This American writer was enthralled with Spain and its bullfight tradition. Through the pages I came to experience the daring, anguish and elation of each strutting bullfighter in his colourful "traje de luces" ["suit of lights"]. Plunging the sword to its hilt between the bull's shoulder blades and into its heart was so decisive, so final. My farm upbringing instilled a respect for bulls – their breeding behaviour, but also their ability to maim and kill. Briefly, bullfighters became my heroes, and I dreamt of seeing a bullfight in person."*

Now I wonder how Hemingway would have dealt with distracted audience members. The crowd was attentive to the activity on the arena sand below. It responded to every nuance, every swagger of the *matador de toros* (killer of bulls). However, one of the two women seated in front of me was a nuisance: she began a tirade complaining about something or other to her woman friend who listened intently but said not a word.

Two bulls died, and the preoccupied woman didn't even care: she was caught up in her own issues. Having emptied her soul, she turned toward the *toreros* (bullfight teams), so all six bulls did not die in vain. I recognize that my early adult infatuation has taken on an element of realism in my senior years: my attention has gone from distinctive colourful brocade to distracting crowd behaviour. I've also discovered that the thrill of man against beast is to be kept in perspective: it is trivial when compared to the thrill of seeing the gleam in your grandchildren's eyes.

Again, I am unsuccessful in meeting the Canadian Ambassador in Madrid. In the morning the embassy answering machine tells me no one is available at reception. In the afternoon the stubborn hostel phone won't connect with the one at the embassy, so I send an e-mail message outlining the progress of my trek and wishing the diplomat all the best (but get no reply). On the plus side, I take that time to get a much-needed haircut and beard trim: tramping the pilgrim path doesn't mean having to look unkempt. I am tidying up to experience the Camino Francés afresh and, as a solo hiker, I'll be missing Peter's company on this next part of my adventure.

The few days in Madrid are a break from walking but this downtime does not feel rewarding: I am eager to get back to my musings on the trail as I catch the bus from Madrid to Pamplona. There I shall make my way to Saint-Jean-Pied-de-Port for the start of my westward hike on the Camino Francés back to Astorga. Although my distant goal lies far to the east in Estonia, I am now travelling west because that is the direction of this route. The crowds are heading westward, and the

Camino signs are facing you as you go west. This time I choose the easier way: I choose the way in which the signs will be obvious, and I can join in with the crowds.

The bus trip is without incident except for an unexpected 15-minute stop in a town somewhere. Wires are being repaired and hanging near the ground across an intersection. Eventually men climb ladders to raise the cables and provide clearance for our vehicle. Some of the electrical current coursing through these wires must originate in the 100 turbines I see spread over distant hills: Spain takes wind energy seriously.

Staying at a four-floor walk-up Pamplona hotel, I visit the bar next door to ask about the location of a shoemaker. I'm still concerned about my hiking boots: they need softer heels than they had been given in Moncton. For the good of my feet, I need to be persistent in finding more flexible heels since they have to absorb the impact of all those steps under my weight. The bartender and the owner of the café are very helpful with directions to a cobbler, and a rough map is drawn on a paper napkin. They are delighted with my gift of two Canadian coasters (with a maple leaf design) to hold their drinks.

The bartender disappears into a backroom and reappears with a neatly folded red neckerchief featuring the words "Pamplona, Iruña" (Pamplona being the Spanish name for the city while Iruña is the Basque name). The men of Pamplona wear this badge of courage at the annual *encierro* (running of the bulls) during the festival of San Fermin in the week of July 6th to the 14th. He advises, "You wear it only during the week of San Fermin," and so I will.

As it turns out, the shoemaker does not have softer heels to place under my boots. I'm resigned to carrying on and to asking my feet for forgiveness as new blisters form. On the positive side, this stroll through the city exposes me to features that include an elevator running at an angle from the bridge of Curtidores up through the city walls. It rises only a few storeys but crosses centuries as it deposits passengers into the old part of the city where I take in the pastel buildings, narrow streets and tourist buzz.

From Pamplona I catch the bus to Roncesvalles (Roncevaux, in French) for the start of my hike on the Camino Francés. I am taken aback by the number of passengers: nearly every seat is occupied. This will spell a hectic pilgrimage though only three of us choose to take a taxi the extra 20 kilometres, crossing the border to Saint-Jean-Pied-de-Port, the starting point in France. The next day we will walk this route back across the border and start our westward trek through northern Spain.

**Obstacles**

The start of my journey is a challenge. The pilgrimage coordinators in Saint-Jean-Pied-de-Port are overwhelmed with the arrival of 200 *pèlerins* (French for "pilgrims). The hostels are filled to capacity, and eight of us are housed in the lounge area of the town's recreation centre. We are each given a gym mat, and we claim a few square metres of floor space. These arrangements are Spartan but meet our needs.

At two in the morning, we awaken to a thunder and lightning storm crashing around the building. Then the rain begins to pelt the skylights. It is a dramatic omen of a miserable day. Short hours later, with the rustle of repacked sleeping bags, comes the hope of an end to the downpour. It continues to rain sporadically, and I decide to wait till the weather settles and the sun shines, but this is not to be.

By 8:00 a.m. we are expected to leave the building and be on our way. Others march through the shower while I sneak off, sprinting to a nearby bistro for breakfast and temporary shelter. In this quaint café, with chairs clothed in earth-toned ponchos, I am met with: *"Qu'est-ce que vous préférez ce matin? Le petit déjeuner?"* ("What would you like this morning? Breakfast?")

I know I am no longer in Spain where breakfast consists of coffee and *tostados* – toasted hunks of bread with pre-packaged marmalade or, when Peter was convincing enough, slabs of cheese. Here I'm served sliced fruit in its juices, natural yoghurt in a cute glass cup, delicate pastries, orange juice and coffee. My boots and hiking gear look out of place among the tourists, so I choose not to linger.

The downpour has become a drizzle, but an onshore breeze carries billowing fog. I can no longer delay leaving the shelter of Saint-Jean-Pied-de-Port, and I set out to conquer the steep slopes of the Pyrenees, assuring myself, "If Napoleon could do it, so can I." That warrior had led his troops along this mountain path instead of taking an easier route into Spain; now I am following his footsteps (though he would have ridden a horse!).

In my late teens, I read a library book about Napoleon Bonaparte: one that weighed a ton. I muse on my resolve in reading a 1,000-page book, and I think of Napoleon's skill in dragging an army all over Europe, and I wonder about the folly of my 6,000-kilometre hike across that same continent. In this Basque region, would Napoleon have appreciated house design? Here the homes look Swiss in their heavy stone features and timber soffits over the gables. Now they are refurbished, but in Napoleon's day they would have housed livestock on the lower level, people in the second storey and laying hens in the attic. And I imagine complaints about noisy neighbours from above and below.

In a moment of quiet reflection before the rigours of my climb, I visit the local church that is part of the regional St. Francis Xavier Parish. Its interior is reverential; walls and ceiling are uncluttered. A recording of Gregorian chant echoes while a pilgrim drops by and sings a few notes, "To test the acoustics." I am captivated by artwork created by and for children: in crayon on poster paper, religious stories decorate entranceway, windowsills and altar table.

Leaving Saint-Jean-Pied-de-Port, I feel the roughhewn stones of the Spanish Gate and realize I'm touching history. At this portal in southern France, millions of pilgrims have grimaced in determination upon starting the trek to Santiago de Compostela. Knights in their finery, monks in muted habits and peasants in rags have filed past these stone pillars over the centuries. Today it is my turn; today I face my own doubts.

The Camino Francés starts at the French border. This section of the Camino de Santiago de Compostela tests our endurance as pilgrims in its meandering route through northern Spain. Over 800 kilometres the trail crosses hills, fields and cities in its westward march. A steady stream of backpackers makes its way through woods, over bridges and under highways.

Camino history dates back several thousand years to journeys taken by the Celts toward a site for viewing the convergence of celestial bodies. The apostle Saint James the Greater (Santiago) is said to have been a missionary in Northern Spain before his martyrdom in the Holy Land and the return of his body to the city of Santiago de Compostela. Hundreds of years later, Saint James is said to have reappeared on horseback in Spain's fight against the Moors.

In the Middle Ages, crowds would trudge this path to pay for their sins and see the world. Recently international status has grown with the Camino's identification as a UNESCO World Heritage Site. A cobweb of European routes merges in Santiago de Compostela while each person's pilgrimage is said to begin "the minute you leave home for the airport."

Through a chance encounter with the German traveller Henry in Mérida, I had discovered this established series of trails with their inexpensive hostels and culture of personal reflection. Here the priority is not the trip but the traveller, and the comradeship of a safe hike allows the opportunity to reflect on one's life. It is said that for some this is a time to consider their relationship with God: they yearn to meet a spiritual need and to become more religious.

This may be true for others; it is not true for me. I have already trod my pilgrim path toward the priesthood – one paved with commitment, but also with loneliness and confusion. That life is in the distant past, but its shadows continue to haunt me. The Camino gives me physical, mental and spiritual space: here I have the freedom to resolve the turmoil of my past. I can come to terms with leaving a life of dedication to God, falling in love and raising a family. During this pilgrimage I may become less religious, but I should become more real.

The rain has lessened, and I dig deep for the courage to face the steep slopes of the Pyrenees Mountains and head into my climb. A half kilometre into the countryside, I meet some hikers in tent-like ponchos they have just bought in town. This rainwear is a wise investment, and I head back to buy this necessity. The woman in the store is helpful, and I settle for the red *capa* with a zipper in the front. I realize how quaint this seems – having started my climb only to head down again for rainwear.

Once more I head uphill as one of the throng of silent images shuffling through the mist. We are a cross between monks going for prayers in their chapel, Inuit women in their amautiks with backpacks in place of babies and Klondike gold prospectors groping through a steep mountain pass. A mutt accompanies us and chases sheep and goats at every turn, but it cannot be stopped from its play.

As we rise higher and higher on a minor road through pastureland, the sheep we have passed become dots down in the distance. Birds soaring over their prey fly far below us. The storm whipping in from the Bay of Biscay tugs at my clothing as nature's wet, cold and wind lay bare my lifelong defences. My spirit is open to change while I depend more and more on momentum provided by the hiking poles Peter left me. On the uphill they give extra thrust; on the downhill they serve as brakes in the mud. The fog and sleet soon eradicate landmarks. Though already mid-May, skiffs of snow are forming trailside, and the gusts numb my fingers. At some point a poorly marked path takes us across the Spanish border.

In late afternoon I slide through the mud into Roncesvalles, the first town on the Spanish side, and seek refuge in its pilgrim hostel. Although arriving wet, cold and grimy, I am delighted with having conquered another test of my personal resources and willpower. I am no longer the little boy – youngest of a dozen children – who needs coddling. In my walk across Europe, I can enjoy self-reliance and self-assurance in the absence of a sibling's commentary.

But what would my brother have said? Would Bill, for once, have recognized my success? Or would he have teased me about my hesitancy in beginning the climb? Or would he, again, have twisted my arm up behind my back to make me cry? Fifty years after his death, I'm old enough to be Bill's grandfather, but he continues to be my older brother and can still undermine my self-confidence.

The Camino de Santiago is named "Le Chemin de Saint-Jacques" in French and "Jacobsweg" in Dutch and German. A Dutch Jacobsweg group adopted the *refugio* in Roncesvalles: teams of a half dozen former pilgrims from the Netherlands take turns serving as *hospitaleros*. I take comfort in the tidiness of the place, and I'm grateful they can do our laundry for a small fee.

I appreciate the patience of the *hospitaleros* in answering questions from our starting group of *peregrinos*. People lived and worked in various countries, left that behind and – days later – are part of the multitude hiking this path. Some adapt more easily than others to the anonymity, rigours and lack of personal space. The *hospitaleros* in Roncesvalles provide a service of support at the first major stop on the Camino Francés.

As I wait my turn at the showers on the first floor, I help myself to a cup of tea in the kitchen area. Here the tea is always on, but I think of the comforts of home – a fluffy bath towel instead of my microfibre cloth and a thick pillow when I've often had to substitute my stuff sack packed with clothing.

Supper is available at the *parador* (historical hotel) next door, and we *peregrinos* are kindly charged less than the standard rate for a gourmet meal. After dinner we are encouraged to go to the local church for a Mass that will end with a special blessing.

To my annoyance, the three co-presiding priests interrupt the liturgy several times to sit and read together sections of their Divine Office (prayers of the day). I have never witnessed this practice and find it disconcerting – putting the people's Mass "on hold" while they carry out part of the daily devotion required of people in religious orders. Either this needs to be a Eucharistic Celebration for the whole assembly, or we shouldn't have been invited. And I recognize this as the first of my irritations with religious institutions along the Camino Francés.

Sharing a room with 120 people in bunk beds serves as initiation to a series of such primitive quarters. Any awkwardness in undressing for bed wears off immediately as all are lost in their own world, and everyone is too tired to care. Sleep's grunting and mumbling is ignored though a neighbour's snoring can be a challenge, and we descend into slumber. Far-off Gregorian chant draws closer; through bleary eyes I catch a *hospitalero* shuffling by and realize his singing is waking us up to morning.

This stopover sets the pattern for the coming weeks – a pattern that becomes comfortable in its repetition. Rising at six o'clock to the stillness of morning, we spend hours walking. At the next lodging, we take our showers, have a nap, launder a few items and buy groceries for the following day. Then we socialize over supper at a café before an early bedtime.

Here our route continues through Basque country. For a week or so, signs are written in both Castilian, the majority language of Spain, and Euskara, the Basque language – one with a liberal use of k's and x's. This area has leanings toward Basque separatism, and Pro-ETA graffiti appear, such as: "Tourists. You are not in Spain." I feel a sense of conflict: the people seem so nice, and they have a right to self-determination, but how does that compare to the same wish for many of the people of Quebec in my home country? I wish I had an easy answer, but I'm really not sure.

During my second day on the Camino Francés, the rain finally lets up. To avoid the mucky path, a group of pilgrims ahead of me chooses to follow the main road to the next hostel. I decide to continue on the pastoral trail laid out in my guidebook and follow a young woman through a field that was ploughed and is now furrows of mud. She is wearing loafers, and I'm grateful for my hiking boots despite their stubborn heels. Hillsides have become quagmires, and I need to watch every step. Despite that close attention and the support of my hiking poles, my foot slips on the downhill. I am exasperated with a pant leg covered in mud. Otherwise, no harm is done, and I stop at the next creek to rinse off the goo.

Maps direct us along a farm lane where a cluster of hikers has come to a halt. They announce, "There's a bull in the middle of the path," and they fear being gored. During my 500 kilometres on the pilgrimage routes, farmers have been careful to keep their bulls behind fences and away from hikers. I would be surprised if this were a bull, and I'm grateful for my farm upbringing in helping me discern the serene look in this creature's eyes.

Walking gently around the beast, I see it's been castrated. "It's actually a steer," I tell them as I lead the group past the placid animal. "But watch its horns. If it turns its head, you could get hurt." Later someone calls me a hero. Aw, shucks!

## Pamplona

Hiking the meandering route into Pamplona, I seek out a *farmacia* for medication to settle my stomach: over a few days, I have worried about feeling nauseous and vomiting from time to time. I suspect that my problem is a reaction to the local bread. Removing bread from my diet seems to help, but that does leave me the challenge of having sufficient food value to keep walking those long distances. A fellow pilgrim advises, "Try Menta Poleo. It's a mint tea you can get at any café here." This local remedy proves soothing.

I discover a restaurant named "Hemingway" that serves a donair the size of my head. Enjoying the tasty filling, I leave the pita wrap to avoid discomfort through the night. I'm intrigued by the collection of photos of Ernest Hemingway decorating the café walls. He had fallen in love with this ancient Spanish city, enjoyed nine visits for the festival of San Fermin and highlighted the e*ncierro* (running of the bulls) in his novel "The Sun Also Rises."

Pamplona boasts evening party activity that continues into the early morning hours. With a few children in tow, adults collect on the streets and in bars, talking and drinking with gusto and keeping us poor *peregrinos* awake till two-thirty in the morning.

Leaving the *refugio* at seven-thirty on this Sunday morning, I encounter a men's choir complete with accordion and guitars. They are gathered around a metre-tall lantern they have placed on the street and are singing exuberantly. In those early morning hours, this scene is quite unexpected – and moving. Meanwhile city crews use paint scrapers to remove posters that have appeared through the night, and street washing units are everywhere. A fire hose drags behind a truck, and a worker directs its nozzle back and forth to wash down the area. Pedestrians cautiously avoid getting drenched.

Trail markers direct me through the campus of the University of Navarra where I cannot find a single yellow arrow. I must have taken a wrong turn and approach one of the hundreds of people out for a Sunday stroll. I am relieved when this elderly gentleman accompanies me to the next yellow arrow – an amble of twenty minutes. This is an odd relationship: I am dependent on his familiarity with the area, but our conversation becomes strained in the ignorance of each other's language.

A few days back, in the middle of supper at the Roncesvalles *parador*, I had a moment of anxiety. When I adjusted my glasses, they snapped in two at the nose-piece. The hostel staff provided me with tape, but this proved to be a temporary fix. I need to stay near the city to have them replaced at an optometrist's office, so I limit the next day's walk to four kilometres. This takes me to De Maribel Albergue in the Pamplona suburb of Cizur Menor. As it turns out,

Maribel is an exceptional character – a community activist who knows everyone. She holds a "clinic" in the afternoon to tend to pilgrims' *ampullas* (blisters). Then she collects a crowd as she scatters cat food into her pond as supper for her turtles. As oversize goldfish swim by, she calls to one of the turtles, and it answers by swimming up to her.

I chat with a young woman who hails from Massachusetts. I've had a song about that state stuck in my head, and she might help stop its merry-go-round. My walking pace has kept triggering lyrics about travel from the tune "Sweet Baby James" by the folksinger James Taylor: "With 10 miles behind me and 10 thousand more to go." But where was he travelling – from somewhere to Boston?

Together, we recall the words of the second stanza: "Now the first of December was covered with snow, and so was the turnpike from Stockridge to Boston." So that's it! With that mystery solved, I am grateful to get the song out of my head.

But, to my surprise, she adds: "Actually, James Taylor's wife is my best friend." And she goes on: "The song they're always asking him to sing is 'You've Got a Friend,' but he never gets tired of it since it helped launch his career."

You just never know who or what you might encounter on the Camino, but now I may have the words of that song stuck in my head: "You just call out my name, and you know wherever I am I'll come running to see you again." But it's impossible to run while wearing a backpack, so I should be all right!

My stomach is again causing problems. At Maribel's suggestion I get a package of dried soup ingredients from the *albergue* dispensing machine and prepare it in the guest kitchen. It tastes great and, thankfully, stays down. However, a banana for dessert comes right back up. My stomach must have thought it was a hunk of bread.

Maribel gives me directions to her optometrist's office in Pamplona, and I'm eager to get that irritant out of the way. I catch the Monday morning bus for the short trip back through the University of Navarra and into the downtown area. It is only four kilometres, which I could have walked in less than an hour, but why walk when I can use public transportation in backtracking?

The optometrist's technician puts me at ease as she helps me choose eyewear that will allow my old lenses to be cut to fit new frames. She takes my silicone temple tip covers and nose-pieces (helpful for my sensitivity to plastic) and fits them to the new glasses. The technician sees me through this complex process with a bit of English and lots of gestures, and my glasses look stunning (if I may say so myself). Not only is the service efficient, but I receive a 15% discount as a *peregrino*.

I make a quick trip to the post office to send a few things on to Astorga as *poste restante* (general delivery). Following the purchase of another disposable camera at El Corte Inglés (a department store chain), I take the bus back to Maribel's haven. She had leant me the key to her storage room, and I retrieve my knapsack while women in white aprons dash throughout the building as they clean it in preparation for that afternoon's influx of pilgrims.

When I find Maribel so I can return the storage room key, she asks about last night's commotion, "Somebody broke a mirror, and other things had fallen on the floor," but it's news to me. This must have happened while I slept, and I'm uncomfortable with having to represent the misbehaviour of fellow pilgrims. Yet, somehow, it sticks to me: we pilgrims – like citizens of a tiny travelling country – are all in it together. But I was asleep, and shouldn't that excuse my lack of action? I try to leave Maribel's troubles behind as I stop at a shining new lunch counter in Cizur Menor. My serving of potato salad is so tasty and attractive that I take its picture while the staff look on amused.

**Hostels**

Maribel's *albergue* is in the process of being enlarged as are other facilities on the Camino Francés. These projects will meet the needs of the horde of *peregrinos* expected to arrive during next year's Holy Year for the Camino de Santiago de Compostela. Holy Years take place whenever July 25th, the feast of Saint James the Greater, occurs on a Sunday. During this year-long celebration, pilgrims receive extra indulgences to free them of future suffering in purgatory. That's bound to attract great crowds, and I'm glad to have beaten the rush despite missing out on the blessings.

Walking the Via de la Plata was a solemn experience, with half a dozen of us sharing space on the trail or at a *refugio*. Now on the Camino Francés, up to 100 pilgrims squeeze into shelter for the night. In most cases people maintain the courtesy of keeping their voices low in the sleeping area – even in the late afternoon – as others may be napping. Sometimes, though, the situation gets the better of the pilgrims: being crammed into tight quarters with only a bunk bed to call your own can become stifling, and it is tempting to let loose.

In one *albergue*, with lights out at 10:00 p.m., the crowd continues to laugh and joke about some incident. As the humour is all in Spanish, I do not understand the source of their amusement. Finally, one of the older men yells for everyone to be quiet. After a few seconds of silence, the commotion starts up again. A half hour later, the group runs out of steam, and we can slip into our much-needed sleep. I welcome their exuberance as I think back on teen years of nighttime imprisonment.

*"In our 90-bed seminary dormitory, the priest supervisor was strict about the rule of silence. We couldn't laugh; we couldn't even talk as our teenage energy had to be controlled. Then lights went out, and my homesickness kicked in. Within the rows of softly snoring teens, I yearned to fall asleep. Only during the black hours of slumber could I escape the bitter loneliness."*

Those were the dark nights of another life. Now I live the adventure of sleeping in a range of *refugios*. The buildings and their *hospitaleros* provide a surprise upon arrival each afternoon. The facility might be large, small, old, new, noisy, quiet, institutional or informal – and no two are alike.

In some cases, the *albergue* is owned by the municipality, which hires former *peregrinos* as attendants. Having completed the pilgrimage themselves, these *hospitaleros* are sensitive to travellers' needs. A few of us finish a long day's walk at a facility where we have heard there might not be sufficient beds for everyone. As we rush in, the *hospitalero* holds out his hand palm down and then raises and lowers it in a gesture of: "Relax; there's plenty of room." I feel calmed and realize that gestures are more essential than words on the pilgrim journey. The two retired men who run the place are quick to hurry outside and bring in the racks of our drying laundry when a sudden rainstorm erupts. A municipal *albergue* generally accepts donations rather than having fixed rates.

A second type of *albergue* is privately owned. Sometimes this seems like a quick way to make money. At one of these, we are irritated with having to line up for sinks and toilets that cannot meet the needs of the crowd. Later we grumble when the toilet tissue is not replenished during the evening and staff with access to the supply have gone home. In other cases, such as De Maribel on the outskirts of Pamplona and mentioned previously, the owners are present and helpful.

A third type is the parish *albergue*. A stay at one of these hostels often includes a shared meal, covered partly by our donations, and we assist with kitchen tasks, such as drying dishes. I enjoy the few hours at a parish *albergue* where the four *hospitaleros* are relaxed and helpful and the cook specializes in oriental cuisine: his supper is delicious. At another I feel on edge as the sole staff member is officious and takes five minutes to register each of us and stamp our pilgrim passport. This usually takes a few seconds, but his procedure includes the review of a long list of house rules. At the supper table, he chats while our meal is getting cold, so someone starts eating; then he scolds her for not waiting till we have said grace. A stay in a parish *albergue* often includes a visit to the priest at the neighbouring church. We might be given a tour of the church and led in a pilgrims' prayer, sometimes with long explanations in Spanish followed by a pilgrim's translation into English.

No matter the type of *albergue*, it boggles the mind to think the whole process – that ends with our departure by 8:00 a.m. – starts again a few hours later when the next group of *peregrinos* arrives. After a quick cleaning of the building, the *hospitaleros* are back to meeting people at the door and applying a *sello* (stamp) to each person's *credencial*.

**Communities**

As our row of ants moves through northern Spain's towns and countryside, we feel removed from the life that occurs all around us. A woman shakes her dust cloth out a window; another waters geraniums on her balcony. Men shovel gravel on construction sites or drive tractors in the fields. In many communities, especially in the Basque region, we hike past the town's outdoor *fronton* (court) for playing *pelota*, a game similar to squash.

Spain has a Camino history of several thousand years, pre-dating Christianity. The people have been born and have grown up with passing pilgrims as a constant fact of life. They've learned a combination of living their lives despite our presence, welcoming us into their communities and finding ways to increase their incomes by meeting our needs. With 100,000 pilgrims passing through every year, many of the towns on the Camino Francés owe their financial well-being to the expenditures of the *peregrinos*.

Whatever those needs, businesses can provide for them. As we approach one of the towns, a car slowly drives along the row of pilgrims ahead of me. As the vehicle approaches, I am amused that it is driven by a hostel owner handing out her business card so we'll choose to spend the night in her *refugio*.

Along the route the rigidity of Spanish meal traditions gives way to pilgrims' wishes, including a Spanish version of bacon and eggs for breakfast. Spanish breakfasts consist of coffee and bread with jam. Now the odd café can fulfill American or Canadian requests for bacon and eggs, but the bacon is a thick chunk instead of thin slices and the eggs come out in an untidy mass. I order this dish only once.

On entering the town of Estella, I take a break in the roadside park that features a memorial to the death of a young Canadian woman. It is said that she was struck by a drunk driver as she rested along the route several years ago. I am dismayed that a hopeful pilgrimage can be so tragically cut short, and I'm reminded to stay alert.

Leaving Estella, we pass a special fountain. Some of the services for pilgrims are the water fountains in each community, but this one is located on the outside wall of a winery and gives the visitor a choice of water or wine. I fill the lid of my water bottle with wine so I can drink a symbolic mouthful while I have someone take my picture. A Web camera on the site (at www.irache.com) shows *peregrinos* quenching their thirst with the local grape product. And I muse: "This Camino has its inconsistencies. At the entrance to Estella, I passed signs of a tragedy caused by drinking; on leaving this town, I could have filled my water bottle with wine."

At a later point on the trail, a cooler holding bottles of juice and water has been placed in the middle of the trail. We are to help ourselves and leave a Euro for each item. As I gulp down a bottle of orange juice, I wonder whether the person left this as an act of kindness or in order to make some money. But it doesn't matter: I appreciate these details and the surprises waiting for us around the next curve in the trail. Our lives have been stripped to the most basic – we eat, drink and move. And we learn to appreciate the little things.

On the Via de la Plata, Peter and I witnessed the early stage of grape cultivation with bare trunks and branches awaiting spring growth. Then we, too, were beginners as we walked Spain's pilgrimage route. Now it is a few weeks later, and I have grown in confidence about the Camino. Here in Rioja wine country, leaves and runners are forming, eager to do their part in grape production. Thin posts holding horizontal support wires have been placed along the sprouting vines. Distant crews are winding the new shoots around these wires while tractors are scuffling to rid the rows of weeds.

Poplar trees along the trail release seed-carrying fuzz in a light snowfall. Mounds of fluff appear on riverbanks and gather in the entrances to buildings, whether *albergues* or eateries. At some cafés the door is always open, allowing the easy entrance of poplar fluff and pilgrims. In one of these, I order a *tubo* (cylindrical glass) of beer as I had in several previous bars. Suddenly, this bartender has never heard that word, and I am left pondering another phenomenon of travel: just when you start to feel confident, things change.

The route through the countryside sometimes takes me under high-tension wires. As these fat lines hang overhead, the dry earth gives off a sound of zapping and crackling. That can't be good!

At a *casa rural* (country inn), I am astonished to learn that my waiter has had a relationship with a young woman from Moncton, New Brunswick and that he had for a time lived in London, Ontario. As I have lived in London and now reside near Moncton, it's a surprisingly small world.

I stop for supplies at a spotless grocery store in Logroño. As is the case in most European supermarkets, the cashier is seated, and we bag our own groceries. It is startling when the patterns of daily life back home are broken elsewhere. Such everyday details catch my attention while the unique features of the Camino have become routine. After my decision to avoid eating bread, I am disappointed that this store is giving a free bread stick with every purchase. My queasy tummy suggests leaving it behind. Twenty minutes later my stomach has no problem with a morning coffee enjoyed along the pedestrian walkway of a bird sanctuary. Flocks rise off the shimmering lake as I drink in another pilgrimage experience.

Having entered and left Rioja wine country, we are hiking the *meseta* (plateau), which mirrors the Canadian prairies. We are snails making our way past endless farm crops while the wind blows in from our right. As we amble westward under cloudless skies, I say, *"Bueno"* ("Nice"), to a farmer about his grain crop.

He motions toward the sky and says, *"Lluvia"* ("Rain"). Farmers everywhere are challenged by the weather, and his crop is thirsty. A 20-kilometre stretch of shadeless trail features fields of oats to the left and wheat on the right stretching into the distance. This monotony is broken by an outside café with plastic chairs and umbrellas set up in the countryside. I enjoy a relaxed half-hour in this open-air eatery managed by an enterprising young couple ready to sell us beer, pop, water and hot dogs (mine without the bread).

## Encounters

An assortment of companions has joined me in our quest. A woman had found her success as a Toronto corporate lawyer to be shallow: "I quit my job, got on a plane and came here to think." A young woman mentions she spent the first night of her hike at an *albergue*, decided not to subject herself to that discomfort again and found hotel rooms from then on.

I admire the perseverance of a Vancouver mother and daughter. They join a few of us for supper at a café, and the mother explains the cast on her arm: "I was slicing bread on one of the first days on the Camino when I cut a tendon in my little finger. We've decided to keep hiking; and, so far, it's working out okay." Heroically, she continues with her arm in a cast while her 20-year-old daughter cuts the meat on her mother's plate.

Some *peregrinos* take the whole process in stride: an American father and his university-age daughter are carefree and unconcerned about their progress. Others plan each day in detail: they explore how far to walk, what kind of terrain will be covered and where to stay each night. So it is that a man and three women from Germany approach each day as a "precision team," scouring maps and guidebooks for distances to be walked and heights to be scaled. The pilgrimage highlights the differences among people.

The pilgrims' personal arrangements now vary from the standard on the Via de la Plata where every hiker wore a backpack. I feel ambiguous about the approach of some travellers: I realize they are free to do what they want, but some seem to lack the dedication that makes the Camino a meaningful experience. So it is that the 38 members of a Belgian women's group are walking the nicest parts of the route with light day packs; they are transported between points in the comfort of a bus.

A yellow Westphalia van has been parked in a few spots near the trail. I approach the driver to find that he is doing Sudoku puzzles while his wife and her friend walk from one town to the next where he joins them for the night. An Irish group of eight is staying in hotels and not wearing knapsacks. One of them explains: "We arrange for a taxi to pick up our bags each morning and take them to the next hotel. It makes the walking much easier."

The Camino welcomes all age groups: they run from 18 to 80, and those over 50 are in the majority. I've met people from most European countries, with the Spanish and German nationals being the greatest in number. It's been especially interesting to meet people from far-flung lands – Russia, Australia, South Korea, India and Israel. The few pilgrims parting each morning and meeting each afternoon on the Via de la Plata have now become a village of hikers. Some travel farther than others each day, and a number of Europeans head for train stations to return home after hiking a section while being replaced by still others in turn.

I am annoyed with those who give the Camino a sense of competition – with pride over an exceptional distance travelled in a day. At some point a group passes through trying to set a Camino record of 50 kilometres per day for the length of the journey. Such competition is not part of the pilgrimage experience: we are searching, not racing.

When I arrive at a hostel one afternoon, a man having a beer at one of the tables set up on the lawn asks me, "Didn't we leave the hostel together this morning? What took you so long? Are you staying here tonight?"

In a split second, I reply: "No, I'm going to the next place. It's a few kilometres away." I interpreted his words as, "I beat you here, and I want to brag about it all evening," so I hoof it out of there.

I surprise fellow travellers with my nonchalance about my schedule for the day and my stops for the night. They ask, "How far are you going today?" And I have no answer: since most *refugios* do not use a reservation system, I simply stop when my mind or body says it is time. In preparation for this trail, I had purchased my second Pili Pala Press guidebook, "Walking the Camino de Santiago." I am thrilled to see this publication, from Canada's West Coast, used by pilgrims from other countries. I have heard it praised as a clear presentation of the information needed on the hike, and I agree.

On an invigorating morning, I keep a steady pace. A few hours later, I pass a park bench and take a break. As I sit back in the warm sunshine, my mind becomes numb to outside sounds. With hat pulled down over my face, I must have attracted attention: at the next café stop, a member of the Irish group says he took a picture of me as a "sleeping *peregrino*." He plans to submit it to one of the Camino Web sites. I'll be eager to look for that when I get home. (I checked later but didn't find this photo on any of the Camino Web sites.)

A university-age lad from Montreal is hiking with a young man from England. They met along the route, and I run into them frequently – catching up on the trail or chatting with them in an *albergue*. The British lad is quiet, but the young man from Montreal is a rebel. In Santo Domingo de la Calzada, he is denied admission to the hostel – something I have not heard of previously. When he walked in complaining loudly about something or other, the *hospitaleros* asked to see his Canadian Passport, but he had misplaced it a few weeks previously. He moans: "My friend is sending it to me by courier. It'll get to me soon. Why won't these people believe me?"

When I see the two companions a few days later, they have walked through the night: "You should walk at night sometime. It's so quiet, and we sleep in a field the next day." The Camino has its share of characters, and these two keep me entertained.

On the walk to Belorado, a rainstorm finds me in front of an *albergue* with its doors open. A few of us enter and wait for the deluge to end. One is a French woman, and I ask what she knows about the pilgrimage route south from Paris. She is able to provide me with two French Web site addresses that might prove useful on my next trip.

Meanwhile other pilgrims – off in the distance – are getting a soaking. If I dare feel complacent, it is short-lived. The next day I go through the turmoil of putting on my rain gear in time for the sun to come out. Then I return it to my backpack in time to be hit with another shower. Changeable weather and unforgiving mud are two of a pilgrim's greatest challenges.

Leaving Belorado in the unsettled weather, I hike along a ridge that takes us through 12 kilometres of pine forest interspersed with purple and pink heather – the first real woods on the Camino Francés. We all feel damp and cold when we arrive at the *refugio* at San Juan de Ortega.

I am the last of the group taking our place in the porch of an adjoining building just as the *hopitalero* arrives to unlock the hostel door. I rush toward it, but a fellow pilgrim remarks that I should be the last one going in as I just arrived. I am taken aback, and – as a joke – I reply: "That's how we do it in Canada." In fact, the Canadian way is to step aside so others can go first. When I get to the door I do just that: I hold the door open and bring up the rear. I really don't understand the man's concern since there is room for all of us.

Mass at the neighbouring church is followed by prayers in a side chapel over the crypt of the local saint Juan de Ortega. Then, back at the *refugio*, we are served bowls of hot garlic soup. This local delicacy hits the spot, and I'm offered a second bowlful. I trust it will warm me up in this stone building that retains its chill day and night, even now in the last week of May when we should be noticing the first hints of summer.

After a nighttime visit to the bathroom, I return to the pitch-dark dormitory but cannot find my bunk. The rows of beds are broken by pillars throughout the area: this becomes a maze in the dark and in the disorientation of yet another sleeping space. Two days previously my flashlight had died, and I planned to buy a new one in the next town. I grope my way back to the bathroom, turn on its light and use that as twilight to my bed. I am relieved at not having disturbed fellow pilgrims, but the purchase of a new flashlight becomes a priority. If the Camino is all about finding yourself, a greater priority is finding your bed!

My few handwashed clothes, hanging to dry in this dank building, are still damp the next morning as we trudge on to the city of Burgos. I sometimes pack my things damp and hope to dry them at the next hostel. When running short of clothes, however, I've had to hang them to dry on my backpack as I walk to the next destination.

Burgos greets us with a monotonous two-hour walk through its industrial and business sections that concludes with a striking image. The old centre of town boasts a magnificent old cathedral and a shining new *albergue* – one that looks like an efficient hotel and feels too cozy: it doesn't offer the discomfort that is part of the pilgrimage. The bed arrangements provide some privacy, and we are each assigned a locker for which we are given our own key. On the one hand, the key is a luxury; on the other, I'm troubled that we might be giving up the trust that is part of the pilgrimage.

To my delight, as I saunter into the facility's common room, I happen upon the four members of the German "precision team." They have gotten ahead of me during the delay in having my glasses repaired in Pamplona. There they are, with maps and booklets spread across the table, planning the next day's conquest. It's comforting to see that some things don't change.

Being a major centre, Burgos sees the departure and arrival of groups of *peregrinos*. People arrive to start this section of the trek; others catch the bus to return home as do some new companions. Over the past week, I have spent time with four people – two couples from Austria, travelling together. I have been asked to join them in a delicious meal they prepared in an *albergue* kitchen. A few days before Burgos, one of the men became ill with an upper respiratory tract infection, and he and his wife took the bus from town to town while the other couple walked the distance. Now in Burgos it is time for them to bid farewell, and – reluctantly – they head home.

Communities along the Camino show their support by displaying images of pilgrims – a stuffed representation of an old man with a walking staff, a yard with colourful statues of walking pilgrims and a roadside bronze cut-out of a hiking Santiago (Saint James). For our part, we long-distance hikers leave our mark through rituals. These might consist of placing two twigs in the form of a cross in a trailside chain-link fence, joining the thousands of others that have gone before. Other pilgrims leave simple statues – like miniature snowmen of stone – along the path. At some point on the trail, each of us adds a rock onto a pile on the ground; this feature is beginning to take the shape of an alligator. In these joint actions, we leave our own isolation to become a community of pilgrims.

This interaction takes a different turn in the village of Hontanas. There several *peregrinos* must have wanted to drink all the wine in Spain, and one of them becomes quite obstinate. He raises his voice and bangs his fist on the table for no apparent reason. A few travellers express concern, and this is the first time I've seen a pilgrim act improperly. We are generally a well-behaved, sociable group – one that respects the facilities, the local people and each other. The anticipated telecast of the *futbol* game between Manchester United (British) and Barcelona (Spanish) dissipates some of the group's energy, and I welcome the morning light when we can start afresh.

Having a coffee at the *refugio* before heading out, I chat with a woman who is employed by a Canadian not-for-profit company. She explains, "We look after the needs of the Inuit from the Eastern Arctic while they are in Ottawa for medical care." Her work is surprisingly similar to some of my duties when we lived in the northern community of Iqaluit (then known as Frobisher Bay) 27 years ago. It is fascinating to compare notes, and – out here along Spain's Camino – I suddenly miss my work as a nurse. That life, too, had been a meaningful journey.

Our morning's walk starts on a trail cut into the hillside. With lush green on my right and a willow-bordered river down on the left, it is a wonderful hike in full sunshine. Then the trail zigzags to take us up onto the ridge and to Castrojeriz where the path runs through the ruins of a convent. In the olden days, the nuns left food on a stone ledge for passing pilgrims. That must have been a welcoming sight.

On a lonely stretch, we see evidence of both free and captive birds. First, goldfinches and greenfinches flit about as if to say, "We'll keep you company for a while." Then, the path is bordered by a series of huts that my guidebook explains are dovecotes: they house pigeons kept for the droppings used as fertilizer.

A climb up Alto de Mostelares is rewarded with a treat of coffee, cookies, water and fruit served by an Italian volunteer group and available for a *donativo* (donation). I appreciate such touches, and they add to the charm of the Camino.

I am beginning to detect in myself the renewal sought by thousands of others over the centuries. Healthier in body and mind, I am able to hike tirelessly and deal with adversity calmly. The trail has been an unpredictable taskmaster. I have grumbled through rough sections with wind and rain lashing my face; I have beamed through flat stretches with breeze and sunshine caressing me. Now I feel content and enjoy the green softness underfoot.

On arrival at the evening's pilgrim hostel in Frómista, I place my backpack by one of a dozen beds to claim it for the night. Then I saunter the few blocks to visit Iglesia de San Martin. This church dates from the eleventh century and has recently been restored. Its ancient artwork was removed since it was beyond repair, so the edifice demonstrates stone simplicity. This is much more to my liking than the resplendence of Europe's cathedrals. Their architecture and artwork feel overdone and do not appeal to my sense of the holy. I find comfort in this simple chapel: it is a church where I would choose to worship.

Back at the hostel, I quietly unzip my knapsack to retrieve my jacket. Napping a few beds over is an elderly woman I had seen on the trail. I had greeted her and her husband with a passing, "Hello," while they were lost in conversation. Out on the hostel patio, a half dozen of us gather for a glass of wine and conversation. One of these is the husband of the woman catching up on her sleep, and I ask about their hike.

Together they have completed the pilgrimage a number of times. "This is our last Camino," he says. At 78 and 80 years of age, the Norwegian couple now skips the more gruelling sections. Their decision to use local buses around uneven terrain allows them this one last hike together. Along the way I have appreciated those with a story that contains a current of heroism, and the age of this couple certainly sets them apart.

This new *refugio* occupies the former Frómista train station. It has been re-built to the point that the station is no longer recognizable. As it is near the entrance to town, half a dozen of us choose to spend the night here. I am much less disturbed by the trains whooshing through the neighbourhood than by the host's lack of attention to detail. Construction leftovers block the way to the clothesline, and the staff members, who appear to be the owner's sons, play loud video games while we try to sleep. Our host asks one of the Spanish-speaking British hikers where all the *peregrinos* are. The reputation of this place is no doubt becoming known in the tight-knit Camino community.

For the first time on the two pilgrimage routes, insects are a menace. As we hike along the banks of the brook that is Rio Ucieza, we can't stop the pesky flies from exploring our ears and eyes. A fellow pilgrim has tied a cloth to a stick and holds it in front of his face as he walks. His fluttering flag keeps the creatures at bay.

Of the three *refugios* in Carrión de los Condes, I choose to stay in the Monasterio de Santa Clara. This convent covers a city block and would have been home to hundreds of nuns in its past. Now only 10 sisters in black habits rattle around within its aging walls. The 30-bed *albergue*, managed by a local resident, is located in a renovated area at the front of the convent, away from the cloistered section. A young Belgian woman arrives, and I strike up an English conversation: "Are you from the Dutch- or French-speaking part of Belgium?"

She responds: "I'm from the Flemish area, but I can manage in French as well."

It dawns on me that we have these three languages in common. "So, both of us speak Dutch, French and English," and I realize she is one of the few people I have met who speaks those three.

A few of the convent rooms serve as a museum, and I enjoy a walk through the paintings and statues donated by religious dignitaries. I am moved by the crafts and trinkets from adults and children – gifts given to the sisters in gratitude for the prayers of this contemplative community. Over the years the items have been carefully stored and are now displayed for our illumination. While an hour of looking up at a cathedral's architecture feels overwhelming, my hour of looking down at these treasures is fulfilling.

Since May is the month of Mary, the convent's evening prayers are preceded by the rosary as have this month's evening Masses along the Camino. The repetitive mantra that is the rosary does not lift my soul heavenward, but I do feel inspired by the high-pitched singing of Divine Office (prayers of the day). This chant is reminiscent of visits to my sister at St. Clare's Monastery in Mission, British Columbia.

St. Francis of Assisi is said to have sought refuge in this facility eight hundred years ago during his pilgrimage to Santiago de Compostela. One of the nuns assures me he wouldn't have stayed at their convent though he may have walked by on the street. I'm not sure whether to believe her or the claim, to the contrary, in my guidebook. In any case, I'm excited by the thought that his path and mine have now crossed.

In our walking environment, people-watching is a universal hobby. A young man from Germany and a young woman from England met just before we reached Burgos. They were together constantly, but now I see them walk alone. I can't help but wonder what will happen in the next episode, or maybe I have too much time on my hands. Now I happen to meet up with Stephan and ask: "You'd been walking with a British woman. What happened to her? Did she go home?" He says they are no longer together because her holiday time is limited, so she prefers to walk faster than he does. At least that's his story.

Unfortunately, the four-person "precision team" has now split up. Two of the women members had gone home, leaving the man and one woman to continue the tradition of dissecting maps and guidebooks in preparation for the next day's walk. I'm curious as to how they'll do as the remaining half of that diligent group.

Occasionally the Camino Francés provides an alternate route that is more remote and, therefore, more authentic. However, signage can be a challenge, and increased distances between towns require enough food and water for the journey. Few *peregrinos* opt for these trails, and I find myself virtually alone – and, suddenly, lonely – on the secondary path to Calzadillas de los Hermanillos. On the main Camino Francés, you see at least 10 fellow travellers within a one-kilometre stretch. As was the case on the Via de la Plata, this minor route reveals only one or two hikers in the far distance.

In fact, as I start on this path, I see no one ahead of me. My guidebook gives vague directions, and there are no yellow arrows to guide me. After a kilometre of worn trail, two possibilities appear. One looks like a sweep of meadow; the other is a winding bit of dirt that seems to head in the wrong direction. Neither looks hopeful. In the distance on my left, I see a pick-up truck beside a barn and wish the person would head my way and give me directions. Magically, the truck moves and comes toward me.

The farmer and his teenage son point to the green swath, and I'm grateful to be on my way. Unfortunately, this grassy section becomes flat, straight and rock-strewn – one of the most tedious Camino stretches so far. It is made more palatable by the croaking of frogs in the channel of water bordering the road. In the monotony their voices are the music that keeps me entertained.

As I approach Calzadillas de los Hermanillos, I catch up to a pilgrim who tells me he's a Dutch filmmaker. He remarks: "With so much immigration in the early 1950's, I'm surprised there's so little information available. I'd like to do a film about the problems that occurred when people left the Netherlands and settled in Canada." As we hike together, I provide Eric with details of our family's immigration, a narrative that has played over and over in my memory.

*"It was spring of 1952, and we were halfway across the Atlantic on our way to Canada when a storm overtook our ship. The Sibajak tossed on the ocean swells while families sat on the floor of the dining hall. To keep us safe, furniture had been tied to the walls with thick ropes, and the floor began to pitch up and down, back and forth, at steep angles. Eventually the sea came back to its senses. A few days later, we steamed into Quebec City and caught a sooty immigrant train to a shabby rented house in Granton, Ontario."*

In leaving our pretty cheese farm in the Netherlands for an economically better life in a foreign country, with its foreign language, our parents showed profound faith. English was to become Mom and Dad's ordeal, and – in Portugal and

Spain – I have become sensitive to the challenge of a foreign tongue. It hampered them in managing the household, running the farm and being part of the community. In my case, this burden is temporary; for them, it was permanent.

**Churches**

As I near the end of my Camino, I realize that churches have been part of the pilgrimage experience – using steeples as guideposts on the journey, visiting cathedrals that pass and attending services while staying in parish hostels. Exposure to these edifices could make you a better Christian: I sense this might work for others, but it doesn't seem to work for me.

Many churches are known for their dazzling *retablos* – massive carved panels, often gold-encrusted, adorning the walls behind the altar. Each time I see another *retablo* in another dusty church that smells of mould, I can't help but wonder: "What's a *retablo* like you doing in a church like this?"

Though *retablos* serve the greater glory of God and local pride, they represent the subjugation of the civilizations of the Americas. From the Inca people, conquistadores seized the riches adorning these monstrous churches. It seems fitting that the billions of Euros worth of gold decorating those buildings now entrap billions more for their continuous reconstruction. If there was a Pilgrim Jesus, is this what he had in mind?

I am both dismayed by this extravagance and confirmed in an old choice to leave my path toward the priesthood after a valiant seven-year effort. My dream of helping people in a special way would have come at the price of accepting intolerable elements within the church. I continue to struggle with a Catholicism that cares for the suffering on the one hand but builds a maze toward heaven on the other.

Having arrived in León (50 kilometres before Astorga), I visit the Gothic cathedral with its two massive towers, its *retablo* of gold and its 1,800 square meters of stained glass. My guidebook has been accurate in its hype: dating from the thirteenth to the fifteenth century, these are said to be among the world's finest stained glass creations.

I take a seat and ignore the throng of visitors as I mull over my reaction to the series of churches and sets of beliefs on the Camino. Early on I had dropped in to see the Baroque retablo at the Iglesia de la Asunción in Navarrete and found it spectacular: even with the church in darkness, it was a glistening cascade of gold.

Then religious fervour infused the folklore back in the town of Santo Domingo de la Calzada, the locale for an old tale about a German pilgrim family. The teenaged son was hanged for the theft of a goblet from an inn when it had, in fact, been placed in his *rucksack* by a worker at the inn, a young woman whose advances he had spurned. Later the parents found their son still alive and approached the local magistrate to have the young man taken down from the gallows. He replied that the son was as dead as the rooster and hen he was set to eat, whereupon the fowl came alive on the official's plate – and the son was set free.

Catholic liturgy is to be kept simple, so it troubled me that the local church supported this fable by housing a rooster and hen in a cage overlooking the assembly. Morning Mass could be interrupted by the crowing of the rooster up in the wall behind the people in the pews. A few extra fowl were kept in a pen outside the hostel in the shadow of the church. I visited them and half-expected a clucked comment: "We think the whole thing is silly. Cluck, cluck."

That church was a mix of poultry and music: its Sunday evening Eucharistic Celebration featured the singing of a choir of engineers that was on tour through the area. I understood they chose music as a hobby to counteract the rigidity of their profession. The Mass was followed by a concert; their rendition of Schubert's "Ave Maria" was exquisite. These proved to be an interesting few hours in Santo Domingo de la Calzada.

As I huddle under the vast sheets of translucent colour within the glory of this cathedral in León, I think back to the

Burgos cathedral where the artwork and gold left me perplexed. There I was more interested in the nearby Iglesia de San Nicholás de Bari. That church displayed a *retablo* that was unusual in its alabaster hues: it looked like an arrangement of breadsticks. I hurried back to the *refugio* for my camera, but upon my return the church was already closed for the evening. On the way out of town at seven o'clock the next morning, the building was still locked. I decided that this was another photo I'd have to locate on the Internet.

On two occasions Mass was followed by the opportunity to kiss a golden reliquary containing a remnant of the local saint. The Camino boasted a saint every few kilometres, and I found religious myths about these people more and more fantastic. Ermita de la Virgen del Rio featured a statue that swam up to the site in a flood, thereby prompting the locals to build a hermitage on that spot.

Our more practical Dutch thinking would squirm at this Latin attitude. Swimming statues, indeed! However, our more rational faith still included angels protecting us and saints pulling us toward heaven, as well as commandments, sacraments and sins. In the face of Spanish fervour, I mull over the faith of my childhood.

*"I was compulsive and found comfort in the certainty of our religion. I could keep my soul pure through a cleansing Confession followed by a healing Holy Communion. The message to love God and serve others was lost in the need to control my guilt."*

Yet the legions of angels and saints had not protected me from Bill's need to ridicule and hurt. Nor did they come to Bill's aid when we were alone in that farm field. "You could have stopped that tractor from flipping over. It crushed the life out of my brother. Where were you then? The whole bunch of you did nothing."

My doubts about our faith were given a different slant a few evenings later. I witnessed a Mass that started with the young priest running to the altar from the back of the church. Then three altar servers raced up, busily adjusting their garments of cassocks and surplices. They must have been late – again – and he was trying to teach them to be on time. I am troubled by this controlling behaviour on the part of the priest, but perhaps nothing else had worked. All in all, this was far from a solemn procession.

I get up from my seat, put on my backpack and leave the León cathedral to make my way through the bustling tourists. I muse on my misgivings about the complex art and mythology that is northern Spain's faith and detect that this may reflect my lack of commitment to the Camino de Santiago de Compostela. Generally, *peregrinos* gaze toward that distant city and its cathedral while I envision my end point in Estonia. I am a "through-walker" (as Peter termed it), so Spain's Camino is important because it provides handy trails and it comes with inexpensive facilities at the end of each day's march. At times I feel like an impostor, but I carry on.

On my way out of León, I again see people selling lottery tickets on the busiest street corners. They wear the slips of paper attached to the front of their jackets, and people approach them for purchases. The salespeople all seem to be disabled, which lends the otherwise depressing enterprise some redeeming value. At a León bookstore, I buy a detailed map of southern France to help me determine where I might start walking in that country. Again, it seems like a huge task: I'll need to take it one step at a time.

Back on the trail, I decide that I owe a visit to the cathedral at the Camino's end point and will take the bus westward to Santiago de Compostela upon my arrival in Astorga, my present destination. I am not hiking those 240 kilometres since they veer away from my journey across Europe, but someday Joanne and I might return to finish the Camino Francés from Astorga to Santiago de Compostela.

**Finish**

Toward the end of my walk through Spain, I begin to feel as though I'll miss the *albergue* experience. The little discomforts, the challenge of sharing space with strangers, the lack of privacy – these grow on you to the point where it all seems normal and routine. It even becomes fun.

With hundreds of kilometres behind me, I'm pleased to be closing in on the culmination of this hike. The walking environment continues to change: for the last day or two, I have not seen churches or houses built of stone. Rather, brick is the material of choice owing to the lack of natural stone in the area. Except for their roof tiles in place of shingles, some of these red-brick houses would feel at home in the older parts of London, Ontario.

A few days back at the *refugio* in the hamlet of Terradillos de los Templarios, two women in the bunk beds next to mine got sick through the night. It was thought they might have been exposed to too much sun. I felt helpless as they took turns running to the bathroom, and by morning both were pondering whether to stay at the *refugio* for an extra day. This is acceptable with good reason, such as illness. As I was putting on my backpack to get back on the trail, one of the women was despondent: "I feel miserable. Maybe I'll just stay here an extra day, or maybe I'll take a taxi to the next town. It's a bigger place, and I could go to a clinic if I don't get better." Among the burdens of hiking the Camino, feeling sick so far from home is especially tough.

The handy Camino "telegraph" system is still functioning: through word of mouth, we receive updates on news in our itinerant community. Further along the trail, I hear that one of the two women who were sick had a stomach infection. Tom, a young British pilgrim, was sick because of "too much sun" but is now feeling better. I seem to be moving more quickly than others, so news only comes to me from behind through those who are travelling even faster.

In La Virgen del Camino, I stop at the Montreal Cafetería for a *café con leche* (coffee with hot milk added). Despite its name, this bar has no connection to the Canadian city. As "Montreal" is Spanish for "Mount Royal," it is probably named after a "royal mountain" somewhere.

Likewise, the local Cañada Real, a traditional sheep-droving route, has nothing to do with Canada.

Approaching the municipal *refugio*, I notice signs with the words "Dominicos" and "Dominicas." These refer to an adjoining series of buildings, and I assume our hostel was built on Dominican religious order property. The role of the *hospitaleros* varies from one facility to the next: they might give advice about the Camino, help sort out medical issues or join in the group discussion. Each has a sense of what is required, but the attendant in La Virgen del Camino stays behind the reception desk the whole evening. This is not a problem, but I am perturbed that her work seems so tedious.

For much of the 100 kilometres before Astorga, we are assigned a sidewalk adjoining the highway. Continuous traffic, with its noise and exhaust, rapidly dull the serenity of the pilgrimage. Any sense of peace eludes us, and over four days the cars whizzing by must see us as statues.

The last few towns appear to have suffered from the placement of the highway through the heart of their communities: the built-up areas look bedraggled and tired. In other places hotels and industrial complexes keep us company. Our peaceful trek has been left behind. I have yet to learn whether there is a Camino authority – a body that regulates the appropriate location of the trail to serve the needs of all. If it doesn't exist, it probably should.

At a local restaurant, I am served *patatas y pulpo*, squid stewed with potatoes in a broth. Despite the description, I find it delicious. Meanwhile, Spanish bars continue to give me a geography lesson in drinks. My previous favourite, Brandy de Jerez, had been displaced by Orujo de León, which tasted somewhat like Dutch genever. Now a bartender has told me that Orujo de Hiervas is even better. A chilled glass of Orujo smooths the roughest Camino.

Each café features a television set, often with Spanish takeoffs of American game shows. Few people are watching, and it only provides background noise, which seems out of place on the Camino. Getting close to the end of my trek through Spain, I regret my lack of exposure to Spanish culture. I've seen numerous churches and their religious art but have yet to hear a flamenco guitar, for example. Over the years I have read about this country's traditions and had looked forward to experiencing them, but they are only to be found in the tourist areas of major cities.

In mid-afternoon I stop at the *albergue* in Hospital de Orbígo just as a spectacular show of thunder and lightning turns to a downpour. I meet Cor, a Dutch traveller slowed down by tendonitis in his left heel, and we discuss the pilgrim belief that this condition can be avoided by drinking enough water. Cor then tells me: "I know a Dutch couple who own a *refugio* in Saint-Jean-Pied-de-Port. They could tell you all about the pilgrimage route south from Paris." He writes down their names and address, and I'm grateful to add this information to the tidbits I've been able to compile.

On my way out of town the next day, several men are fly-fishing in a stream below, oblivious to groups of us passing on a nearby ridge. Yesterday afternoon's rainfall spells a wet walk this morning. I find the dripping vegetation irritating but enjoy a sky filled with a menagerie of clouds – the kind in which children and the child-like see a zoo full of creatures. In contrast, on Spain's *meseta* I'd often seen a cloudless sky, blue from one horizon to the other.

Cyclists and dogs continue to agitate me. While I'm watching swallows flit in and out of the holes in a sand cliff, a stone pings on the trail behind me and a bike zips by, its handlebar grazing my elbow. Then the Camino's yellow arrows direct me through a farmyard where half a dozen dogs begin yapping and licking my calves. The chance to lick the bare legs of a *peregrino* must be a novelty for these animals. And I think back to 50 years ago – to bikes and dogs and Bill.

*"Bill and I biked to elementary school during the last two years of our attendance there. I lumbered on my sensible Dutch women's bike; Bill streaked along on his sporty Canadian model. On the way home in the autumn, we collected sugar beets that had fallen from passing wagons and aimed*

*them at the farm dogs frothing at our ankles. A direct hit sent the dog yelping into the distance."*

A bicycle would mean a quicker Camino, but I'm resigned to walking, and I finally approach Astorga. That tourist city will be my end point on this trip and give me the chance to step off the treadmill. A fellow pilgrim had warned me that the hour-long trek upward into the centre of Astorga was one of the steepest of the Camino, so I take my time and absorb every sensation.

I have now hiked the distance from Cabo de São Vicente, Portugal through Spain and into France – over 1500 kilometres. Tomorrow I'll take the bus westward past the last 240-kilometre section of the Camino Francés to Santiago de Compostela to appreciate its sites. From there I'll head for France to start preparing for my next walk, south from Paris to Saint-Jean-Pied-de-Port. I'm jubilant during my homecoming in Astorga – walking into the *albergue* Peter and I had used during our previous stay and, thus, "connecting the dots" once again. I collect my items from the *correos* (mail service) and reorganize my backpack.

Awakening early, I savour the experience of listening as others scurry to prepare for a long day's walk while I lie in comfort. I gawk at the wares in the Pilgrim's Shop –postcards, t-shirts and trinkets, all displaying Camino logos. Out on the street, a guitar player entertains with a lengthy song about being a *peregrino* on the Camino de Santiago. I enjoy the attention he gives us pilgrims. Later I realize he plays the same song over and over as pilgrims pass by. The emotional nature of the tune ensures that many coins are tossed his way.

Near the *albergue* I find a park bench along the Camino route, and several old companions stop for a final goodbye. I meet young Tom from England; the young Belgian woman who speaks Dutch, French and English; a Dutch man who stops at every tourist attraction along the way; the rebellious young fellow from Montreal travelling with the young man from England and, finally, Lisa (one of the two women who were sick at the hostel in Terradillos de los Templarios and a member of the original "precision team").

I watch with a touch of envy as each backpack disappears around the next corner. I was concerned about "wasting" the extra time in Astorga while waiting for the afternoon bus to Santiago de Compostela but now appreciate letting the Camino experience pass by in review. I could have taken an earlier bus, but it left Astorga at four in the morning. That seems like the middle of the night, even for a pilgrim.

As I bid, *"Bon camino"* ("Farewell"), to passing acquaintances, Astorga's Bishop's Palace rises up across the plaza. With its pinnacles and stained glass, it is the most lavish church rectory I've seen and annoys me as a symbol of the shortcomings in the church: making luxury a priority is intolerable in an organization dedicated to our spiritual needs.

Amid bursts of rain, the bus from Astorga to Santiago de Compostela transports me past medians lush with the yellow of broom bushes in flower. I relish the comfort of moving through space on a modern bus and not having to endure the downpour. My mind becomes numb, and I adjust the seat to nap position for much of the four-hour ride.

## Santiago

Arriving in Santiago de Compostela, I make my way to the local *albergue*, the dormitory of the Seminario Menor – a "retired" minor seminary. Others have just completed their trek, and I had assumed their joy would be palpable. Instead, all is low key in this formal atmosphere. Having spent five of my teen years in residence at such a school, I sense that the ghosts of former seminarians are still haunting the building. They ensure the place could not be a happy one, and – once again – I can't help but be reminded of those seminary days.

*"I was homesick every day and every night. I disliked the team sports we had to play – football, soccer, hockey and basketball. I didn't mix easily and felt awkward in the group. My five teen years in the minor seminary were five years of sadness. No seminarian was totally happy with the path he had*

*chosen, but others found release in camaraderie on the sports field. I did not; I felt so alone."*

Now I feel comfort in being alone and free to explore. During the evening I saunter to the centre of the old city and enjoy the singing of a men's group. They sport traditional Galician costumes of black pants with red cummerbunds and red vests over white shirts. Melodic tunes on stringed instruments attract a cluster of *peregrinos*.

Santiago is located in Galicia, which has its own dialect: now "Plaza" has become "Praza," "Junta" has become "Xunta," "Hiervas" has become "Hierbas." The city thrives on tourism, and shops are everywhere. Santiago's winding streets are the most complex I've encountered. I use my compass a number of times to find my way back to the minor seminary and a good night's sleep.

I miss the pilgrims that Peter and I met on the Via de la Plata and wonder whether I might encounter some of them here. However, considering the distance I have travelled since then, they probably reached Santiago a week or two back. By now they have returned to the comfort of their homes, and the Via de la Plata has become a memory.

I watch *peregrinos* file up the church steps after completing their journey. I admit to mixed emotions – appreciating their efforts but wishing I could be one of them. However, as my nephew Peter assures me in an e-mail message, I probably walked farther on the two pilgrimage paths (over 1000 kilometres) than most of the people who finish in Santiago de Compostela. They would likely have done only the Camino Francés or the last part of it. I remind myself that it is not meant to be a competition, so the walking any of us has done is a meaningful journey.

The cathedral's Saturday noon Mass is packed, and many of us cluster in the church doorway. With a half dozen priests around the altar, the service ends with longwinded speeches, only a few words of which are in English. Then the *botafumeiro* – an 80-kilogram golden vessel – is filled with incense and hoisted by eight men tugging ropes. Through a crescendo of organ music, our bodies arch back and strain to view this spectacle high above as the censer swings back and forth, back and forth, grazing the arched ceiling. Instead of filling me with awe and wonder, this ritual strikes me as a Hollywood production. At the music's orgastic conclusion comes a burst of applause from the spectators, and so Mass ends with a bang.

As they file out, people are chatting about the spectacle when an announcement in various languages advises us to be silent in this holy place. You would think they could make this announcement beforehand as this exuberance must occur every day and the service itself is what sparks the assembly's enthusiasm. The whole thing is surreal, and I feel justified in my doubts. Thus, ends my Camino: enlightened, yes; converted, no.

I return to the retired seminary that is my *refugio* and find the woman in the bed next to mine still asleep. Her Camino must have left her exhausted as I do not see her awake in my two days there. I repack and look forward to my visit to southern France where I'll prepare for my hike through that country a year from now. I'll begin with the complex train-bus-taxi ride back to Saint-Jean-Pied-de-Port, the starting point of the Camino Francés.

On Sunday morning the eight-hour train ride takes me back through Astorga, and I enjoy sliding through towns I passed during my hike. Then I transfer to the slow local in Vitoria for the train ride into Pamplona. A couple's two unruly children become the centre of attention for the resigned passengers: their squealing and jumping from seat to seat keep us on edge.

When I arrive back at the Pamplona *albergue* I had used on my hike through this area, things look as they did a few hundred kilometres ago. However, in the morning it again feels odd that I am not in a rush to get walking. Instead, I get a haircut, though the two women – the shopkeeper and her assistant – seem to hesitate in cutting the hair and beard of this foreigner. By the time the owner finishes an excellent haircut followed by a shampoo in a chair massaging my back, we are communicating non-verbally and non-stop.

From Pamplona I take the bus – crowded with starting *peregrinos* – to Roncesvalles, a dozen kilometres short of the Spanish-French border. There 10 of us pile into a taxi van for the 30-minute ride through the Pyrenees and across the French border to Saint-Jean-Pied-de-Port. As on my last taxi ride through these hills, I am surprised so few are beginning the pilgrimage in that traditional starting point: most of the bus passengers have decided to skip the challenge of the Pyrenees and to start in Roncesvalles, Spain. They will be missing one of the more interesting parts of the Camino.

One of the passengers is biking the route, and neither he nor the taxi driver can reach a clamp on the van's bike rack. I can't help but grin when my Dutch height comes to the rescue in securing this attachment; then we are on our way.

In Saint-Jean-Pied-de-Port I meet with the couple Cor had mentioned back in Hospital de Orbígo. Their *refugio* has no vacancy, but they are able to provide a printout of information on the route from Paris to the Spanish border. I relax over two nights in "Sur le Chemin au Chant du Coq," an *albergue* within the owner's home. The kitchen serves as a pen for rooster and hen with a litter of chicks. You'd think the health department might object to that.

In these two days, I can prepare for next year's walk from Paris south to Saint-Jean-Pied-de-Port. I talk to the people at l'Accueil Saint-Jacques (the Saint James Welcome Centre), locate a guidebook in French at the local bookstore and chat with a young man who had walked the route. I have breakfast at the tearoom I had visited a few weeks ago during my hesitation in starting the Camino Francés in the rain. Later I chance upon an outdoor café where the hot chocolate is so rich and tasty, I can't help but order a second mug.

**Sojourn**

My flight back to Canada is booked for a week from now. I feel physically fit but lack the psychic energy to tackle any of the hike from Paris down to Saint-Jean-Pied-de-Port. After gathering information for my future walk south from Paris, I decide to go for a holiday somewhere in France. I choose Toulouse but – at the last minute – opt for Marseille as I am attracted by its location on the Mediterranean Sea. An unhurried train gives me picturesque views of farms and villages on the way to Bayonne. Then high-speed trains whisk me to Toulouse and on to Marseille.

Upon arrival in Marseille, I go against my practice of using only public transportation. It is late in the evening, so I call a taxi to take me to the *auberge de jeunesse* (youth hostel) kilometres from the train station. The cab takes me through rundown tenements that I hadn't thought to include in my classy image of this city.

The hostel, a renovated mansion, is away from restaurants or bus stop and lacks the normal features of Internet access and coffee or pop machines. The grim elderly couple serving as the facility's staff stay locked in their reception office and give brusque answers to our questions. Others are grumbling about the shortcomings of this hostel, and we try to talk about more interesting things. As it turns out, this unhappy facility has a bed available for one night only. I stay the night and am glad to be returning, by bus and subway, to the train station the next morning.

Despite the brevity of my visit to Marseille, I have a few noteworthy experiences – a taxi driver who provided running commentary on the community; a glimpse of some of the less-attractive parts of the city; a fascinating, but sad, hostel in a mansion of classical design; a bus and subway leading to a beautiful new train station with a dozen staff eager to assist visitors. I also caught a glimpse of fancy tourist hotels near the beach area as well as two massive churches.

During this whirlwind visit to Marseille, my fellow travellers have been the highlight. The chatty folks in my room (especially a Swedish retiree named Hans) made up for the dour staff. Someone suggested: "You should visit Sète. It's an interesting little city on the Mediterranean Sea, and its hostel staff are really friendly." So Sète becomes my next stop. Its hostel proves to be a vast improvement over the one in Marseille, and I feel this is a home – at the end of a steep climb – where I could spend a few days.

Near the hostel someone's yard gate opens into a tunnel of shrubbery. With a bower of branches overhead, this is a beautifully kept garden of green. The owner happens to be talking to a neighbour, and I compliment him on the appearance of his property. Bernard is delighted to give me a tour through his yard and house, which features a magnificent natural stone fireplace.

I present him with two coasters with a maple leaf design and a Canada lapel pin, and he suggests I stay for a drink. He pours us each an anisette with water on ice complemented by a bowl of olives. He is a doctor who recently both retired and divorced, and the precious house has to be sold as part of the settlement. His son is studying in Italy, and his daughter is attending university and living at home. This gentleman's French is rapid-fire, his expression sad. We enjoy the visit, and he asks that I come for supper before I leave town.

I enjoy a relaxing few days in Sète. I ramble along the Corniche (the broad seaside walkway), plan the next draft of my memoirs and chat with other travellers. Before leaving the city, I take Bernard up on his offer of joining him for supper. He performs magic, filling the various cooking surfaces of the elaborate barbeque he had been given as a retirement gift. Bernard serves us slices of potato, eggplant and peppers as well as a great slab of meat. With an accompanying bottle of wine, the meal is delicious and is followed by a rum and raisin ice cream treat for dessert. Afterwards the incline up to the hostel has become even steeper.

I meant to leave Sète after three days, but I am too late for the morning train. This gives me an extra day in this tourist haven with its dozen restaurants in a row, and I go window shopping, watch a fishing boat unload a catch of sardines and have a salmon pizza for lunch.

On the way back to the hostel, I cross through an urban park where a group of retirees is socializing. I take a seat on a bench in the mid-June sunshine and begin to tune into their French conversation. A jovial acquaintance of theirs arrives with a suitcase, which he says contains the lottery winnings he is taking to the bank. Then he goes on at length about computers and how they spell the end of human resources in the workplace. My limited functioning in Portuguese and Spanish during visits to those countries has now been left behind as I understand at least 75% of what is being said.

If I hadn't paid close attention while typing my blog entry, that last sentence would have come out: "?y li,ited functioning in Portuguese qnd Spqnish during visits to those countries hqs noz been left behind qs I understqnd qt leqst è(% of zhqt is being sqid:" With my arrival in France, I have left behind the familiar QWERTY keyboard (named for its upper left row of letters) and need to adapt to the AZERTY and its accent options. As I type my blog entry, I need to stay alert to each typing finger and to keep making corrections. The creative side of me is under pressure to keep the account interesting while hampered by the concentration required to type legibly. It feels like learning to type all over again, and I think back on being taught to use a typewriter.

*"In the novitiate building in Sainte Marie, Illinois, USA, a dozen of us in our late teens sat at desks in a well-worn classroom that smelled of ancient furniture wax. The young man teaching us to type was a fellow novice who had arrived from a junior seminary for late vocations. He had a West Virginia drawl and had been in the US Navy where he typed documents for senior staff. He told of having been one of a team of typists racing to complete the same report where the first piece with not a single mistake would be used. This became a feat of endurance."*

And I think of discipline – that needed in typing the perfect document, in accepting a life of seminary piety or in walking across Europe. And I wrestle with the thought that none of it really makes sense.

The woman managing the hostel in Sète suggests: "You should go and see Dominique. He owns two hostels in the Biarritz area in the southwest of France. It's not far from Saint-Jean-Pied-de-Port, and he has probably met pilgrims who walked from Paris." I'm hopeful that she's right – that Dominique has detailed information on that route south through France.

Always ready to follow another lead, I take the train to Biarritz and book into the hostel there. A staff member makes arrangements for me to meet Dominique. As happens so often regarding particulars about Europe's pilgrimage routes, this man's information is less than enlightening. I am not interested in his irrelevant details: he knows a 73-year-old man who has walked from Switzerland to Santiago de Compostela. That information isn't helpful as it is not the route I have chosen. He says he could ask another acquaintance who knows more about the trail from Paris down to Saint-Jean-Pied-de-Port. So, I leave Dominique my e-mail address, and we'll see what comes of the information he might send me. (In fact, I don't hear from him again.)

The Biarritz hostel is within easy walking distance of bus stop and train station, and it stands out as one that is exceptionally well designed. Each four-bed room has its own bathroom with toilet, sink and shower, and each occupant is provided a cupboard. The attractive features of this hostel include a lounge with bar, a spacious dining room and an outside sitting area with ping-pong tables. Supper is available at a reasonable price, and I order the spaghetti. I savour one of the largest plates of pasta I have ever tackled. Many Canadian youth find their way to Europe for their summer travels. In the case of this hostel, about half of the guests are Canadian.

With sandy beaches skirting the downtown, Biarritz is a surfer's paradise. This city had been the French playground for the rich and famous until overtaken by the Riviera. Stopping for a coffee at an outdoor café, I feel underdressed and lacking in fashion sense. Everyone around me is sporting designer-label clothing from stores that are not Mark's Work

Wearhouse. Hydrangea bushes with full pink, purple and mauve blossoms appear everywhere, decorating this city of pastel mansions and exclusive hotels.

## José

I rise early to catch the train to Madrid for the flight home and have been instructed to help myself to the cereal, juice and coffee I would find in the hostel kitchen. It is well before 6:00 a.m., and I search out light switches to bring the space to life. As a nurse, I would rummage through hospital kitchens in the night to find a meal for a patient. All that food and gleaming equipment have an eerie loneliness in the silence of those early morning hours.

I have my breakfast and head for the train station where half a dozen American men and women are returning home after a carbon conference in Biarritz. This group is employed in a lab in the state of Kentucky where they research alternative uses for coal. I laugh at their anecdote of having to concentrate on the words of a droning speaker while, through the conference room window, they watch people enjoy themselves on the beach.

A significant number of police are on board the French train as we approach the Spanish border at Irún. They seem more thorough in checking identity cards and passports than I would have expected in travel between neighbouring European Union countries. A young police officer has a concern about one of the stamps in my passport; I am relieved when his supervisor says it is not a problem.

On the fast train from Irún to Madrid, my seatmate hails from San Salvador in Spain. I appreciate Pedro's questions: "How was the Camino? Did you like it? What do you think of Spain?" He works for a company that provides "trenchless" technology – inserting water pipes and other conduits underground without the need to dig trenches. As I understand it, a hole is dug in which they place a powerful diesel unit. This machine inserts a prong horizontally into an existing outdated pipe or through the ground itself; then a plastic tube is pushed through. It even allows a conduit to be inserted under a railway track without stopping the trains. Pedro is enthusiastic over the potential for this system. He enjoys the chance to practise English as knowledge of the language is required in his work, and he insists I come and see him on my next visit to Spain.

A wall screen in the train car shows our initial speed through mountainous area as 90 kilometres per hour. Then the rail gauge widens to make travel through curves more stable, and I inwardly encourage the indicator till it shows we have reached 200 kilometres per hour. We easily pass cars on the neighbouring highway and race through a 30-kilometre tunnel piercing a mountain west of Madrid.

It occurs to me how fortunate I am to be doing all this travelling. My next thought is how badly my clothes need laundering after all those handwashings that were actually more of a rinse. Oh well, I'll soon be home.

I had looked forward to the new municipal hostel in Madrid, but it has no vacancy. The staff check with another facility in the neighbourhood, and it has a few spaces available. This happens to be the hostel where I had stayed a year ago and that had no vacancy when Peter and I arrived on our flight from Toronto. I am honoured that one of the staff, a middle-aged man, still remembers me from a year back and gives me a firm handshake.

In the intervening year, I have learned so much about Spain. As I scour local restaurants for a later meal, I now know that *"menu del dia"* refers to the day's selection – at a set price – of soup or salad, main course, dessert and a bottle of wine. Interestingly, each table gets a bottle of wine, whether one is alone (as in my case) or in a group. I haven't yet been able to finish the whole bottle!

The hostel men's bathroom is being renovated, and that limits us to the use of one small washroom. In the comradeship of hostel life, such inconveniences are accepted with a nonchalance that would be healthy to follow in our daily routine.

A few weeks back, with my last visit to Madrid at Peter's departure, I had been unsuccessful in contacting the Canadian Ambassador by phone. I had wanted to meet with him and describe my interesting hiking project; instead, I sent an e-mail message to advise him of my progress. I have not received a reply. This time I arrive too late on Friday afternoon to pursue this matter. Now I'm looking forward to contacting the Canadian Ambassador in Paris when I start my trek in that city. Perhaps I'll have more luck.

In Madrid I have a small beer at my favourite sidewalk café near the hostel and then a caffè mocha at Starbucks. At this outlet they ask your name when you place your order so they can call it out when the item is ready. I muse that it is time to add another name to my lifetime list. I was called Josephus at my birth and baptism, Jos in my early childhood, Jossie by Mom, Shauntsie by Bill, Jo (pronounced "Yo") by Dad, Joe in later childhood and Joseph in retirement. Each reflected a period of my lifetime, an element of my life as recounted in my memoir "Looking for Bill, Finding Myself." I give the Starbucks server my Spanish name and take delight in being addressed as "José."

Later at Bergantino's Restaurante, I enjoy my last *menu del dia* supper, priced at eight Euros (about 12 Canadian dollars). One of the patrons greets me: "Hi, I'm Kevin. I'm a university student from Philadelphia and here to learn more Spanish. The couple who own this restaurant kind of adopted me for my two months in Madrid." Kevin is a great conversationalist and provides translation services for English-speaking customers.

On the *metro* to the Madrid airport, I am concerned that my flight information doesn't state whether I fly from Terminal 1 or 4. A buzz among the more knowledgeable passengers provides the suggestion that Air Canada probably uses Terminal 1 (which proves to be correct).

On the flight home, I enjoy the Canadian film "One Week" about a man taking a motorcycle trip across Canada when he is diagnosed with terminal cancer. I seem to have peers with parallel stories in all sorts of places.

A five-hour wait between flights at Toronto Airport leads me to the airport's Sheraton Hotel for a coffee and banana split. I'm glad to be back in a Canadian restaurant, and I muse on my experiences across the Atlantic. In Spain anything to do with meals seemed complicated, whether meal times (supper between 8:00 and 11:00 p.m.), menu choices (especially when given in rapid Spanish by a rushed server), facility usage (such as needing to locate a café with the required *comedor* dining area) or *tapas* traditions (with some being free with a drink and others available for purchase but those rules changing at the next café). Rural communities did simplify the meal-purchasing process by rounding out prices to the nearest Euro so you were freed from managing small change.

I ponder my luck in chancing upon Marie and Anna as initial fellow pilgrims. On this trip my nephew Peter was a relaxed companion, and I have enjoyed the company of others on the way. With Joanne's support I am fulfilling a dream. My flight is delayed, and I don't arrive at Moncton Airport till well after midnight. This makes seeing Joanne even more heartwarming. A two-month absence can give your life a refreshing new meaning.

Settling back into retirement, I appreciate the simple things – the conveniences of home with its predictable shower, comfortable bed and recognizable food. My clothes are clean and less basic than those of my hiking days. Family and friends are interested in anecdotes of my trip, and I delight in providing more detail to those who have plans to walk their own Camino. And each of these discussions brings the urge to continue the journey – to get back on the trail.

# Trip 4: Encore en Route

*May 11 to June 28, 2010 – 988 kilometres*
*Paris southwest to Saint-Jean-Pied-de-Port, France*

**Paris**

My fourth walk through a section of Europe will take me through France, and I think: "I am *encore en route*, again on my way." The first three trips have taught me so much that I should feel confident in this venture. Instead, the preparations still give me a sense of uncertainty – as though this is my first hike. An acquaintance expressed an interest in joining me, but he had other commitments, so I am again on my own.

With no pilgrim hostels on this trail, I am taking a tent so I can use campgrounds, which are less expensive than other lodging. If it sees little use, I'll feel free to give the tent away as it has already served us well over the years. I have also compiled a list of the few youth hostels *en route*. Once again, I am following an ancient pilgrimage path Via Turonensis – and modern signs – that will lead me southeast from Paris to Saint-Jean-Pied-de-Port at the Spanish border.

The flight from Montreal is uneventful except for a detour around clouds of volcanic dust from Iceland. This makes us only a half-hour late on arrival at Orly airport. A young woman in an information booth arranges for my stay in a Paris hostel near the headquarters of the Chemin de Saint-Jacques (Path of Saint James).

In a visit to that office, the coordinator tells me that details on the pilgrimage route through France are sketchy. The

French guidebook I purchased on my last visit to Saint-Jean-Pied-de-Port is likely the most up to date. I wish I had a set of local maps to help me search out trails, but the length of this hike would make that impractical. I am told: "If you took all those maps, you would need a wheelbarrow!"

Both the weather and the hostel guests are cold. I wait in line to register while a Christian college group from Michigan confronts the hostel receptionist with a series of complaints. "You put eight of our students in one room. Can they be split up so it's not so crowded?" "Each room has only one receptacle to power up our phones and laptops. Do you have other receptacles we can use?"

Over the few years of my struggle to cross Europe on foot, people's expectations have changed: gadgets have become a priority. Some of those, with GPS features, would make my hike simpler, but I enjoy the challenge of being close to getting lost. I shall need to rely on inner resources and the French people to find my way.

In visiting Saint Sulpice, I explore another church that is under repair and could continue in that state for many years: so much remains to be done. Then I browse through a used book store, looking for topics I would not see back home. The loose flooring in this old shop causes a bookshelf to wobble, and a book on display comes crashing down on my head. The owner informs me that this is a very expensive book and I should be more careful. I know how I would like to respond, but I'm limited in my knowledge of local language and social convention, so I leave quietly.

My roommate at the hostel is a young man from South America looking for work and an apartment in Paris. In an earnest voice, he describes his interest in the ancient study of alchemy: "I'm sure it exists; we just need to figure out how to make alchemy work. Then we could easily turn iron into gold." My travels keep challenging me, and I'm not sure how to respond to these ideas when my roommate is so sincere. I decide to listen politely and then change the subject.

After one night at the hostel, I look forward to the challenge of starting my hike. I begin by walking around the nearby Tour Saint-Jacques (Tower of Saint James). This is the Paris landmark near the River Seine where thousands of pilgrims have begun their journey over the centuries as they headed for Tours and on to Spain. The 52-metre Gothic tower is all that is left of the 16th-century Church of Saint-Jacques-de-la-Boucherie (Saint James of the Butchery). That church was named after its patrons, the wholesale butchers of the nearby Les Halles market. On top of the tower of muted greystone stands a statue of the apostle Saint James the Greater guiding us toward Spain. A motorcycle is parked nearby, and I'm tempted to borrow it. I could be in the south of France in no time!

It is Ascension Thursday, and I pass a church just as Mass is starting, so I make my way inside. The church is busy, and a university student squeezes in next to me. In hushed tones Alexandre asks: "Could I get your e-mail address? I plan to visit Canada and would like to contact you for more information." (However, I do not hear from him again.) Here I am at a weekday Mass in a crowded French Catholic church, and I think back on how important we held holy days of obligation in my Ontario Catholic childhood.

*"In our Baltimore Catechism we learned about Ascension Thursday as the day Jesus rose into heaven. Six 'holy days of obligation' occurred throughout the year. On those days the Public School students, all of whom were Protestant, attended school; those of us at the Catholic Separate School could stay home. We went to church and treated those days as though they were Sundays. The days were special, and so were we."*

Here in France it is unfortunate that Ascension Day is taken so seriously because no businesses are open. I knock at the door of a tourist information office in hope someone will answer, but no one is there on this religious holiday. A locked door stands in the way of accessing the list of families who take in pilgrims in exchange for a donation.

Instead, I stop to ask a man who is out for a stroll the way to the hotel in the nearby city of Massy. I'm tall, but he towers over me. I give him a Canada lapel pin and take a break on a park bench before continuing to my lodging for the night. The man returns to give me a card for my wallet. It pictures the Eiffel Tower, and he squeezes the card to light a tiny bulb at the tip of that Paris landmark. He grins as he hands me this handy flashlight – a great start to encountering the kindness of strangers in yet another country of Europe.

On this Christian holy day that is a French holiday, the hotel has only skeleton staff. There are few guests, so the two employees relax in an alcove watching a soccer game on TV. Many restaurants are closed, and the few that are open have non-Christian owners and staff. I locate one that serves dishes from the Middle East and enjoy a tasty shish kebab. Upon my arrival at the hotel, the staff promised, "We serve a big breakfast that is part of the cost of the room," and the following morning they deliver on that promise.

**Irritants**

Paris is a widespread city, and it proves to be a slog to escape this metropolis. In this trek through built-up areas, I seek out cafés for their toilets: when I need to pee, I order a cup of coffee so I can use their facilities, but – when that coffee does its work – I need to use another toilet at another café and order yet another cup of coffee. I soon realize that the process is actually counterproductive!

I know I have made it past the endless city sidewalks when I pass Orly Airport. My hike takes me under the flight paths of the great winged engines swooping out of the sky to find their landing place. So sleek in flight, they rumble to an awkward conclusion on the ground.

I am relieved to finally be walking through French countryside but encounter the irritations that come with such a trip. Traveller's constipation leads me to a grocery store in a search of a bottle of prune juice. When I enter a store, the size and weight of my backpack are problematic: its size brings me close to knocking items from shelves, and its weight seems to increase as I comb through the shelves for an item.

As I pass rows of milk cartons, I am surprised that they are not kept refrigerated in Europe as they are in Canada. Apparently, they have been subjected to the "ultra high-temperature pasteurization" that kills more bacteria and gives the milk a longer shelf life. I find the juice section but not the prune nectar. I'm about to give up when one of the staff directs me to the section entitled *"biologiques"* ("organics"). There I find my treasure and think of my childhood constipation and hours on a bedpan.

*"There I sat in the living room, with family members coming and going and asking if I hadn't gone yet and what was taking so long. Bill would be outside playing while I was consigned to be seated on that ring of numbness."*

Armed with my prune juice, I am on my way and check my guidebook for the address of a facility in Longpont-sur-Orge. This complex of houses serves as a getaway for children from the inner-city neighbourhoods of Paris and has a few beds available to pilgrims. Unfortunately, the place is full to capacity, but I am told I can pitch my tent in the backyard.

Both staff and children feel intrusive: although I start short conversations, I become the object of their whispers throughout the evening. The park-like setting reminds me of the *jardim* in Aljustrel, Portugal where I was assaulted. I have pangs of anxiety as darkness sets in – vague notions of people looking to do me harm. I walk over to check out the three-metre high rock wall around the yard and decide I'm safe. I sleep well.

The next morning I see a McDonald's restaurant in the distance and go looking for a cup of coffee. I'm surprised to find the doors still locked; a sign indicates the opening time is 10:30 a.m. This is a striking example of the difference between our two countries. Here people of all ages start the day by carrying baguettes home from the bakery – under their arms, in bicycle baskets and in handbags.

The Canadian custom of going to a coffee shop on the way to work must seem foreign to the people of France where the early morning hours provide a rare place to eat or drink. Even sizable towns may have no breakfast or coffee available whereas my hometown of Sackville, with only 6,000 people, provides about eight such establishments as early as 7:00 a.m. I can understand neither the lack of such services in Europe nor the need – or the availability of customers – for so many of those businesses in our part of Canada.

The next day my guidebook suggests I seek shelter at a convent of Dominican sisters. A nun answers the door, and she explains: "We have a group here on retreat, and there may not be room for you. I'll check with the sister who looks after visitors." I bide my time in the parlour while the search is on. I'm flabbergasted that it takes a half hour to find a nun in a closed convent, but I'm finally given the answer, *"Non,"* there is no room for me.

I continue on to the farm of a former pilgrim who has a cottage available for a night's stay. Thierry grows a cash crop of wheat, sugar beets and canola. He has made the long trek from Paris through Le Puy-en-Velay to Saint-Jacques-de-Compostelle (or, in Spanish, Santiago de Compostela). A few years later, he made the hike "in reverse" – returning home from Santiago. The family is warm and welcoming, and my guest house is a wonderful example of post-and-beam construction. In the evening their teen son Jacques-Henri entertains us with his prowess on the unicycle. I hold my breath as he performs, only centimetres from the dishwasher's open door!

In the town of Étampes, my guidebook states I need to turn left at a stadium, and I see signs toward the building but cannot locate it. (Later I learn that a new housing development blocks it from view.) An important-looking man with a briefcase escorts me for the next twenty minutes as he is headed where I need to be. A sign at his office indicates he is an accountant. *"Merci beaucoup,"* I say as I hand him a Canada pin, now confident I'm on the right track.

I phone home at the next town and, on its outskirts, come upon a pleasant campground that had not been listed in my guidebook. A winding road ends in several S-curves that lead into the campground. This is a haven for tourists from the Netherlands. Since they are only staying overnight, they do not socialize but retire early. I am disappointed as I had hoped to practice my Dutch conversational skills on these weary, unsuspecting travellers. This is my first glimpse of recreational vehicles being parked using remote control. People look like they are switching television channels or adjusting the volume while they walk beside their units to park them.

When I leave the next morning, I follow the instructions in my booklet and take the path leading from a bend in the road. As it turns out, there are several such paths at several such curves, and I chose the wrong one. The trail takes me through farm fields for two or three kilometres only to reach a dead end. I am annoyed at starting the day this way and have unpleasant thoughts about the authors of my guidebook since they could have added more detail. I meet up with a farmer who tells me, "You can keep going through the fields, but a stream will block your path." I follow his advice, trudge back to the campground and start the day's hike over.

I find the municipal campground on the outskirts of Toury, but it has no staff in attendance. Instead, a young well-dressed couple seem to take charge from their trailer and tell me I'm not to camp here. My discomfort increases with the whispering among other campers, and I have a vague sense of re-experiencing that fateful night in Aljustrel, Portugal.

Desperate for accommodation, I make my way into town and ask a young man who is waiting for a ride outside the bus depot if he has any suggestions. When his father arrives, they have a *tête-à-tête*, and I breathe a sigh of relief when invited to camp in their backyard. So, I come to spend the night at the home of Alain, Sylvie and their four children. Alain is the perfect host and makes sure I have everything I need – use of their shower, a few drinks, meat for my little barbeque and breakfast the next morning. Alain is self-employed: he travels to China to import electronic components into France. This is another of those tidbits that only a walk through Europe would reveal.

The next morning Alain buys me a card to use in pay phones so I have an easier time of finding shelter for the night. He gives directions to an apartment they own in Orléans should I need it. Then he says: "I'll drive you into the country, and you can just walk south from there."

But I respond: "No. Just drop me off at the bus depot where you picked me up. I need to walk every step of the way across Europe." This trek continues to be all about "connecting the dots" as Peter said. I turn to wave goodbye to another helpful person, and he waves back at someone who must be a puzzle for him.

My trek through Portugal and Spain and into France has left me surprised at the dryness of the soil and the need for extensive watering. I count nine irrigation plumes rising into the air over farm fields as I drop by a farm *gîte* (bed and breakfast) for directions. It is coffee time, and I'm invited to join the hostess and her farmer husband at the wooden kitchen table. We get into a complicated French discussion on farming in Canada, and I'm glad to be walking again to clear my head after racking my brain for all those French words.

When I had put on my backpack to leave, photos were taken to appear on the farm Web site. This farm with its Internet presence opens memories of my old-fashioned farm childhood. I see my father lugging pails of water then and look at myself with my knapsack now, and I know that my perseverance is reflected in that of my father.

*"Dad struggled through rain and cold to water the livestock. Over and over he walked from the pump beside the house back to the barn with a pail weighing down each arm. During winter storms Bill and I would take turns opening the barn door as Dad trudged through."*

Over the seven years on that farm, Dad must have made 50,000 of those trips. He had a purpose: he had a family to feed. I have no purpose other than a dream to fulfill.

Later I check the "Ferme d'Abbonville" Web site (www.ferme-abbonville.fr). I am pleased at having been given a spot on their home page with my picture and its caption: *"Un petit coucou du pèlerin Joseph"* ("A little hello from the pilgrim Joseph").

With no vacancies in the town of Gidy, I visit the *mairie* (town hall) for advice, and I'm given the key to an apartment. It serves as their shelter for abused women and for pilgrims and proves to be a tidy unit with a few beds, a simple kitchen and a great shower. Once again, I am grateful that a community has provided me with a home for the night.

This hike has been all about searching: I've had to find my way down the trail and locate places to spend the night. My preparations had started with a search for the right hiking boots. A three-hour drive took me to a shoe store in Fredericton that specializes in big feet. This had been a wise decision as my size 15 medium-width hiking boots are working well although a few blisters have made their presence felt. Such is the cost of folly.

**Orléans**

Just north of Orléans, I take a few pictures of a phenomenon known locally as *"la folie"* ("the madness"). On five-metre-high pillars, a concrete viaduct soars over farm fields. This is a section of the Aérotrain (Skytrain) test track of the 1970's that was to become part of the Paris-to-Orléans line. Powered by an airplane engine, the train could reach speeds of 400 kilometres per hour. The 18-kilometre line is now abandoned as the project was dropped in favour of the European-model Train à Grande Vitesse (High-Speed Train). Cost of destroying the kilometres of concrete was deemed prohibitive, and its presence causes little inconvenience to those below. However, local farmers see it as an example of political folly, and I'd be inclined to agree.

A hot trudge into the city of Orléans is eased by the shade of a sweep of acacia trees and brings me to the door of Sergio, Gaëlle and her two little boys. It is in their building that

Alain and Sylvie (from back in the Toury area) own an apartment I can use during my stop in Orléans.

These folks have heard I was on my way and express words of welcome. Sergio speaks a clipped French, and I keep calling on Gaëlle to "translate" into a French I can understand. He continues talking while she's in the kitchen preparing supper, and I notice that, after each of his sentences, I need to ask: *"Pardon?"*

My stomach has been in turmoil again, and I have trouble making it through my serving of pasta and salad. While Gaëlle retreats into the kitchen to prepare desserts, Sergio asks if I'm okay. My stomach is unsettled, and I must look green. I excuse myself, swoop down the stairs to my tiny apartment and get to the toilet just in time. I wash hands and face and brush teeth, return to Sergio who asks if everything is all right (I tell him I feel fine, which is true!) and welcome a delicious dessert. Suddenly I'm hungry, and it goes down well. My stomach is settled, and I feel refreshed.

Sergio entertains me with a CD of Portuguese songs produced by his rock band. He explains the choice of language for the lyrics: "My parents and three older brothers emigrated from Portugal. I was born after our family came to France." In my wanderings through life, I have had similar experiences: the person most interested in maintaining the original culture and language is often the youngest in the family.

When Sergio says he has something for me, I guess what it is and think, "Oh no, not another thing to carry." He presents me with their old laptop and insists I accept it since my story has given him more than he could give me. The personal computer will certainly make it easier to maintain e-mail correspondence with home and to enter my blog information. Considering the convenience provided by this device, the extra weight is something to which I can adapt.

It will be one of many adaptations on this trip. Spain's Camino was straightforward; France's Chemin is convoluted. This hike has been an ordeal: sections of the trail are lacking the blue and yellow *coquilles de Saint-Jacques* (scallop shells of St. James) pointing the way, and guidebook instructions have been far from clear. Furthermore, in Spain I could simply appear at a hostel and be given a bed; here each night's stay needs to be arranged upon arrival.

Towns in Portugal and Spain provided a café, store, telephone booth and library with Internet access. Other than bakeries, no businesses can be found in French towns since people do their shopping in nearby cities, and a telephone booth is a rare find. Access to the Internet is only available in large centres because the French government had arranged for each household to have a simple computer, making public Internet facilities unnecessary.

I am annoyed by this lack of basic services and by the weather: two days of cold during the trek out of the greater Paris area have been followed by two weeks of sun-drenched stretches in unseasonably hot conditions. Now, in the third week of May, I am left wondering, "How long is this worthwhile?" On a more positive note, the interior of the Gothic cathedral in Orléans is an example of those said to lift the soul heavenward.

As you enter its great doors, the narrow nave draws your eyes up to the arched ceiling towering overhead. Despite my sceptisism about monstrous cathedrals, I find this one uplifting. I am intrigued by the tale of St. Joan of Arc, whose statues appear throughout the community and give a glimpse into her role during England's 1429 Siege of Orléans. The blockade had lasted six months when, only nine days after her arrival, Joan of Arc led the troops to victory – a remarkable feat, considering she was a mere teenager at the time.

## Loire

Beginning in Orléans my hike follows the course of the Loire River. This majestic expanse gives me a sense of calm, and the croaking of frogs is the loudest I've heard.

In Saint-Ay I have another uncomfortable experience in a campground. As I walk into the area, a few men begin to harass me about hiking the Chemin de Saint-Jacques: they taunt me for no apparent reason, and one sticks his tongue out at me. When I ask one of the *riverains* (local people) about this attitude, he explains, "They are the 'caravan people,' and that's how they behave."

I choose not to camp there but proceed to Meung-sur-Loire where a former pilgrim welcomes me to his estate that serves as a religious retreat. He takes me through a complex of buildings to show me where the bathroom with shower is located and assigns me to one in a row of bedrooms each of which has a doorway onto the extensive lawns. I pay him a few Euros, and he disappears as he has meetings to attend. Several other visitors seem fervent and lost in prayer, so I enjoy a quiet evening.

No matter how well intentioned, neither the local people nor the tourist information centres seem to understand the vagaries of walking the Chemin de Saint-Jacques. If you are not driving a car – or, at the very least, a bicycle – your needs remain mysterious. So it is that the people at an information centre advise me: "Just follow the trail along the Loire River. It takes you right into Beaugency."

They are correct for a few kilometres. Then the path abruptly ends in the woods, and my way is blocked by a stream that is too deep to ford. In frustration, I hike back (almost to the information centre!) to cross the river tributary at a bridge back in town. An elderly man out for a stroll gives me proper directions and the comment: "Those tourism people don't know what they're talking about."

A *gîte* in the town of Avaray is the former home of an elderly couple who had farmed the small acreage. They have retired elsewhere, and their son rents it to visitors for overnight stays. The son says, "Breakfast is not included," but only when he and his family drive away do I realize I shall be alone in the house.

I make myself at home and look forward to my afternoon shower when I discover there is no hot water. I opt for a shallow bath, rummage through cupboards and find an electric kettle. A pan serves to heat water on the one electric element of the stove as its gas elements will not light. This feels eerie – like a remake of the movie "Home Alone." The son happens to arrive on his tractor, phones his parents for instructions and opens the gas valve that had inadvertently been closed. I pay myself for my efforts by an hour-long soak in a tub brimming with warm water. After today's long stretch, it feels great.

The house is within a kilometre of the looming double evaporation silos of an electric generating nuclear plant. In my home community, a heated discussion on wind turbines continues, but I am more comfortable with those than with the dangers of a nuclear meltdown. I muse on packing my bag quickly in case of an evacuation of the area and trust the nuclear plant staff to stay vigilant overnight. They do their job, and in the morning I leave with no regrets.

As was the case in Beja, Portugal, the morning begins with people shaking hands with others they meet. As I enjoy my morning *café au lait*, several customers shake my hand while they make the rounds. I am honoured to be included in the ranks of the citizens of Avaray.

During much of the day, I follow kilometres of trail on the *digue* (levee) built to keep the Loire River from flooding surrounding farmland. Black insects swarm around my face and are an irritation till I realize they do not bite or sting. Since they don't even land, I welcome them as a flying escort.

In Paris I had been told that several *pèlerins* (pilgrims) start on this route each week. I hoped to encounter others but have not yet come across a single fellow hiker. On the other hand, groups of non-pilgrim cyclists are plentiful, particularly along the Loire River – in one case, a dozen or so from New Zealand.

With 400 conventioneers in the tourist trap of Blois, no lodging is available. A young woman at the tourism office suggests an alternative: "I live near a campground about six kilometres away. When I finish work, I can drive you there on my way home." I appreciate her offer and arrive at my home for the night. The owners are a retired man and woman who show attention to detail: although the place is not extravagant, I am pleased to see that its bathrooms are exceptionally clean.

The next morning the owners flag down a couple who are going to the Maison de la Magie (Museum of Magic) in town so I can catch a ride and continue my trek. People just keep being nice to this Canadian stranger – or, perhaps, this "strange Canadian" who is intent on walking across Europe.

At the end of the day's hike, a private campground magically appears, and I seek shelter for the night. Unfortunately, one of my tent poles begins to split, and my best Red Green imitation with a borrowed role of duct tape does not stop the pole from snapping in two. I could have worked more diligently at solving the problem, but in the morning I roll up the tent, place it in its bright blue bag and give it a proper burial in the garbage bin.

A week and a half ago, Thierry (the cash crop farmer) suggested I throw the tent in the *poubelle* (garbage can): "You can always find places to stay, and the tent is just extra weight." Later, I had had two uncomfortable encounters with campground clients in Toury and Saint-Ay. A week ago I bought a warmer sleeping bag: it was the only one available at that store but fit my lanky frame. Despite the hot days and my new sleeping bag, cold was awakening me in the hours before sunrise. So, when my tent suggested it was time to depart, I agreed.

The French tradition of enjoying civic holidays in celebration of religious feasts holds true for the Monday following Pentecost Sunday. This day commemorates the descent of the Holy Spirit upon the disciples of Jesus. Once again, businesses are closed, and I have trouble finding food, shelter and tourist information. These holy days are getting to be a nuisance.

As I leave the hive of tourist activity that is Chaumont-sur-Loire, I enter grapevine country and enjoy a sample of local wine at a *cave* (temperature-controlled wine storage building). It is located in the country, but I would soon see more of these tasting-purchasing enterprises in the towns.

Among these fields of grapes and barrels of wine, I think of grapes and wine in my youth.

*"When we bought our farm in Arkona, Ontario in 1954, it came with a hedge of grapevines stretching from our garden to the distant road. During a bountiful year, bushels of these grapes became jam and juice. Mom found a new use for the tub that had served to make cheese in the Netherlands and to bathe us as youngsters and soak the laundry in Canada. She surprised us with her ability to turn it into a vat of wine to be bottled for an upcoming family wedding. It met the approval of guests and family, particularly my brother Tony who – along with a few friends – stumbled up the stairs from the basement and announced that it tasted great."*

Meanwhile, I am soberly climbing hills above the vineyards as I consider the experience of the pilgrims of old. Theirs was a rare chance to explore the sights – like row upon row of grapevines – that those at home could only imagine. Now television, airplanes and a variety of gadgets have brought distant locations to us with little effort on our part.

I pass a group having lunch at a picnic table, and they want to hear about my trek and hand me a tasty piece of fried chicken. After a brief stop, I keep walking as I munch and muse on such consideration: for a moment my isolated activity is recognized by the local community. I finish the snack and pick up speed when I'm brought to a halt by a group of a dozen gathered on a lawn around tables laden with food: "Do you want some fruit and a cup of coffee? We get together once a year, and everybody brings something. We always end up with too much food."

*"Oui, s'il vous plaît."* I'm offered a chair and join them for a bit of conversation. So that's two snacks and a cup of coffee thanks to the generosity of strangers. This interesting day ends at a tiny hotel next to a monstrous chateau in the tourist city of Amboise. Signage to do with "Léonard de Vinci" indicates that the famous Italian spent the last few years of his life here as guest of the king.

That evening I am overcome with a longing for home, its comforts and Joanne, so I phone her the next day. I am given details of a family celebration that included a feed of lobster. The convenience of our remodelled bathroom also arises during the conversation. Meanwhile I continue my lonely quest: I cope with shared bathrooms and no lobster.

Right after the phone call, I am faced with the most agonizing of my several fears, and no one else is there to share the anguish. My guidebook directs me onto the narrow walkway of a bridge spanning the Loire River. It is a half-kilometre trek a nauseating distance above the swirling water. Halfway across, my knees feel rubbery, but I force myself to put my pace on automatic and to avoid looking down. This trestle also serves as a river crossing for trains; thankfully, none whoosh by me during my unending passage. On the positive side, room is available for a few of us in the guest area of a convent in Tours where we help the nuns set up our cots.

Half a dozen Benedictine nuns serve as support staff at the Basilica of Saint Martin. There have been several saints named Martin, and I wonder for which of these the church is named. Then it strikes me that – of course – it has to be Saint Martin of Tours since I'm in Tours, France. It can be difficult to make the jump from our "Lives of the Saints" books years ago to my presence in these foreign countries now.

The sisters provide tasty meals, welcome visitors to their Divine Office and are gracious and understanding. The smile of one of the nuns is delightful: it reflects the twinkle in God's eyes. In France soup is not available outside the winter season, but the sisters' dining area – with its gathering of two dozen middle-school students and a few pilgrims – is the exception. When we are served a rich broth, I am overjoyed and consume three bowlfuls much to the amusement of my two fellow pilgrims.

One of these is Hank who has travelled from the Netherlands by bike and who, interestingly, always responds in English to my Dutch comments. The other is Thomas from Saskatoon who explains: "I finished an undergraduate degree in philosophy and decided to come and walk in Europe. So, I did the Portuguese Camino from Porto to Santiago, now I'm hiking the Chemin de Saint-Jacques."

"Did you start in Paris? That's what I did."

"No, I started in Santiago de Compostela, and I'm heading for Paris." I'm flabbergasted: Thomas must have been hiking for months, and he's so relaxed about it. And he's doing it "in reverse" – from Santiago, instead of to Santiago. That means he doesn't see the yellow arrows or scallop shells telling us where to turn. Here's another person who has become my hero. His studies in philosophy must be gelling on this endless trek: he seems to take the whole thing in stride.

Thomas arrived ahead of us, so he gets his own room while Hank and I share a room. In our brief time together, Hank becomes a nuisance. He begins with a question I have been asked in France but never in Spain: "Are you doing this for religious reasons?"

Perhaps the number of pilgrims in Spain made the question less pertinent since the reasons could be as numerous as the travellers. During my time in France, I could not come up with a proper response: the answer depends on what is meant by "religious reasons." Given a broad enough definition, the spiritual part of me may have played a role in my decision to walk across Europe. I'm not really sure, and I don't really care.

Hank's religious ideas take on interesting features, and at bedtime he expounds on them from his cot in the dark. He is solid in his belief in a God Creator who watches over each of us individually but adds that he doesn't follow a faith tradition and does not go to church. He criticizes my questioning of anything to do with spiritual beliefs, and his sermonizing becomes irritating.

When he says he knows of the existence of God through all the good things that have happened to him over the years, I respond: "John of the Cross might disagree. That great mystic said we know of the existence of God as much through the bad things that happen to us as through the good." A moment later I wonder whether that was really said by Saint John of the Cross. Perhaps it was another mystic – maybe Saint Catherine of Siena or Saint Teresa of Avila? In any case, my comment lets me interrupt the one-sided conversation, "I'm going to sleep now," but his diatribe leaves me with the uncomfortable feeling that we create God as much as He created us.

But I'm not done with Hank, or he's not done with me: twice through the night, he appears at my bedside to awaken me because I was snoring. I welcome his morning's departure and watch as his bike turns the corner on a Tours street and Hank becomes a grating memory.

Thomas has decided to take the day "off" (that is, not to spend the day walking), and this appeals to me as well. I catch up on my wash and participate in the sisters' Mass, which is attended by a sizable group from the community. Mass is held in the "crypt" in the church cellar where a reliquary holds fragments of the bones of Saint Martin, a soldier turned bishop of Tours.

I span the centuries by sauntering through the great Gothic cathedral and then visiting a McDonald's restaurant. Using their Wi-Fi service and the laptop given to me by Sergio, I catch up on my e-mail correspondence while I enjoy a *café au lait* and a McFlurry. Even in this treat, I see European adaptations as the chocolate syrup is on top of the ice cream and not mixed throughout as it is in Canada.

**Countryside**

The Loire River, my companion from Orléans to Tours, is left behind, and I encounter two forms of racing, in the air and on the ground. Low-flying jets (equipment of the French air force) streak through the sky – amusing themselves in sets of two and four. Then I pass a horse-riding oval where a man is honing his skills on the sulky. I keep being surprised at what appears around the next bend.

The cold weather at my arrival in France has been replaced with a blast of heat. I am frequently threatened by rain, but it provides little more than a few sprinkles. The shape of the walking environment has changed. My several days of walking out of the city of Paris and its metropolitan area were followed with the remoteness of great fields of canola and wheat that could have been the Canadian prairies. Then came the friendliness of an old Southern Ontario patchwork quilt – fields of hay or crops interspersed with woodlots and roaming herds of milking cows. I see piles of manure near the road, at the top end of hills overlooking the fields. I conclude this must be a means of getting the goodness of the manure into the soil without the need to spread it on the land. Rain would simply wash the nutrients down the slope.

I turn right off the trail taking me through farmland so I can stop for a cup of coffee at a passing hamlet. In the middle of several houses is a small café, but it is only open a few hours a day and this isn't one of them. A neighbouring couple notices and invites me for a delicious cup of coffee and a chat at their picnic table. The elderly couple are long-time residents and tell me which road to take to get back on the trail. Their advice goes against my instincts – and my compass – but I follow their suggestion, and the road eventually leads me to my path southward.

A strange contraption over a distant garden catches my eye. As I draw closer, I realize it is a black plastic bird about two metres across and dangling in the breeze from a pole. I am impressed with this monster as it is successful in keeping predatory birds at bay and unnerving me as well.

As I walk through the countryside, my upset stomach continues to be a distraction: it won't let me just enjoy the hike. I have stopped eating baguettes, and that has helped. Two things that have been effective are Coke and herbal tea – here those are "Coca Cola" (not "Coke") and *"infusion."* When I translated "herbal tea" from the English and called it *"thé herbal,"* I was quickly corrected, *"Non, c'est 'infusion.'"* The verbena *infusion* is especially pleasant.

A bowl of soup would be easy to digest, but French food culture allows for soup only on the winter menu, not now

123

in the late spring. I like soup at all times of the year and would like to see that tradition change. I fantasize a network of outlets specializing in soup and salad. The name would be "Vitasoupe," and – with the right branding – it could make a fortune.

By one of the strange coincidences that seem part of the hiking experience, I meet a group of young people sitting on the grass for a break from their classes. They are students at a cooking school in a grouping of houses here in the countryside, and I ask: "Why is there no soup on restaurant menus now?" But they seem disinterested and light another cigarette. Oh well, it's their loss. They could have made a bundle with "Vitasoupe."

An *auberge* (country inn) near Sorigny has a complex system of codes for hooking into its Wi-Fi service. The people are welcoming, but their Internet access causes me an hour of frustration in trying to get a connection. Finally, I realize the signal up to my room is too weak. I head down to the bar area where I find the Internet service to work more smoothly and where documenting my adventures can be complemented with a *café au lait*.

A fellow guest is Parisian and has made it this far after a long struggle. He explains: "I have 'foot problems,' and the doctor suggested I do more walking. So, I walked from our house in Paris, just a few kilometres, and my wife came to drive me home. Then I walked farther, and she would bring me fresh clothes and the other things I needed." Over time he was able to hike longer stretches and is now using a small backpack and reaching 20 kilometres a day. I am impressed with his perseverance, which makes my story seem tame.

The next afternoon I reach Sainte-Maure-de-Touraine, which is famous for its goat cheese, traditionally cured in cinders and still given a gritty texture. It is part of the menu Jean-Luc has prepared for our supper of a slice of pork loin with spaghetti and lettuce. He is a member of the Amis de Saint-Jacques (Friends of Saint James) and picked me up at the town's *office de tourisme* to provide a bed for the night.

During the meal he pulls great pieces from his baguette while I take small portions in deference to my sensitive stomach. When we have finished eating, his section of the table is a mass of crumbs. I wonder what his mother would have said since mine wouldn't have been pleased, and I think of Mom's attentiveness at our meals.

*"With a dozen of us gathered around the table in our country kitchen, we prepared our sandwiches – spreading bread with margarine and layering them with Dutch sandwich meat or Gouda cheese, and with chocolate sprinkles in our last sandwich. Children drank milk while adults had tea. We were careful to keep spills and crumbs under control. We just knew it wasn't right to leave clutter behind."*

I realize I have seen this kind of mealtime messiness throughout France. It seems to be accepted practice: Jean-Luc's mother may have made as much of a mess and simply cleaned it up at meal's end.

In his public presentations about the Chemins de Compostelle (Compostela Paths), Jean-Luc compares the story of Saint-Jacques (Saint James) and Père Noël (Father Christmas, our Santa Claus). He explains, "This makes the pilgrimage legends more understandable for the average person," but I muse on the possibility that Santa is in fact Santiago.

The Dutch fable of Sinterklaas who arrives on a steamship from Spain with his helper Zwarte Piet (Black Peter) may be a combination of the bishop Saint Nicholas of Myra (in present-day Turkey) and Saint James the Greater. This apostle is said to have travelled through Spain with a bag on his back, doing good deeds and serving the Lord.

The Dutch story has parallels in other European countries, and it follows the literary tradition of taking one of the subjugated people – in this case the Moors – as a companion. Just as Robinson Crusoe had Friday and the Lone Ranger had Tonto so the Dutch Sinterklaas has Zwarte Piet. And so, the Christianization of pagan beliefs has been reversed: the Christian Saint James has become the Dutch holy man Sinterklaas who became the modern pagan Santa Claus.

Jean-Luc knows the people who wrote the guide I am using, and he contributed some of its photos. I realize he may be able to answer a question about the pilgrimage through France: "Why is the Camino Francés through Spain so simple and the Chemin de Saint-Jacques so complex?"

He explains: "In Spain the communities have agreed on the direction of each trail, and they use yellow arrows as markers everywhere. In France we're still working on that." As traditional local paths intersect with long-distance trails, some communities have up to four sets of puzzling signage. I need to follow the shell signs of the Chemin de Saint-Jacques (Path of Saint James) in some cases and the red and white stripes on signs for the Grande Randonnée (Great Rambling, e.g. GR-3 or GR-655) in others. The Grande Randonnée is a network of long-distance footpaths, covering about 60,000 kilometres in France and continuing into other European countries.

The guidebook authors do not agree on the route to be followed, so you proceed with caution. Some prefer to take their readers through interesting, winding trails while others would rather get them to destinations quickly. For most of one day, I'm delighted to be able to put my guidebook aside and simply follow yellow and blue signs featuring the Saint-Jacques scallop shells. They appear at every turn, but this is too good to last and comes to an abrupt halt.

On another day cartons of juice provide both my highs and lows. I had been yearning for vegetable juice but cannot find it in the grocery stores. Instead, I see a litre carton of "Gazpacho by Tropicana" that is advertised as number one in Spain and can be served hot or cold. Taking a few sips throughout the day proves satisfying.

At some point I stop for a rest and, as usual, recline against my backpack on the soft green. When I get up and put on my pack, it is damp and starts dripping. Then I discover that the lid to my carton of prune juice has popped off. I spend a half hour sopping up the gooey mess with my mosquito netting (which I had not used till now) and Baby Wipes. For the next few days, my little world smells sweet and feels sticky.

The tourist office at Dangé-Saint-Romain provides a list of families who take in pilgrims for the night. I am fortunate in being directed to the rural home of Cécile and Jean-Michel and their university-aged sons, Florent and Vincent. Vincent's visit home from university and recent family birthdays are reasons for champagne and a special meal. At this home again, I am part of the French pre-supper ritual: at six o'clock supper is on the stove and allowed to simmer while everything stops for an *apéritif*, a social drink of wine or liquor. They are warm, wonderful people who make sure I have lots to eat and drink.

Florent has the breakfast table ready for me the next morning, and I'm thrilled to be sent on my way with a sandwich layered with items from each food group. As I go out the door, I hear Jean-Michel mumble to Cécile, *"Sur la table"* ("On the table").

He is referring to the Euros I had left there as a *don* (gift), and she returns them to me, *"Non, non. Ce n'est pas nécessaire"* ("No, no. That's not necessary"). A Canadian pin for each of them is welcomed with enthusiasm.

That Sunday morning sees me repeatedly put on and take off my rain poncho in the unsettled weather. Over the next three days, I become frustrated as the weather changes from warm to rainy, back and forth. On the good side, donning this big red cape by throwing it back over my head and backpack had been a challenge but is now becoming second nature.

By now I am convinced of the existence of a "dog disobedience school." It specializes in teaching hounds to wait till the last second when the pilgrim is beside the residence gate. Then the beast is to jump up against the enclosure, bark viciously and show its fangs – all at the same time. They have rattled me every time, as have the guns in the fields. These are meant to keep birds away from crops but succeed in keeping me from complacency in my reveries.

In the village of Fontaine-le-Comte, an ancient abbey – with chapel, courtyards and crumbling walls – serves as a tourist attraction, and I stop for a peek. I had been desperate for a toilet, this place is not staffed and I am the only visitor. I contemplate peeing in one of its little yards when I notice a sign that leads to a surprisingly ultra-modern *toilette* with "touchless" soap dispenser and hand dryer and with stainless steel throughout.

In France I have been advised not to use the expression *"salle de bain"* ("bathroom") that I had learned at school. In most homes these facilities don't include a bath or shower, which are in a different room, so I have been instructed to call them *"toilettes"* ("toilets"). In Canada we might call it a bathroom no matter what porcelain features it harbours, but the people of France are very precise in such language issues.

I am always relieved at the point in my walking when the initial adaptations are behind me and my body is starting to understand the stressful activity that is expected of it. Then just placing one foot in front of the other begins to feel like the most natural thing to be doing, and the irritations disappear. As I speed along a meandering country road, a woman stops her car to chat. On the passenger seat, I notice a basket of cherries, and she says they were freshly picked at a friend's house. I'm pleased when she leaves me with a handful of sweet, juicy cherries and with the standard greeting for long-distance walkers: *"Bon courage."*

## Towns

At one of my accommodations, "La Barque," I am directed upstairs through a small door that leads into a garret with a comfortable little apartment. The owner is an elderly woman who describes herself as *"non-voyante"* ("non-seeing") and feels her way through her kitchen tasks. This house serves as a retreat centre and is located in Naintré near the Vieux-Poitiers site of a battle in AD 732 between Charles Martel and the Moors.

128

The next day the interplay of old and new is brought home to me when I pass "Matériaux d'Autrefois" ("Materials of Olden Days"). This business looks like a lumberyard and sells found stone decorations, such as carvings and pillars. Then a few kilometres on, I seek refuge from the rain and enjoy a hot chocolate, followed by a second one, in the wood-panelled café of the 18-hole Golf du Haut-Poitou.

The contradictions continue, and for 20 kilometres my feet tread the remains of *"la voie romaine"* ("the Roman road.") In fact, none of the ancient narrow thoroughfare is visible: long ago it turned into sections of gravel road or paved surface. Now *bandes rugueuses* (grooved strips) warn drivers of an upcoming stop sign. I amuse myself with an image of the original Roman road with a warning sign: "Slow down your chariot here."

Meanwhile the ultra-modern appears off in the distance: the angular buildings of Futuroscope rise above the trees. This theme park is based on multimedia presentations and has several 3D and 4D cinemas. I had heard that the place was worth a visit, but I can't bring myself to walk a few kilometres out of my way and to leave my commitment to the peaceful trail. I would need to store my backpack, become excited about modern technology and find an expensive room for the night. Futuroscope passes in the distance.

Entering Poitiers, I'm sorting out which street to take when a man approaches: "I'm from the local Chemin de Saint-Jacques committee. Welcome to Poitiers. If you need a room for the night, go to the tourism office in the centre of town. It's up that way." At the end of a steep climb, I arrive at the pinnacle where the information people book me a room near the base of my climb. So down I go again to an Auberge de Jeunesse (Youth Hostel) serving a boisterous group of young people with special needs and having a few beds available for pilgrims. It is a well-managed place, but the shower only produces a dribble. On a long hike, that is distressing.

As an outsider, I have aimed for a balanced attitude toward France. Although some of their ways are not what I am used to, people have been very nice. However, I make an exception for the town of Lusignan where I end up spending the following night: the town appears old and worn; the people seem tired and sad. At the same time, the menu at my inexpensive little hotel features cuisine in the 80-Canadian-dollar range.

The proprietor seems to say – in complex French – that the building is locked. If I leave, I won't be able to come back inside, so I'll need to have supper here. I tell him I'm not spending that kind of money on a dinner without my wife, and he backtracks. He shows me a back door I can use, and I treat myself to a great bowl of spaghetti at the Italian eatery across the street. It is excellent and reasonably priced.

This part of France was a home for French Protestantism, a minority group about whom I have heard very little. The guidebook directs me past a derelict non-Catholic cemetery enclosed by a high wall and locked iron gates: it is not maintained since the Protestant community here long ago dispersed or, apparently, were forcefully converted to Catholicism or massacred.

A display of historical information mentions the Protestant practice of teaching girls and boys together in the same classes. To the Catholic Church of the time, that was an abomination – a response that now seems bizarre. Catholic-Protestant differences played a major role in my youth, and I come up with a whole list.

*"On the farm in Arkona, Ontario, we were Dutch Catholics within a solidly Canadian Protestant community. When we arrived there, we attended the Public School as the only Catholic students and were excused when the Baptist minister arrived for a weekly talk. Then the Catholic Separate School was built in the country next to a rural Public School, and each group became distinct from the other. Catholic and Protestant peers just did not mix; we didn't even know their names."*

Those differences in faith led to intolerance, suffering and death in this part of France – a region that now consists of peaceful farms. I spend days making my way past farm crops and notice that the canola has left its flowering stage and the pods are filling out nicely. I pass an experimental farm where soil and growing conditions are studied using little plots of land and large greenhouses. Always interested in discoveries to do with farming, I take a picture of fence posts capped with black metal cones to delay their weathering.

Hiking through countryside I arrive at the home of Matthieu and Naïssé to spend the night. Naïssé is the sister of Gaëlle from back in Orléans, and Gaëlle had arranged for my stay here. Matthieu and Naïssé are a friendly couple, and I feel at home immediately. They offer a bed for the night; in return, I put up with the over-friendliness of their huge slobbery dog and with the stealthiness of their four cats in a disorganized house.

As I walk through residential area into the city of Melle, I meet an older man in front of his house beside a pile of stones. He has a trowel of cement in his right hand and is building an ornate rock wall by his garden. A few blocks further on, I'm surprised to see exactly the same scene – another man building another wall. I give a second, *"Bonjour. Il fait beau, n'est-ce pas?"* ("Good day. It's nice weather, isn't it?") But I can't help musing about these activities of our senior years: while I'm exploring, they are shutting in and shutting out; while I'm free to hike the roads of Europe, they are building walls.

A few blocks further on, I chance upon a restaurant that specializes in oriental cuisine. The menu at this family-owned business features eight kinds of soup. With a cup of green tea, a little salad and a big bowl of soup with pork and noodles, I'm in my element.

The previous day I had been waiting in the village square for Naïssé to get home from work. There I met Natalie, and we had a pleasant chat. She said: "I'm here for a meeting of leaders in community development. I walked the pilgrimage to Santiago a few years ago, so I know what it's like. If you need a place to stay, I live near the trail." As it turns out, when

I reach Natalie's community, I can find no accommodation, so I take her up on her offer to pick me up in a town *en route*.

We drive back to her house, I take a quick shower and we hurry to a *spectacle* (performance) of songs written and sung by community activists who share in her volunteer work. I find it impossible to stay awake: the day's trek has worn me out, the French lyrics leave my mind numb and the chair is too comfortable. My nodding head becomes noticeable as the presentation lulls me to sleep. After the concert and my snooze, I shake myself awake so I can redeem myself with conversations during the drinks and munchies following the production.

Driving through the twilight back to her house, Natalie detours to two of the *lavoirs* (laundry areas) that have been reclaimed as historical features. These are stone cisterns through which part of a river's course had been redirected to serve as the laundry-socializing area for women in days gone by. The region is scattered with such remains – crumbling walls in marshy spots where once stone cisterns of clear running water were fitted with steps, benches and a roof. Volunteer groups, with which Natalie is associated, have rebuilt several *lavoirs* to their original condition. I am moved by her respect for the past and for the struggle of women in that past.

The next morning Natalie takes me back to my spot on the Chemin de Saint-Jacques. I enjoy a careening ride through curved roads headed up and down the rolling countryside, and she leaves me with a bag of cherries for a snack. Munching on cherries provides a pleasant diversion till, further along, I am distracted by a startling apparition: three hikers are taking a break in the shade of a village churchyard.

I approach the middle-aged couple and a younger woman (who is a doctor and family friend) and remark: "Since I left Paris, you are the first walking pilgrims going my way. Where are you staying tonight?" As it turns out, we are heading to the same hostel in Aulnay where they invite me to join in their simple pasta supper. Wanting to contribute something to the meal, I scour the shelves of the grocery store and settle on fresh cherries. (I've had my fill of cherries by now but have still not tired of them.)

During our conversations a number of people have interjected that my French is certainly better than their English. I've been surprised at the lack of familiarity with the English language here in comparison to that in other European countries. I now feel less hesitant in finding the right French words and more confident in applying the complex rules of grammar. Uttering sentences like, *"Je suis en train de traverser l'Europe"* ("I am crossing Europe"), has become automatic. However, I am taken aback when someone says my French is much better than that of the people from Quebec as they are very hard to understand. Sometimes you must simply appreciate – and not question – a compliment.

## Bornes

Starting in the town of Aulnay, metre-tall stone *bornes* (pillars) appear along the pilgrimage route. These have been placed by the Département de Charente-Maritime (the local administrative district) as waymarks. They are essential: despite constant use of my compass, I was getting lost several times a day; now I can be certain about the route.

I look forward to taking a week-long break from hiking to attend a family reunion in the Netherlands. To avoid taking slow local trains for part of that trip, I'd like to leave from the railway hub of Bordeaux and now quicken my hike to that city. I need to meet my sisters in Amsterdam on Friday June 11th, so I put in two 40-kilometre days to feel more caught up. As I dash through the kilometres, I am reminded of "Sherman's March to the Sea," which I see as the American Civil War equivalent of the bombing of Hiroshima and Nagasaki to end the "War with Japan." There is no stopping me, though a motorcycle contest – of all things – causes aggravation.

Near Saint-Jean-d'Angely I am perturbed that an international Motocross competition has booked all lodging, and the tourist information people can find me no place to stay.

However, they tell me: "An Englishwoman named Jill has offered a room at her house if visitors cannot find anything else. She's an artist and lives about 20 kilometres south of here near the Chemin de Saint-Jacques. She was just here to talk about arranging a display of her art in the information centre. She was leaving when you came in." They cannot reach Jill, so I take the contact information and start walking, with the sound of Motocross engines revving in the distance.

A local man, originally from England, drives by slowly and then stops. He has hiked some of the route and wants to meet this fellow pilgrim. He knows of a place to stay at a town about 20 kilometres distant: "Just wait on this park bench, and I'll go home for the information. I'll be back in 10 or 15 minutes."

I've already hiked for a few hours and am nowhere near a bed for the night. Twenty minutes later I begin to get anxious just as he drives up with a map, address and phone number for a *gîte*. He joins me in my hike for a kilometre or two and sends me on my way, grateful that I'll have a bed at the end of the day's trail. I no sooner arrive at this home for the night than in walks the neighbour, Jill the Englishwoman artist! I ask about her art and later join her for a cup of coffee and a look at her colourful modernistic oils.

This home for the night is a farm converted into a country inn. The man, who had farmed all his life, does the cooking. It goes against my expectations to see this old farmer folding tablecloths and making sure the cutlery is straight. He is an excellent cook and takes pride in his work. I can't help but get an image of Dad at our kitchen range.

*"Mom had gone for a visit to family in the Netherlands, my siblings had all left home and Dad and I managed kitchen duties. I had wondered what we'd have for supper before we headed to the barn to do the milking, but Dad surprised me with his abilities at cooking. He made a delicious meal, and I did the dishes."*

The farmer's wife has prepared two salads to go with our supper. As we sit down to dinner, she says: "I forgot to ask if there is anything you cannot eat?"

I reply, "The only thing that bothers me is cucumber," and – a second later – I realize one of her salads is 90% cucumber. She rushes inside to make me an alternate salad while I feel bad and insist on eating some anyway. I make it through the night with no evidence of a cucumber-related tummy ache.

The next morning starts with a downpour, and I spend much of the day slogging through puddles on a trail in the woods. My approach to the city of Saintes proves as circuitous as the one Peter and I experienced in arriving at Benavente, Spain. Here the directions are unclear, the *bornes* are long distances apart and an archaeological dig directs hikers away from the travelled route.

Wet undergrowth slaps my bare legs and is endlessly irritating while my boots become waterlogged. I feel defeated in covering only five kilometres in two hours, and I'm not even sure this is the right trail. I finally make my way out of the muddy up-and-down paths in the woods – and right onto the 18th hole of a golf course! It seems otherworldly. A lone golfer directs me toward the city, and I'm on my way.

In this case, he simply points to the sand road through the golf course leading to the clubhouse and toward the city below. Other responses have not been as helpful for finding my way, and I've needed help many times. The hike through Spain had been straightforward, but the one through France has been tricky: my guidebook can be unclear, the trail is often not well marked and local people are unfamiliar with the hiking paths. On a number of occasions, when I ask for directions from residents, they express surprise: "The guide is saying to go where? That's the long way around. Here, let me see." I'm alarmed that, in frustration, they will rip my guidebook pages to bits.

Usually the book takes me through woods and fields, and the local people insist highways provide quicker access.

Simple requests – for the direction to the next town, for example – are met with straightforward answers. Anything more complicated becomes a discussion over the best driving routes. The suggestions are similar to advising a hiker in Southern Ontario to take the major Highway 401 from London to Toronto as it is quick and efficient: "You'll be there in no time." The thought of a leisurely stroll just doesn't fit into modern high-speed thinking. More useful has been my humble compass that I count on at least half a dozen times a day.

## Characters

In the city of Pons, I look for a bed on a late Sunday afternoon. I pass several hotels but hold out hope for the pilgrim hostel. I've heard it is priced at only eight Euros per night, and it would have a more interesting atmosphere with discussion among the hikers. However, those beds must be booked in advance by phoning the local tourism office. I tried to do so earlier in the morning, but the tourism office was closed for the day (as are most places on Sundays in France). Past the downtown area, I reach the hostel, and I'm in luck: it happens to be one of the Sundays a tourism staff member is present for a re-enactment of some of the city's medieval history.

The tourism person reminds me that I should have booked the hostel bed in advance. She is friendly (and holds the key to the hostel), so I feel guilty about my unkind thoughts in response to her comments. However, I'm tired of hearing over and over from tourism staff that the pilgrimage route requires proper planning so reservations can be made ahead of time.

I understand that some pilgrims have their route planned in detail months in advance. I probably should have done this. I likely should have a *portable* (cellphone) to reserve my accommodation. I could have used a smart phone to help me find my way. Then I might add a GPS-enabled car for the extra convenience. Oh, and a hired driver, leaving me free to daydream. There. I'm all set for my pilgrimage!

I seem to approach my trek in an old-fashioned way that is suitable to our hostel building since, a half millennium ago, it served as a hospital for the destitute and for pilgrims. I am assigned a bed and chat with Benoit, a young man whose flowing hair cascades down his back. In our evening together, he says only a handful of words: "I'm from northern France and going to Santiago" and "Back in Saintes did you end up on the golf course too?"

And I think: "What did he just say? I must have been on the right track after all, or – at least – we were consistent in our error."

Before leaving Pons, I want to take a picture of a grouping of pilgrim statues a block or two away. Turning to snap the photo of these characters, I realize I had reached the end of the film in my disposable camera, and the debate begins: "Should I climb up the steep road to the city centre to look for a camera? Or shall I just let those statues be? Shouldn't I buy the camera here in the city when I may be stuck in countryside for a while? But it's so early, and that hill is so steep." In resignation, I climb the hill, buy the camera, head back down, take the picture and hike past fields of metre-tall sunflower plants. They would certainly be worth photographing in full flower later in the season.

In this day's hike, I come across two ends of the housing spectrum – the large, old, abandoned and the small, new, ready-to-occupy. I experience the former along a road running beside a two-metre-high stone wall. The wall goes on and on – for more than a kilometre – and ends at a crossroad. At that point a set of iron gates mark the entrance to this abandoned monastery and the wall starts again as it encloses a massive property. I imagine the life that would have been lived in that set of buildings and the farming required to feed this contemplative community.

A few kilometres along, I come to a new housing development, and a contractor takes pride in the house that is almost complete, "It's a wooden house, the kind you have in Canada." In other words, this style of construction does not follow the traditional post-and-beam or stone construction of France. Rather, it incorporates modern wooden framing and vinyl siding. In the course of an hour, I have come across two types of shelter that span the centuries.

By mid-afternoon, I arrive at a *halte jacquaire* (Saint James stopover) in the house of a couple babysitting their grandson. I find the husband baffling, and he remains a puzzle throughout my stay. At my arrival I ring the doorbell as directed by a sign. I hear activity in the house, but no one answers. I knock and then knock louder still, and a man with a gruff appearance answers and grunts at my presence. He shows me my apartment attached to the far end of the house. On the spacious lawn, beside a swimming pool, is a cottage with meeting room and bar, none of which seem to be in use.

When his wife gets home, the man becomes less morose. He takes me along when he gets in his car with his toddler grandson to drive down a country lane and look for wild boar in a fenced area in the woods. We have a delicious supper during which I am disturbed by the man's several put-downs of minority groups. This becomes an odd interaction when his rant emphasizes the word, *"Musulmans,"* and I wonder what he has against musclemen, and I ask *"Musulmans? Musulmans, qu'est-ce que c'est?"* ("What's *Musulmans*?")

He replies, "You know. Those people, the *Musulmans*." Finally, I dig into the recesses of my memory and realize he means "Moslem." Then I find it difficult to express tactful disagreement in a language that still provides challenges. He realizes I'm irritated and directs the conversation to his family's strong Catholic faith. They are active in the local parish, but many people are not. He regrets that their priest now has 36 church buildings under his care, most of which are no longer used.

Churches often serve as markers in my guidebook – places to turn or to pass on the way to the next point. Then I mock the children's fingerplay with my own version, "Here is the church, here is the steeple; you open the door, but where are the people?" Most churches in southern France range from being in need of extensive and expensive repair, to being unsafe, to being closed permanently. If the heart of these thousands of isolated communities was once the churches, then cardiopulmonary resuscitation is desperately needed!

With few young parishioners among the assembly at any church, the input of their more liberal ideas is absent, and I surmise the survival of these struggling buildings is uncertain. A modern miracle would be the regular attendance at Mass of young people as the majority of services are ceremonies without celebration.

I continue my musings as I relax in one of the white moulded chairs on the lawn outside my room and think of this man's comments. The religious art in churches has one common flaw – the appearance of European models as Bible characters. We understand now that Jesus and his people would have looked more like inhabitants of northern Africa particularly in skin tone. The decision not to picture Jesus on the cross as naked (though that was integral to the Roman practice of crucifixion) is understandable. But the decision to make the race of Jesus more acceptable to the European churchgoer is regrettable.

Several of my French conversations with active Catholics have hinted at their anti-Middle-Eastern biases. Now I muse that, perhaps, the Good Samaritan account was added to the Jesus stories later and is not really part of the example we should follow. Perhaps Moslems are not really our neighbours. Or, perhaps, this prejudice would be diminished if religious artists had told the truth.

My pilgrim reveries about the history of the Roman Catholic faith that I inherited bring me a feeling of loss. Our simple faith based on the Christian scriptures seems to have been taken hostage by theologians, artists, hierarchy and bureaucracy. The local get-togethers of believers of the first and second century – in family homes and led by women – became monstrous church buildings, a complex path toward heaven and an anti-female bias.

The early Church easily adapted the new Christian faith to "pagan" (that is, country folk) ways as evidenced in the old pagan seasonal celebrations (including Christmas and Easter) that became the Church calendar. Even a pagan route westward through northern Spain was given an apostle, Saint James the Greater, to sanctify it so it could become the French "Chemin de Saint-Jacques-de-Compostelle" or the Spanish "Camino de Santiago de Compostela."

Over the centuries the Church accepted the rebellious inclinations of revolutionaries like St. Joan of Arc and St. Francis of Assisi whose shadows I encountered on the Camino. However, I see Roman Catholic Church history as a failed experiment in which the Church took a long, continuous curve to the right with a shift to conservatism and limited free thought. Parishes in southern France serve as examples of this failure with closed buildings, few priests, aged assemblies and irrelevance in their local communities.

I am shaken from my reveries when my host calls out: "At eight o'clock tomorrow morning, there will be prayers and coffee time for visitors at our church in Mirambeau. It's important that you attend. I'll drive you there; then we'll come back here for breakfast, and you can continue your hike." We discuss what I might like for breakfast, and he wishes me good night.

The next morning I am up early as usual. By 7:15 there is no sign of him, and I rap on the front door. I knock louder and realize I need to leave now to walk the few kilometres to the church and get there in time for those prayers. I grab my backpack and arrive at the church when the service is about to start. Afterwards I meet a few parishioners and visitors, and we are well into our coffee and pastries when my host breezes in and says he overslept. I am not sure how to respond to this mystery of a man, so I say, *"Merci, au revoir"* ("Thank you, goodbye"), and continue on my way. I've missed his breakfast, but departing is more important than eating. He left his mark, and I carried him quite a distance through France and, now, into my book.

In Mirambeau I enjoy a visit to a hardware store that prides itself on being 150 years old. The owner shows me an inscription in a cupboard indicating that the business dates from the reign of Napoleon III (1852 to 1870). Besides the usual plumbing and electrical items, there are regional crafts and oddities. I happen upon a universal plug, a flat plastic disc that fits any sink. Way back, in our walk on Spain's Via de la Plata, Peter had said Rick Steeve's travel guide suggested each traveller carry one of these because sink plugs may be missing. After all the times of using a sock as a stopper, I can now act refined.

During this second week in June, the morning started cool, and I wore my jacket and trouser combination. Now I am finding it warm and look for a place to change into my shorts. A woman is walking from her drive shed toward her house, and I ask if I can change in the outbuilding she just left. She says that's fine, and – beside the farm tractor – I spend ten minutes removing backpack, opening stuff sack and changing clothes while balancing on my hiking boots to keep from soiling my socks.

Finally, I'm done and find her standing outside the building waiting for me to leave. I thought she was back in her house, but she may have been suspicious of this stranger and anxious for me to be on my way. In any case, she appreciates the gift of a Canada pin, and I go back on the trail.

I pass near the village of Cognac, the birthplace of that type of brandy, and signs everywhere tell us we're in cognac country. I have continued my "research" on local drinks to relish another favourite: this is *pineau*, which is a mix of cognac and wine that has been fermented one last time. According to legend it was accidentally discovered in this area in 1589 and proves to be very tasty.

Cartelègue, a friendly village, is the site of the cleanest and brightest accommodation, village office and church to date. One of the village councillors provides me with the key to the room attached to the village office. It is a spotless mini-hostel with bunk beds, kitchenette and laundry, and I wish I

141

could stay for a week. She takes great pride in their office area that is a modern space within a stone building where sections of natural stone appear in corners and around windows.

Across a square stands the church; its interior has been repainted to brighten the religious art spread across the ceiling. I ask her why this village is so well looked after, and she replies: "It's because of our mayor. He's a special person and works hard to make this a nice community. Every detail is important to him." The mayor seems to be a proud homeowner for whom the whole community is his home.

My guidebook advises that, at this point on the Chemin de Saint-Jacques, I am to head westward to Blaye to take the *bac* (ferry) across the Gironde Estuary. This route is intended to expose pilgrims to the extravagance of the Bordeaux wine region. It sounds like a wonderful walk, but I choose to avoid the ferry in order to walk the whole distance across Europe. Leaving Cartelègue, I head south and develop my own itinerary following secondary roads. To my amazement, trailside markers indicate that the route I have "discovered" is an alternate pilgrimage path that my book fails to mention.

The more southerly latitude is now evident in the subtropical vegetation, the greater intensity of the sunshine and the more advanced stage of growth of the farm crops. The Basque influence in house design is beginning to show: a few houses have the wide wooden features so evident in the Basque region 200 kilometres to the south.

My hiking gives me free time to think about any number of things, including the workings of local communities. This area, for example, must feature manufacturing plants as I keep seeing trucks with signs *"convoi special"* (Canada's "extra-wide load"), and the shipment consists of a section of a new home or a boat mysteriously wrapped in coloured plastic. I notice that every service van is white in colour, and I wonder if that's a tradition or a regulation. The monotony could be overwhelming, so my mind keeps busy by looking for answers to unimportant questions.

After the interestingly named town of Saint-André-de-Cubzac, the road enters a half-kilometre-long bridge high over the river known as La Dordogne, and the sidewalk hugs the bridge wall that is of steel latticework construction. I fear that I'm about to fall through the holes in the grillwork beside me and to my death in the water twenty metres below, but once again I arrive at the other end intact.

High bridges are my enemies; low bridges are my friends. When I come to one of the latter, I cross from one side of the road to the other to check on the difference in current as it approaches the bridge and as it continues on its way. The upstream side is slow moving and quiet; the downstream side is turbulent and loud. Through careful study I have concluded that this is attributable to the narrowing of the stream at the bridge, which forces the downstream water to move more quickly. Over time this increased flow wears away riverbed materials producing little rapids and waterfalls. My long, lonely path gives my brain time to study details of all kinds, and crossing hundreds of bridges is making me an amateur hydrologist.

In Portugal such bridges spanned dry or marshy areas, and I assumed they were useful in directing runoff during the rainy season. Here in France the bridges span gentle streams that meander through the countryside and gurgle as I pass, and I recall a scary low bridge on our farm in Arkona, Ontario.

*"We would cross a culvert in our farm lane on the way to the fields to get the cows for milking. I didn't like walking this path alone and hoped Bill would be along, for inside that pipe lived a family of muskrats. Being rodents, they were frightening."*

And I ponder a variety of things: "Why is the beaver not nearly as scary as the muskrat? Why are we so wary of certain people with a culture or religion different from ours? Who was more afraid – the muskrat or I?" And I keep on walking.

## Bordeaux

From an Office de Tourisme, I received a print-out of directions to a hotel in the town of Bassens in suburban Bordeaux, but the information is complex: I need to go left, right or straight ahead at a dozen roundabouts through the town of Ambarès-et-Lagrave. When the signs for entering and leaving that town appear four or five times in a row, I realize I must be walking in circles.

I'm tired at the end of this day of 40 kilometres that is meant to help me get to Bordeaux in time to catch the train and meet my sisters in Amsterdam. Finally, two women doing their power walking – "This is our exercise, so you have to keep up with us" – lead me to the hotel hidden within a subdivision at the edge of an industrial park in Bassens.

When I arrive, the bartender, who is in charge of registering guests, is busy with a restaurant full of customers spilling out into the courtyard. I decide to join in the revelry and have a beer and a well-earned supper. Then I have a second beer – which is unusual for me – and I think of my brother Bill. I get tears in my eyes as I struggle with wishing our childhood had been less troublesome, witnessing his death under that tractor and wondering what he would think of me now. All these people and their families and friends start to head home, and the bartender finds time to direct me to my room.

The next day I end up getting lost on entering Bordeaux and ask for directions from two well-dressed gentlemen. They set me on the right path, and in return I agree to take one of their Jehovah's Witnesses pamphlets.

After registering at the hostel in Bordeaux, I make my way through the cavernous train station to purchase a ticket to Amsterdam. Bordeaux proves to be another European city with a wealth of architecture from those hundreds of years back. I pay a visit to the city's cathedral, and a young man with a ponytail says, *"Bonjour."* Without his great quantity of hair cascading down, I hardly recognize Benoit from our stay at the hostel in Pons five days earlier. Meeting a pilgrim a second time is always heartwarming, and this reflects a bond peculiar to us.

My purchase of a jacket and pants combination from the Running Room in Moncton has proven to be wise. This outfit can be rolled tightly to take little room in my backpack. It has been lightweight enough to be comfortable in these warmer climes, and it looks presentable as evening wear in people's homes. Now the coin-operated laundromat just around the corner from the hostel in Bordeaux serves to freshen my clothes after four weeks of handwashing.

I return from the laundromat just as a rock band is setting up for a beer party in the hostel's back yard. I watch and listen for a song or two but don't feel part of the activity and head for bed. The band disrupts my sleep as does the persistent cough of a German pilgrim-cyclist. Before retiring for the night, I suggest he see a doctor as he seems short of breath. He replies: "No, I'll be all right. I'm not biking tomorrow so I can rest."

Morning comes quickly, and I catch the early train from Bordeaux to Paris through countryside I had just crossed on foot – like a review of subject matter covered during a school term. Arriving in Paris, I take the *métro* (subway) from one train station to another, from Gare Montparnasse to the massive Gare du Nord, as I head for the train to Amsterdam. With Michael Bublé concert posters in *métro* hallways and Justin Bieber smiling from magazine covers, it's as though I hadn't left Canada.

Paris train stations are patrolled by soldiers sporting dangerous looking weapons they appear ready to use. It is unnerving when one of them points to my hip pack. Wondering what I have done wrong, I notice the light on my personal alarm is on: I must have pressed it inadvertently. Relieved at not being in trouble, I proclaim a heartfelt, *"Merci beaucoup!"*

The first view of my native country, the Netherlands, normally occurs through the window of an airplane as we descend. This time I am racing in from the south on a high-speed train, and it is a moving experience. Crossing the swollen mass of water known as Hollands Diep and then the gentle South Holland countryside is transfixing. A week with my sisters and brothers-in-law, the visiting of old neighbours and relatives (including Dad's sister, our 100-year-old aunt, as well as her 102-year-old husband) and the celebration of a family reunion leave me softer upon return to Bordeaux to continue my walk a week later.

## Landes

Over three or four days, my feet weigh down in a path of loose sand. This endless stretch provides some of my most frustrating walking in Europe to date. At times I am faced with a straight, boring tunnel between the trees as it stretches kilometres ahead of me. Then it feels as though I'm alone in this world and standing still. The monotony is relieved by a dear little fawn I surprise in its path.

The route takes me through the Landes, a triangular 40-by-90-kilometre area with a fascinating history. This ancient seabed, with a 15-metre depth of sand, had been a swamp and useless for anything except housing *"brigands."* Then Emperor Napoleon III ordered the planting of millions of pine trees. The greenery absorbs the groundwater and dissipates it into the atmosphere although some water still seeps up to form the odd puddle.

Along the unending trail, patches of coal have migrated to the surface, and concrete tanks appear from time to time to provide water for fighting fires in this flammable environment. The Landes region reminds me of the Pinery Provincial Park near Grand Bend, Ontario with its pine trees and sand. This area is rich in the lumbering of pinewood and the sale of piles of firewood – activities I had not seen elsewhere in France.

Kilometres of boredom are finally relieved by the odd patch of corn as I stop at a *gîte rural* (country bed and breakfast) for the night. The owner mentions, "I have distant family members that are Acadian and living in New Brunswick." She is an exception to the lack of knowledge of Canada's rich Acadian history, culture and dialect.

At other times I have heard people in France voice vague complaints about the dialect and attitude of tourists from Quebec. France's enthusiasm for its language and tradition does not translate into support for minorities in the French diaspora such as those in Quebec or New Brunswick. And I muse on cultural differences and ethnocentricity: we see ourselves as the centre of our own cultural universe. The people of France are challenged with accepting the upstart French-speakers from the New World. They are so different – even, an embarrassment – *vis-à-vis* the established language and culture of real France.

At a service centre, a secondary road taking me through Belin-Béliet intersects with the major highway that is the Route des Estuaires. Hikers are directed to a path behind the restaurant and gas station and separated from those services by two-metre-high chain link fencing. I think, "It sure would be nice to have a cup of coffee," and realize I am not the first pilgrim with that thought: a hole has been cut in the fence to give us access to the treats passing by so closely.

The instructions and map in my guidebook prove to be confusing. The booklet states, *"Laissez à droite le tunnel"* ("Leave the tunnel on the right"), which I misread as, "Take the tunnel on the right." Owing to a recent rainstorm, the tunnel is flooded, and I carefully cross the superhighway. I am headed for Saugnacq-et-Muret to spend the night and realize I am quite lost; my compass is of no help. After forays into several rural roads, rechecking of compass and maps and asking several *riverains* (local people), I am relieved to hike into my goal, a resort of lodges and cabins that provides a few rooms for pilgrims.

There I meet two fellow hikers who are recent university graduates and who pitch their tents in the backyard at no charge. We socialize into the evening with packages of chicken soup and a wineskin, and they tell me: "We have a tradition of pouring some wine into the last few spoonfuls of chicken soup. Then we drink it. Try it; it tastes really good." Pierre leads us in song on his miniature guitar and harmonica while Damien and I do our best to hum the more or less familiar tunes. They plan to take a break from hiking as a girlfriend is giving them a ride to a beach somewhere.

In this southern part of France, several churches sport a hut beside the steeple. I understand that these are dovecotes, and I wonder why I haven't seen such structures on church roofs elsewhere. In any case, there they are, collecting droppings for use as fertilizer.

As I relax on a park bench in the town of Pissos the next day, a boy of about 12 years of age waits outside a store while his mother shops. He seems awkward on old roller skates that must be new to him and cautiously rolls up to me on the uneven paving stones. The youngster may be mixing together some of the stories he's heard but poses the most profound question asked during my pilgrimage – a simple question with complex answers: *"Allez-vous à Jérusalem?"* ("Are you going to Jerusalem?") Perhaps I am.

The guest room of a *gîte d'étape* (wayside hostel) in Labouheyre is immaculate: the elderly couple keeps it ready for grandchildren to come and visit. I enjoy a community event in the town square where, for a few Euros, I get a feed of duck heart and fries while a pipe and drum band plays in the background. Later a rock band performs at full volume, and my host couple suggest, "Close the shutters on your windows to keep out the noise." This helps deaden the raucous music forcing itself into my space from a block away as I get some much-needed sleep.

As I continue on secondary roads during this fourth week of June, tractors pass with steel high-sided wagons brimming with carrots. I am impressed with the size of the harvesting machines that travel back and forth through the fields. The Landes area grows some farm crops but mainly caters to vacationers: campgrounds, cabins and canoes are everywhere.

In Lesperon I visit the village office to book a bed in their hostel. A Dutch couple, Gerard and Ria, arrive on their bicycles when the office has already closed. This leaves me in a quandary since I have the keys but do not have the authority to give them a bed for the night. I decide that letting them enter is the pilgrim thing to do, and they can pay for their lodging the next morning when the village office opens. (As it turns out, I leave early and can only assume that took place.) While we enjoy their beer and wine, Gerard insists on calling me "Peter." He explains, "Pictures of St. Peter show him holding the keys to heaven, and you have the keys that let us into this paradise."

Out in the country the next day, a car stops half a kilometre ahead of me. Two people get out and start walking, and the car speeds into the distance. When I catch up to them, it is Damien and Pierre, now taking a smoke break as they relax in the roadside grass. They tell me: "We need to take a break every half hour or so. How far can you walk in one stretch?"

I haven't given that much thought, but I tell them: "That would likely be about 10 kilometres, taking me about two hours." They are astounded, and I just keep walking.

Near Taller I am baffled by the choices at an intersection. I notice a woman by her house some distance away and wave my hand toward one of the crossing roads. She responds in the affirmative by giving a large nod that is visible from afar. Once again, I am on my way until the next bit of confusion. Residents are more aware of the vagaries of the Chemin de Saint-Jacques the closer I get to my end point near the Spanish border.

Entering the town of Saint-Paul-lès-Dax (usually shortened to "Dax"), I walk by a police checkpoint where vehicles are being stopped to monitor for infractions. Lost in pilgrimage thoughts, I easily forget how normal life continues all around me.

When Pierre and Damien appear at the Dax hostel, I treat us all to pizza and beer at an Italian restaurant. So many people have been so good to me that I want to give something back somehow. While we discuss whether we want two or three large pizzas, the waitress interrupts: "Each customer has to have a pizza."

I suggest: "Then we might want to get three medium-sized pizzas."

She responds: "You might as well order the large ones. They are all the same price." Some customer service issues are difficult to understand when you travel outside your own cocoon. The pizzas prove to be delicious, particularly those with a *"crème fraiche"* ("fresh cream") topping. Unemployed and hungry, my guests are delighted: they consume every morsel.

Dax is located on a series of geysers, and the downtown area features fountains of steaming water rising into the air and splattering into a decorative pool. The commercial spa Calicéo is situated on one of the local geysers, and the contact person for the hostel suggests, "I'll drive you to the spa, and you can find your way back from there." However, when we arrive, the complex is set to close for the evening, so we opt for a beer at a Tex-Mex Bar. I enjoy a touch of North America in the country music and Wild West theme that seem out of place in southern France, particularly the twang of English lyrics as background to French conversations.

**Target**

The bridge taking me across the Gave d'Oloron waterway into Sorde-l'Abbaye shows a construction date of 1943. I have been hiking along the World War II border between the Wehrmacht-occupied zone and the Vichy Regime of Marshal Philippe Pétain. That boundary ran parallel to the Atlantic Coast, and the bridge must have been built during this German control of southern France. During the destruction of World War II, Vichy collaboration with the Nazis allowed such construction: their bridge was being built while others across Europe were being destroyed. And I'm struck by the historical peculiarities that keep arising in unexpected places.

In Sorde-l'Abbaye I meet two Belgian cyclists whom I had seen in Pissos, 110 kilometres – and four days – back. They are astonished I have kept up to them on foot while they are on bicycles. Either I'm doing some tough walking, or they're doing some relaxed pedalling and plenty of sightseeing. I try to avoid seeing my project as a competition, but – in light of the energy I am expending – I'm pleased with their recognition of my diligence.

Fields of vines are a major source of kiwi fruit for the European market. This is another fact that catches my attention in the scenery around me while I remain attentive to the uneven trail underfoot. Frequently the guidebook mentions the high-tension power lines under which the path crosses: these wires provide a distant waymark – a feature to guide us. At one point I look behind me to see if I have passed the indicated set of wires. Then I look ahead of me, see no wires and assume I have made a wrong turn. Finally, I look directly overhead, and there they are. Then I know I've been lost in thought.

As I follow the trail down a farm lane, an elderly farmer stops his tractor for a chat. He suggests: "You might want to take a break at our hostel in Arancou. It's a nice place and only a few kilometres from here." When I approach the building, I assume the door must be locked as it is now late morning. I'm pleased that it's open, though not staffed, and as welcoming as the man had described it. In many places the citizenry has been involved in fund-raising or contributing in some way, and they take pride in caring for pilgrims, a service many take seriously.

Here the small village of Arancou has been able to develop this excellent facility for hikers: it is clean and bright with comfortable furniture that could give me a relaxed overnight stay, but I must keep hiking as it is still early in the day. I make a real mug of coffee and add milk from the fridge. I find some goodies to go with the coffee, leave a donation and return to the trail refreshed. Interestingly, a carved stone plaque set into the wall of this structure shows it to be exactly halfway – at 830 kilometres – between Paris and Saint-Jacques-de-Compostelle (the Spanish, Santiago de Compostela).

The two churches in the joint communities of Bergouey and Viellenave date from the 13th century. Both are of the sturdy, unpretentious nature attributed to the Basque people themselves, and the robust countryside now features corn, corn and more corn. Unfortunately, *balisages* (route indicators) are less common, and I go for kilometres without being reminded that I am on the right path. One might assume the route would be better marked as it approaches Saint-Jean-Pied-de-Port, the launching point of the Camino Francés. That is not the case: here the trail confuses me as often as it has anywhere in France.

The fault lies in the age of the *balisages*: having been placed years ago, the small plastic signs are deteriorating with age and many have fallen from tree or fencepost. I get a spring in my step on finding a marker that shows I am on the right path after a number of uncertain twists and turns. Now I am also feeling giddy at the thought of nearing the "finish line" at Saint-Jean-Pied-de-Port, 40 kilometres in the distance.

The "Franciscan" *gîte d'étape* (wayside hostel) at Saint-Palais is an old monastery but has not a monk in sight. I understand it is still owned by the Franciscan order, which counts on a Belgian pilgrimage group to manage it. Taking my backpack up the stairs to the dormitory, I pass a guest who asks where I am from, and I tell her: "New Brunswick. It's in the eastern part of Canada."

She responds: "I'm from Poland, but I now live in Paris."

I comment: "That's like the pianist-composer Frédéric Chopin who was Polish but living in France."

She is taken aback and says: "Actually, I'm a classical pianist. I'm going down to the chapel to practice for my concert tomorrow evening. It's part of my music tour through southern France."

She seems distracted, and the hostel staff later mention that the concert will go ahead although the pianist's *copain* (male partner) died at this hostel a few hours earlier. Outside the chapel I see a sign for the concert to be held on Thursday, July 1st and featuring works by Schumann, Schubert, Chopin and Bach. I suddenly feel ill at ease: we pilgrims encroach on the personal space of others but from an uncomfortable angle

152

that feels intrusive rather than committed. I continue to travel through glimpses of the countryside and the edges of people's lives.

## Pyrenees

With the foothills of the Pyrenees Mountains come some tough climbs. Setting out in the morning, I am struck by the photogenic haze on distant hills. Throughout France the mornings have shown a mistiness that appears as something out of a well-crafted piece of art. I hope to capture this perfect morning on my disposable camera but realize it is out of film. Instead, I take a longer gaze to capture the scene more fully in my memory.

The closer I get to Saint-Jean-Pied-de-Port (which stays tantalizingly out of reach), the easier my French communication becomes. Stopping at a convenience store for a new camera, I understand every word. It's rewarding to reach the point where I can carry on a French conversation without the need to struggle through vocabulary and verb tenses.

At the edge of a village a half hour's walk from my end point of this trip, I take a picture of a few dozen sheep huddled together and staying very still. Then I realize many of these animals look sick with a limping walk, a putrid smell and a general listlessness. I feel an urgency to tell someone of the condition of these creatures. I am tired and burdened with a backpack but wait for a car to pass. However, no one passes on this country road, and the few houses show no signs of anyone being home.

I feel as though I'm deserting these creatures when I continue on the last few kilometres of my walk. Still haunted by the sight of those sheep, I enter Saint-Jean-Pied-de-Port through the "Porte Saint-Jacques" stone archway that has been the arrival point of pilgrims over the centuries. I get a tourist to snap my picture as I have now – incredibly – completed the 2500 kilometres from Cabo de São Vicente, Portugal to Paris, France.

Information at the Amis de Saint-Jacques (Friends of Saint James) welcome centre shows that the 471 Canadian pilgrims who passed through town by June 2nd of this year represent the fifth largest group. The top national groupings (in order of greatest to least) are those from France, Germany, Spain, Italy, Canada and the Netherlands. Starting hikers are being given *carnets de pèlerin* (pilgrim passports, *credencials* in Spanish), of which I now have three that hold a total of 101 stamps. I realize I have completed a long, long pilgrimage.

The staff assign me to a bed at La Caserna, the parish hostel run by an elderly couple who have made the pilgrimage journey themselves. Upon arrival I am offered a glass of homemade spiced peach-pear juice. It hits the spot, and I decide it is my celebration drink. The hostess comments on the size of my boots (50 European, 15 Canadian) as she would several times over the next day or so. Having arrived late in the afternoon on Saturday, I ask: "Could I stay an extra day? I need to arrange my train ride north for Monday morning." They agree but remind me that, normally, pilgrims only stay one night in any hostel as the whole idea of a pilgrimage is to keep moving.

Sharing my quarters are an anxious young Hungarian woman and a young man from Montreal named Gabriel who has just finished a section of the pilgrimage. Apparently, the woman is worried about a number of issues in her life: they seem to have to do with family and politics back home. Foremost among her concerns are the pressures of being ready for the upcoming pilgrimage. I am impressed with Gabriel who is very helpful in his understanding of both her broken English and her concerns. After the hostel's excellent supper, he kindly takes her for a walk through the first part of the route so she'll be more confident when setting out the next morning.

The 8:30 a.m. Sunday Mass at l'Église Notre Dame du Bout du Pont (the Church of Our Lady at the End of the Bridge) is in the Basque language, Euskara. After Mass the announcements about upcoming parish activities are, interestingly, in French. Some parts of the hymns are sung by the whole assembly; in other parts the men and women take turns, probably following an age-old tradition. I am moved by the men's voices as they reflect a robustness and enthusiasm that bounces off the rafters.

It's a quiet Sunday morning and shops are still closed, so I return to the church to experience the late Sunday morning Mass. I appreciate the chance to compare these Sunday Celebrations to those back home, and this becomes learning opportunity for me. At the 11:00 a.m. Mass, only the singing is in Euskara; the rest of the service is in French. Based on the number of priests, I assume the church is administered by a religious order as there are enough priests for two to concelebrate the 8:30 a.m. Mass while three do so at the 11:00 a.m. Mass. And I think of the closed churches of southern France and toy with the thought that the diminishing resource of priests should be redistributed.

One of many Camino-related coincidences lies in the content of the Holy Gospel (Luke 9:51-62) for that Sunday's Eucharistic Celebration. The story is about hiking, about Jesus and his disciples following their own Camino into Jerusalem. They found a particular village less welcoming than others had been; at times I have had that feeling as well, though most have been very good to me. I could identify with the Gospel's words of Jesus that he did not really have a home – a condition I experienced throughout France when, each morning, I had no idea where I would be resting my head that evening.

In the afternoon I return to the church and enjoy the singing of a touring Basque choir. Harmonies intertwine in a mix of Basque melodies and Latin hymns. I am inspired to walk back to the sick sheep I had seen the previous day. This trek "in reverse" proves disorienting: after a few wrong turns, I finally find the pasture. To my surprise, the sheep are nowhere in sight although the stench lingers. I can only hope their condition has been recognized and they are receiving proper treatment.

Early the next morning, I catch the TGV (Train à Grande Vitesse, the High-Speed Train) for the trip to the

Netherlands. In this race through the countryside, the distance by train seems much longer than I could possibly have walked in those six weeks. I recognize mine as a lengthy trek.

Joanne will arrive in a few days for a shared holiday in Europe. Meanwhile I stay at the youth hostel in Haarlem where I meet Adam, a student from the University of North Carolina in Chapel Hill. He developed an interest in European train stations and is now travelling from one to the other to take photos, record details and interview the staff who manage them. His story is one of accidental connections with people who happen to know others who run the rail system. His was meant to be a holiday, but it turned into an informal summer course that he'll pursue into his university program. And so, interesting people keep appearing in my travels.

I also take this opportunity to visit the city of Leiden for a bit of my own research into the most traumatic incident of my early childhood. On the one-hour bus ride from Haarlem, I think once again of that terrible moment on our farm in the Netherlands.

*"Just after my fourth birthday, our cows had been let outside for the summer, and I watched Dad and my brother Tony scrub the stable with soda water. A fresh pail of boiling hot water was placed on the walkway, and the adults went into the house at tea time. I stayed behind and walked backward to watch the reflection of a barn window follow me in the wet floor. The backs of my legs bumped the rim of the steaming pail, I lost my balance, and my bum splashed into the sizzling water. I screamed, and family members came running. Dad held me, wrapped in a blanket, for the drive to a six-week stay at the Academisch Ziekenhuis [Academic Hospital] at the University of Leiden."*

As I step off the bus in Leiden, the hospital rises right across from the bus station. Most of it is now concrete, glass and steel and goes by the unwieldy name of Leids Universitair Medisch Centrum (Leiden University Medical Centre). A man from their communications department takes an interest in my story, and I ask him for copies of my old medical files. (Days later he advises me by e-mail that those records from 1951 no longer exist – unfortunately.)

On that horrible day, my father would have carried me through the entrance archway at the base of a five-storey building. That Poortgebouw (Gatehouse) still exists, and I take some pictures. The whole complex has been rebuilt since those days, but the Poortgebouw continues as a waymark on my path through life.

I pick up items I had stored at Central Station and proceed to Schiphol Airport to meet Joanne with a fistful of tulips. I'm eager to see her again and look forward to our relaxed holiday in Europe.

*JOSEPH KOOT*

# Trip 5: Across Borders

*May 14 to July 7, 2011 – 1133 kilometres*
*Alphen aan den Rijn, the Netherlands south to Paris, France*
*(694 km)*
*Alphen aan den Rijn, the Netherlands east to Oldenburg,*
*Germany (439 km)*

**Preamble**

Here I am, ready for my next trip into the great unknown with a new pair of size 14 boots. My last pair was a size 15 and felt similar to these new boots – the fit depending on the manufacturer. My boots are of such significance that I take my time in finding the right ones: they can be my greatest friends in helping me through hazardous terrain while, at the same time, being my constant enemies in causing blisters.

Just as my boots need to feel right, so the plans for my next hike have to feel ready. Before each of my walks through Europe, I have felt differently than during the previous hikes. Now on my fifth trip, I have a sense of being unsettled as though I'm missing that strong urge to walk. Perhaps my memoir writing has resolved some of the childhood issues around being the youngest in the family – issues that may have given me the determination for such an unusual project. I do not feel the urgency to search my memories as I have on previous trips.

Yet, starting this hike in the Netherlands, where I was born in 1947 and from which we emigrated when I was five years old, brings with it a whole set of emotions about going

159

"home" again. I could have chosen a more direct route from Paris to Estonia but chose this detour through the country of my birth. I wanted to share this hike – this highlight of my life – with the place where my life started.

With Joanne away for a few days, I arrive at Moncton Airport for my evening flight and look forward to a pre-flight supper. However, I learn that the food service closes at 6:00 p.m. on Saturdays and Sundays, so my hunger pangs will have to be patient till meals are served on the plane.

After the flight from Moncton to Montreal, I board the Air France Boeing 777 that will transport us to Paris. I search out my seat in the distance through the obstacle course of people straining to lift massive suitcases into overhead bins. I thank Air France for the convenience of checked baggage and wonder: "Why do passengers do that? It's not a hotel room."

The main course of shepherd's pie for supper is a disappointment: it is too salty for my taste. On the other hand, the breakfast of orange juice, sweet muffin (with an orange zest) and yoghurt is delicious. Being in a pensive mood, I don't bother turning on my personal television set; instead, I read two newspapers and daydream.

In the Paris airport, I witness what might happen if your passport is suspect. Entering a routine checkpoint, I look for the shortest line. As it turns out, I choose incorrectly. The officers in the two cubicles in front of my line seem suspicious of the passports the people ahead of me have presented. After 10 minutes of intense questioning, both cubicles close and the two travellers are escorted elsewhere. I feel uncomfortable at the head of the line but with nowhere to lead the people behind me. An official arrives to move pylons so we can go through another checkpoint. Fifteen minutes after reaching the front of the line, I can proceed, so I had definitely chosen the slower one!

A flight from Paris delivers me to Schiphol Airport near Amsterdam and the short train ride into the city. I know I am back in the Netherlands when I order a restaurant meal of two Dutch favourites – a bowl of white asparagus soup and a dessert pancake slathered in the thick Dutch syrup with its hint of molasses.

I seek out a hostel near the train station as my home for the night and plan some big city shopping – maps of trails through the Netherlands and Germany, a cellphone, sandals and a night light. I purchase the maps at Reisboekhandel Pied à Terre, an Amsterdam bookstore that specializes in travel materials. The cellphone will help me arrange my homes for the night as listed in my "Vrienden op de Fiets" ("Friends by Bike") guide. In the evenings the sandals will give my feet a break from their boots, and the night light will keep me from getting disoriented in dark bedrooms.

On each of my trips, soccer has been a local highlight, and this one is no exception. Honks, shouts and firecrackers in support of the Ajax (Amsterdam) team continue into the night. At about one in the morning, our 16-bed room is awakened by a raucous group that takes a while to settle. Even more irritating is the bunch that arrives at about four o'clock: they turn on the light and sound as though they had too much to drink. Finally, they calm down, and we can get back to sleep. I feel bad for the young man in the bunk above mine. Before bedtime he told me: "I feel really sick. I had an allergic reaction in Austria yesterday, so I have to go home." His travels have been cut short, and he's flying home to Brazil in the morning while my trip is beginning with my hike toward Paris.

I plan to follow the Dutch Pelgrimspad (Pilgrim Path) that will take me south toward Belgium. Although I am starting this trail south of Amsterdam, I am intrigued by an Internet entry that says the Pelgrimspad starts at Amsterdam's Central Station, so I seek out details. At the information centre in the train station and at another in the nearby VVV (Dutch tourism office), nothing indicates that this is the starting point of the Pelgrimspad. Neither of these offices has heard that the trail starts here, and the woman at the VVV checks on-line, "In case someone else asks me." The mysteries around European pilgrimage routes continue.

To my annoyance, my brand new sock liners are not holding up: I now have a hole in the toe area after only one day of use. I wear the sock liners inside my wool socks, and their smooth finish helps prevent blisters, so I don't want to be without them. I would have trouble finding new ones in Amsterdam, so Joanne will send some of my old ones to her Oom (Uncle) Jozef since my route will go near his house.

In preparation for my journey, I cut up and mark the maps I bought – one outlining the Pelgrimspad, the other providing a detailed view of the Netherlands. I am left with only the parts covering my route. On a serious hiking trip, anything extra becomes a burden, and I relegate the leftover sections to the nearest garbage bin.

## Lope

On my first day, I take the early morning train from Amsterdam to Alphen aan den Rijn, in the province of South Holland, where I begin my walk southward through the Netherlands. I chose this starting point so that – when I head northward from here a month from now – I can stroll through the street where I was born. As I begin this trek, I am excited about hiking among towns with names I heard in my parents' conversations all those years back, towns like Boskoop and Bodegraven.

I greet a man spading his garden, and he wonders whether I'm doing the trail around a series of windmills. I answer, *"Nee, ik loop naar Parijs"* ("No, I'm walking to Paris").

He responds: *"Da's 600 kilometer!"* ("That's 600 kilometres!")

I could have thanked him for the information or agreed it was far. Instead, my buried Dutch brusqueness springs to life, and I answer, *"Dat wou ik eigenlijk niet horen"* ("I really didn't want to hear that"). And I remind myself to speak pleasantly – as a visiting Canadian should.

Distracted by the Dutch countryside, I forget to check my map and end up veering from the pilgrim route: instead of

162

turning south at Zwammerdam, I walk on to Bodegraven. I thoroughly enjoy this walk along the Oude Rijn (Old Rhine) featuring watercraft of all sorts, from rowboats to freighters. As I am soon to discover, the walk laid out in the guidebook is intended as a quiet stroll over dikes and through nature while I prefer experiencing Dutch activity – shops, houses and farms.

Along the way a sign indicates that Gouda is four kilometres distant, which should take me just under an hour. However, the Pelgrimspad takes me into the Reeuwijksche Plassen (Pools of Reeuwijk), a peat bog that had served as a source of fuel over a century ago and was then flooded. These hundreds of acres look like Ducks Unlimited wetlands back home: they are nice puddles – but no Bay of Fundy.

Then the route continues toward an historic village where pilgrims can stop for a cup of coffee. I'm frustrated that the four kilometres to Gouda are about to become 10 or 12 kilometres, so I skip the village with its coffee. Instead, I seek out a trail that provides a shortcut through the puddles back toward Gouda. Finally, I enter the town and try to bring back details of a hazy recollection – a rare arrival at its cheese market as a five-year-old.

*"A few siblings and I would perch beside Dad, and the horse was given its signal. Off we went to deliver our cheese to the market in Gouda and to live an adventure beyond our farm neighbourhood."*

Now, almost 60 years later, I arrive on foot and go in search of the address of my first night's accommodation on the Pelgrimspad. My hostess is one of over four thousand addresses listed in the "Vrienden op de Fiets" booklet and available for guests who hike or arrive by bike. The visitor pays 19 Euros for a night's stay, which includes breakfast.

This home is busy with two auto mechanic apprentices from Denmark and several carpenters from Germany in short-term lodging. I tell the hostess I would like to handwash some items (t-shirt, socks and underwear) in the sink in my bathroom and ask if she has a place where I can hang them to dry. She replies that doing laundry is forbidden as I might get the floor wet, *"Ik heb boven helemaal nieuwe laminaat"* ("I have new laminate flooring throughout the upstairs").

I'm perturbed by her remarks and want to answer, "Lady, I'm not starting a laundry service, just washing my few little things," but think better of it. I'll save my dirty laundry for another lodging that may be more understanding.

In the morning I hike along a channel where white swans glide between lily pads while yellow irises provide the backdrop. In the village of Vlist, I stop at a restaurant with old rock and roll music playing on its satellite radio system. As I finish my coffee, I'm surprised to hear the familiar intro of the next old song, one with a catchy refrain: "It was an itsy-bitsy, teeny-weeny yellow polka-dot bikini that she wore for the first time today." You never know what you might come across here.

Playing old American hits in public spaces is common in Europe, and in the Netherlands my exposure to local songs is limited once again. On my iPod back in Canada, I have 2,000 songs playing continuously, and perhaps 100 of those are Dutch tunes, mainly traditional songs from our pre-immigration years. In some ways I can feel more Dutch there – and be in touch with that part of my past – than I can here.

In Schoonhoven I find a clothing repair shop to mend the ravelling cuff of my jacket. The young Turkish immigrant handles this repair expertly while he, his Moroccan friend and I converse in our broken Dutch. They are interested in details about Canada and about my trek across Europe. The tailor insists he doesn't want to be paid for the repair; instead, I am to treat myself to a cup of coffee the next morning using the money I would have given him. I wonder why he is adamant about not being paid and suspect he wishes he were in my shoes, walking across Europe.

For the 200-metre crossing of the Lek River, I need to take a ferry since there is no bridge in the area. This is my first non-walking section across Europe, and I decide to keep pacing on board during the 10-minute crossing. I ask myself: "That should count, shouldn't it? I did the best I could, didn't

EUROPE, ONE STEP AT A TIME

I?" I can't convince myself that my continual stroll during the crossing counts as a walk across the Lek. In light of my accomplishment so far, this hole in my journey leaves me dissatisfied.

I step off the ferry and locate the road taking me south. It passes a family business – a fish-packing plant with attached restaurant – where I can enjoy the "free" coffee suggested by the tailor the preceding day. It is lunchtime, and the three women are spellbound by my hiking story, but the five men ignore my Dutch narrative and wear permanent scowls. I feel some tension in this dining area and hurry on my way with fond memories of the pleasant conversation with the tailor and his friend the previous evening.

In Gorinchem (also called Gorkum), I enquire about the memorial to the 19 monks who had been hanged in 1572 because they would not renounce their Catholic faith during the Dutch religious wars. They were known as the Martelaren van Gorkum (Martyrs of Gorkum), and my mother went on pilgrimages to this holy site in her youth. I am eager to experience a bit of what she might have seen over 90 years ago, and I search out City Hall for information. The woman at the tourism desk tells me, "The old church was torn down, and they built a new smaller one there." Apparently, a crypt in the base of the building houses the bones of the martyrs.

I find the church, but it only opens for Mass on Sundays, so I take some pictures of this tan brick structure and hurry on my way as I reflect on our Catholic traditions and modern sensibilities. Dutch Catholics once flocked to this site that commemorated the Protestant brutality that murdered holy men of our faith. Now a modest new church keeps this lone visitor outside its doors, which only open a few hours each week. Over the years Catholic-Protestant differences have decreased, but has that come at the price of respecting our heritage?

The couple at my Gorinchem home for the night have a shrine to St. Clare with statue and flowers set up in their living room. My host is a retired accountant who engages in lots of chitchat. My hostess is more stern and comments: "You shouldn't take shortcuts on the Pelgrimspad. They planned it so you would walk the whole thing." She doesn't seem to understand that I am more enthused in coming across Dutch daily routine than in nature's peace and quiet of which I can get plenty in our rustic home on the Bay of Fundy. Besides, this is my journey, which doesn't include sightseeing detours but does go by my rule of walking every step of the way. However, having used a ferry to cross the Lek, I've bent the rule of always walking the distance.

Now in Gorinchem I have a choice of a long four-lane bridge up in the air over the river or a friendly little ferry to the other side. I catch the ferry, but my host's words, "Take the ferry: that's a lot easier," haunt me. Since my start in southwest Portugal, I have not chosen the easy route. Why start now? By its very nature, my hike has been tough, and there would be no end to the process of making this journey easier. Avoiding an unending, terrifying bridge would be the first step to the crumbling of this venture. I need to stay committed to the toughness of the process: I need to take the ferry back and walk that bridge.

Stepping off the ferry a second time and now back on the north shore, I make my way through two kilometres of streets toward the highway traffic starting its ascent onto the bridge above me only to find I cannot enter the pedestrian walkway from that point. This is the four-lane expressway entrance, and a high fence stops me from even considering this approach. Instead, I have to return to a point near the ferry crossing and take a bicycle path around to the bridge as a pedestrian. Before arriving at a scary bridge, I have told myself out loud, "Cross that bridge when you come to it," but this time it's as though I'll never reach it.

Finally, two hours after starting out this morning, I come face to face with my fear of high bridges as I start across. Through an expansion joint in the walkway, I glimpse the ground far below and wonder if my next step will land or whether I'll be hurtling through the air. The next step holds, and I try to ignore my wobbly knees as I repeat aloud the chorus of "You've Got to Walk that Lonesome Valley." On the way across, I meet other pedestrians and children on bicycles, and I think, "Crossing in a car is safe, but don't those others know they're exposed to danger?" A young cyclist turns to look at his friend behind him, and I want to scream, but I keep trudging.

Eventually the water far below becomes land far below that begins to slope toward me as I'm being deposited back onto level ground. I have mixed feelings: "I made it!" and "When will I have to endure this torture again?" I turn off the highway onto a narrow road, leaving traffic fumes for country air, and I'm rewarded with a delicious cup of coffee on the patio of a farm café. I've survived once again.

## Brabant

I enter North Brabant, and in Heusden my hostess does not mind my doing a bit of laundry in the bathroom. She suggests I put my items at my feet while showering, so the soap residue and my tramping will start the cleaning process. Then I need only give them a final rinse before hanging things to dry.

Later she entertains two neighbouring women on lawn chairs in the garden while I join in the wine and conversation. I sense she may have invited them to meet this interesting Canadian, and she comments: "You have such a cute Dutch accent. How would you have developed that dialect through your immigration to Canada? Your way of talking Dutch is like that of our little children." I am not amused: I try so hard and find it a challenge to speak their proper Dutch.

For a few kilometres, my route through the Loonse and Drunense Duinen (a dune area distant from the ocean) is a tough hike in loose sand. After a bit of confusion over small roads that aren't on my Pelgrimspad map – "Do I take this one or that one since they're both going the wrong way?" – I arrive in Helvoirt, North Brabant. A detour of a few kilometres brings me to the home of Joanne's Oom (Uncle) Jozef and Tante

(Aunt) Sjaan, to await a package with jacket and sock liners sent from home through UPS (United Parcel Service). In my solo trek southward, it feels odd to be hiking into their yard and to be greeted by people I know.

I relish three days with Oom Jozef and Tante Sjaan that include lots of visiting and good food while Tante An does some of her great cooking as well. On Sunday morning Oom Jozef and I go to the Basiliek Sint Jan (St. John's Basilica) in 's-Hertogenbosch (also called "Den Bosch") for one of the special Masses held in May, the month of Mary.

The people of North Brabant have a special devotion to "De Zoete Lieve Vrouw" ("The Sweet Dear Lady"), and the Mass includes a parade of banners representing various community groups. Oom Jozef rummages through memories of his childhood and tells of the one Sunday each May when the family walked the few hours to church from Helvoirt. During that long procession, they would pray three rosaries (which would take about an hour) but only one on the way home so the children could play as well.

I meet two of their three sons whom I haven't seen since 1977 when they were young boys, and Tante Sjaan kindly does my laundry. Oom Jozef and I enjoy a visit to the Museum 't Brabants Leven (Museum of Life in Brabant). The owner-guide is a fast-talking character with a great sense of humour. The thousands of items on display include some (such as coffee grinders and bean-slicing gadgets) that recall images from the kitchen of my childhood.

We go for a car ride to preview my next day's hike to the area of Oirschot as Oom Jozef wants to make sure I know where to turn. It's unfortunate he cannot provide that service all the way to Paris. That would certainly decrease the number of times I have to ask for directions. After lots of socializing, food and coffee, I pose for a last photo with my backpack, and they wave as I return to my trek.

The further south you travel in Europe, the greater are the number of miracles witnessed by the community. Now signs lead me to a chapel called De Heilige Eik (The Holy

Oak) where I attend the early afternoon Mass. This chapel in a glen attracts a crowd, and small buses bring people from seniors' homes.

Someone explains: "A local person carved a statue of Mary and put it on the branch of a tree. A rich lady came along and said a statue shouldn't be in a tree, so she placed it in the local church, but it returned to its home in the tree. They kept putting it back in the church, and each time it found its way back to the tree. Finally, they built this chapel in the woods, and here it has stayed. It has brought many miracles." My opportunity to join this enthusiastic crowd in singing "God Groet U, Zuivere Bloemen" ("God Greet You, Pure Flowers") is heartwarming. This is a hymn to Mary that I remember Mom and my sisters singing in harmony so many years ago.

In the same area, white asparagus is in mid-harvest during this fourth week of May. I'm enthralled by the half-metre high mounds of earth: they stretch the length of each field and are covered in sheets of white plastic to keep the plant from turning green. Teams of a half dozen workers move through the field to harvest the asparagus tips. They briefly lift the plastic from an area, use a rod to pry the white stems out of the ground and place them in baskets to send to market or sell locally. Each "asparagus for sale" sign also mentions "strawberries for sale," so those two crops must need the same soil type, which continues to be very sandy. Apparently, glacial action from 10 thousand years ago is behind the nature of the soil.

The Pelgrimspad takes me through farm fields toward the airport serving the city of Eindhoven. In the distance two passenger jets take off with a roar. I'm excited to see my path lead past the end of the runway, so I stop at that point to experience the exhilaration of watching one of these giants rise into the sky right above me. I stand and wait. Then I sit and wait. Finally, 45 minutes later, a tiny plane takes off, and I catch a photo of it from below. (Later, in the developed picture, it looks even smaller!) That's the only plane I get to see, and it definitely wasn't worth the pause in my hiking.

I miss the distinct smell of pig manure as I traverse the area. The farm tradition is fast coming to an end in parts of North Brabant. The subsistence farm with a few cows, a couple of pigs and some chickens on a small acreage are no longer to be found. Now people don't farm, or – in a few cases – they farm in a big way.

I now come across the odd low hill that will become rolling countryside as I get to Limburg. Until now the ground has been flat, especially in South Holland, but I did have to face some serious climbing. In a few of the guest homes, the staircases were almost vertical, which created some tricky manoeuvring to get my backpack up to my room. One spiral staircase took up a footprint of little more than a square metre. I suspect that Canadian building codes would not allow that type of construction.

Fields of potatoes are beginning to appear. These require irrigation, as some areas have had as little as a few days of rain over the last month or two – and that in a rainy country. On the other hand, New Brunswick has had more than its share of precipitation, and we'd welcome sending some to North Brabant.

Between fields I cut through an area of woods displaying an unusual sign: "Laagvliegende Buizerd" ("Low-flying Buzzard"). For a kilometre or two, I focus on the lower branches, prepared to duck should the bird see me as prey. Thankfully, he stays home, and I exit the woods intact. Efforts at environmental protection have resulted in ponds busy with frogs and in twittering birds everywhere. A local person mentions: "They were building a road not far from here and stopped construction because a bird's nest was in the way. When the young birds flew off, the work continued."

People pay a great deal of attention to their houses and yards: many are busy with outdoor chores. I can't feel comfortable with all that effort. Whether in my childhood or later years, bending over to coax seedlings out of the ground or to control weeds has seemed like a waste of energy. I suggest they take that time to go for a walk instead.

In Valkenswaard I seek out the Stayokay Hostel – one of the Dutch hostel chain that is part of Hostelling International. Here a handful of teachers are coordinating activities for a rabble of children. The young people are noisy, but the teachers take it all in stride. I escape the buzz of the hostel to find a restaurant that features an Indonesische Rijsttafel (Indonesian Rice Table) at a reasonable price. Thanks to the food culture brought to the Netherlands from its former colony of Indonesia, I get to enjoy a meal of rice with side dishes – satay, fish and vegetables.

The number of questions and comments about immigration are unending. On my hike through the Netherlands, I have met only one person who did not know anyone who had emigrated. Everyone else has family or acquaintances overseas, particularly in Canada. People's comments have left me intrigued as to how different our lives have been from the lives of those who did not emigrate. I see myself as Canadian, but with the benefits of our Dutch heritage with its food, songs and stories. I find it difficult to imagine being otherwise.

Again, on this trip I have a longing for my home in faraway Canada. This time I ponder my time in the kitchen making applesauce or liver paste or soup. I miss preparing supper while waiting for Joanne to return from work. Margarine seems to be the standard here, and I prefer the real butter we use at home. When drying myself with my microfibre cloth, I especially long for our big fluffy bath towels.

Before leaving Valkenswaard the next morning, I locate the tourist information office for details on how to get to Weert for the evening. I could take the road, but would like to cross "'t Linderbos," a woodsy area that looks Canadian with its birch, oak and pine. A young worker provides me with a map through that park while the woman managing the office informs me: "You can't walk to Weert today. It's too far."

Weert is about 30 kilometres distant, just past the boundary into the province of Limburg. Her words become a challenge, and I take off, not stopping in Weert but continuing to the next town, Stramproy. I'm tired and don't understand why I do these things. I certainly don't plan to walk back and tell her she'd been wrong!

During this hike I cross a corner of the district known as "De Peel," which straddles the border between the provinces of North Brabant and Limburg. The region is best known for the extraction of peat for fuel over hundreds of years, but it is significant to me for another reason. In my lifetime I have managed to struggle through three books in the Dutch language, and one of those was the novel "Parochie in de Peel" ("Parish in the Peel"), by Toon Kortooms.

I found this book in the "other languages" section upon my arrival at Sacred Heart Novitiate in Ste. Marie, Illinois in July 1965. Scouring the library shelves, I noticed a few works in Dutch and took the opportunity to improve my mother tongue. This story was told from the point of view of the priest and was interesting enough to keep my attention for the duration. It recounted the challenges of this young priest assigned a parish in a poverty-stricken neighbourhood of De Peel. Since my use of the Dutch language had consisted solely of informal conversation, it was a chore to go from cover to cover, but I challenged myself to read the whole book. Now I pass through De Peel in the challenge of hiking the whole distance across Europe and have entered the province of Limburg.

In Stramproy – "That looks like 'Strathroy,' the Ontario town," I think to myself – I stay with a couple whose residence could grace the cover of a house and garden magazine. I take in the paintings and carvings displayed strategically throughout their orderly home overlooking the manicured back yard. They tell me, "We've made several pilgrimages to Santiago de Compostela on foot and by bike," and it shows in how they care for guests. My room is charming, the bed is comforting and at breakfast the couple disappear behind sliding doors that are closed with precision in the way of ensuring privacy for a king.

The next day a rainstorm catches me off guard. In the howling wind, I'm soaked by the time I don my rain poncho. My next lodging is at an address named "Dijk" ("Dike"), and I have trouble finding it till someone points out the dike on the edge of town: "Just walk beside the dike and look for the house number." It turns out to be as simple as that.

Still damp, I arrive at my home for the night, a house in a state of repair. I'm warned to avoid the wet paint on hallway walls as I climb the ladder to place my backpack in my attic room. They are sincere people, and I enjoy my host's chatter about the area as we relax in their sunroom and look out at the countryside. "That's Belgium," he says of nearby farmland, and I feel a flicker of warmth as my heart counts down the countries still to be crossed in my international trek.

Stopping at a roadside café with an "Open" sign, I look forward to a morning coffee. However, the owner is still in her housecoat, so the bread delivery person serves me instead. I guess that's the way it is in small towns, whether here or back in Canada. However, the details around restaurant meals show you are no longer in Canada: your dinner entrée arrives on a plate surrounded by little bowls of vegetables, one of which may be *snijbiet* (swiss chard) in a light cream sauce. A cup of coffee comes with a glass of water, a sliver of pound cake and a jigger of whipping cream flavoured with Irish Cream. I'm feeling spoiled here.

Groups of spandexed bikers seem to use this area as a training ground for the Tour de France or some such thing. Cars, bikes and uneven walking surfaces continue to keep me on guard as they could spell the end of my hike: my body needs to stay intact, and one wrong move could send me home to recover from injuries.

In a few towns in the Netherlands, I have seen schoolchildren take bicycle driving tests while parents in hunter orange vests occupy folding chairs at street corners and mark the children's performance on clipboards. Despite such standards, cyclists seem as unconcerned about my welfare as are car drivers. I wonder: "Aren't vehicles supposed to slow down when they pass a pedestrian? These speed up instead, making it look like a sport." They and I now find ourselves among expanses of barley and wheat. These stretches must seem short to them on their speeding contraptions; for me, as a hiker, they are endless.

At one point I ask someone for directions, and I'm told that the shortest way is through the part of town that is *"op de berg"* ("on the mountain"). This rounded hill would certainly not qualify as a mountain in Canada, but I'm impressed with its appearance in this flat country.

## Maas

My first view of the majestic Maas River is disturbing: the power shovel on the deck of a barge makes a racket as the maw on its boom dips down to scoop another tonne of gravel. A local person explains: "Along the river a layer of good gravel goes down about four metres and is used at construction sites all over the Netherlands. They have broken through the riverbank to keep digging."

When these excavated areas are flooded, they create more Maas Plassen (Maas Pools), a series of lakes along the Maas River. The Netherlands has been preoccupied with controlling land and water – draining water to create arable land in the north, removing gravel to create wetlands in the south.

When I was walking southeastward through North Brabant toward Limburg, I was told: "You should turn south here. That will give you a shortcut into Belgium on your way to Paris." Instead, I insisted on continuing through the Netherlands to take in all of Limburg from top to bottom so I would explore as much of my fatherland as possible.

Now, just past the town of Thorn, geography makes that impossible: the Maas River lies in my way. I cannot hike southward through the northwestern corner of Limburg without leaving the Netherlands after all. I ask several people, hoping one will know of a secret road I can take, but all agree. So, I'm forced to make a 10-kilometre detour around a curve in the

Maas River by crossing into Belgium, hiking through the town of Maaseik and walking back into Limburg. Surprisingly, no road signs tell me I'm leaving or entering either country.

When you sleep in the dorm room of a hostel, you don't know what will happen that night. It may be quiet or there may be coughing, mumbling or snoring. Generally, though, your peers are respectful of your need for sleep. I don't find that kind of consideration at the Stayokay hostel in Maastricht.

As we prepare for the night, I enjoy a chat with the young woman from Brazil assigned to the next bed. Charmingly, her English is tinged with Spanish intonation. She informs me, "I'm a Ph.D. candidate in psychology, and I plan to study how older people spend their free time." I start telling her about writing my memoirs and hiking across Europe during my retirement years. However, it does not pique her interest, and she keeps talking about herself till I shut off my light.

At two o'clock in the morning, three young Dutchmen burst into the room. They are loud and drunk. They turn on the overhead lights so they can make their beds, and they do a lot of swearing, all of which brings us fully awake. I'm in a lower bunk and facing the wall when they come in, so I feel as though I won't be noticed. I'm annoyed but pretend to be asleep and assume the storm will pass.

The young woman does not keep a low profile, but starts talking to the goons, even mentioning where she is from. When she complains about their behaviour, they rebuke her and call her "Brazil." She storms out and returns with the night manager who assigns her to another room. She has several large suitcases, so it takes her a while to pack up while I sense the sparks between the two sides in this conflict. Finally, she leaves, they settle down and I get back to sleep. In the morning I leave the room quietly so I don't disturb the sleeping monsters.

On my way out of the hostel, I track down the manager and complain about these three being assigned to our room. In response I receive a free *lunchpakketje* (packed lunch) of sandwiches, fruit and a drink. Having been a manager, I know

175

all about giving people a little something to get them out of your office and on their way.

I had bought a cellphone and its minutes at an Albert Heijn department store in Amsterdam and assume I can buy more Albert Heijn minutes at another store of that chain. When I do, my phone won't accept them. In frustration, I go into the next Albert Heijn store on my route, and I'm told: "Those weren't Albert Heijn minutes you bought the first time. They were from T-mobile NL, the phone's provider."

As it turns out, that purchase was useless and can only be refunded by providing their head office near Amsterdam with my receipt. As a visitor without a bank account in the Netherlands, I would be caught up in a complex project to see the return of my Euros. I think better of it, buy T-mobile NL minutes and muse on this latest of the mysteries that come with my hike: "Another of many lessons learned."

As I walk along the Albert Canal that accompanies the Maas River into Belgium where the river becomes the Meuse, I'm excited to meet up with a group of hikers with day packs on their backs. One of them explains: "We spend a few Sunday afternoons looking for wild orchids behind the roadside bushes." And I thought they were headed for Santiago!

I've appreciated the built-in language lessons that come with my hike. I travelled through South Holland with its more studied Dutch and its hard guttural "g" sounds. I arrived in North Brabant with its softer, more Germanic, "g" sounds and its own dialect, including a picturesque vocabulary. Then in Limburg I would overhear a few words of a conversation and think I had understood when the patter suddenly took a turn and sounded like nothing I'd ever heard before – perhaps more akin to the German language.

Now entering Belgium, I'm surprised at the sudden change at the border – from Dutch to French. Generally, the northern part of Belgium speaks a form of Dutch called Flemish; the southern part uses a French dialect known as Walloon. It hadn't occurred to me that the Dutch province of Limburg extends so deeply southward into Belgium that, past its southern tip, the French language would suddenly appear. But so it does.

I'm finally in Belgium to come to terms with one of the most traumatic moments of my career as a registered nurse. In the late 1970's, I worked in the Intensive Care Unit at Norfolk General Hospital in Simcoe, Ontario when a horrible car accident forever affected the families of five Belgian college-aged men. These young people had come to Canada for a summer of picking tobacco, had driven to see a movie in town and ended up in hospital and – for two of them – on steel carts in the hospital morgue.

When the mother of two of the boys arrived from Belgium and wanted to see her son in the morgue, the evening shift nursing supervisor recruited me to accompany this woman since I spoke Dutch. I was moved by the way she stroked her son's face, talked to him in her grief and warmed that ice-cold room. Now she is back in my heart as I start my trek through Belgium.

As in South Holland, canals are teeming with barges, each of which can hold the contents of a fleet of transport trucks. The groups of bikers have now given way to a few of us walking, and I find myself strolling with the local people. I'm surprised that I have not met other hikers finding their way to Paris or points beyond.

Someone suggests: "Just follow this path along the river all the way to Liège." As in my past experiences, local information may not hold true. A dozen kilometres before I reach Liège, the end of the trail forces me to detour around impenetrable woods and past a mysterious chain-link fence with "no trespassing" signs. Eventually I arrive in an industrial area, puzzled as to what to do next, when my cellphone rings. It's Joanne saying hello, but she can't help me in my confusion. A few more requests for directions from local people, and I'm on my way into the city.

Belgium's political parties have been unable to form a government for some time, and I wonder how things might look. A young waiter mentions that everything worked fairly well when they had a government; now it still works fairly well without one. "Do we really need one?" he muses. I know it's a rhetorical question, but I search for an answer and can't find one.

Liège looks like a typical northern European city – one steeped in history – and the hostel is a modern rebirth of an old Récollet monastery. In a nearby quadrangle lies a memorial to the great Belgian novelist of the last century, Georges Simenon. This monument consists of a round boulder held down by heavy chains. Etched into encircling granite blocks is a series of words about walking in sun and shade – words I find comforting in my own travels.

I sense an active cross-cultural buzz in this city: at an outdoor café, three senior citizens – appearing to be from three different minority groups – are caught up in a discussion. The talkative Kurd tailor who repairs the second ravelling cuff of my jacket is another of many people with whom I would choose to spend more time. But I need to stay on the move – perhaps staying young by constantly adapting to change, both physically and mentally, including that imposed by this keyboard. In the French-speaking part of Belgium, the familiar QWERTY keyboard is left behind, and I need to deal with the frustrating AZERTY system: the placement of its letters and accent options are slowly coming back to me from last year's travels through France.

My first of two nights at the Liège hostel are peaceful despite having four roommates in a six-bed room. However, on the second night, I become irritated by the ruckus when a group of teachers have lost control of their charges. Late in the evening, a few hours past my bedtime, a police car pulls into the driveway – perhaps summoned by a fellow guest – and the building falls silent.

Starting my morning hike to Huy, I'm aggravated by a lack of sleep and the persistent rain. The way out of Liège takes me along 20 kilometres of smoky industrial complex along the Meuse, effectively hiding the river from view. Suddenly I see the odd sign indicating that "Le Festival du

Cirque Franco Canadien" ("The Festival of the French-Canadian Circus") will take place at the nearby village of Hermalle-Sous-Huy. I'm tempted to hang around for a few days and meet these fellow Canadians, but – as always – I need to keep moving. I have a continent to cross.

After all the smoke and noise as I left Liège, the small city of Huy is an impressive sight – orderly and with a sense of growth. It reminds me of the resurgence of the Moncton area back home in New Brunswick. As Huy is pronounced like the French for "yes," I decide their branding should include the double sound: "Huy? Oui!" I would suggest this to city representatives, but it is now late afternoon, and I can't linger.

Having left the Netherlands with its profusion of "Vrienden op de Fiets" homes and now hiking Belgium's Via Mosana pilgrimage route, I find fewer of those host families and need to seek out other accommodation. The Huy tourist bureau provides the name of a bed and breakfast at a seven-kilometre distance in the pretty town of Ben-Ahin.

When I arrive at the home of this couple that have "done the Camino," I feel welcome once again. Our discussion extends over a range of issues, and my hostess has strong feelings on every topic. She is concerned about pollution from all those factories along the Meuse as they are outdated and feels the lack of a Belgian government is a concern since democracy is fragile and needs to be made to work.

She also talks of the challenge of adapting to local conditions while you travel: "Two young men stayed here for a few days. They were students from Australia, and one of them missed peanut butter, so he bought a jar. We don't use peanut butter much, and ours must be different from the kind used in Australia. He took one mouthful and threw the rest in the garbage."

The next day I feel a sense of loss in leaving these good folks behind. It seems to be the story of a pilgrim – meet interesting people and leave them just as quickly. My wordless stretches through the day prepare me for lots of socializing in the evening. Everyone continues to be interested in Canada, particularly its geography, and wishing to learn more.

Unfortunately, my queasy stomach is still bothering me. It certainly would be easier to carry out my venture if I had no fear of high bridges over those numerous rivers, if my stomach behaved and if I could easily sleep through the night. But I guess that would need to be someone else leaving footsteps across Europe.

When I stop at a fancy restaurant for a cup of coffee, their banana split is calling me. It tastes great, but I feel bedraggled among the well-dressed clientele. I pull out my cellphone and begin to reread Joanne's messages as I try to fit in. I'm sure they see right through me since my cheap model looks unimpressive among their iPhones.

My hike is full of coincidences, and one occurs as I pass a sign (strangely, near the village of Wartet) that reads, in French, "commando training centre." The exact moment I glance at the sign, the air shakes with an explosion from the next hill as though to reinforce what I'm reading. Further along soldiers climb dolomite cliffs that border the Meuse River: my quiet reveries are replaced with military activity. Rock-climbing enthusiasts are everywhere, and much is made of the 1934 death of King Albert I of Belgium in a solo climb at the Marche-les-Dames, which I had passed a day or two earlier.

I enter the city of Namur and retrieve the next guidebook from my backpack as I've completed the Via Mosana and I'm now starting on the Via Monastica. This pilgrimage route takes me through the perfect pedestrian walkway over a set of railway tracks. The modern, fully enclosed bridge makes me wish all others were constructed in the same comforting way.

Then a sidewalk runs through a park, serving as playground for Canada Goose families. Parts of Europe have been plagued with these birds: they consume corn and wheat, eating into farmers' profits. As a Canadian, I feel a twinge of guilt, as though the Canada Goose habits are my fault. However, like everyone else, I need to get around their droppings by taking awkward steps like those of the knight on a chessboard.

Past the Namur Casino, I find my home for the night, and it comes with its own set of irritations. I had called earlier and was told no one would be home till late afternoon so I sit beside my backpack on the front steps of this row house and look out at the shrubbery on neighbouring lawns. Then the family car pulls up, and it is my hostess and her adult daughter. A boy and girl, of about eight and six years of age, bound out of the vehicle to embrace their next bit of mischief while their mother's shouting does not help to improve their behaviour.

Over the few hours, the boy keeps the family on edge: he throws a ball in the kitchen, knocking cute little glass bottles off a shelf. After supper he climbs a stepladder in their garden to retrieve a Frisbee that is still out of reach on a neighbouring wall. I'd joined the family in the backyard, and I'm watching his antics when I realize they have fled into the house: if the boy fell, I'd be out there alone to pick up the pieces. I head indoors, my host – a doctor – has come home and we have a little chat.

The mother of the children is a nurse and complains: "We are always being told to follow Canadian nursing standards. That's not fair because Canadian staffing levels are so much higher than those in Belgian health services." I feel caught in the web of having to defend my previous nursing profession, and I retire to my room early. There I find a bed with sheets that are far from fresh and decide to use my sleeping bag instead.

As I plan to leave early the next morning, my hostess has shown me around the kitchen – how to prepare the coffee and where to find the breakfast foods. She gets up just as I am leaving and in time to reprimand me for having eaten the wrong bread – it is her husband's special diet bread. It tasted good to me, and I don't feel bad: she hadn't told me not to eat that bread, and I'll consider it payment for the discomfort of my stay. I'm just glad to be zipping away from that house and down the trail to my next adventure.

I pass through the friendly town of Profondeville, and the church doors are open, so I peek inside. An older woman interrupts her pre-Mass prayers to say hello and to tell me the Ascension Day Mass will soon begin. With my backpack and all, I attract both the attention and the helpfulness of locals: during Mass she leans toward me to show me the page numbers of songs in the hymnal. This parishioner certainly makes me feel welcome.

When I return to the trail, the odd yellow Camino arrow or stylized shell appears. These put an extra spring in my step – knowing I'm on the right path and that others have left their footsteps.

My Via Monastica guidebook suggests seeking out L'Abbaye de Leffe in Dinant as a home for the night. It's an old Norbertine monastery that had developed an exceptional beer. The abbey no longer produces the ale but receives residual payments from the Belgian brewing giant that bought the rights. This community of about a dozen monks and half a dozen visitors who are "on retreat" welcome me into their family atmosphere. Visitors have supper and breakfast together and help wash dishes. We also attend Benediction and take part in the Divine Office in the evening and the next morning.

Apparently, the "paying guests" (all except me) have nice rooms. Any pilgrims that find their way here (there had been two the previous day but only myself this evening) are given a bare floor in a neglected classroom with no shower available and only cold water to wash. They take the monastic atmosphere seriously here! I am uncomfortable among the crates of books, discarded furniture and a sink full of water with a putrid stench.

I plug in my night light, get into my sleeping bag and prepare to doze off when I raise my head for one last look around and see something moving along the floor against the far wall. When it moves in time with my head, I realize it is not a rat after all but my own shadow. Reluctantly, I go to sleep as I muse on my teenage seminary days in another pious milieu.

*"As seminarians, our talk was all about helping others. In reality we were a closed community intent on helping ourselves – living a life of piety on our own way to heaven."*

Now that old sensation finds me enduring the monks' lack of care as I lie in my sleeping bag in this abandoned building. The next morning I give a donation for the community – to cover the meals anyway, I figure. The monk who looks after visitors seems surprised, and I have second thoughts. But by then his hand has closed around my few Euros. I suggest it's time they use those beer residuals to fix up their pilgrim quarters.

The next day I welcome departing from this artificial family and exploring the world of nature as I pass a profusion of flowers in the roadside ditches. These are tended by buzzing bees while groups of butterflies swoop up from their flower-related activity and serve as my escort. Now, at the beginning of June, these busy insects provide comfort as I struggle with a blister. I had hoped to be blister free on this trip, but a small sore has appeared on the back of my left heel. I'll have to tend it carefully.

As I enter France and come to the town of Givet, someone stops his car to tell me the municipality has a shelter for pilgrims and the key is kept at the police station. I am pleased and make my way there. Over the next two hours, attempts are made to locate the key.

After several phone calls, the man who normally looks after this key arrives. However, when he had left for a month's vacation in China, he entrusted it to someone whom we can't find even when we drive to look for him. I suggest we simply get one of the police officers in the adjoining room to kick the door in. No one laughs. In the end I'm directed to an inexpensive hotel where I'm given the last room available and spend a comfortable night although the bed is one of the narrowest I've seen.

I leave Givet in the early sunshine and see a bridge that would take me to a quiet bicycle path on the east side of the Meuse River. However, it is headed into countryside and could well come to an end, which would lead to detours on the way to Fumay. Instead, I stay on the west bank of the Meuse, choose the shoulder of the highway heading southwest and fight traffic for an hour before I exit onto a pleasant country road. This trail leads through the village of Chooz and continues in a southwesterly direction, which is perfect: that's where I'm headed.

Perhaps things are going too well, and I'm becoming complacent. If I had checked the detailed map in my guidebook, I would have noticed my path was leading into a dead end: it was taking me into a peninsula of the Meuse River where the road becomes a loop with no bridge out of the area. I am caught and need to continue southwest around that peninsula and northward again to get out of this trap. Eventually, I reach the houses at the narrowest part of the peninsula – houses I had seen two hours earlier! – and I'm finally free to turn southwest again toward Fumay. "Always check maps for every detail," I remind myself.

In mid-afternoon I stop at a restaurant in the village of Haybes for a cup of coffee and a review of the map so I can make sense of the above missteps. A middle-aged woman seems to be the owner, and a young woman waits on me. Suddenly, the owner is asking if everything is okay, and I realize I have fallen asleep with chin resting on my palms and elbows on the table. It seems the young waitress didn't know what to do about this sleeping guest and asked the boss. Once again, I explain, *"Je suis en train de traverser l'Europe"* ("I am crossing Europe"), but I have the feeling they don't care why I'm tired. They prefer customers who are wide awake.

A few kilometres down the road, I arrive in the town of Fumay where the parish provides a shelter, but this time the people who look after it cannot be found. I end up at a bed and breakfast where I close the shutters against an impending electrical storm. Even then, the booming and crashing awaken me from a sound sleep. Things simply stay interesting.

People have been kind in helping me find ways to record my progress. Parts of my weekly blog entry were written in a secretary's office at the hostel in Liège, at a café where the owner let me use his family's laptop and at a *mairie* (village office) where the mayor gave permission for me to use one of their computers. And, of course, the French AZERTY keyboard continues as one of my challenges.

The river that started as the Maas in Dutch and continued as the Meuse in French has been a pleasant companion over nine days. I first came across it in Thorn in the northern part of Limburg and enjoyed its features through Belgium and finally to Fumay in France.

At times the river was busy with the traffic of barges decorated with geranium boxes and landscaping. One of my first hostesses on this walk spoke of the years she and her husband had spent on Europe's waterways delivering goods. I'm fascinated by this way of life where the home is definitely the workplace.

Then, around the next bend, a flotilla of pleasure boats would appear. In spots the water looked clean; in other places sludge and garbage were collecting. Occasionally a low dam interrupted the wide channel to maintain the water level for river traffic that detoured through canal locks around those barriers. Of course, the river had a series of bridges: I appreciated the low friendly ones; others, intended for cars only, felt overwhelming as they soared on stilts from opposing cliffs high above the water.

Then there were groups of bikers and pedestrians seeing the sights, and the next day I would be alone. Sometimes the sides of the river were 10-metre-high concrete walls on top of which families strolled pleasantly – but foolishly, I thought, given the lack of barriers along those walkways. At other times my grass and dirt paths meandered down to the river's edge as water lapped at my feet. And, of course, fishermen relaxed in the shade while tourists rushed around, bound to take in all the sights.

The length of this exploration caused it to be more meaningful than my brief companionship with the Loire River on my previous hike or with the Marne River a few days later. Now in Fumay the river and I share a heartfelt goodbye.

**Help**

Leaving Fumay I enter the French Ardennes region – green rolling hills interrupted with groves of trees. As I pass through the town of Rocroi, I pause to examine its star-shaped walled fortification. Built in the mid-sixteenth century, the fortress surrounding the town is well maintained and impressive: it provides a real view of medieval history. Rocroi is also the end point of my hike along Europe's formal pilgrimage paths.

I had taken the Via de la Plata northward from southern Spain and followed the Camino Francés eastward in northern Spain. In France, I had hiked the Via Turonensis from Paris southward toward the Spanish border. Then in the Netherlands, I had used the Pelgrimspad, heading south from Amsterdam to Maastricht where I joined the Via Mosana bringing me southeastward through Belgium to Namur. Now, finally, the Via Monastica has guided me from Namur south to Rocroi. From now on I'll be charting my own course, as I did in Portugal. I'll be searching without a guidebook for the remainder of my trek through Europe and counting on map and compass to direct me.

From time to time, I'll still come across a section of trail that a local group has designated as part of the pilgrimage system. In fact, just past Rocroi I am surprised (and grateful) to be guided by a profusion of yellow arrows. They are plentiful and easy to follow – with one exception.

I am directed along a trail into the woods when the signs end. To continue in the right direction, I climb through two barbed-wire fences, throwing my backpack over and manoeuvring between the strands. I find myself in a pasture with a herd of cattle bearing down on me. Despite my farm background, I feel uneasy with this attention and make it through a third fence just in time. I see a farm lane and follow it between a cluster of outbuildings when yellow arrows appear on the odd fencepost. I'm sure the route I took couldn't have been the intended one but am glad to see I have not gone too far wrong.

On parts of this trail, farm gates consist of sections of iron rods at 45-degree angles that let upright creatures – like me – lean over to walk through while securing cattle in their pastures. Other gates look as though they are folded almost in half at the hinges, allowing me to walk in and out of this arrangement while keeping cattle secure. After the frequent opening and closing of gates, I appreciate these innovations that make it effortless to go from one field into another.

I arrive in Signy-L'Abbaye early enough in the afternoon that the tourist office should still be open so I can check on a place to stay. Two men, in their late teens, are chatting as they lean against a car, and I ask where to find the *office de tourisme*. One of them points to the stairs going down to the next street: "Go down those steps beside the church, and at the bottom you will find your information." I follow his instructions and see no information centre, but an old woman is sweeping her walk, so I ask her about places to stay. She has a wealth of knowledge, and I follow up on her recommendation to stay at the least expensive place, which is a cross between a hotel and a *gîte* (bed and breakfast).

I stay there and am pleased with the choice. As it turns out this is one of the few nights on my European adventure when I make it through the night (from 9:30 p.m. to 5:30 a.m.) without waking up even once. In the morning I learn that no tourist office exists in this town, and the young man's directions leading to the old woman's details remain baffling – and somewhat biblical.

After a good night's sleep, I'm ready for breakfast and peruse the menu. While waiting to be served, I'm amused to see a middle-aged woman come down the stairs to take her tiny dog outside for whatever dogs do outside in the morning. Seconds later another woman appears with her tiny dog and follows the same process. Then another. It just seems like the stuff of an interesting French film.

This part of my route shows some local efforts to develop a section of pilgrimage trail, but they haven't yet produced a guidebook to lead hikers through the area. In fact, few people seem to know the path exists. From my hotel-*gîte* I head in a southerly direction through town, aiming for Paris off in the distance. I'm not sure which way to turn next when, down the main street, I see a man and woman wearing backpacks and entering a bakery.

They are an older couple (okay, about my age!) from North Holland who tell me, "We left home at the beginning of May and plan to arrive in Santiago de Compostela in October." That's a gruelling distance, and I ask whether they might not tire of each other's company, but they ran a business together for years, so that's not a concern. This couple has both a guidebook describing the Grande Randonnée (Great Rambling) and a gadget accessing the Global Positioning System (GPS). They are pleased with how helpful this apparatus can be in the middle of nowhere.

A week or so earlier, a local person had seen me looking down at the device in my hand and asked: "Is that one of those modern things?" He had thought it was a GPS contraption, but it was far from modern though it may have been a novelty hundreds of years ago; now it was simply my plastic Canadian Tire compass, complete with whistle and magnifying glass. I am pleased with how well it has served me: at the more complicated turns on the path, I proceed with detailed map in my right hand and compass in my left.

The Dutch couple is following the signs with red and white stripes marking the Grande Randonnée route while I'm trying to follow the yellow arrows of the pilgrimage route. Outside the bakery they check their information and point me in the right direction. Then, a kilometre out of town, we meet again. They say they got there so quickly because their GPS showed them a shortcut.

As we walk along, I happen to mention taking shortcuts on the Pelgrimspad through the Netherlands, and they assure me they follow each step of the trail. ("But you just took a shortcut," I muse. "Sometimes people are a puzzle.") A few kilometres on, yellow arrows veer away from the Grande Randonnée route, and I follow those, so we go our separate ways. I do not see them again and appreciate returning to the peace of my solo hike.

This is productive farmland: I travel past herds of beef cattle, large rectangular hay bales and crops of wheat, canola, barley, corn and sugar beets. Heading through the country toward Château-Porcien, I meet an elderly man who is pulling weeds from in front of his garage door. He is enthusiastic about the area and points to distant crops that I should appreciate as I pass. The route takes me between fields forming a quilt into the distance and under the turning blades of a row of 10 wind turbines. For all the talk about the noise these machines make, I can barely hear them above the sound of the breeze in my ears.

The *abri* (shelter) in Château-Porcien proves plain but clean and well maintained. The staff and customers at the café across the street are pleasant. This is another town where patrons shake hands with everyone, including me, upon entering. Again, I feel part of the community.

On my way out of town the next morning, I follow a series of yellow arrows. Then at an intersection there is no indication as to which way I should go. I check into each road for a few hundred metres, hoping for a yellow arrow in the distance. I finally give up, take the most likely route and meet a profusion of yellow arrows a kilometre later. You never know what to expect, and this time I'm grateful to be led through a village with another comfortable pilgrim shelter and a memorable restaurant.

Before turning in for the night in this village of Asfeld, I stop for a serving of lasagna and salad at a bistro named "Le Christina." This is one of the best meals I've had in Europe since the Mexican food at Taco´Mex Restaurant in Biarritz, France two years ago. Flavourful lasagna, served hot with a cool, interesting salad – these can be truly memorable.

The next day I round a curve in a village, and my map is unclear as to where the road will lead. A woman is about to get into her car, and I ask her the way. She seems eager to chat and says she's a teacher but has the day off. Then she bursts into tears. She motions to the cemetery where she has just visited the grave of her husband who died a year ago at 51 years of age. She confides: "He was such a good man. I was the eldest in my family, and we had no father. So, I had a tough life, looking after my brothers and sisters while my mother went to work. I was lucky to have such a great companion as a husband."

I suggest to her it hadn't been luck but that she had chosen wisely. (At times like this, what does one say, especially in an unfamiliar language? On reflection now, I'm still not sure what would have been my most supportive comment – even in English.) I understand they had one child, a son, and I suggest she may want to write her memoirs. Then I ask if she wants a hug, and it turns into the French air-kissing with cheeks barely grazing – a ritual I find quite meaningless. In any case, I leave it at that and continue on my way while memories of her tag along.

In the town of Bétheny on the outskirts of Rheims, I pass Floralie's Garden, a family-run business and the largest independent, stand-alone garden centre in France. In front of this expanse of plants for sale, I see a kiosk that can be my source for a meal. A man is baking crepes on round black iron surfaces, and I order the *sucre vanillé* (vanilla sugar) type. Near the end of my day's hike, I'm famished, and the rolled-up crepe with a fresh cup of coffee makes this treat the standard for all others to follow.

I hike into Rheims and get to appreciate another of the profusion of European cathedrals. This one is special owing to its age of 800 years and its state of disrepair, having suffered a catastrophic fire in the last century. I feel more comfortable with this suffering building than with those that seem proud of their resplendence. As usual with these old churches, scaffolding is in place and likely will be for years.

I search out the retired seminary that is available for the use of pilgrims and other travellers, and I settle in there. This building houses a diocesan library where a local author gives an evening lecture on the "Religious Ardennes." As in so many areas in Europe, local saints, monasteries and religious buildings are numerous and good for a two-hour presentation with PowerPoint photos. I am pleased with the amount of his French I understand – though I must add that he speaks very clearly. Of course, after a 30-kilometre hike, staying awake proves a challenge, but I do not too badly.

At this hostel my two fellow pilgrims are a young man from Quebec and a young woman from the German-speaking part of Belgium (and I hadn't even known of such an area). They are heading southward in France and on to the Camino through northern Spain while I continue west toward Paris. I find comfort in the stillness of the peaceful chapel, within the quiet of this seminary, within the peace of my solitary march. My troubled seminary past must be starting to heal. Later the distant practice session of a classical pianist lulls me to sleep.

At breakfast we are served only orange juice, coffee and baguettes with jam. A group of two dozen visitors takes up both sides of the row of tables in the centre of the room while we few pilgrims look on from the fringes. The uniformity of that throng – breaking apart their bread, spreading some jam and chatting all the while – is disconcerting. They all act so alike, and I wait for one of them to break out of the pack and say, "You know, I could go for some Corn Flakes right about now." But it doesn't happen. Unfortunately.

One of the women attendees at the previous evening's lecture had mentioned: "I know somebody who is gathering information for a new pilgrimage trail from Rheims to Paris. You might want to contact him." It would be interesting to try that path, so I seek out the man in his bookstore, and he provides me with a few photocopied pages of "Les Chemins de St Jacques de Compostelle: Reims-Paris" ("The Paths of St. James of Compostela: Rheims-Paris").

Apparently, a group has followed this draft version of his route, and they left the odd scallop shell painted on a tree. However, the directions prove to be confusing, and I end up in isolated woods where trails lead in odd directions and I need to guess which to take. I quickly give up on this route in favour of my map and compass. I have more confidence in them: I'm sure they will get me to Paris.

Nearing Hautvillers, I am impressed with productive fields and affluent buildings in champagne country. Tasting-purchasing facilities are everywhere, and I stop at one that is an ivy-covered mansion to see what happens within its walls. A young couple from New York is just leaving the shop's perfectly appointed interior with several bottles. I pay a Euro to enjoy a sample glass poured by the university-age son of the owners. He asks about my hike and dreams of doing something similar. I suggest he just leave the shop behind, and he replies, *"Mais mes parents!"* ("But my parents!")

I gulp the champagne as it's nearing five o'clock and I still need to find a bed for the night. Sometimes I find myself rebelling against the grind of always having to look for a place to stay. The parent in me says, "You'd better find a room," while the child says, "Just let me enjoy this champagne first." This time the parent wins. As I hand the champagne server my empty glass, I suggest: *"Allez!"* ("Go!") He looks wistful as I shut the door behind me, keeping his dreams within its walls.

I finish the glass of champagne just in time to catch the tourist information person while she is closing up shop. She directs me to a bed and breakfast where my elderly hostess makes me feel like a long-lost son catching up on family news: "The picture on the wall beside you shows our six children. That one was taken of the whole group of our grandchildren. And here are the great-grandchildren: yes, we have two of them now."

Her husband stays quietly in the background and becomes a bit more talkative when I join them for a supper of soup, salad and dessert (at five Euros). They own the house next door, and it serves as my home for the night. Its gate leads to a curved and walled alleyway perfectly suited to champagne country and leading to the artistry of wrought iron signs on homes and businesses throughout the photogenic town.

In the immediate area of Hautvillers, the homes, gardens and outbuildings show signs of wealth thanks to the sale of champagne. With my farm background, I find myself admiring the farm machinery designed for these crops, including an apparatus that looks like a mid-sized tractor rising on stilts above its wheels so that it can clear the vines. The belly of the beast hangs down between the rows while a tangle of fat black plastic pipes leads to spray nozzles to cover the rows with fungicide or insecticide or whatever. In the next field, I marvel at a similar piece of equipment – now armed with a series of chattering rotating knives – pruning the tips of grape stems. Over a distant set of fields, a helicopter swoops back and forth as it sprays a luxuriant crop.

Though I am still exploring champagne country the next day, I feel as though I have left the richer area behind. As I approach Dormans, homes are not as nice, and equipment looks as though it has been bought from the Hautvillers growers as they upgraded.

## Adventures

Entering the dusty community of Dormans, I look for a place for the night. The tourist information person is not helpful: "There are a few small hotels in town and an old church rectory. Here's a map. Just check around; you'll probably find something." She could have considered phoning those places about a vacancy so I didn't have to trudge all over, but she was too busy chatting with a friend who dropped by. Over the next hour, I become more and more discouraged: the nun at the rectory says I cannot stay there, and both hotels as well as the *gîte* (bed and breakfast) are *complet* (full). This is wedding season, and everything is booked.

A waitress and young client at one of the hotel bars proves helpful as she knows the community and he has a smart phone. They suggest I go to a bigger town with more hotels, and the young man adds: "My phone shows that the train is leaving for Château-Thierry in an hour. That town is a 15-minute train ride west of here." Out of the machine at the deserted station, I extract my ticket, and – for the first time on this trek across Europe – I travel to a different community to spend the night.

When I step off the train in Château-Thierry, the first two hotels near the station are *complet*, so I walk toward the downtown. Desperate for a room, I pass a bookstore where a young woman is closing up. She is the owner and phones around till she finds me a hotel bed three kilometres away. When her husband comes to pick her up after work, he kindly drives me up an unending slope to the hotel. After today's 23-kilometre hike from Hautvillers to Dormans, trudging through Dormans with no success, taking the train to Château-Thierry and running into hurdles there – after all that, I'm exhausted. My backpack becomes lighter whenever I speed along the trail; when I plod from one hotel desk to the next, it is filling with bricks.

The next morning I am hopeful for a better day: I zip downhill past the bookstore and board the train taking me back to Dormans. Once again, my rule of walking every step across Europe takes on a hint of silliness. Here I am, riding through country I rode through yesterday and that I shall be crossing on foot later today.

Arriving in Dormans, I start the hike back along the Marne River, finding a path I had seen from the train. This trail through woods along the river continues for 10 kilometres and becomes a country road taking me to the edge of Château-Thierry. There a railway crossing becomes a challenge: its open grillwork structure rises several storeys into the air, and I climb its stairs only to find there is no way I can control my panic and walk across it. I climb back down and cautiously cross the rail lines instead. That is less safe, but – in my mind – so much safer.

Once again I arrive in Château-Thierry and find another hotel with a bed for the night. The hotels must compete on the quality of their buffet breakfasts as they are substantial (eggs, cereal, sausages, meats, cheeses, yogurt, baguettes and sliced bread), and I fill up before each day's trek.

My tos-and-fros between Dormans and Château-Thierry leave me eager to escape the area. The desk clerk at the Hexagone Hotel in Château-Thierry uses her computer to come to my rescue: "Here is the list of places you could stay tomorrow night. They are about 20 or 30 kilometres from here. The least expensive is the Mission Polonaise in La Ferté-sous-Jouarre." I wonder what this "Polish Mission" might be, but it is reasonably priced (at 22 Euros) and shows up in the travel information, so it's worth a try.

When I arrived in Dormans yesterday afternoon, I needed a bed for the night and the person at the tourist centre was too busy talking to her friend to advise me. Since then, I have been grateful for the help of four people, none of whom were tourism staff. Looking back over my trips, assistance from the tourist information people has been disappointing, and they have, at times, suggested trails that led nowhere. They could certainly learn from the waitress and patron at the bar in Dormans or the bookstore owner in Château-Thierry or, now, the clerk at the Hexagone Hotel – or any number of other people I have met along the way.

Waking up refreshed at the Hexagone Hotel on Sunday morning, I feel ready to cover the 30 kilometres to my bed for the night. As churches are plentiful but Masses are few, I decide to attend the first service I come across. Over the next few hours, I pass five churches, but all of them are closed tightly. Finally, in a larger town, I catch the end of a Mass that includes a First Communion celebration and is being followed by a baptism. Families are beaming with pride at the first communicants – girls in white gowns, boys in their Sunday best. On the church steps, many photos are taken.

Finding my way through the next town, I pass a young priest on the sidewalk and greet him, *"Bonjour, Mon Père"* ("Hello, Father"). He is dealing with an electronic device in his hands and briefly glances up to give me a distracted response.

Those days when the parish priest warmly greeted passersby seem to be in the past. "We've come a long way from the days of the Curé d'Ars," I muse as I recall stories about the pastoral work of the French parish priest known in English as St. John Vianney, the patron saint of priests.

As I pass a small yacht with two couples on board, they wave enthusiastically. I walk over to chat and am invited on board for a cup of coffee. They are cruising from Paris to Strasbourg and tell me the system of European rivers and canals will let them get to any number of destinations. They are interesting people and interested in my story, but disconcerting nonetheless.

Each time one of them asks me something, the other three get into a heated debate over elements of the question. One asks: "What time will you get to your destination this afternoon?" This causes the other three to launch into a discussion on how fast hikers walk while I try to be polite and wait for them to finish, but the questioner is looking at me expecting an answer. It's a strange experience. All the while their little dog is huddled at my feet, and one of the men warns me not to step on the dog's paw. It has occasionally lashed out and bitten an ankle, he says. I sit perfectly still, finish my coffee and return to the peace of my walk.

In La Ferté-sous-Jouarre I need to approach several people to find the Polish Mission. Set back on a side street, it is not well known by the community but proves to be a welcoming home for the night. The convent is owned by the Sisters of Saint Joseph; in their simple grey habits, they now run it as an efficient hotel. Its chapel features an iconic image of a Madonna and Child with dark features – one that appears daringly non-European and follows the "Black Madonna" tradition.

The sisters, originally from Poland, cater to the Polish community in this part of France. A few people are staying overnight, and relatives are celebrating a boy's First Communion as we gather on the patio looking out at shrubbery and flower beds. One of the families had moved from Poland to England and is now visiting for this reunion. The daughter, in her early teens, strikes up a conversation with me as she feels out of place in the French chit-chat she hardly understands. Instead, my English language is a relief to her, and she is fascinated with the tales of my travels.

Late in the afternoon, a bus full of children from Poland arrives for a few days of hiking in the nearby hills. At check-in I was promised, "We'll give you a light supper," but I receive the same meal at my card table as do the groups at banquet tables stretching down the hall. This turns out to be a large bowl of soup, two slabs of pork roast with an apple purée dressing, green beans and boiled potatoes. And a delicious cream puff for dessert.

Despite the barrier of their Polish conversation, the nuns and guests are friendly, and they pass the test I had set for them. I'd been concerned about my future walk through Germany and on into Poland: I wondered how accepting I would find the people in the eastern part of Europe. Now I'm reminded that nice people can be found everywhere, and I have no need to be anxious.

In my eagerness to reach Paris and finish this leg of the trip, I put in a day of almost 40 kilometres that terminates at a hotel in Lagny-sur-Marne. As soon as the owner comes from behind the desk to show me my room, his big hound gets up from its place in the lobby and lies down in the office his master just left – as though guarding the area. When I ask about it, the owner says, "He does that all the time and surprises everybody," and adds to my mixed feelings about dogs. Just when I feel as though I can't handle the aggressive bark of another one or the cooing by an owner, I see something like this and find it quite nifty.

Exhausted after the trek, I lie on the bed and fall asleep. I awaken when my cellphone tells me Joanne has sent a text message that has to do with Air Canada's impending strike. I text a few words back, and then the phone rings, and it's Joanne. I tap my resources to come fully awake but don't succeed because Joanne comments: "You sound really tired. Is everything okay?" A rigorous day's walk has an effect beyond the physical: it drains me of mental energy as well. I finish talking through the fog and go back to my nap.

The hotel's attractive buffet breakfast includes ham and cheese slices, boiled eggs, croissants, chocolate filled pastries, yoghurt, fruit, juice and coffee. I again appreciate every morsel as I set out to seek the most direct path to Paris.

## Metropolis

As I expected, June 14th consisted of a long day's walk into Paris. The anticipation of arriving at another end point in my wanderings makes it feel as though that goal keeps slipping into the distance. The whole day is spent in the towns and cities that are part of this great metropolis, and I concentrate on dealing with vehicle traffic, waiting for "walk" lights, enduring the unyielding pavement and finding the shortest distance. As I approach Paris from the east, the grid patterns extend diagonally through communities, and streets do not run in a neat westerly direction. I hike northwest for a few blocks and then southwest for a few blocks, hoping to discover a path that leads directly to downtown Paris. A couple on their bicycles tell me of just such a path, but it comes to an abrupt halt after a few kilometres, and I am back to hiking back and forth.

Eventually I reach central Paris and ask an older woman for directions. She is going my way and follows me through the cobweb of streets. Twice she calls from behind me to tell me I missed a turn, and I go back to the spot where she's waiting and pointing down a side street. I turn a final corner, and there it is on the bank of the River Seine across from Notre Dame Cathedral – the Tour Saint-Jacques.

This is the tower I had left a year ago on the trek southward through France. Now I arrive after completing another section of Europe. With tears in my eyes, I walk around this traditional pilgrimage starting point and have someone take my picture. I have now hiked the distance from Cabo de São Vicente in Portugal to Alphen aan den Rijn in the

Netherlands – a total of 3200 kilometres. Who would have thought?

I need to find a bed for the night but do not have the contact information for the pilgrimage hostel in Paris. I start to enter the cathedral to talk to the information people there, but knapsacks are not allowed inside, so I'm frustrated in being stuck outside. Someone tells me the nearest tourist information office is kilometres away, and I do not have the interest or energy to hunt it down.

Suddenly the clouds part, and I see a solution: I text Joanne for the phone number she will be able to find on the good-old Internet. Joanne doesn't answer right away, and she's had phone issues, so I go to Plan B. A young man is squatting beside his rickshaw – a contraption designed to show the pilgrims the sights and to keep students employed and fit. I think, "Someone like that would have information for me," and he suggests I visit the tourist office a stone's throw from where we are standing – a cubicle at the edge of the street.

They search the Internet but can find no information about a pilgrim hostel in Paris and suggest a nearby youth hostel instead. While I'm registering at this *auberge de jeunesse*, Joanne texts the pilgrimage hostel information, but by then I have decided to stay in this attractive facility. I know I'll enjoy my stay here: it is one of three old Parisian buildings that an organization has converted to hostels, and it displays charm with corner courtyards in the shadow of the building while guests are protected from the street by walls and gates.

Meanwhile I settle in and celebrate my accomplishment with a trout dinner at a nearby restaurant. The dessert of French toast covered in chocolate ice cream and a liqueur sauce is memorable. Just down the street, I locate an Internet facility that lets me begin to catch up on my blog entries. To my surprise, the manager leads me directly to a QWERTY keyboard. After my frustrations with the French AZERTY layout, I am delighted: touches like that can make life much simpler.

I consider staying at the hostel for an extra day and seeing a few of the Paris sights. However, the place is fully booked for the next night: the present group of university students from South Carolina will be joined by a larger group of young guests. At 7:15 in the morning, as I wait in the courtyard for breakfast to begin, the gate swings open, and a stream of about 100 children marches in. They chat while awaiting further instructions from the lead teacher. I am astonished at the size of the group and their arrival at that strange hour, but perhaps they travelled on overnight buses. In any case, there is no room for me, so I decide to catch the high-speed train for Amsterdam.

On the way to the Netherlands, I need to switch trains and train stations in Paris, and there I experience one of the variety of irritations that come with mass transit. I follow arrows toward the *métro* (subway), which I need to take to the other train station. These signs lead me into a hall where an attendant is monitoring the traffic flowing through a turnstile leading to the trains. I ask him if that is the way to the *métro*, and he says: *"Non. C'est de l'autre côté."* ("No. It's on the other side.")

I assume he is referring to the other end of the building and head for it. I don't find the *métro* entrance there, but signs point to the area I just left. It suddenly dawns on me that the guard was not talking about the other end of the building but the other side of the room – only steps from where we had been standing. He could simply have pointed to the other turnstile a few metres away and saved me 20 minutes of searching. "Another lesson learned," I muse as I make my way through the confusion of pedestrian rush hour in the Paris *métro*. I find the monstrosity that is the Gare du Nord (one of six Paris train stations and the busiest one in Europe), and I'm on my way back to the Netherlands.

In Amsterdam I take the tram to the Stayokay hostel at Vondelpark where I had lodged previously. It's a well-organized facility, and I'm glad to be back. Part of it is housed in the former Amsterdamsche Huishoudschool (Amsterdam

Housekeeping School) that once provided training for housekeepers, maids and housewives. That five-storey square brick building, with its old name inscribed across the third storey, hints at an interesting history. During this hike I had wondered where all the Canadian young people were as there are usually so many travelling in Europe. Walking into the hostel, I realize they have all made their way here: they form quite a crowd.

I take the opportunity to find an outdoor eatery where I can catch up on our Dutch cuisine and savour a feed of *poffertjes in een kraam* (tiny pancakes in a booth, though the English doesn't sound nearly as picturesque). This complements the *gerookte paling* (smoked eel) from earlier on this trip. It's good to be back.

Again I visit the sociable white-haired man at Pied à Terre, the Amsterdam bookstore (located on Overtoom Street just south of the Leidseplein) that specializes in travel information. In his upstairs office, he's surrounded by maps and clients, and I wait my turn to tell him: "I'll be hiking through northern Germany when I finish in the Netherlands. Do you have a map of that area?" Then it occurs to me that – of course – he has a map of that area. He has thousands of maps; he has a map of every area, and he's familiar with each one. I only need to decide how much detail I want as he shows me maps of various scales; I settle on one that provides enough information without being overwhelming.

I treat my clothes to a well-deserved wash in the hostel's laundry and find a shop to get a haircut. Not only does the young woman cut my hair expertly, but she provides a delicious cup of coffee as well. I'll have to bring that to my hairstylist's attention when I get my next haircut back home.

## Completion

An outsider watching me on this journey would often wonder: "What is he up to now?" We like things to make sense, but some of my actions must be hard to understand. I drop in at a sporting goods shop at the end of the Zandpad

201

(Sand Path), which is actually a paved alley of a few hundred metres running from the hostel to the street. At this store I buy a day pack, a simple cloth bag with strings, so I can carry a few items on my back.

I have a plan – one that is forming more quickly than I had expected. This plan has to do with my need to correct the 200-metre ferry crossing of the Lek in Schoonhoven. On my map I located a bridge 20 kilometres distant and thought: "Some day I'll go back and 'connect the dots.' I'll walk the extra 40 kilometres that will take me from the ferry crossing, over the nearest bridge and back again."

Then the previous afternoon it occurred to me that now was as good a time as any to have really walked every step from Cabo de São Vicente to Alphen aan den Rijn. To carry out this plan, I decide to stay at the Vondelpark Hostel in Amsterdam for an extra day. They are filling up fast: they can accommodate me, but I'll have to move to a different room. I deduce the hostel business must be lucrative as there is no shortage of patrons.

The next morning I am up early because I need to sort out which train to catch and the ensuing walk will take all day. I am on a tram by six-thirty to catch the train at Amsterdam's Central Station and am left craving the sizable Stayokay breakfast – three kinds of cold cereal, Dutch cheese, sliced meats, boiled eggs, three kinds of bread, Dutch rusk, *ontbijt koek* (breakfast cake, also known as *snijkoek*), *gekleurde hageltjes* (fruit-flavoured hail), chocolate spread, jams, yoghurt and fresh fruit. Instead, I buy a coffee and chocolate-filled croissant at the train station to tide me over. I have placed my backpack in a hostel locker for safekeeping and carry a few items in the day pack I bought yesterday just for this purpose.

The train takes me to Utrecht where I catch the bus to the town of Vianen on the Lek, and there I start my walk at eight-thirty. I find the bridge over the Lek, and it turns out to be a comfortable, wide bridge for bicycles and pedestrians next to a new higher bridge for vehicles. Having crossed over, I enjoy the pleasant morning as I hike down the quiet road that lies on the dike on the north side of the Lek.

I'm concerned that my breakfast of coffee and croissant was not enough to keep me going and check my map for the next town that is still some distance away. Suddenly I come upon a recreation area of trailers and boats, and I'm in luck since it has its own restaurant. The owner and his wife enjoy the tales of my adventure, and he whips up a delicious three-egg *uitsmijter* (eggs, cheese and ham on bread). As I pay my bill, he tells me: "The two cups of coffee were free because you came so far to visit us." Again, very nice people.

A kilometre further on, I come across a three-metre-high pole stuck into the ground and waving a Dutch flag above the three bookbags tied to the pole. It is the Dutch tradition to display the school bags of those graduating from secondary school on flagpoles. As there are three bags, I wonder: "Would these three children have been triplets?" I'll never know as I need to keep hiking.

About halfway through my walk, I feel overwhelmed as an indescribable noise envelops me. It's coming fast, from behind, and I feel exposed on top of the dike. I jump to the side, away from the monster, and look up to discover two fighter jets streaking above the treetops. I am still shaking minutes later and can identify with the anguish people must have experienced during the bombing of the Second World War.

I stop to watch a tractor crawl through a field spreading liquid manure behind it. I had previously seen a tractor pull a tank on wheels to distribute the stuff. In this case, there is no tank, and this seems to be a feat of magic. The procedure makes no sense till I see a four-inch diameter hose dragging through the long grass beside the tractor, which drives to and fro. Back at the barn, manure would be vacuumed out of a pit and sent through this hose to the field where it is spread. In his enclosed – and, possibly, air-conditioned – cab, the driver may well be enjoying the music on his iPod or satellite radio while I think of Bill, Dad and manure.

*"Every Saturday, on our farm in Arkona, Ontario, Bill and I would load wheelbarrows of the stuff from our pigs and calves and drive it up the boards onto our barnyard manure pile. Every few summers Dad would borrow a manure spreader, and we would stand side by side on the pile to pitch forkfuls into its bucket. In the field the mechanism would be engaged and create a moving shower of nourishment for the soil."*

Now I wonder what Bill and Dad would think of my 40-kilometre hike to make up for the 200-metre ferry crossing. Dad may have grunted, and Bill may have punched me, but I trust they would have been silently proud of me.

I'm halfway through the day's jaunt when I arrive at Schoonhoven, take the ferry across to the other side and begin my walk back to Vianen. I stop at a fruit market to buy some cherries for a snack, and I learn that even that transaction can be puzzling. A few weeks ago, in my hike southward through the Netherlands, I stopped at a fruit stand. I waited to be served when the clerk said: "No, you just help yourself. I can't serve everybody: I'm too busy."

Now I see an elderly couple taking a paper bag from the counter and filling it with fruit, so I do likewise but get reprimanded again. This time I'm supposed to wait for the clerk to help me. I'm confused but then deduce from the conversation that the older couple are the clerk's parents and likely own the fruit farm. They don't even pay for their "purchase," so definitely the wrong people to imitate.

Back in Vianen, as I search through side streets to get back to the main road and the bus stop, gusts of wind drive a sudden lashing rain. I pull the rain poncho out of my day pack, struggle to put it on in the storm and end up as one of many soaked passengers on the bus. A Starbuck's caffè mocha at the Utrecht train station warms me as I make my way back by train to Amsterdam and by tram to the hostel.

The day's experience – a 40-kilometre hike to compensate for a 200-metre crossing – leaves me feeling unsettled. It seems silly, almost embarrassing. But at least I have now walked every step of the distance: though not in chronological order, I have gone southward to the ferry terminal, between that point and Vianen, over the bridge, along the other side and south to the next town.

At some point during my hike through France someone said: "Oh, you don't walk it all in the same direction?" He seemed disappointed that I could change the rules by sometimes going northeast, sometimes southwest. In fact, there are no standards to this game since so few people would do anything as peculiar as hiking across Europe. I still have only two rules of my own in this venture – walk every step across the continent and keep writing about the experience. Admittedly, the whole thing is a bizarre project, a constant struggle to ensure I hike the distance. It makes little sense, even to me, but it has to be pursued.

**Birthplace**

This is going to be a big day for me. Today, June 18th, I am excited about the prospect of walking De Lagewaard, the street where I was born and from which we emigrated when I was five years old. However, the day becomes not so much the fulfillment of a dream as a series of hurdles.

This is my last morning in the Amsterdam hostel, and I may not have access to Wi-Fi over the next few days, so I finish the e-mail message that becomes my blog entry for the week. I'm awake at dawn and should have plenty of time to finish my computer work and cover the 24 kilometres to Katwijk aan Zee by late afternoon. As it turns out, I should have hit the trail earlier.

Leaving the Amsterdam hostel, I walk down the Zandpad to cross into the Leidseplein area. With the morning traffic comes the mental and physical exercise of checking for bicycles from the left before leaving the sidewalk, checking for cars from the left, crossing three rows of tracks while wary of approaching trams, checking for cars from the right, watching for bicycles from the right and finally reaching the safety of the sidewalk on the other side. As I wait for the tram going to the train station, I watch the morning hive of traffic and marvel at seeing not a single accident.

I leave from Amsterdam's Central Station and need to switch trains in Utrecht. This gives me the opportunity – two days in a row, this is getting to be a habit – to savour a Starbuck's grande-sized caffè mocha in the Utrecht station. One of the outlets has a line-up, so I head over to the Starbuck's diagonally across from it. Two of these businesses in this new station – who would have thought? Finally my next train arrives at Alphen aan den Rijn. From this spot I walked southward to Paris a few weeks ago; now I'm heading to the northern part of the Netherlands and on into Germany.

Outside the train station at Alphen aan den Rijn, I ask passersby the way to our old community of Koudekerk aan den Rijn. They are unsure of how to get there on foot but try to be helpful by guessing at the best route. Later, when I check a local map, I realize this hike through town should have taken me less than an hour and covered four kilometres. Instead, the suggestions lead me into the country where I get lost twice and take a winding road to my destination. At some point, I seek shelter beside a building to put on my rain poncho when, minutes later, the rain stops. And this happens another two times later in the day.

I feel confident when I recognize the path along the Old Rhine River from previous visits, so I seek out the bridge that is the Koudekerkse Brug in Hazerswoude-Rijndijk. I am excited about crossing this bridge to enter our old village of Koudekerk aan den Rijn, and I stop for a cup of coffee before the hike into my past. Seated at one of the café tables is a group of a dozen people who call out: "The meeting is just getting started. It's nice that you could join us." They assume I'm here to enlist in this group who hike local paths, get together to compare notes and receive a stamp for each section they have walked. The club president tries to explain this to me, but I'm baffled by his clipped Dutch speech, so others "interpret" for him.

When I tell of my trek across Europe, they cannot relate to my experience, and I feel ill at ease since my dream seems to belittle their successes. I finish my coffee and change into my shorts in the café washroom because I was starting to feel warm before I entered the café. When I leave, a cold wind arises from the west, but I decide not to return inside to change back into my trousers. It would be uncomfortable to have to explain to the hikers why I'm back. I just want to get on the road and have to explain only to myself.

I'm euphoric in walking down De Lagewaard, the street of my early childhood memories. In our pre-emigration days, it was a one-lane street of red brick. It remains narrow, but the bricks have been paved over with a layer of asphalt – unfortunately. Farms along this street have a narrow frontage and a channel of water between properties in place of fences. These farms are 50 acres in size, so they stretch back into the distance away from the road. As I daydream and gawk at the old homes, I realize how things have changed from 60 years ago. Now patios and awnings have been added, and the landscaping is elaborate.

I look for the original name of our homestead, "Nooit Volmaakt" ("Never Perfect"), but now "Eben Haeser" is inscribed on the two posts guarding the driveway, and I walk right by our old farm. I was born in *"het huisie van Lex"* ("the little house of the Lex family") across the road but can't use it as a guide since it was replaced with a modern house about thirty years ago. I stop to ask someone the location of our farm and make my way back to it.

As I stare at the house and stable, I'm distracted by an unruly horse being led down the street by two young women. They walk beside it, holding its reins while the animal turns, first one way then the other, and looks as though it might gallop off. One of the women stops coaxing the beast long enough to take my picture as I tell them, "This is the house where I lived 60 years ago." But the horse has their attention and reminds us this is no time to chat, so we all continue on our way.

As a five-year-old child whose life was limited to our house and barn, I did not know what lay beyond our laneway. Now I'm still unsure and head the wrong way, ending up going east toward Alphen again instead of heading west to Leiden as I had intended. With all this back and forth, the walk to the evening's bed in Katwijk aan Zee is much farther than I intended, and I arrive there an hour late.

Today I learned that a map of the area would have made the hike shorter, that I could not trust my old memories and that I cannot mix walking and sightseeing. Having a place to stay and to leave my backpack while strolling around in a relaxed way would have been much more pleasant.

Though it resulted from taking the long way, I enjoyed entering our street from the bridge as that is such a pretty area with its frog ponds and bulrushes in front of Hansel and Gretel homes. I appreciated the chance to reminisce when I recognized the barn door of our neighbouring uncle and aunt from which I had seen a man remove blistering paint with a kerosene burner 60 years ago. Family history veered into the present when I read the plaque on the front of our old house stating that our late brother Bill had laid the first stone. I had seen that inscription on previous visits, but the emotions that came with this hike now led me to read it through my tears.

On my trek across Europe, I had taken a detour to hike through the street of my birth, and I was pleased with that decision. But, as so often happens, they were the peculiarities of the day – the hikers' meeting, the wrong turns and that silly horse – that made it memorable.

**North**

My home for the night in Katwijk aan Zee is near the *vuurtoren* (fire tower), which I assume is a tall structure to watch for forest fires in the oceanside wooded areas. I don't see such a tower, but I do notice the lighthouse and learn that this is the *"vuurtoren"* and is old enough to have used a fire as its source of light. And so, my education in details of the Dutch language continues.

On my way to my lodging, I ask a man for directions as he strolls with his wife and two children. They are headed my way, so I walk with them. The man says: "Your family's immigration was the right thing to do. I'd like to do something like that." He seems eager to change the course of his life, and I would like to have heard more, but we reach their parked car and part ways.

The talk in the resort community of Katwijk aan Zee is all about the weather. The month of May had been so nice; June has been cold and rainy with few tourists. The next day I hoped to find my way along the ocean as I headed out of town, but the cold wind ("Like November in Dorchester Cape," I think) and the driving sand have me decide otherwise. At times my path straddles a dike, and I'm exposed to constant wind; at other times the leeward side of this embankment can be quite pleasant, but then the rain starts – again.

I skirt Noordwijk aan Zee (a town on the seashore) and decide to explore Noordwijk-Binnen (Noordwijk-Inside, away from the coast). At a two-day street bazaar "Markt onder de Linden 2011" ("Market under the Linden Trees 2011"), booths sell crafts, plants and food items. I enjoy the music provided by a trio of teens playing classical melodies on stringed instruments but, more movingly, that of my father's favourite, the *draaiorgel* (street organ).

This is my chance to have another feed of *poffertjes* (tiny pancakes) and a *nieuwe verse haring* (new fresh herring). These fish have been caught in the new season although one of my hostesses comments, "Some of the merchants cheat and use last year's frozen supply instead." In any case, held up by the tail to dangle into my mouth in the traditional manner, the *nieuwe verse* tastes great.

On this June 19th, the famous Keukenhof tulip garden complex is deserted. Acres of headless tulip plants are remnants of the glory that had been a rainbow of colour only a month ago. Patches of canna lilies are still in bloom, which makes the tulip fields look even more forlorn. I pass the locked gates with regret at what I missed while they – in turn – beg for company.

By now I have experienced a range of personalities and services among my homes for the night. Some folks tell a detailed story of their life, others ask pointed questions about our immigration; some provide a well-appointed room with a few extra comforts, others give you a sparse environment. In all cases, the hosts and hostesses have been friendly.

Today is Father's Day, and I'm feeling lonely, so I long for a home here in Hillegom where I shall be left on my own without a lot of interaction. That's exactly what I get. The man runs a bed and breakfast, and I'm assigned one of the rooms. He introduces himself, shows me the room, explains how to use the coffee maker, gives me a key, takes my money and is gone. It's perfect. His shower is great – lots of water and the biggest, fluffiest towel I have seen in Europe.

I had asked about restaurants, and he said: "Go to Massada just around the corner. You'll like it." He was right: Massada's mixed fish platter is delicious. With a glass of red wine and then a glass of *citroen jenever* (lemon-flavoured Dutch gin) for dessert, this isn't bad as Father's Days go. And a dark-chocolate covered ice cream bar from a variety store on the way back to my lonely room – now that's luxury. Even my stomach has become more settled: I have tried tying the front clip of my backpack lower on my tummy, and that seems to be helping. I watch little television here, but a BBC program on the geography of the Dutch coastline is fascinating and fits right in. My day is complete.

The difference between the architecture of Roman Catholic and Dutch Reformed churches has been striking. The tall, thin Catholic ones look spiritually uplifting; the wide, solid Protestant ones are sensibly rational. I wonder: "In such a small country, how can worship involve such divergent points of view?" I've wanted to take a picture that shows both styles in one photo but haven't succeeded: it's as if the two faiths don't want to be seen together.

I have now entered the province of North Holland and stop in Haarlem at a café that advertises homemade *appeltaart* (a cross between apple pie and cake). I have had a piece of *appeltaart* elsewhere: it came from a factory and had hard bits of apple core throughout. With a mound of whipping cream, this one is heavenly.

I've been in the Netherlands long enough on this trip to join in worrying about the condition of the dikes. The long period of dry weather (which is now, thankfully, coming to an end) has left some of the dikes unstable. I understand they are designed to have a wet interior; if they become too dry, it can lead to *"dijken scheuren"* ("tearing of the dikes"). An unsound dike could cause disaster in this nation where a third of the land lies below the level of the ocean's surface.

On my route northward, I need to cross the Noordzeekanaal (North Sea Canal). Several ferries take people across, but – again – I need to follow my rule of hiking every step. I look for a walking route across this canal and find it in IJmuiden, only a dozen kilometres north of here. That isn't a long distance and should have been an easy stroll.

However, this is one of those days when people join forces to irritate me. Without a local map, it's easy to get lost on trails through parks and on winding streets through subdivisions. So, I count on passersby, whose comments include: "You're going where? Those locks are a long way from here." and "Do you know how far that is? And you're walking!" Those responses make the hike feel longer, and I would have preferred, "You're our hero," but no one comes up with that.

"Op de Sluizen van IJmuiden" ("On the Locks of IJmuiden") is the title of a romantic song, one of the Dutch tunes in which a man leaves a woman to go to sea. However, the reality of a skyline of smoky blast furnaces and the arduous nature of my hike are far from romantic. This part of the trip takes me on a westerly course and away from the northerly direction I was headed, and – when I finally reach the area – I become frustrated with my to-and-fro steps in crossing the broad canal.

The four swing bridges over side-by-side locks are almost a kilometre apart. This means crossing one bridge, walking along the canal to the next distant bridge, crossing it and walking back, sometimes toward the area I have just left. This zigzag becomes a five-kilometre hike over what could have been a half-kilometre distance if all those bridges had been placed in a row. In some stretches I need to share the road with cars. They swerve around me as they speed to catch the traffic signal at the next one-lane bridge before it changes to red. I trust that Dutch engineering has a reason for this distant placement of bridges, but I find it frustrating and finally get to the freedom of the other side.

I have come to recognize my cellphone as invaluable in making arrangements for "Vrienden op de Fiets" accommodation. After the Sluizen I'm uncertain of the direction to that night's home in Beverwijk, so I phone the host family for information, and they tell me I'm only blocks from their house. I am half-listening and have one eye on the action headed toward me: two men approach and are arguing over their dog on its leash. I'm no expert on dog breeds, but this one sure looks like a pit bull terrier. It grazes my leg as it passes on the narrow sidewalk, and I give a start and finish my phone call very suddenly: "So we'll see you in – ooh! – ten minutes." Click.

At my home in Beverwijk, the couple is welcoming and relaxed. I enjoy a good night's sleep, which is helpful in being fully awake at dawn in preparing for each day's hike. On my first trips, the early morning was a test in arranging the items in my backpack. This being the fifth of my walking sessions, the morning ritual has become more automatic, and I have resorted to simplicity in packing my things. I have long ago stopped trying to keep my clean and dirty clothes separate. Considering how few clothing items I carry with me, everything is used within a day or two anyway. On my initial trip, I had items that were clean, half dirty and completely dirty. By now my need to maintain control over my space no longer includes having numerous containers.

Now I have a stuff sack of clothing and a smaller one with the few items I use occasionally (like a thin long-sleeved sweater). I keep toiletry items in one zip-lock bag and other items in another: the transparency of these bags allows me to see what is where. With the addition of a few maps, first aid kit, sleeping bag and rain poncho, that pretty well completes my earthly goods on the trip. A zip-lock bag with some extra items – Canada coasters as gifts, an extra bottle of Camp Soap and one of contact lens solution – is almost empty in this latter part of the trip. To avoid a constant search through my knapsack, keeping it simple becomes as important as keeping it light.

A walk along another great canal – the Noordhollandskanaal (North Holland Canal) – brings me to Alkmaar. The scenery is a postcard: on its opposite bank, the broad canal is bordered by perfectly spaced, perfectly rounded trees; a line of cars flows beneath them.

Alkmaar is known for its colourful cheese market, which Joanne and I missed when we arrived on a non-market weekday 37 years ago. I miss it again as the market is now held only on Fridays. Apparently, men in traditional garb carry long sleighs of cheese, and it looks as though these are being sold. I am told they have changed hands well before the event and what you see is simply a tourist attraction.

As I enjoy a cup of coffee at an outdoor café, several police cars stop in the middle of a side street in response to a disturbance. The reaction of the crowd is fascinating as all conversation stops while everyone zooms in on the distant action. Finally two young men are taken away, and we can all go back to our routine lives. Interestingly, this is the only time in all my years when I have witnessed someone's arrest. You don't often see that, and it's certainly not something you first expect to see in a sleepy little city like Alkmaar.

Later I return to that outdoor café for supper, and I'm looking for something typically Dutch. Soup and pancakes sound good. On my hike through the Netherlands, I have not been successful in finding soup that meets my standards. A bowl of beef bouillon, advertised as *"groentensoep"* ("vegetable soup"), had only a few sprigs of chives floating in it. A shrimp soup had two pieces of shrimp, a whole lot of potato and a few strands of half-raw onion. This time I settle for the tomato soup, and it is delicious. For dessert I order a Dutch pancake: the menu picture promises it will be the size of its plate. The waitress reappears to tell me: "I'm sorry, but we have a very strict cook. At five o'clock the lunch menu ends, so he can't make your pancake." I look at my watch: it's 5:02.

I feel bad about my English response – "That's crazy!" – and leave the waitress an extra tip. Then I move over a few tables, to the section run by a different restaurant, and enjoy a delicious Dutch pancake. Perhaps my inflexibility in trying to enforce prison health standards is coming back to haunt me. But not giving me a moment or two when I'd already been there for 20 minutes – for heaven's sake, that's irritating.

As their home would be hard to find, my host for the evening kindly walks to meet me while I wait beside the Grote Kerk (Big Church). As a high school math teacher, this man is trying to mark student exams at the dining room table while his wife and I sit there lost in conversation. Finally he gives up and joins us. His teaching profession gives him a special interest in my immigrant dialect: he finds it intriguing that I use noun genders so well – for example, it is *"het" huis* (the house), but *"de" stal* (the stable) – but that my vocabulary is so limited. I enjoy the discussion but head upstairs soon after since he seems to have a few hours of work ahead of him and the pile of student papers hasn't decreased.

On my European venture, beds have featured a duvet that is the exact length of the mattress. I keep getting frustrated in trying to stretch this item to meet the needs of my tall frame. Either I tuck in the end and lose warmth around my neck and shoulders, or I leave it untucked and my feet get cold. This "comforter" is far from comforting. You would think that someone somewhere would have found a way to add an extra half-metre of material. That would certainly give me a better night's sleep.

I've found disorienting the local practice of keeping all inside doors closed. I'm usually assigned a loft bedroom, so I need to go down to the second floor (or the "first floor" as they call it here) to use the toilet, which is normally in a separate room from the bathroom. At the foot of the stairs, I'm faced with a series of closed doors, and I wouldn't want to walk into someone's bedroom in the middle of the night. I've learned to pay close attention during the initial tour so I know which is the toilet door as that can save a great deal of embarrassment later.

From the Running Room in Moncton, I had purchased two high-energy candy bars in case of an emergency lack of food. I had now used both although this had more to do with yearning for a snack than with starving on the trail. Now I find a Runner's World store in Alkmaar where I buy two more bars in anticipation of the coming trek across the Afsluitdijk (literally, "closing off dike"), the 30-kilometre dike separating the North Sea from the Zuider Zee.

Leaving Alkmaar, I pass through the friendly town of Sint Pancras. I stop in a café for a lemon tea and a chat with the woman who owns the place and a customer whose parents-in-law have moved to Ireland to get away from the hectic Dutch lifestyle. The owner's big brown dog lazes around and at one point places its head on my lap.

As I'm leaving, it lets out a fierce bark and nips at my leg. It is not really a bite and, thankfully, does not break the skin, but it takes me completely by surprise. Even more shocked is the owner who turns pale. Apparently, the dog had never done such a thing. The customer suggests: "I think it was bothered when you put on your backpack. That made you look scary." He could be right. To the list of things I find dangerous – cars, bikes, uneven walking surfaces – I'll now have to add "dogs."

The farm building that serves as both house and stable in North Holland is a square structure with a long sloping roof (of thatch or tile) that swoops toward the ground, stopping at the low brick walls. Cash crops of grain, potatoes and sugar beets are plentiful; though the fields are not as large as those of France and Spain, they remind me of those expanses.

One of my hostesses remarks, "It is not always windy in North Holland, but you really notice it when it is a quiet day," And I'm reminded of – but don't miss – the constant wind while hiking the Spanish *meseta* or living in the Canadian Prairies. There are more groves of trees than in the province of South Holland, but I find few cows: herds of cattle are simply not as common as they were in years gone by.

My path beside the Amstelmeer runs beside a dike, hiding the immense lake from view. This hike is serene with a channel of water on my right and birds singing contentedly. I climb the grassy dike on my left to explore its other side and receive a blast of wind in my face as the shimmering expanse of the Amstelmeer stretches out to the horizon. It's so vast as to be disorienting.

## Dike

I'm making my walking days shorter in preparation for the long trek on the Afsluitdijk. On the last day, I walk only 15 kilometres and arrive in Hippolytushoef before noon. I'm not expected at my hostess's home before 6:00 p.m. and learn how difficult it can be to fill six hours with activity when not walking. I have lunch in a restaurant and stretch one cup of coffee to take up about an hour, which includes nodding off while poring over the map covering my route of the next few days.

I spend a moment or two on a park bench, but the cold and rain urge me to keep moving, so I take my time looking at every item in each of the half dozen stores. This area had been the island of Wieringen in the Waddenzee before the Afsluitdijk was built: the lowering of water levels and the creation of *polder* (land claimed from the sea) changed all that. The people now see themselves as inhabitants of a mythical island.

Early the next morning, I prepare for my trek along the Afsluitdijk by taking an anti-inflammatory medication. Normally, I'm sensitive to my body and let it advise me, but this is going to be long hike before I can stop the stress my feet will be enduring. I had found a room in Hippolytushoef as close to the Afsluitdijk as possible, but that is still an extra seven kilometres at the beginning of the day. Then there will be the 30-kilometre dike and another six or seven kilometres to get to my next home in Makkum. So, a total of almost 45 kilometres.

I'm pleased when this walk starts with a *gerookte paling* (smoked eel) that is advertised at someone's house on the way out of town. The young woman says: "If you're only getting one, you don't have to pay. That's okay." As always, the *paling* is delicious, but the smelly paper wrapper stays with me till I find a garbage can halfway through my day's trek.

Worrying about my hike on the Afsluitdijk proved to be a new experience. I have always avoided dwelling on the next day's walk: concerns about the weather, the terrain and the traffic can doom the day before it starts. However, I now thought about the straight, boring stretch, and it bothered me. This worry was fuelled by people's comments, *"'t Is ver, hoor"* ("Listen, it's far").

Until now my path had been a solitary experience – unfamiliar to others – and I could choose to ignore the next day's issues. Or it had been shared by others back on the Camino, and I could avoid those who dwelt on the following day's hike. Here people have driven the length of the Afsluitdijk, can't imagine walking that distance and feel obliged to warn me. Suddenly everyone is an expert.

As it turns out, I don't find this part of my walk through Europe nearly as difficult as I had predicted. Furthermore, there are no hills to climb. And, on this narrow strip, I always know exactly where I'm headed. Not once do I need to ask for directions!

For 30 kilometres the North Sea lies hidden behind the four-metre high grassy berm on my left, the paved bicycle path stretches before me, the four lanes of highway traffic flow on my right and the Zuider Zee lies on my far right. This scene becomes monotonous. However, monotony is something I've learned to manage by filling the time with old memories and new discoveries. This trek feels like a combination of the long, straight trail through the Landes of southern France (although loose sand in that path made it more difficult to navigate) and the sidewalk next to the highway over much of the last 100 Camino kilometres before Astorga, Spain.

From the constant stream of cars, people wave and honk. I pass a few cyclists, but it seems unusual for someone to walk the distance. Among this traffic I feel special in the freedom to simply walk up the side of the dike and over to its other side to discover the odd ship on the horizon or a distant sailboat skimming the North Sea. It is remarkable how loud and busy is one side of the dike and how quiet and undisturbed the other. And, of course, this provides private toilet facilities at any point on my walk!

I approach a group of parked cars and notice they have stopped at the information centre. I'm sure it provides a wealth of details about the building of the dike and could be interesting, but I won't be one of its visitors. The visit means using a tower of stairs, crossing a walkway above two lanes of streaming traffic to enter the centre and doing that again on the way out. I see people chatting as they casually cross that walkway in the air, and I wonder how they can do that. I keep my feet on solid ground and leave the information centre behind.

Halfway along the dike, I stop to replace damp socks and to enjoy the *lunchpakketje* (packed lunch) I had prepared at breakfast. I relax at one of a half dozen picnic tables to enjoy sandwiches of cheese, *"boeren ham"* ("farm ham") and sliced boiled egg; *gekleurde hageltjes* (coloured sprinkles) on a raisin bun; slices of apple; orange juice and a yoghurt drink. Two cycling women stop to tell me: "You must be the Canadian hiker. We heard about you from the waitress who served you lunch yesterday."

I have little problem making it to the other end of the dike where two other women say, "We're friends of the woman whose house you stayed at last night," and I ask them to let her know I've made it. Later, as I stop for a cup of coffee at the day's destination of Makkum, a family comments that they saw me on the Afsluitdijk hours earlier. Sometimes I find the world very small indeed.

**Friesland**

Halfway across the Afsluitdijk, I entered the province of Friesland. Further along there was a sign indicating the exit toward Makkum, my home for the night. This sign was on the opposite (south) side of the road and seemed to be meant for automobiles and not for hikers, so I continued walking the bicycle path to the end of the Afsluitdijk. Then I needed to turn right, but it was impossible to cross the streams of traffic that were entering and exiting the dike and racing down the highway.

An overpass appeared in the distance, and I hoped I could cross there. It was tricky making it across merge lanes and onto the grass hill leading to the overpass, but eventually I ended up on the right road, having gone only a kilometre or two out of my way. I'm still uncertain as to where I should have exited the dike. Perhaps there are so few hikers that no provisions are made for us. In any case, I survived crossing both the dike and the road, and I made it to Makkum.

In that tourist village, I find restaurant patios brimming with clients. Now, toward the end of June, many customers have disembarked from the hundreds of sailboats that decorate the area. I'm intrigued to hear the waitress effortlessly switch from Dutch to German to the Friesian language. I overhear three or four words of a conversation and think it is not that hard to understand Friesian, but then the next 20 or 30 words are totally foreign and collect speed as though on ball bearings. In its written form, this language seems to have the vowel-consonant combinations of pre-modern English to which I was exposed in an English literature university course years back.

Joanne and I visited the towns of Sneek (pronounced like the English "snake") and Heeg last year. We were impressed with the tourist activity in Friesland. Now I'm even more certain that my 1950's view of the province is well in the past. Half a century ago, the poorer of the Dutch immigrants seem to have come from North Brabant and Friesland. We from South Holland were not well off, but the people from those two provinces seemed destitute. And I think of a Friesian immigrant who became dear to us.

*"Hank Westenbroek was a young man from Friesland who became part of our family in the 1950's. Hank would appear on our farm, help Dad for a few months and – just as suddenly – leave for construction work somewhere. We enjoyed the clipped syllables of Hank's Friesian accent and his ready sense of humour."*

Now Friesland seems even more commercially successful than was North Brabant when I crossed it a month ago. Friesland has used its assortment of lakes to brand itself as a boating-leisure area for visitors from the Netherlands and Germany. Adding to the province's charm are the cottages of bright red brick and the friendly people. Here everyone constantly says hello to everyone else, including visitors to the area. I feel welcome as I search roads and bike trails for the best route eastward.

During my hike the next day, I come across the cute village of Allingawier, one of those that have been turned into living museums. There must be interest in this step back into history as its parking lot is full by mid-morning. Then comes the touristy town of Bolsward with a four-day community celebration in full swing. Music, food, circus acts and a historical drama production are getting started as I walk through. I would have enjoyed dawdling, but that wouldn't take me across Europe, so on I go.

I reach the Stayokay youth hostel in Sneek where Joanne and I stayed a year ago and discover that its sailing school is still hopping. I appreciate the enthusiasm of young people from Germany and the Netherlands who are learning navigation skills in a social setting. The next day, Sunday, is a good time to take a break from my walking. My clothes need washing once again, and I'm in luck because the hostel staff provide laundry service for a reasonable fee. With Saturday's busy group of young people having left, Sunday is sombre.

I seek out a Catholic church for my attendance at Mass, and the woman at the hostel desk gives me directions to Sint-Martinuskerk (Church of St. Martin). She adds, "Years ago my grandfather was the custodian there," and I get the sense of being five years old as my father's words come drifting back.

*"In May of 1952, our immigrant train passed numerous churches on its trek westward from the harbour in Quebec City. We would be looking for a farm to buy in Southern Ontario, but Dad suggested, if that didn't work out, he could always become a custodian as there were so many churches to choose from."*

Things have certainly changed since those days: now I check for Mass times using the Internet on the hostel computer. I am disappointed as the Mass is less reverent than that of our home parish in Sackville, New Brunswick. Here the priest and two university-aged male altar servers carry out the whole ritual with one of the servers doing all the readings. The choir sings beautifully – and the assembly could join in on the singing and give a few responses – but it has the appearance of a theatre production rather than a celebration.

And I think fondly of Sunday mornings back home at St. Vincent's Church in Sackville where about 20 different members of the assembly – besides the choir – provide ministries during our Sunday celebration. They greet people at the door, proclaim the readings, announce the prayers of the faithful, provide altar server support, collect the donations and distribute communion. Ours has the sense of interaction that befits a celebration of the Paschal Mystery, I think. It encourages the fully conscious and active participation in the liturgy that the church advocates.

In the outdoor café called De Walrus, I chance upon a lunch menu item that includes three kinds of soup. These are served in white cups on a white tray, and I get to enjoy *kokos-kerriesoep* (a spicy chicken soup), *champignonsoep* (mushroom soup, though not nearly as good as Joanne's) and *mosterdsoep* (mustard soup with diced Friesian ham). As a soup lover, I'm in my glory.

The next horde of young people is expected to arrive tomorrow, and at Sunday's supper only seven of us remain in the building – a German man, a Dutch woman with two children, two staff members and me. The man is loud, using an outside voice for indoor conversation, and I look forward to the end of the meal. Then I slip out to the patio area to enjoy the cool evening with a glass of *jonge jenever* (young Dutch gin).

On Monday morning I leave Sneek, and the walking seems simple. I have again reached the point where it is easier to keep walking than to stop: stopping then takes effort while walking becomes automatic. At home my self-talk includes, "I need to go for a walk," but here it becomes, "I need to stop walking." I also get to a point where it feels more natural to be wearing the backpack than to be walking without it. This trek across Europe keeps surprising me: I'm looking for life's deeper meanings, but the process of hiking can be just as remarkable.

During my hike of a year ago – from Paris to the Spanish border – my thoughts ran uncontrollably toward my unfinished memoir and the anecdotes I still wished to add. This time my ideas swarm around plans to publish and distribute the memoir. I look forward to getting home and making those plans reality.

The lakes enjoyed by tourists can be a nuisance for the hiker. Highway construction in Spain and the canals earlier in the Netherlands had been the cause of detours. Here I become frustrated as bodies of water impede my progress and force me to veer from my intended path. Now I need to follow a route that swerves north in an arc up and around Snitser Mar.

I hike beside a canal and pass a small yacht that is proudly sitting high out of the water and creeping toward a bridge. The chrome features protruding above its cabin stop the boat from making it under the bridge, and the two couples that are its crew and passengers engage in some discussion as to how to proceed. Finally they back away and turn around but have no idea of the *schadenfreude* (German for "enjoyment of another's misfortune") felt by this Canadian stranger watching from metres away. It's refreshing to see that the rich also have to face reality.

Akkrum is another active community: it has so many businesses that there seem to be more stores than homes. After Akkrum I head out of the recreational district into dairy country. Herds of up to 100 Holstein-Friesian cows graze in the bright green. I am impressed with the well-tended homes and the clusters of shrubs and flowers. Farm equipment appears new, clean and bright with a massive baler wrapping each round bale in plastic before gently placing it on the ground. In the next field, I see a chute on a harvesting machine blow haylage into wagons headed for farm bunker silos.

During my first walk in Europe, I had "spoken" to a Portuguese farmer in gestures as he dismounted from his tractor to fix a stubborn piece of irrigation equipment. I had motioned for him to join me on my walk, but he had declined. Now I think he could have enjoyed comparing notes since farmers everywhere have a lot in common.

In Drachten I stay with a curious family in a well-worn house. Their conversation is disjointed, but I understand from the husband that he and their young adult son have done some travelling – to bible school in the state of Kansas and to the country of Suriname as missionaries. Their dysfunctional relationships and reactions to each other seem odd, and I have mixed feelings: I find the dynamics fascinating but look forward to morning when I can leave this confusing family behind.

As it turns out, the next morning the town of Drachten won't let me leave while I become more and more frustrated. I know I need to be on the other side of the *snelweg* (superhighway) to continue eastward, but I'm stuck in a wooded area west of it. I hike back and forth through several bike paths and hope to meet someone I can ask, but it's early morning, so I'm alone in these woods. I can hear the zooming of traffic and even catch the odd glimpse of the highway through the trees. Finally I chance upon a bicycle path that meanders through a tunnel to the other side, and I'm free.

In this part of the Netherlands, I'm intrigued by the number of motor-assisted bicycles. The elderly must find it useful to have the motor do some of the work on a lengthy trip. I am also entertained by signs that reflect the characteristics of Friesian names, many of which end in "stra" or "sma." "Bergsma" seems common, and – curiously – "Dragstra" is the name of a local business that deals in classic cars.

Passing by the village of Siegerswoude, I long for a cup of coffee, but the presence of a café does not look hopeful. Suddenly, around the next bend, a campground features a patio near the road. A sign on the door of the adjacent house says to phone their number for service. My cellphone is answered immediately: "We're just driving through the campground in our truck. We'll be right there."

Five minutes later the couple take my order, and the man brings me a steaming Canadian-sized mug of coffee – a nice change from those cute European cups that hold two mouthfuls. The woman serves a slab of warmed *appeltaart* (apple pie-cake) smothered in *slagroom* (whipping cream). They tell me to take my time while they go to town to do their grocery shopping. I finish, leave them each a Canada pin and continue on my way satisfied.

One of my hostesses back in North Holland had mentioned that her job involved providing services to people residing in that province. She commented on the boundary between the provinces of North Holland and South Holland and said: "I had to keep checking the map for the line between North and South," as it did not run straight or follow any pattern that reflected conditions on the ground. Now, as I enter the northern end of the province of Drenthe for a hike of a day and a half, I'm surprised to see that the outskirts of the city of Groningen (capital of the province of Groningen), including its airport, lie within Drenthe. As in Canada, so here, historical anomalies don't always make sense in terms of the present reality.

## Drenthe

Suddenly the affluent farms of Friesland are left behind at the Drenthe boundary. I'm disappointed as everything now looks poor and worn including the farm buildings, equipment and crops. Even some of the bicycle route signs are rough and hand-painted though still helpful in pointing the way. A few beef cattle and sheep graze the scrubland.

However, within 10 kilometres or so, I find myself in the midst of luxuriant trees and hordes of tourists. They are immersed in the stillness that comes with Drenthe's country lifestyle and its unhurried way of life. Many historical homes have been converted to opulent mansions with impeccable landscaping. I continue to be astonished at how quickly things change, even at a walking pace.

At the end of one of the first consistently warm days, I arrive in Eelde-Paterswolde and have trouble finding my home for the night. The local people point me in the right direction, and I receive a warm welcome and enjoy our conversation on lawn chairs in the back yard. My host is an engineer who is home to look after their pre-school son while his wife is away. He explains, "I work on the systems that control water and that ensure we have good drinking water," and I remember the great pumps pouring tons of water out of the country and into the ocean at the start of the Afsluitdijk. Considering this country's 24-hour-per-day vigilance in emptying rainwater from the land and keeping ocean water up behind its dike, I'm sure he has a full-time job well into the future.

I happen to be this family's first "Vrienden op de Fiets" visitor, but they have had experience with the hospitality of others: a few years back, the couple biked through China and travelled throughout Asia. As a new host, the man asks me: "What should I change in your room so it will be set up well for visitors?" I suggest fewer knickknacks and more level surfaces to spread things out: he appreciates the information.

In some of the houses, I have started my night's stay by removing vases or photos from side tables so I could unpack my bag, and I tried to replace those items in the right spots when leaving in the early hours. As I depart this morning, my host draws a complex map of trails to help me find my way through an underpass since a major highway could block my path out of town. His sketch proves to be essential.

People make their way from various parts of the Netherlands to bike in Drenthe's park-like setting. They are an unhurried group, and I'm glad their activity has no semblance to the bicycle madness of Amsterdam. School groups ride bicycles to points of interest in the company of teachers and adult supervisors. I see young people do some hands-free biking while manipulating a hand-held apparatus to text some important message, and I think of Bill.

*"When my brother was given a used bicycle, he couldn't just ride it in a normal way. Bill wouldn't bother holding the handlebars and would zoom downhill with his feet up in the basket while leaning back with arms crossed. Danger meant nothing to him."*

Now bikers are left behind as I suddenly find myself among hikers – walking alone or in pairs – on the Pieterpad. This path runs the length of the Netherlands from north to south and is named for two places with "Pieter" ("Peter") in their name – Pieterburen in northern Groningen and St. Pietersberg at the south end of Limburg. I finally have company on the hike and can take a break from checking map and compass. However, our trails separate after only a few kilometres as I look for the next bike route taking me east toward Germany.

During my previous walks, I avoided highways in favour of country roads. Now in the Netherlands, bike paths are usually found running along medium-sized roads. These paths suit me perfectly, and so far I have chanced upon them by accident. I could have used a bicycle route map, but at this point I'm not starting over to do it right.

Even though we share bike paths, the speed of bikers and the fact that they are limited to level surfaces makes their journey different from mine. Throughout my European hike, I have seen bike riders glance down at the page attached above their handlebars. These charts are set up as tables showing the distance from one town or natural feature to the next. I assume similar charts are not made for hikers because we don't have odometers although, by this point in my long-distance hike, I automatically convert hiking speed to distance covered: I have a built-in odometer.

Despite their access to route data, bike riders still can't give me, as a walker, complete information. However, it has been an improvement over that provided by the hordes of car drivers who don't understand the route requirements of the hiker at all and could leave me quite lost. I have started to see unattended gas stations to satisfy the thirst of all these automobiles. People use their credit cards to purchase fuel with not a staff member in sight.

I approach Zuidlaarderveen (in Drenthe but on the Groningen boundary) and my next home for the night. This proves to be another interesting family: my hostess looks after households when a baby is born (and in the Netherlands most are born at home), her husband has trouble walking and looks sickly and their teenage adopted son has a pyramid-shaped recording studio in the backyard. The area is infested with moles, and the woman takes me along as she walks through the yard to check the traps.

I notice great herds of milking cows as I saw in Friesland. Sometimes the smell and bawling sound from a huge barn informs me that some cows are not "free range," and I feel sad at their imprisonment. Wheat and barley thrive in large fields, and I'm told the sandy soil is suited to potato crops.

This area has an interesting history: from the 16th to the 20th centuries, hundreds of square kilometres of two-metre-deep *veen* (peat) had been removed to serve as a source of combustion for homes and factories. Peat had also been used as construction material for some of the smaller Dutch dikes and – as their interiors were meant to stay moist – dry conditions could cause instability in those dikes. The clay content of the larger dikes (such as the Afsluitdijk) ensures those are not in danger.

Just north of here, a section of several hundred square kilometres is being considered for the creation of a diked containment area. Should water need to be removed from the region more quickly than is possible through existing channels, excess water would be fed into this emergency reservoir. Unfortunately, that would result in the flooding of many farms, but it would serve as an alternative to greater damage elsewhere. I find this dilemma to be surprisingly similar to the controversial flood-plain issues of southern Manitoba in western Canada.

On this trip I made extensive use of the "Vrienden op de Fiets" list of host families. I have now stayed at my last of these homes and realize that this too has been a rewarding experience. Each home was different – whether its bed, bathroom or breakfast – and I wouldn't know what to expect upon arrival. Some houses were modern, others were old; some were fancy, others were plain.

In the mornings I would come downstairs to find breakfast ready for me. I delighted in seeing which kind of bread this family used and how the sliced meat was arranged. In one home the items had been placed so close to my plate that they were crowding it out, and I moved things away so my plate and I wouldn't feel claustrophobic.

Interestingly, most of the host families had a connection to social services of some kind: they had adopted a needy child, worked in a field that involved the care of others or were volunteers in their community. I always felt welcome and could briefly pause from my continuous search. "Vrienden op de Fiets" is a resource I recommend.

Sometimes a family proposed that I stay for a few hours after breakfast before heading out or even suggested, "You could stay an extra night if you want to take a break from all that walking." I felt uneasy about accepting those offers and didn't ever do so because an extended stay would make me part of their world. I've enjoyed casual chatting but have avoided commitment. I wanted to protect my investment, to use my resources by walking away from these folks and continuing my tussle with the trail. Like the German Shepherd dog, the "Littlest Hobo" of Canadian television (imagine my use of a canine analogy!), "I'll just keep moving on."

## Groningen

In Tripscompagnie I am entertained by a dredging machine: at the edge of a waterway, it grunts in scooping bucketfuls of mud from the channel bed and slopping them into a truck. Meanwhile a worker sits in a boat to check the depths and ensure enough of the stuff has been removed. This is another of those things you don't run into everyday and reminds me of a gentler process during my youth.

*"As a four-year-old, I went with Dad and my brother Tony in our punt. They had scraped mud from the edges of the ditch bordering our property and had filled our little boat with the stuff. Now Tony was poling the boat as we glided through water channels to a back field. There they used pails attached to poles to scoop and spread the squishy fertilizer."*

I pull myself away from watching this polder scene of keeping water channels clear and turn toward Zuidbroek where I ask a hairstylist for directions to the nearest café. She thinks none are open and adds: "I have coffee ready for my customers. Sit down, and I'll pour you a cup." I enjoy a chat and the chance to respond to her clientele's questions about Canada, and I'm on my way refreshed.

Less than a kilometre on, a sign directs me toward a bicycle path. However, a paved trail runs between canal and highway and looks more interesting, so I choose it and have a nice walk – till the trail ends about 10 minutes later. The next half hour sees me slogging through tall wet grass and wondering where I'll end up. I check my map, and a few detours bring me to another bike path. My boots eventually dry and – with a change of socks – no harm has been done. It has simply been another adventure.

I find it interesting that one youth hostel can be so different from the next. Some serve as places for young adults to party, others house visiting school groups, still others serve as family vacation spots. The hostel in Scheemda has hardly a child in attendance. Most of the guests are middle-aged or older folks biking in this quiet part of the Netherlands, and some come from quite a distance. One couple of about my age has stayed here often on their bicycle rides through this area, and I'm pleased to join them in the hostel's supper.

The man and I discover we both have *hoogtevrees* (fear of heights). He hits one aspect of the problem precisely when he suggests, "Everything is fine until the ground starts to move." That's exactly my experience as well, but it's more than that. As I head back to my room after supper, I ponder the fact that Europe's bridges, overpasses and outside staircases have made me an expert and that it's not so much "fear" as a form of panic.

In crossing a high bridge, I'm fine till suddenly waves of a panicky sensation surge through my chest, abdomen and knees. This response seems to be connected to my sight more than to my mind: it's not so much fear of being high in the air as it is a reaction of my eyes to that shimmering distance. These feelings of discomfort are then increased by a strange worry about having to escape the panic by dropping over the edge. A high wall along a bridge, for example, keeps this worry over falling under control and allows me to cross with little difficulty. Much of this doesn't make sense, but that makes it all the more troublesome – as is true of any panic reaction.

The hostel serves as a community meeting spot, and a group of regional government representatives is lost in discussion on finding ways to save money on their projects. I feel uncomfortable in the way their earnestness stirs memories of my role in government bureaucracy – only four years back but a lifetime ago. I was a nurse manager in the federal prison system, but my work involved more managing than nursing. Systems needed to be maintained, whether or not they contributed to the health of the inmates. Feeding the monster that was the organization required a string of meetings.

In their search for more money, these folks seem to take a lot of breaks outside, or perhaps they enjoy the evening air during a small-group discussion and a cigarette. The meeting was to run from 6:00 to 8:00 p.m., but at 11:30, when I go down for a cup of herbal tea after a first sleep, I'm amused that the last of the participants is finally leaving. This "first sleep" has become part of my adult sleep pattern: I go to bed early, awaken before midnight and – an hour or so later – return to sleep till early morning when I'm up for the day. This process has become automatic and continues during my European nights.

On July 1st I am destined to celebrate Canada Day with the adventure of entering Germany. Over the last 10 or 15 kilometres before the border, a series of mansions appears. These impressive homes are of brick or stucco and boast ornamental features. In many cases, the home is now a farmhouse with a huge barn recently built onto the back of the manor. I am overwhelmed by the extravagance.

In the eastern part of Groningen, I find conversations in the local dialect difficult to understand: although the language is Dutch, words are given a German pronunciation. It is astonishing that this dialect has such a German sound that residents across the border from each other have no trouble communicating although one side speaks Dutch while the other speaks German.

On my trek through the Netherlands, I explored features of the Dutch language that I'll share before my narrative enters Germany. A week or so back, one of my hostesses mentioned: "Recently I talked to a man who was visiting from New Zealand. He moved there from the Netherlands as a boy. You sound exactly like him." (And I wonder whether his Dutch wouldn't be affected by the Kiwi idiom.) Apparently, we immigrants have developed speech patterns that Dutch people group together as an immigrant dialect. These patterns would stem from an imitation of our parents' diction in faraway Canada and our lack of exposure to constant changes in the Dutch language. I have mixed feelings about this woman's generalization: I wish my Dutch were better but take pride in maintaining the language in the 60 odd years since our immigration.

My hike through the Netherlands revealed words and expressions that are either new or now used in novel ways. *"Alstublieft"* (literally, "if it pleases you," and sometimes shortened to *"alstu"*) means "please" but has so many uses now that it could mean almost anything from "Can I help you?" to "Here is your meal" to "Glad I could help." However, on entering a store, I was often taken aback when the salesperson skipped the niceties and uttered, *"Zeg het maar"* ("Just say it"), which seemed an abrupt way to ask what I needed.

I was amused at the way English words had migrated into the Dutch language. Making travel reservations has become *"boeken"* (from the English "booking"), and *"tosti"* is the new word for a toasted sandwich. The verb *"pinnen"* has to do with use of a debit card and its PIN (personal identification number), and a cash machine is a *"pin automaat"*. The Dutch have developed a handy way to answer the phone: there I could simply say, *"Met Joseph"* ("With Joseph"), in place of our rather meaningless "Hello." I least wanted to hear *"Helaas!"* ("Alas!") as its annoying sound preceded statements about no vacancy at a possible abode for the night.

To my relief, people were accepting of my limited Dutch and overlooked the errors I must have made – with one exception, which they constantly corrected. That was my use of the word *"weiniger"* as a translation for the English "less" or "fewer" (as in "less money" or "fewer people"). Even though *"weinig"* means "little," saying *"weiniger"* would be like saying "littler" instead of "less" in English. Each time I used that word in a sentence, someone would remind me that the proper word was *"minder,"* and this happened over and over. I got to the point where I anticipated this correction within the thousands of words I must have spoken during breaks from my walking. In fact, I tried to switch from *"weiniger"* to *"minder,"* but a childhood of immersion in the verbal patterns of one's parents is not easily dismissed.

The border with Germany bulges to include the entire town of Bad Nieuweschans on its Dutch side. I ask for directions to a restaurant and take a seat on its patio. When a rainstorm brings us inside, I am delighted to discover one of the coziest eating establishments I have ever seen. In tones of mid-brown, the simple furniture complements a quiet atmosphere that includes a playroom for children. I order my meal and rehash experiences with food during the Netherlands part of my hike.

Breakfasts provided Dutch sandwich spreads of meat, cheese or sweet sprinkles, but I was disappointed at how often food seemed artificial or was mass-produced. Chocolate milk came out of a carton; butter had usually been replaced with margarine; cheese had become perfect slices in plastic packaging, which eliminated the charming chore of slicing from the section of a cheese wheel; the Dutch chocolate tradition had been replaced with artificial-tasting American chocolate bars.

Thanks to the rounds of the "Dutch Truck" in our Maritime community, Joanne and I consume a greater variety of traditional Dutch food than I tasted during my hike through the Netherlands. At home I happily consume Dutch cookies and chocolate treats, I use real Dutch cocoa in my homemade hot chocolate and I slice Gouda cheese onto my homemade bread.

Of course, during the hike I sometimes had *"gerookte paling," "poffertjes," "witte aspergesoep"* and *"appeltaart"* (smoked eel, tiny pancakes, white asparagus soup and apple pie-cake). These delights triggered my Dutch taste buds. And, throughout the countries I have visited, the rich flavour of their coffee has been impressive.

Here in my final Dutch restaurant before entering Germany, my mustard soup, hot chocolate drink and layered pudding cake are heavenly. I'm surprised that – though this is a classy establishment – the washroom tap only provides cold water as is the case in many European lavatories. Maybe it's assumed the cold will scare the bacteria to death.

## Germany

If I had expected border-related activity, I was mistaken. I had been amused by an anecdote of the map expert at the Pied à Terre bookstore in Amsterdam. He mentioned that the old guard post at one of the Netherlands-Germany border points had actually been turned into a café. The bicycle path I'm following crosses a narrow wooden bridge at the edge of Bad Nieuweschans and delivers me into farmland. No signs indicate my entry into another nation, but I realize the countryside around me must be Germany.

The simple cellphone I purchased upon arrival in Amsterdam has proven invaluable in calling homes to arrange my nightly stays. Joanne and I have also maintained contact using short text messages that let her know where I am and let me know what she's been up to. Any concerns I may have had about the intrusiveness of the cellphone have not materialized: I have found it an enjoyable and useful tool. Being able to share with an important person in your life, "Just entered Germany!" and receiving the reply, "Hooray!" is kind of neat.

Despite all the walking I have now done and all the hurdles I have overcome, my entrance into Germany unnerves me. My childhood included a constant sense of foreboding: no matter how happy the moment, something was about to go wrong. This feeling of impending doom now finds a home on the trail. I have easily grown comfortable in each country, but then a new country arrives, and with it a few days of unease, of not knowing what to expect.

Now in Germany I feel even more apprehensive as I return to the communication gaps I experienced in Portugal. Thanks to the hostel system and the frequent use of English, the Camino in Spain was easy enough to muddle through, and my French and Dutch language abilities served me well in France, Belgium and the Netherlands. Now, however, I would be in a very foreign country. I need not have worried as people prove to be pleasant and helpful, and the combination of smiles and gestures can serve you well.

As I enter the town of Bunde, a woman calls from her porch. She sees me puzzle over my map and wonders if she can help. Speaking English well enough that we converse easily, she also helps me sort out my telephone number confusion in contacting the next hostel for a bed for the night. She describes the intricacies of the route I am to follow. "There you must turn left," reflects a German manner of speaking and her confidence in knowledge of the area.

I thank her for the information and add that I now no longer need to visit the tourist centre a short distance past her house. Then she says something I find truly baffling: "It's two o'clock on Friday afternoon. The tourist office is closed now." I have not yet been able to understand or negotiate the intricacies as to which European businesses or public services are open at what time. However, you would think the potential arrival of weekend tourists on a Friday afternoon would be an excellent reason for the tourism staff to be available.

The first 20 kilometres in Germany take me through flat countryside similar to that of Groningen, which I just left, or of the South Holland of my early childhood. Much of this land is polder, land claimed from the sea, and now consists of mixed farms among the many channels of water. Dairy cows and beef cattle roam the pastures. On a number of barns and houses, the southerly facing half of the roof is covered in solar panels, and I see a profusion of wind turbines.

My approach to the town of Leer leads me on a bicycle path heading east for about a kilometre, then north for about a kilometre, then east again, north again and so on. I am reminded of the road to "Rock Glen" in my childhood.

*"On summer Sunday afternoons, Bill and I would hike from our farm and through the village of Arkona, Ontario to*

235

*the natural area of Rock Glen Falls. The last stretch was a gravel road that zigzagged back and forth a half dozen times before straightening out to lead us to a ravine of youthful adventures among its fossils, cliffs and waterfalls."*

In my present zigzag approach, I become frustrated as the city stays temptingly out of reach. I think to myself, "It would be easier if there were a diagonal path from here to the centre of Leer over there," when I see its tallest building slowly falling over. This is alarming till I realize it is actually a bridge that is closing. This is Jan-Berghaus-Brücke (Jan-Berghaus Bridge), which is a "bascule," a type of bridge with a pivoting section that is raised and lowered using counterweights. When it is open, the bridge deck extends a length of five stories into the air. No wonder I could see it from a distance.

When I arrive in Leer and guess that I might have walked far enough into town to be near the hostel, I stop to ask a man who is vacuuming his car. He turns off his vacuum cleaner and points out the location of the hostel – a mere two blocks away. I had had a similar experience in being very near the Badajoz train station way back in early Spain. And this surprising closeness to a hidden goal has happened a number of times since.

The Leer hostel is a family setting where the majority of guests are parents with children. A small group of adults is biking the Ostfriesland Wanderweg route that runs between Leer and Bensersiel 70 kilometres to the north on the North Sea. I'm fascinated by the shape of the men: they have muscular upper bodies that tower over spindly legs. They look like cartoon characters, and I expect them to fall over at any moment. Despite their infatuation with travel by bicycle, my hiking receives supportive comments and smiles of approval.

On my way down the street to find something to eat, I pass a church where people drift in to enjoy a musical performance. The mixed choir of adults and children – accompanied by the dance routine of the little ones – is entertaining till my rumbling stomach suggests I move on.

When I pay my restaurant bill for supper, the waiter returns one of the coins: "This is a baht, a coin from Thailand. It looks a bit like a Euro but is almost worthless. Somebody must have snuck it into the change they gave you." I feel used and wonder what to do with this coin that is of no value to me.

So far the local building style doesn't show any particular pattern, but I am comforted in finding everything so well tended. I hike next to a thick hedge that runs along the edge of the sidewalk, and into its greenery I throw the offending baht coin, and I think, "Good riddance." Local idiosyncrasies continue to surprise me: here machines for dispensing packages of cigarettes are located throughout suburban areas. I have not seen that elsewhere in Europe. Past Leer a variety of houses lies within a mix of landscapes – groves of trees, fields with crops and forest areas.

Bicycle paths are twinned with roads as they were in the Netherlands, but in Germany these paths see much less traffic. Now I notice a strange phenomenon: people use their bicycle bells. Bike racers in their spandex still speed by within inches of me, but local folks give a "D-r-r-ring" or a cheery greeting as they approach from behind. I'm quickly getting to like these people.

With so few "Vrienden op de Fiets" host families in Germany, I decide to stay in youth hostels that happen to be a full day's walk apart. This takes me from Leer to Westerstede, but the hostel there is closed – for reconstruction, it appears. I opt for a hotel room at a reasonable rate and come to the first downtown inn only to be told it is full, as is the next. At the third I am fortunate to be assigned their very last room. It has a comfortable bed (with two short duvets so I can put one over my feet) and a breakfast of great variety where I'm famished once again and need to try everything.

On my way to breakfast, I negotiate the maze of rooms near the hotel lobby. This path leads to the stairs and the upstairs dining area where the meal will be served. In the half-light and the eerie silence of a seven o'clock Sunday morning, I suddenly see someone standing next to me. I let out a gasp and then realize it's my own image in a full-length mirror. I'm now certain it's time to go home.

## Melancholy

On my Sunday morning hikes, a certain melancholy overtakes me. As I read over my blog entries, I can identify which incidents occurred on a Sunday morning by the information fixed in the feeling part of my memory. I pass homes where people are gathered as families or sleeping in while I trudge the road alone to face another day of challenges. As Johnny Cash sang, "'Cause there's something in a Sunday that makes a body feel alone."

At that point in my reverie, a distant church bell may peel out the hour or, more rarely, the start of Sunday Mass. Now on this Sunday morning, I pass a herd of young beef cattle, and a few of the tan-coloured beasts wander up to the fence out of curiosity and perhaps a wish to come with me. This is a routine occurrence where a few critters make me feel special by running up to the barrier that separates us. If I had responded to these wordless pleas, I could now be leading a great herd of cattle down the bicycle paths of Germany. Of course, I would need to train them to hug the path's shoulder and leave room for passing bikes.

I appreciate the lushness of a half dozen *"baumschulen"* (tree nurseries, literally "tree schools") with their neat rows of plants, shrubs and trees. In one of these, great irrigation plumes are spraying a vast acreage. Moments later I chance upon a restaurant where I stop for a pot of tea. I feel honoured in being served a fancy long-spouted ceramic pot – white with blue decorative features. A candle within its base ensures that my tea stays hot to the last drop. New to me is a stainless steel gizmo that lets me squeeze the juice from a thin lemon slice into my tea effortlessly and without having to use my fingers.

Nothing is without imperfections, and the ice cream with berries mentioned on the menu proves to be a great disappointment. The berry portion has the texture of Canadian cherry pie filling straight out of the can – a product that becomes palatable when eaten warm. The thickener in my berry topping congeals further in the presence of the ice cream and becomes nauseating. I eat it anyway – for the energy I need, not for the food value. Meanwhile a group of five well-dressed elderly men at a round corner table reflect the easy repartee of long-term friendships. I understand few of their words, but the feeling is one of gentlemanly sociability and makes my trek seem even more solitary.

In the rural combination of woods and fields, homes are impeccable – red-brick with shiny roofs of black tile – and surrounded by carefully chosen landscaping. Suddenly two neighbouring houses are dilapidated and have a profusion of debris in their yards. I find it refreshing that, even in this northern European orderliness, there are exceptions.

Of personal concern this morning is a chipped tooth. Each such incident becomes a distraction pulling my mind away from concentrating on my journey. This physical issue is additional to the pain in my right leg that has troubled me over the last few days. Anything longer than a 20-kilometre hike has resulted in a cramp in my calf, so I have cut a few days shorter than usual. This means I may not reach my goal of Bremen, Germany where I intend to take the train back to Amsterdam for my flight home. This inability to meet my expectations can play greater havoc than can the pain itself. And I think of the races of my youth.

*"With my 'touch of asthma' diagnosed years later, schoolyard races left me gasping for air. I didn't share the enthusiasm for sport of my brother Bill or my peers. Making sure that our side had a higher score than the other side didn't mean much to me."*

My hike across Europe is so different from those schoolyard games. Then, I was locked into having to compete. Now, this hike is liberating: I can walk long distances and feel in charge of my body. However, I struggle with mixed feelings: my hike is not a race against anyone else or against myself; yet, my inability to reach Bremen seems a defeat. And so, I tussle with my ego in the face of the reality that Oldenburg (about 50 kilometres short of Bremen) may be my end point on this trip.

The lack of vacancy at a more distant hostel, the wish not to rush to the finish and concern about missing my flight home lead me to settle into the hostel in Oldenburg with the knowledge that this is likely the end of the road for this trip. At the last I still hold out hope for reaching Bremen, but my legs, feet and I have a meeting and unanimously decide it is time to head home.

At the Oldenburg hostel, I share a room with a sociable young man who was born in Vietnam and had been living with an uncle in Germany. He is now working as a cook in Oldenburg, and the lack of available housing has forced him to take a room at the hostel. I appreciate his dreams of rejoining his parents in their more relaxed life in Vietnam.

I join in the buffet supper at the hostel and find that everything tastes great – all except the *spätzle*. Others at the meal, particularly the German children, exclaim, "It's delicious. Can I get some more?" However, in my exploration of local foods over the five trips, these tasteless strands of homemade noodle stand out as something for which this foreigner cannot acquire a taste.

Avoiding a line-up at the train station, I use the ticket machine to pay my fare to Haarlem (near Amsterdam). I punch in my bits of information, and magically a ticket flows out. I'm grateful that these things can work easily after all.

My train won't arrive for another half hour, so I have plenty of time for the peculiar procedure that prepares me for my arrival here on my next trip. When I return to Oldenburg by train to resume walking, I might exit the station in a different direction since the building has two entrance areas. Depending on where I get off the train and through which doors I exit, I could end up minus a few metres in my walk across Europe. That will never do.

As a solution to this bewildering problem – that only I would understand – I go to the doors at one end of the station and walk across that entrance from one wall to the other while avoiding people rushing through the doors because they're late for a train. Then I walk through the great hall that echoes with the screech of braking trains and the multilingual announcements about platform changes and arrive at the distant doors of the other entrance.

I walk along the row of doors at that end of the station and can now sit and wait for my train, secure in the knowledge that I have this crucial issue covered. No matter where I exit next time, my footsteps will connect. I can't let carelessness prevent me from walking all of Europe, one step at a time.

The series of trains taking me from Oldenburg to Haarlem involve about 20 station stops and require five transfers. I don't feel inconvenienced since the trip allows time to normalize my mind as I relive this part of my hike. Strangely, all transfer times except one are exactly seven minutes long – just enough time to locate and board the next train – and, in the process, I enter the Netherlands. At the Amersfoort transfer to a connecting train, I buy a *gehaktbal* sandwich (sliced meatball with mayonnaise and lettuce) that reminds me I am not yet back in Canada.

As a mini-Amsterdam, Haarlem is easy to enjoy and to navigate, and I purchase an OV Chipkaart (a smart card used for public transport) that simplifies the use of local buses. Having appreciated my stay at Haarlem's pleasant hostel a year earlier, I choose this repeat visit. The building has all the amenities (laundry, Internet, bar) of a larger facility but without the crowds.

I do my laundry one last time, get the pictures on my disposable camera developed and wander the streets of this tourist haven. I enjoy a last feed of *poffertjes* within the sound of the carillon of the "Grote Kerk" ("Big Church") that dominates Haarlem's city centre. This is actually St. Bavokerk (St. Bavo Church) named for a seventh-century wealthy Frankish nobleman of Belgium who converted to Christianity, became a monk and lived a life of penance as a recluse. Then a visit to "The Dutch Landscape in Art" exhibit at De Hallen art gallery lets me connect the artists' interpretation of Dutch scenery to my own poetic instincts.

On the last evening, I welcome two men who arrive separately to share quarters in my six-bed room. One is a white-haired retired bakery owner from California, the other a pony-tailed deep-sea diver from Perth, Australia. So, there we are, three men breaking out of our individual job-related isolation – early mornings mixing dough and preparing baked goods, weeks in an underwater chamber to perform dive after dive, years in a prison environment coordinating health services. Each of us is now free to explore the culture that is Europe.

The urgency to get to the airport in time for my flight home requires arising at 5:30 a.m. and sadly missing the hostel's extensive breakfast. I catch the 6:30 bus into Haarlem for the train to Amsterdam's Sloterdijk station and muse on this 1100-kilometre escapade through parts of the Netherlands, Belgium, France and Germany. Late in the eight-week period, I began to see my journey as two distinct adventures: one occurring while I was walking, the other taking place whenever I stopped. The things I experienced and the talking I did depended on whether I was moving or paused in my journey.

My many hours of walking proved to be solitary and reflective with little input from anyone. Having left my iPod at home, my hiking was accompanied with the sounds of nature – birds, frogs and the breeze. The natural world also provided a variety of smells during my trek. These ranged from the scent of flowers to the odour of a manure-spread hayfield. Each time I passed the roses in a flower bed, I couldn't help but stop to smell them. I was surprised at how often there was little perceptible scent, but the odd fragrant rose made up for this lack of aroma in so many others.

One might think that my sense of touch during the hike would consist solely of the breeze against my skin. In fact, I resumed a childhood habit of letting the taller of the hay stalks, farm crops or flowers along my path run through my hands to cause a tingling sensation. Over time my feet became sensitive enough to distinguish among the types of road surface, so that pavement felt quite different from gravel, sand or grass.

My hike provided an endless series of views. I took in towns and villages with their houses and businesses, streets and roads with their cars and bikes, barns and fields with their livestock and tractors, paths and trails with their nature and scenery, as well as planes and birds above me, rivers and valleys below.

After hours of hiking in solitude, taking a break for a coffee or entering my dwelling for the night meant a time of conversation in Dutch, French or English. I shared thoughts on immigration, details of Canada's geography and tidbits about my hiking experiences. In their several languages and various dialects, I was helped to appreciate local people – their family stories and their work and play activities.

I have now come to the end of another trek or, rather, two intertwined treks – a moving one and a still one. I ponder the two sides of my next trip as I arrive in Amsterdam and transfer onto the train to Schiphol Airport. Once again, I am thrown into the madness that is air travel: my reverie is over.

The segments of my flight from Amsterdam to Paris and Paris to Montreal involve Air France flights while I shall be on Air Canada from Montreal to Moncton. On the first plane at Schiphol, I locate my seat in the very back on my left – thus the furthest from the exit doors at the time of disembarking. In French I joke with the flight attendant: "The bible says the first shall be last and the last first."

He responds: "That's not true for Air France although a few airlines have planes that can disembark the rear first." Then on the Paris to Montreal flight, I have been assigned to the front row of the plane. A passenger asks the flight attendant if her husband could switch seats with me so they can sit together. Incredibly, this puts me in the front row seat right next to the main exit door! Considering the many incidents in a long trip, coincidences are bound to occur. However, this one seems eerily unlikely. I guess the last can be first on Air France after all.

# Trip 6: A Tough Finish

*April 26 to July 5, 2012 – 2,371 Kilometres*
*Oldenburg, Germany northeast to Narva-Jõesuu, Estonia*

**Finale**

"Here I go again." Those words appeared in a tune (from the 1940's) entitled "Taking a Chance on Love" while I'm taking a chance on making it all the way to Estonia's northeastern shore. On this trip I am under pressure to finish my journey across Europe before Joanne's upcoming retirement from the teaching profession. This could be my last chance to reach my goal, and it will be challenging to cover a few thousand kilometres in one trip. I'll simply need to keep moving.

I have felt more troubled than usual about the upcoming walk. This may have to do with a recent cold and flu, with being one year older, with having to deal with five unfamiliar languages on this trip – or all of the above. Joanne, Rebecca and Jessica are at Moncton Airport to say goodbye, and the grandchildren's eyes looking up at me make me realize, again, that it would be nice to stay home. Our dreams don't always make sense.

Then, while walking to my gate at Toronto airport, I am intrigued when an announcement about the boarding of a flight to Abu Dhabi comes through the background noise. For a moment I imagine spending two and half months being spoiled by our daughter Laura who lives in that distant city. But I think better of it; I need to keep finding my way through Europe. On the plane a toddler in the row behind me is cranky and noisy enough that the people beside me are assigned other seats. Moments later the child falls asleep, and I have lots of room and enjoy a quiet flight to Frankfurt, Germany.

At Frankfurt Airport I search out a shop to get a German SIM card for the phone I bought in Amsterdam last year. I was worried that this might be a complex process in a foreign language, but they speak some English, and it is quite simple. When I say, "I need a SIM card and some minutes," they spring into action, and I am all set and out of the store within a few minutes.

The connecting flight to Bremen is less than an hour in duration – so just enough time for a cup of coffee. I relax during the train ride to Oldenburg as I scan the countryside I had planned to cover last year. Cramps in my right calf forced me to leave that section for this trip. A review by the physiotherapist in Sackville identified the problem, and his suggested set of exercises has, hopefully, resolved it.

To my surprise, I do not feel the usual thrill in arriving at my previous end point – in this case, the hostel in Oldenburg. The bustling airports have kept my mind on the practical aspects of travel and not allowed me to enjoy the anticipation of returning to the peace of this hostel. Now a group of middle school children makes sure I don't get too complacent in my reveries. They are an active group but settle down at about nine in the evening for the sake of us older folks.

A long-haired university student is the only other guest in my six-person dorm. He explains why he's there: "I've been looking for a place in Oldenburg while I study chemistry at the university here. But I haven't found anything yet." This lack of housing for young people is one I've heard over and over in my travels through Europe.

My first day of walking brings all three setbacks I experienced from time to time on previous legs of this journey – disappointing food, faulty advice and too long a day. I am dissatisfied with a restaurant serving of spaghetti Bolognese with its thick strands and little sauce: I need the food energy for my trek, so I make it through the whole plate, but it's a struggle. Later I ask a man for directions to my home for the night, and he responds, "I've driven there many times, so I know a shortcut," which never bodes well: this country road swings around to a point away from my destination, forces me to double back through pastureland and gets me there over an hour late.

With each of my trips, I plan (and don't usually succeed) to ease into walking by covering short distances on the first few days. Now, in order to walk the whole distance across Europe, I've detoured to avoid the ferry crossing that would have taken me on a direct route toward Bremen. I've also gone an extra six kilometres in that loop through the countryside. All of this results in a 35-kilometre hike – much too long to be a warm-up exercise!

This troublesome day marks the beginning of my last trip to Europe and the end of the journey that has taken chunks of my last five years. I think of my teen journey that was seven years in length. I see similarities in the enormity of the task, the energy required and the distance to the goal.

*"That trek took me halfway to entering God's Holy Priesthood. The experience came with an overwhelming homesickness, a nagging piety and intensive studies. It also came with one of the most troublesome experiences of my life – telling my parents I had quit. I was distraught, not because I had disappointed them but because I had disappointed myself."*

Quitting my path to Estonia now would be unthinkable, and I wonder where I get the determination to set such lofty goals. And I continue on the trek of making this dream a reality.

Ruth Neuke's *Gästezimmer* (guest room) in Deichshausen proves to be welcoming. I have phoned her to let her know I have been delayed, and she is waiting at the road to direct me around a cluster of houses to her door. She and her husband are a gentle couple who give me quiet time to recover from the day's hike. I appreciate both their thoughtfulness and their oversized, fluffy bath towels.

I am surprised that the area between Oldenburg and Bremen looks like much of the Netherlands with its dikes and with channels separating flat fields. This Moorland area skirts the North Sea and is the valley of the Weser River.

A stretch through an industrial park brings me into Bremen. Within a grouping of office buildings overlooking the river, the square yellow hostel is clearly visible from a distance. Two men in my room are walking 200 kilometres southward in Germany. Meeting other hikers always cheers me up: it's good to know I'm not alone.

One of the men speaks English well, and I ask about the irritatingly short duvets on beds during much of my walk and again at this hostel. He explains: "They are the standard one-by-two metres. People might want them longer, but that is the standard." This response seems typical of Europe where tradition trumps initiative; in North America we would have questioned the small size of these items and done something about it.

In fact, I immediately formulate a plan for longer duvets, outsourced to a factory in China and supported by Kevin How-Can-I-Make-Money O'Leary of television's "Dragon's Den." They'll be so popular we won't be able to make them fast enough. But I'm busy hiking right now, so this remains a dream.

A Bremen church is featuring a half-hour organ recital, and I find a seat among the audience to daydream through the loud booming and gentle strains. I probably don't have a full appreciation because each piece starts to sound the same as the last, but I do find it relaxing.

During the first few mornings of my walk, it rained till seven or seven-thirty when I was ready to leave. Then it cleared up, and I had a cool, cloudy day – perfect for a brisk stroll. This morning again, the streets are damp from last night's rain, and it looks like good hiking weather.

Finding my way out of Bremen, I pass through a street market, and a booth with Dutch cheese catches my attention. The owner says: "We're from Woerden in South Holland. My wife, my son and I travel between the Netherlands and Germany selling all kinds of cheese." They are diligent people, arranging their display in front of a colourful Dutch tapestry of farm children in wooden shoes. As customers start to line up, I'm pleased to see they have a thriving business.

I stop for a bowl of pepper cream soup and discover a mixture of bits of yellow, green and red peppers spiced with peppercorns. It's tasty and colourful – a recipe I look forward to trying at home.

I'm astonished at the age of the communities here. In the town of Tarmstedt, a sign indicates that it had its 750th anniversary a few years ago; then a bit further along, Kirchtimke outdoes it at just over 850 years. That's old!

I stay at an inn where a crowd is celebrating a woman's 60th birthday in the banquet area. My room is near the festivities, and I relax to strains of German drinking songs interspersed with the unexpected less traditional, such as Credence Clearwater Revival's "Bad Moon Rising."

The flat pastureland of the first few days is giving way to rolling hills and expansive crops of wheat, canola and potatoes separated by park-like areas. As in the southern part of the Netherlands, I come across white asparagus being harvested and for sale fresh from the field.

I am curious about a half dozen forest-green buildings that look like overgrown yurts but with metal walls and plastic roofs, so I approach a man scanning his yard for a daring weed. He explains in German while I try to follow and sort out the details. I understand the installation is fed grass that creates biogas to fuel a generator. The man comments that it produces enough electricity for 20,000 homes.

I am prepared for a relaxed overnight at a hostel in the woods near Zeven. After a trek into this idyllic spot, I'm disappointed that it is deserted: a sign indicates it is temporarily closed. It's still mid-afternoon so I stop at the hotel in Zeven to ask what might be available in the town of Heeslingen, 10 kilometres on. The staff is buzzing, filling bowls of ice cream for five Lutheran confirmation celebrations, and they direct me to the owner in the reception area.

I introduce myself as a Canadian walking across Europe, and he rambles on in English: "We're very busy, but I can give you five minutes of my time. We got along well with the Canadian soldiers at the base near here; they were there for 43 years. I'm the seventh generation in my family to run this hotel; our son will be number eight." In a flash he gives me a photocopied map of his favourite jogging trail through the woods that will be more scenic than following the road. Then he phones the *Gasthaus* (guest house) in the next town to make a reservation for me. This is an outgoing, sincere individual – one with a hyperactive streak – and it would be nice to stay for a chat, but we both have other priorities.

Lost in thought on this trail, I come upon a stylized yellow and blue shell sign that marks this as a *Pilgerweg* (pilgrimage route). I have stumbled upon the Via Baltica, part of the European network of pilgrimage paths that interconnect to lead to Spain's Camino, which was so much part of my travels a few years back. The Via Baltica runs through this area but is not well defined – whether by signposts or in guidebooks.

A woman who is heading west on this *Pilgerweg* joins me for breakfast at the guest house in Heeslingen the next morning. I ask her about trails lying east of here, and she suggests: "You might want to go and see Pastor Lose in Hamburg. He has an interest in pilgrimage routes and could give you more information." She is taking only a week of holiday time, so hurries to catch the bus to a stretch further on.

This time I am consistently using my hiking poles. It will be a long couple of thousand kilometres, and my arm and shoulder muscles have to do their share. So far, it's not going badly – the usual discomforts and a small blister behind my right heel, but I carry on.

On the first day or two, I have walked past farmyards smelling of sour ensilage. This is nauseating, even to my "farm nose." As in the past, I often stop to smell the flowers in peoples' gardens beside the path, but I have not yet smelled one that is aromatic, perhaps because it is early in the season. So far, the smells of Germany have not been comforting to me.

On the other hand, I feel acknowledged by the people as they have been charming and helpful. All services seem to be closed on this Monday, and I see a welcome sign outside the building housing a men's club. In their café area, three elderly men are chatting, and I interrupt them to order a mug of coffee, which one of them serves me while he keeps up his conversation with his peers. As friends, they probably have their own lingo in a language that is foreign to me though my German is getting to the point where I now automatically say, *"Tschüss,"* for "Goodbye."

I pass seven roadside crosses as a memorial to what must have been a horrible accident and realize that I am walking in and out of the hearts of communities. Zooming past these crosses by car would be much less intrusive, and I appreciate entering these neighbourhoods and being accepted, if ever so briefly.

On my way eastward, a sign indicates that the distance from Apensen to Buxtehude is 6 kilometres by car while an adjoining sign shows it to be 12 kilometres by bike. I am often bemused by such discrepancies. Now I need to decipher whether it would be preferable to follow a longer, easy bicycle path or a shorter, busy road into Buxtehude, a sprawling city that seems to go on forever. I choose the road, which provides me with a wide shoulder and – soon after – treats me to its own sidewalk.

Patrons tend to keep their voices under control in German restaurants, but the seniors' group at the Hotel Stemmann in Buxtehude is deafening. They are about 40 people travelling in a fancy bus and enjoying themselves thoroughly – and lifting my spirits as a result. The very relaxed owner asks where I'm headed on my trek and warns me about the next day: "Tomorrow is May 1st. It is a 'bank day,' so everything will be closed. It's a chance for workers to have the day off. It has to do with what Jesus Christ did. Something like that."

Mischievously, I ask him: "Oh, will you be going to church?"

He replies, "No, I have to work," and the next morning he appears – still unshaven and having just rolled out of bed – and struggles with the buffet breakfast for a horde of us older folk. He is obviously not used to setting up tables with their variety of foods and keeping the coffee topped up. But we are patient and do little things to help out. In the few hours, he has appreciated my hiking adventure; I have enjoyed his relaxed attitude. We share in a heartfelt goodbye, and I start my search for a road that will get me around the city of Hamburg.

**Hamburg**

I thought a bridge east of Buxtehude would take me across the Elbe River and lead me eastward while I stayed north of – and avoided – the metropolis of Hamburg. As I get closer, I learn that this is not a bridge but another ferry, so I need to detour southeastward through kilometres of parkland to take the pedestrian tunnel to the other side of the Elbe River in Hamburg. This "rule" of avoiding ferries is getting to be a nuisance. This time it costs me 20 extra kilometres, and now no one seems to know where I can find the tunnel. It reminds me of the challenges in getting up to and through the "Sluizen van IJmuiden" on my walk through the Netherlands: here again people keep questioning me on walking such a long distance.

A glass of chocolaty café mocha at a McDonald's McCafé helps make my struggle bearable. Then three people try to use their smart phones to help me find my way to the tunnel, but none succeeds. Twice their batteries are low; another time the man cannot access a map, but he is pleased to tell me that – wherever the tunnel is – I have only 19 kilometres to go! I hail a young woman coming toward me on her bicycle, and she says: "I moved here from Munich a few months ago, and I spend my free time exploring Hamburg by bike. Here, I'll show you where to go."

Her paper street map clearly shows me the route, and I even follow her recommendation to take a break at Veritas Beach. I have a quick beer at this recreation spot of sand, picnic tables and music along the Elbe. Then I pass a set of apartment buildings and appreciate the sight of families of visible minorities gathered for barbecues along the river on this holiday afternoon. I finally make it through the half-kilometre tunnel. At its far end will be my hostel and a well-deserved rest.

Straining in the glare of sunlight as I emerge from the Alter Elbtunnel, I am overwhelmed at having to make my way through a crowd of thousands gathered for the May Day workers' celebration. A speech reverberates through the square as a union leader rallies the workers. I pop in at an information centre, and I'm told, "Just take the stairs up the hill, and you'll find the hostel." That's easy enough to say, but getting there is a different matter: both staircases have become bleachers for the crowds. I try one of the stairways, but partway up it is closed with construction boarding.

An ambulance is waiting on the sidelines, and I deduce that emergency personnel must know the way. They suggest: "Take those stairs on the left up to a walkway. It crosses over a street and leads to the hostel." Though hampered by my backpack, I manage to excuse my way through the crowd, pass a solemn expensive hotel and, next door, find the bustling inexpensive *Jugendherberge* (youth hostel). During my stay I half expect guests from the hotel next door to come and enjoy the spontaneity of the young people in the hostel. I'm disappointed that it doesn't happen. I guess they need to stay earnest.

The next day I use the hostel washer and dryer to bring some order back into my stuff sack of clothing. Then I make my way to St. Jacobi Evangelisch-Lutherische Kirche (St. Jacob Lutheran Church). There I hope to meet Pastor Bernd

253

Lose whom the woman pilgrim I met in Heeslingen recommended as having pilgrimage route information.

Back in Sackville our non-Catholic family physician had advised me: "You're Catholic, aren't you? You should wear a cross when you go through Poland. That will help you find places to stay because it's such a Catholic country." I search through my things for the small wooden cross from McLean's religious goods store in Moncton and loop its cord around my neck for my initiation as to how it will feel when I get to Poland.

Unfortunately, Pastor Lose is away, and no one in the church office has the information I need. I do learn that the pilgrimage route comes to Hamburg from the north, so the trail would not help me since my path leads eastward. I am told that many churches in small communities here are shared between the Catholic and Lutheran faiths and that Catholicism is a minority religion in this part of Germany. In any case, being Catholic and wearing a cross did not guarantee success in finding the perfect pilgrimage route eastward. We'll see if it will get me a bed in Poland.

In a Hamburg outdoor café, I order a cup of mint tea and expect the usual gauze tea bag. Instead, this comes as a glass mug with real mint leaves in steaming water. Both the appearance and taste are exquisite. As I near the bottom of this delicious serving, I ask for more hot water and eventually see the kitchen staff bring out a glass cup of water and place it on a sideboard. The waitress asks if I got the requested hot water, and I remark, "It seems to have been lost unless that's it over there."

The waitress interrupts me, "Oh, I'll get it from the kitchen myself," and she does. But this would have been so simple in Canada where asking for more hot water for your tea is routine, where it's sometimes the wait staff who suggest it. This is not the practice in those areas where I hiked on my way through Europe, and I learned not to change local procedures as that can become frustrating.

To type my first blog entry of this trip, I find an Internet café among the acres of electronic equipment in a Saturn store (like Future Shop, but fancier – and with coffee). Accessing a computer has been a challenge: German hostels do not usually furnish them, and I haven't seen a library that provides that service. Again, I need to adapt to a distinctive keyboard: this time only the letters "z" and "y" are switched, but the punctuation marks are in unusual spots and take me a while to locate. I fluctuate between typing carefully so I get everything right and typing briskly, which requires going back to make corrections. Both methods are a challenge.

I face another avoiding-ferries moment as a result of having taken the pedestrian tunnel into Hamburg. The tunnel started with an elevator ride: we went down at one end and up again at the other. I could have used the incredibly scary stairs leading downward in the silo-like interior, and – to my surprise – a few brave souls did. Would taking the elevator be acceptable in my walking every step across Europe? After all, it moved me vertically and did not make the route shorter.

As it turns out, this is not an issue since I explored the north side of the river during my visit and would like to see its south bank on the way out of Hamburg. I now simply take the elevator-tunnel-elevator across and rejoin the footsteps in the spot where I arrived at the elevator the first time.

This city seems to be all about water, with restaurants on ships and with smaller boats everywhere. The south side of the river is an area of water transport, with shipping companies and long-haul trucks starting their day. Now I seek out a bridge several kilometres to the east: it takes me northward across the Elbe River, and I turn right to continue my trek.

From a distance I notice a glass monstrosity that turns out to be the Hamburg office for Der Spiegel, the weekly newsmagazine. I see a sign for a newsstand on its street level and drop in to scan the variety of reading material on sale. I ask the young clerk: "Is there a European Union newspaper or magazine that I might contact about my walk?" I had been looking at a way to publicize my feat after I finish it, but he knows of no publication serving all of Europe. He sells copy for European media every day: if anyone would know, he would.

My lunch at the Hamburg oriental restaurant "4 Mosa" is a pleasant hour of choosing from the dishes passing by each table on a conveyor system. For the set price of 8,90 Euros, I get to take portions as they pass in a glass channel beside me. It's not easy to fill up on sushi, and I try a wide variety of the items offered. Including my first taste of roasted rice tea, everything is delicious.

**Country**
My trek lets me explore this corner of Schleswig-Holstein, which is the most northerly of the 16 states that make up Germany. In the nineteenth century, this area found itself caught between Denmark and Prussian Germany, and the resulting conflicts were part of my history courses many years back. On a more personal level, I appreciate this being the home of the Holstein cows of my farm childhood.

I hike along a park, and a mother smiles as her child points to me and says, "*Opa.*" I smile inside since my grandchildren give me that title, which is German and Dutch for "Grandpa." Further along I hear a boy tell his friend that I am "power walking." This is late in the day, and it is not much power – just walking. I keep using the hiking poles although they initially caused a cramping in my shoulders. The pain eased, and the bathroom mirror shows developing shoulder muscles, and I think of my brother.

"*Bill loved sports; he was always active with ball, bat or bicycle. I liked the quiet activities of reading, listening and thinking. Bill's developed into a muscular body; mine stayed a pudgy one.*"

Now my body is developing into that of an athlete, like Bill's. I like to think my brother would have enthused over its appearance, and I would have been pleased. Or maybe, as in "Stand Tall," the award-winning Burton Cummings song, "It's silly human pride."

Many yards have signs of *Kartoffeln* (potatoes) for sale, and I assume these must be last year's crop as it's still early in the growing season. Other notices are about upcoming elections, and a young man is engaged in a discussion over his sign, which includes the word "Nazi." I am taken aback when he scowls at me as I pass.

In the next village, the Union Jack is waving in a front yard. As I approach, an Audi pulls into the driveway and a nattily dressed woman steps out and talks to the man who is working around the flower beds. I ask why they are flying the flag of the United Kingdom, and the woman explains: "I moved here from Britain 40 years ago when we got married. My husband here is from this area." We have a brief chat during which I enjoy the husband's speech patterns: he speaks excellent English sprinkled with a mixed German-British accent.

In Portugal I had been encouraged by a German visitor to the area, "They don't have a walking culture here, but you'll meet more hikers when you get to countries further north." Maybe it's still early in the season, but I see little evidence of walking – mostly (again) cars, cars, cars. Canadians are at least as active as people here in Germany.

When I arrive at the hostel in Mölln, I recognize a theme of harlequins: a colourful buffoon is painted on each window – somewhat overdone, I think. The place is lively as six dragon boat teams, each in its colours, prepare for competition on a local lake. They tell me, "We are not supposed to drink on the evening before a competition," but the many bottles of wine tell a different tale. A young woman is alone at the hostel to attend a local chess competition. And so, hostels serve a wide variety of clientele, but long-distance walkers continue to be the exception.

Just before Hamburg I had crossed a bridge with a massive stone entrance while the rest of it was more recently built of steel girders. I assume the war had destroyed all except the stone archway since bridges had been vulnerable to attack as a way of disrupting supply lines. Entering Hamburg, I saw a city of new architecture while historic buildings are to be found in towns like Mölln. Bombing during the horror of the Second World War must have decimated German cities while many towns survived intact. I get the impression of sensitivity to those times since I hear the words "newer" and "older" here but no reference to the war.

Exploring the route out of Mölln on Saturday morning, I continue to see images of harlequins. These have become part of local fables. I am amused as I pass a man biking with a fat unlit cigar in his mouth. Then I meet merchants setting up their displays and see a baby-poop green couch being prepared for the Green Party candidate to meet voters later in the day. I do not linger but wonder whether they could not have chosen a less nauseating green.

At times my hike takes me through wooded areas, and I think that will be the last of the farms. Then after the forest, kilometres of farmland spread out, and in Salem I come upon a farm business with a store selling natural products and a café serving a delicious *spargel* (white asparagus) soup. In the deciduous trees, the birdsong is the most beautiful I've heard on my journey, and a bullfrog throws in its croaking as the bass section. The number of bike paths is decreasing as I continue eastward, so I look for small roads with less traffic.

I stop to admire a machine pulled by a modern blue tractor. The top of this unit, which looks like a giant vertical pencil sharpener, is fed large round bales of straw that it spreads across strawberry fields. Further along, the strawberry plants are peeking through black plastic, and people are pulling shoots up through the holes. The workers have been brought here on two big buses that sport pictures of plump strawberries and the Web address "www.frische-erdbeeren.de," (for "fresh strawberries"). The fields must cover a thousand acres: it's quite a sight. In contrast, I later pass a community garden. Each family has its own tidy plot, and I find the whole arrangement well organized and pleasant.

In public spaces people seem reserved. The aggressiveness of their dogs makes up for this as they bark from behind enclosures. A man heads toward me on the path, restraining his muscular hound on its leash. Just as we pass, the dog tries to lunge toward me almost pulling the man off balance. I just can't accept the passion for these troublesome creatures.

Moments later I say, *"Guten Tag"* ("Good day"), to a young couple biking past and distract the man whose bicycle strays over the edge of the curb so he almost loses his balance. His wife looks aghast, as do I, and we envision scraped hands and ripped clothes. He controls his wobbling bike and catches his balance, and on they go.

In Gadebusch I discover a nice hotel and pleasant people in an otherwise dull-looking city. Perhaps it's this combination of friendliness and dreariness that leads me to question what I'm doing. Here I have to accept whatever comes my way; at home I have some control over my life – and someday I'll be home again and in control. My project seems to have gone from having to walk, to having to finish walking. I honestly don't understand. Perhaps when I'm done, it will become clear to me, but now it does seem a ridiculous undertaking.

Passing a donair shop, I stop for a Coke to quench a serious thirst. The man running the place draws me into a sad tale. In broken English he says his parents and siblings moved from Iraq to Chicago. Because he had served in the Iraqi army, he could not join them there. Let's say he has no good words for George Bush whom he blames for this isolation from his family. And so, I discover yet another side of conflicts.

## East

I have now entered the Mecklenburg-Vorpommern area that was part of East Germany after the war and until the fall of Russian communism. Finding my way through the city of Schwerin to the hostel at its other end is a challenge because it is Sunday afternoon and there is no one to ask for directions. This city of 100,000 people may have fewer businesses open on Sunday than does my hometown of Sackville, New

Brunswick with its 6,000 residents. They take their day of rest seriously here.

I approach a family at a car wash, and one of the children is excited at this chance to practice the English he learns in school. He points toward the south, "My dad says the hostel is about two kilometres that way, and we can drive you there," but I try to explain that I need to walk every step of the way across their continent. Then I spot a taxi driver, and I'm delighted by his real map that shows me exactly where to go in this city of lakes: in a flash I see that I need to pass a small lake and arrive at a larger one where I'll find the hostel. In place of smart phones, paper maps are a great invention!

The day ends in a strange way. When I arrive at the hostel, it looks closed, but I see a long-haired young man cleaning up rubble in the yard. He is the sole employee and takes a break from those duties to arrange my stay for the night. I ask about a meal, and he says: "There's a café at the entrance to the zoo a block away." When I get there, it is closed for the evening, so my supper becomes a light beer and two chocolate bars from the hostel canteen.

Fortunately, the hostel has a computer as I'm eager to catch up on my blog entries; unfortunately, it is out of order. I feel lost as the only guest in a building that can sleep 100 people, and at 8:00 p.m. the young man locks up and goes home. That leaves me alone except for the squawking and groaning from the zoo. Despite the setting, I enjoy a restful sleep thanks to an extra-long duvet comforting my lanky frame.

The next morning I finally use my rain poncho still stuck together in its pouch after my careful drying and storage last year. Through the drizzle I pass a grieving woman with her head bowed. This is a memorial to the Second World War at a spot where Russian and American forces met at war's end. The marks of their tanks have been preserved in the roadway adjacent to the statue. A few kilometres on, a wild boar piglet – mangled as roadkill – lies on the edge of the street. I'm disturbed by a thought: "Somewhere out there is a sow mother grieving the loss of her child."

*Spargel* (white asparagus) is so popular that it even comes as dessert in combination with strawberries, nuts, caramel sauce and ice cream. I try it and find it isn't bad although the bitterness of the *Spargel* refuses to disappear despite the sweetness of the other ingredients.

I ask a man doing yard work about a five-kilometre shortcut through the woods to the next town. Wordlessly, he bends down and draws a map of the trail in the sand, including a rough sketch of a house where I need to stay to the left. I appreciate his silent helpfulness.

I come upon a group of six apartment buildings in the middle of nowhere. Now abandoned, they must have been part of a communist project of some kind. As I walk along, gawking at these buildings, the point of my hiking pole catches in the grate of a storm drain, which pulls off the rubber tip. Without that tip the stick would make clicking sounds on hard surfaces: that would be tough to endure over a few thousand kilometres. I'm desperate to retrieve the tip – now slippery with muck – so I use the handles of my hiking poles as a set of chopsticks. They barely fit through the grooves in the grate, and I am able to pull the tip up toward me but not to grab it as my hands are holding the poles.

A lone car comes to a halt at a nearby stop sign, and I make a beckoning motion with my head for the woman driver to come and help me. I even mouth, "Please," but I'm not sure if she sees me. If she does, I can't blame her for deciding not to get out of her car for this strange hiker: I'm kneeling on the ground with bum in the air and holding walking poles that disappear into a grate. I must have been a sight! As she drives away, I manage to pull the sticks out through the grate without having the tip fall back into the muck. I can continue with my equipment intact.

I discover complexes that consist of up to six barns attached together and that must have been part of farm collectivization under communism. Recalling the simple farm of my childhood, I can't imagine the commotion of farmers and livestock in that grouping of barns surrounded by unending fields. As an artifact of that period, one of the farms retains a stretch of fence with concrete posts that are three metres tall and angle outward near the top. These bring to mind similar poles around the Ipperwash Army Base in my youth.

*"As youngsters on the way to Ipperwash Beach on a hot Sunday afternoon, we would huddle in the back of Hank Westenbroek's pick-up truck and comment on the scenery. We knew the beach was near when we passed the 'army camp' with its fences of 'upside-down hockey sticks.'"*

Here the old communist barrier consists of chain-link fencing running from one post to the next and, on the angled tops of the posts, strands of barbed wire. Now only of historic interest, these communist fences could have been meant to keep the hungry masses from trespassing.

Many towns seem to be pulling out of their drabness to catch up to the vigour of former West Germany. Several fortresses of apartment buildings have now been replaced with bright ones across the street. The old just need to be demolished.

Then I enter Sternberg, a pretty town of historic buildings, and it is far from drab. This seaside resort, hugging the Grosser Sternberger See, feels pleasant and relaxed. The next day truckers kindly pull over for me as I hug the shoulder. I get to a restaurant where I'm told: "Your tea is half price because you have a *Rucksack*." Here my backpack is recognized, so the walking culture does seem to be supported. And so, I continue to come across a range of experiences, both gloomy and bright.

Halfway between Sternberg and Güstrow, I discover the pastoral setting of a family-owned restaurant within a petting farm for children. As I enjoy my lunch, the speaker system entertains us with German music, mostly polkas. I mention, "I like this music a lot more than the piped-in American music in other German restaurants," and the owner replies that a lot of Americans prefer German music. I'm sure many from the Milwaukee area would agree. That city in Wisconsin had been the haven for waves of immigration from Germany, the last of which took place from 1880 to 1893 and originated in this area of northeastern Germany.

The hostel in Güstrow lists potato salad on the menu. Adding some lettuce, I am in my glory. It also features the standard rabble of children, but well behaved. When I arrived at this hostel, the woman at the desk said: "We have a nice room for you. You'll like it." Yesterday the desk clerk at the hotel in Sternberg had said something similar. It is eerie: in both cases, it was as though they had been expecting me and had set aside a special room. Both accommodations were quiet and spacious: I couldn't have asked for better.

Hostel employees perform duties (serving food, doing paperwork) and provide care (organizing children's activities, comforting those who miss their parents), but here the staff are even more compassionate than usual. They are mothering-fathering types, and I appreciate their kindness so far from home. The facility even includes a building where people take seminars on childcare techniques. It seems the perfect place for it.

In Portugal my Dutch appearance led everyone to conclude correctly that I did not speak Portuguese. Here my looks make people think I'm German, and a moment later they see through my awkward attempts at speaking my own form of the German language. Many old Dutch words slid into English without change; however, when these Dutch words entered the German language, t's became s's, and p's became f's. Thus, the Dutch and English "water" is "*wasser*" in German, and "open" is "*offen.*"

With this in mind, I try to mispronounce my Dutch so it will become German. This hasn't worked since the two languages are quite distinct. For example, "It's tasty" is "*'T is lekker*" in Dutch but becomes "*'T schmeckt*" in German. The favoured expression is "*Alles klar,*" which would translate into our "Okay."

At this point in my journey, I need to control the tricks my mind can play. I'll fantasize about the end of the walk – doing the last kilometre on Estonia's coast – and realize I'd better get back to the reality of just taking one step at a time. Each step is work; each needs my full attention because a stumble could be disastrous. Every kilometre or two, I come upon a series of half a dozen molehills at the roadside – many with a neat round hole at the top. I see this as a lesson and tell myself: "Don't make mountains out of the daily molehills you face. Just keep walking."

During the first 10 days in May, I've enjoyed a few warm days and have considered changing into my shorts, but then the wind comes up. With the arrival of warmer weather, the lilacs are finally giving off a fragrance. They seem to be everywhere.

I continue to be surprised at the differences between this area and my earlier experiences in Belgium, the Netherlands and western Germany. Here trains are almost non-existent – only the odd passenger train of two cars shuttling between communities – and bicycle paths are few. I spend a lot of time hiking through roadside grass as cars and trucks zoom by. Guardrails are a menace: cars pass within centimeters of these barriers and force me to walk on the overgrown ditch side. Trudging along a slanted surface of tangled vegetation becomes disheartening and promotes blisters; then, suddenly, a bicycle path appears, and I can zip right along. Once I was so overjoyed that I kissed my fingers and reached down to touch the bike path in gratitude.

I've been amused at an experience in German guest houses and hostels that I call the "breakfast dance." *Frühstück* (breakfast) is usually included, and only the time needs to be negotiated. They ask at what time I'd like to have breakfast, and I say: "Is 6:00 okay? I like to start out early."

"No, that's too early."

"How about 8:00 then?"

"We can give it to you at 7:00. *Alles klar.*" Only twice was my breakfast served at 6:30 a.m.

While doing the breakfast dance, I have struggled with the way fingers are held up to indicate numbers. Here the thumb is used to indicate "one," the thumb and index finger indicate "two," and so on. Showing that you would like breakfast at six o'clock – using five fingers of one hand and the thumb of the other – takes concentration. If you then want to indicate eight o'clock, adding the index finger and middle finger is really challenging, especially after a full day's hike.

The hostel at Teterow is buzzing with 30 children and teachers from an alternative school in Berlin. "Like Montessori, but different," I am told, and they are quick to add, "We make only half of what state teachers do." Both staff and students are a less regimented lot than yesterday's group who came with a schedule and expectations. Now the children are free to engage in crafts, games and exploring: the whole scene has a sense of freedom where I see little competition, lots of interaction and frequent recognition of accomplishments.

I feel comfortable here as it reminds me of my employment, soon after my university years, at White Oaks Village, a facility for troubled boys. Each summer we would take the group to a Scouts Canada camp in the Haliburton Highlands of Ontario. There they could swim in the lake, paddle canoes and do wood crafts. Each evening's campfire, with songs and stories, was a highlight.

This group of children and adults reminds me of those days, more than 40 years ago. Then we were a team of adults organizing the next day's adventures. Now, alone in my quest to cross Europe, I wish I had fellow travellers – others passing through. The hostel staff inform me: "You can have your supper at six, and all the others eat at six-thirty. Breakfast will be at seven o'clock, and your room is upstairs in the garage behind the main building."

I make my way to a wooden structure in the back yard, open the shed door and am met with the smell of oil. I wonder what I'm getting into as I climb the creaky stairs, but I find a sleeping area that is clean and comfortable and in which I am the only guest. There are two bedrooms with two beds in each and no decorative features of any kind. My bathroom is a cubicle downstairs, off the garage, so this is no four-star hotel. I close the door at the top of the stairs to keep the smell of oil to a minimum, and I have a good night.

The next day I pass another oversized yurt next to an arrangement of tanks and pipes. This is part of the ReFood company that collects restaurant waste as a source of gases to power the generation of electricity. I have seen this company's trucks collect food leftovers from bins behind city restaurants.

As I hike down the road, an elderly couple, biking with packs indicating a long trip, head toward me. They are negotiating a steep hill, stopping half a dozen cars and trucks that are trying to get by on the narrow road. The bikers don't flinch, and I realize they are much more daring than I.

At a hotel stop, two guests are interested in my hike. One suggests: "When you've finished in Poland, you need to hike through Kaliningrad. You'll find that it's the nicest part of Germany." The man mocks Russia for owning the area lying between Poland and Lithuania that had been – but is no longer – part of Germany.

His comments encourage his friend to throw in another historical tidbit: "When I went to visit the old colony of German East Africa [now Namibia], I was surprised that the people there speak German. And they speak it very well."

I'm not sure how to handle their nationalistic fervour and manage to change the subject. (Note to self: "When talking to foreign visitors, do not get into a conversation on Quebec sovereignty aspirations. It will be a one-sided, unhelpful discussion.")

Hiking out of Stavenhagen, I'm surprised to find eight padlocks on the sidewalks, all of them with their shackles cut and with one lock appearing in front of every third house or so. The trail of locks even leads around the corner in the direction I'm headed. Perhaps the work of a busy bicycle thief. Strange.

I enter an area of parkland in which the road is so enclosed in green that it seems like twilight. Signs warn to use headlights for cars to be visible to each other since daytime running lights are the exception here. I notice a wooden cross nailed to a tree trunk and commemorating the death of 20-year-old Lars. I stop to take a picture as cars fly by this warning sign.

This part of my journey seems most like the route through Portugal with its busy, narrow roads and lack of local information. Spain had its pilgrimage services. France had its trail and *mairie* (town hall) staff. The Netherlands and Belgium had bike paths and "Vrienden op de Fiets." Those supports made the trek so much simpler.

Seeking directions to the next town, I approach a group of women waiting on the sidewalk for the last few attendees to arrive for their meeting. They are members of the "Diakonie," a group that serves both Lutheran and Catholic faiths. I am entertained by their relaxed manner, and one of the women jokes: "The Diakonie helps people with problems. If you had a blister, we could come and help you." That sounds worthwhile, and I suggest they continue on with me, but they decline.

Borders have often seemed less wholesome than the area that came before or after. They have been areas of transition, like the awkwardness of teen years. So, it was with the abandoned town of Retiro at the Portuguese border and the sad city of Badajoz on the Spanish side; so, it was as well with the scrubland between Friesland and Drenthe. When I entered the Mecklenburg-Vorpommern area at the former border into East Germany, I saw rundown remnants of the communist period. Then things looked better as I travelled through the eastern part of Germany. Now near the Polish border, I find the same disorder, including crumbling, uninhabited buildings. I assume someone with an interest in the American Southern States lives in this area as I pass a Confederate flag and an advertisement for "Line Dance."

It's a windy day, and I sense frustration among a group of about 30 people on a bike tour. They are facing a stiff breeze and are spread over several kilometres, waiting for each other to catch up and not wanting to leave anyone behind. At times like this, walking seems easier.

As I step off the road into the woods for a pee break, a gust arises and stirs the trees overhead. There is groaning and creaking and the sound of breaking branches. With this area of foxes (earlier one ran by in a field), oversized snails and wild boars, I can see why it has become a land of fables. And the cuckoo's call reverberates through nature till it echoes in my head. If I were a youngster, I wouldn't dare go and visit grandma through these woods!

A few days back, I happened to catch up to a man walking his dog, and he commented that my hike must cost a lot. Now, at an inn where I stop for the night, the owner asks: "How can you afford such a long hike? Did you win the lottery?"

My German lessons have not yet taught me how to say, "Mind your own business." I suppose they have a point: this is a crazy, expensive dream, but a dream that pushes me onward.

I'm passing vegetable patches (each with its own tool shed) and a farmyard with hundreds of geese and a sign indicating they are butchered "fresh" daily. Paths of square stones, that are a local specialty and hard on the feet, lead to an overpass across the famous *Autobahn* with its drivers who know no speed limits. The size of European fields keeps surprising me: a crop of barley takes me almost half an hour to pass. That's more than two kilometres long by almost a kilometre into the distance. That's a lot of barley.

At my stop on Sunday afternoon, the Pasewalk Hotel is fancy and expensive but has no meal available. The kitchen closes after lunch on Sundays, so I settle for reheated soup and a salad in the hotel's bar. Three meals are provided every day, but for supper on Sunday – just when guests arrive – we need to go elsewhere for a meal. Here is another oddity I have trouble grasping.

This is advertised as a "resort hotel," but – other than a few lawn chairs in the back yard – it seems more like a hotel than a resort. It does provide a computer for the use of guests, and I go in search of it so I can check my e-mail later. As I walk through the central meeting room looking at this computer, I stumble: my shoulder bangs into a chair that smashes into a table, and I hit the floor.

Two staff come running: "Are you okay?" I realize I have been the victim of Europe's crazy idea of putting a riser in the middle of a room where the floor should be level. My boots have been great at protecting me from uneven surfaces, but here my sandals are of no use. I lie there with bruised pride and a scraped knee; otherwise, I seem to be in one piece. One never knows: I can lose my footing in an instant.

Before I leave Germany, here is a note on a favourite topic, "soup." Early on, the German variety had floating cubes of egg – like an omelet material – not to my liking in soup. Then came the delicious white asparagus soup that was everywhere (and had no floating egg). Now those days are over, and I'm experiencing *"soljanka,"* a tomato-based recipe with sausage slices and pieces of boiled egg – a tasty soup, but no white asparagus.

My map seems to indicate a border post at the entrance to Poland. I'm not surprised to see cars lined up ahead of me, as well as a man in a yellow vest stopping traffic. When I reach that point, I find that it is simply a construction zone with a new road replacing the old customs plaza at the border crossing. Only the language on the signs and the advertising for gasoline and cigarettes – "cheaper than in Germany" – tell me I just arrived in Poland.

## Poland

Moments after crossing the border from Germany into Poland, I get a text message that says, in German, something about saving money on my phone plan outside the country. I'm astonished that a computer in Berlin, or wherever, knows I have crossed the border before I do. How do they manage those things?

While I'm having a McCafé coffee and a chocolate sundae as my cross-the-border reward, something buzzes in my pocket, and it's Joanne texting me to phone home. She likes to hear my voice once a week: I guess it is melodious after all.

I'm dismayed that the call ends halfway through as I run out of minutes. Because I have left Germany, the roaming charges eat them up in no time.

Upon arrival in the city of Szczecin for a two-night rest, I go in search of a Polish phone card, and I'm back in business. This is at a sparkling Saturn store in a new shopping centre. When I arrive just after 8:00 a.m., the store is already hopping, and 20 of us are in line for one checkout. The security guard seems bored, and I think perhaps he could help out, but this is not to be.

The hostel in Szczecin is a great disappointment. It does not provide breakfast, which is unusual for Hostelling International facilities. I plan to catch up on my laundry, but the washer is broken, and they have no dryer. The way to the clothesline is blocked with branches recently pruned from the trees in the backyard. I notice that the staff doesn't once leave their office-reception area. That never bodes well: you can't manage a place from behind a counter.

Of the four computer terminals, three are out of order, so I take turns with the group of young people on a school trip: "Go ahead and order your pizza. When you're done, I'll work on my blog." On the good side, I find that the Polish keyboard is similar to ours back home, reducing the stress of typing.

Szczecin is a well-worn city with lots of grey buildings and a sidewalk in dangerous disrepair, leading me to be vigilant after my tumble in that hotel. This feels like a miniature Prague but without the glitter. Someone had suggested: "You'll find real Polish food at the Restauracja Karczma Polska." The meal there is tasty and typical of northern Europe with lots of potatoes, red cabbage and chunks of meat – a working person's diet. The next day I return for a bowl of "hunters' game soup," which consists of cabbage, mushroom and bits of pork, bacon and sausage. It is satisfying as well.

A helpful young woman in the tourist information office loads me up with maps and booklets. She explains, "These show you the bike trail that runs for a few hundred kilometres along our north coast." It sounds attractive, and I envision a well-marked trail taking me through this part of Europe. Then I recheck my map and realize I would have to walk several extra days to get to a path that goes in a semicircle up and around the coast. When I get there, I may find that it doesn't meet my needs as a hiker: for example, places to stay may be distant from each other.

I decide to stick to my own path, a more direct route eastward. In fact, a year ago I had thought: "On my next trip, I'll follow the trail along the north coast of Germany and Poland." I had trimmed the bottom half from my detailed German maps as I would not need those parts. Now, on my trek through Germany, I had been limited to staying just north of my overenthusiastic scissor work. This is not a problem, but it's funny how things work out.

During my stay in the city of Szczecin, an ordinary walk leads to a thunderbolt of insight. I take the twenty-minute hike from the hostel to downtown, leading me along the main boulevard named after the previous pope, Jana Pawła II (also written as Jan Paweł II). At a department store, I purchase a disposable camera and head back toward the hostel. Crossing the tram tracks, I enter a circular park with its shrubbery and brick pathways, and there I see a father pushing the wheelchair of his teenage son. The father stops and wipes the drool from around the young man's mouth, and my chest tightens.

At that instant I have my answer: I am walking across Europe for this young man and for all those who can't, including my brother Bill. I hadn't been able to explain – to others or myself – why I undertook this challenge, why I had to fulfill this baffling dream. Other than my determination, nothing prepared me for this feat. Why me? It didn't make sense. Now, somehow, it does. I have searched my head for a reason and find it in my heart.

Suddenly I am overcome with a feeling of relief. I now have an answer and can stop fixating on questions about my childhood: I am free of the pressure of reliving my past. Now I can concentrate on the daily grind, and my childhood is free to become words in my upcoming memoir, "Looking for Bill, Finding Myself."

During my second morning at this hostel, I can leave on my own schedule as no breakfast is served. I'm always surprised at the early morning activity in Europe. By six-thirty I discover streets busy with traffic, people walking dogs and the group of students from the hostel boarding a bus for their day's outing.

Many people are cutting grass this morning. Lawn mowers seem to be the exception; the majority use string trimmers. Then I pass another church with scaffolding up to the distant roof. A man way up there is casually doing his work, walking back and forth. I don't know how people dare do that.

My hike takes me along a highway when a bicycle path appears. I followed this easy trail wishing it would continue forever, but it abruptly ends after a kilometre or two forcing me back onto the shoulder of the road to deal with the constant traffic. It seems unfair to tease me with such simple walking among the hundreds of kilometres of struggle.

And, of course, my blisters continue to remind me: "Don't walk across Europe again." On each of my walks, I hope not to have any blisters as I'm sure I've found the perfect hiking boots. (Not only do my present boots fit well, but the top eyelets are clips that hold the laces in place and make them easy to tie.) The first week with new boots is hopeful. Then a blister springs up. It subsides, and two more arrive. Smearing any potential problem area with Vaseline is an old Camino trick. I have some faith in that. Obviously, my blisters do not.

After a long day, I stop for a cup of green tea at the restaurant of a hotel in the country. The young woman in reception is so welcoming and helpful I realize it would be foolish to take another step. I settle in for the night along with the travelling salespeople, all of whom seem to be men in their thirties.

It's a comfortable stay, and breakfast includes a variety of vegetable salads – the Polish standard. On my way out, the same woman in reception asks, "Will you be in the Guinness Book of World Records?" This takes me by surprise: it hadn't occurred to me that my trek might be so noteworthy. I tell her I plan to write a book about my adventures, and she says she will be watching for it.

In each of the towns, people visit kiosks for their cigarettes, magazines and grocery items. I'm surprised at the number of people walking and biking. More people are active than I had seen in any country outside the bicycle craze of the Netherlands.

I am perturbed that many people look so sad and suspicious, and older men look particularly unhappy. Each time I entered another European country, I quickly learned how people said, "Good day," to each other. Here I went days without hearing, "*Dzień dobry,*" as people met. It's hard to learn the niceties of a language when you don't hear them used. The buildings, cars and farm equipment seem much poorer than those in Germany, and a beautiful home or new tractor stands out in the crowd.

As I hike into Stargard Szczecinski, a man sees me studying my map and asks if I need help. I tell him I'm looking for the tourist office, and he points in its direction. Then he insists I pay him a *złoty* for the information. This is my third such experience on my journey across Europe, and I simply say, "No," but it continues to irritate me. I feel that pointing a visitor in the right direction is part of life; it does not qualify as a tourism business.

I drop by the local church, and its dimensions seem unusual. For being short and narrow at its base, it is exceptionally tall. Its arched ceiling rises high above me: the blue decorations on a white background soar a nauseating distance overhead.

At the tourist information office next door, I ask the woman for the best route to the next town. She says she knows that area well as her "mother-in-love" lives there. I appreciate her effort at mastering the English language, but this slip-up would be enjoyed by mothers-in-law everywhere. She insists on using English although I mention she can speak to me in German with which she is more familiar.

In Poland the second language is German, and I have surprised myself at speaking it – in my limited way – as necessary. I seem to have become European in just using a small amount of a number of languages and not worrying about it. In Canada we want to get the second language right, and it becomes a chore. Here you just relax over your efforts.

In Chociwel a sign directs me to a mansion of a hotel, Pałac Nad Jeziorem, with a dour older man at reception. In the parking lot, men in camouflage are greeting each other in various languages while a young woman acts as interpreter. During an early supper, I get to overhear the details of what I thought was a military exercise. They are four young men from Denmark, negotiating with local guides for that afternoon's deer hunt.

A woman at the hotel is washing curtains, and I ask if she can give my clothes a much-needed laundering. For five *złoty* I am pleased to have clean clothes, but they come back damp. Careful draping over lukewarm radiators gets them dry enough to pack by morning.

Later the son of the couple who own the hotel – the dour man and the woman who washed my clothes – takes over from his father to cover the reception area and the bar. He suggests I try a drink of Old Krupnik, a mix of vodka and honey. It may be the best yet, and its smoothness relaxes me as he relates their family story.

He tells me of his parents' ambition in leaving their jobs as teachers of agricultural technology to turn this dilapidated building into a hotel. He speaks English with pauses to search for the odd word: "It was my father's dream. One day he saw the end of a rainbow over this building. Then he knew he had to turn it into a hotel. In the past it was a school, but there was a lot of storm damage, and part of the roof was missing. We sanded and scrubbed everything because it was full of mould. If I stole something then, the police wouldn't have been able to catch me because I had no fingerprints left."

He goes into a back room, returns with a scrapbook and says, "Not everybody gets to see this." I glance through photos of a family working together to turn a disaster into a simple but sound building. It's another heart-warming story that is so much bigger than my solitary hike.

The hunters return from their tracking, and three of them have each shot a deer. One of the deer's racks was of "silver medal" standard. It's too bad the deer didn't live to enjoy the fame.

Over an Old Krupnik refill, I ask the young man why Polish older men seem so sad. He says they are not sad, "Just tired because they had such a hard life."

That is generally true of Europeans. It may be especially so for the people of Poland, always following a path between superpowers – Russia/the Soviet Union on one side, the Austro-Hungarian Empire/Germany on the other – they could never be their own bosses. Everybody wanted part of them, and they had to struggle to maintain their self-determination. "Kind of like being the youngest in a family of a dozen children," I muse. Interesting.

I am left with a regret. Having met thousands of people over the course of my hike, I am missing many of their names. In most cases, my meeting was brief, and these personal details were not significant. However, this young man's story left such an impression on me that I wish I could record his name. Unfortunately, I didn't ask, and he is destined to remain anonymous in this anecdote. My plod through Europe includes highlights that would be worth a return visit, and this family's dream is one of those.

On the next day's hike, I'm surprised to see a house only a metre and half from the highway road surface. You don't see that in Canada. Then a dozen children, finishing school for the day, form a ragtag group behind me. A pink backpack in front of me leads the parade as its owner's arms swing up and back while her head is held high as though in victory. Later two women spontaneously greet me as I pass – the first time that has happened in this country. Then a dozen dogs run out from a distant trailer. They are friendly and keep their barking under control.

And so, my hike continues into the next town, Drawsko Pomorskie, where my information shows a hostel. Two women walk by, and I ask if they know the street I need. They're not sure and flag down a van whose driver does not know either. We proceed to a nearby garage where someone phones somebody about this hidden street.

One of the men in the garage has me put my stuff in his car and drives me to the hostel, which – as it turns out – is closed for renovation. We go back to the garage, and I find a hotel in which to spend the night. The moral of the story is that I had rather someone just point in the general direction, and I could ask another person nearer the spot. Here I felt uncomfortable in being the centre of attention while a dozen people helped me find a bed that wasn't available.

**Spontaneity**

In the continuous tunnel that is my hike, I come upon orchards and rows of berry bushes. Now that tunnel is widening: the landscape is opening up and so are the people. I can peer far into a distance of green fields and woods while people seem happier. A man walks into his neighbour's yard where they laugh with gusto over a shared joke. I'm glad to hear it.

I surprise two ducks that come flapping out of a creek, and they surprise me in turn. The cars flying by miss a gurgling conversation among a crowd of bullfrogs while an owl provides background music. In some cars the stereo systems are so loud I hear the boosted bass before I hear the engine itself. Then I pause for a bit of peace on the corner of busy roads where grottos with statues of Mary or crucifixes are adorned with flowers. By the end of the third week of May, the light green juvenile leaves at my arrival on this trip have matured into thick summer foliage. The hills are getting longer and steeper in this park-like setting.

As I crest a hill, I see two vehicles stop at the side of the road in the distance. Then people get out of the cars, and one of them starts gesticulating toward the adjacent property and the distant scenery, including a lake shimmering through the trees. As I approach the group, I become more curious and see that one of the cars has a German license plate. This seems to be a real estate salesperson trying to convince a set of foreign potential buyers. At a walking pace, I can watch such scenarios develop – something that would be missed when travelling by car or, even, by bike. "Maybe they'll seal the deal by the time I disappear behind the next hill," I muse.

The town of Połczyn-Zdrój has at least five hotels, all of a health-resort nature, and people arrive to be invigorated and spoiled in a quiet setting. I look forward to joining in this relaxation and get a room at one of these hotels where no one looks under 50 years of age, except me (just kidding!). For $35.00 Canadian I get a room, breakfast and supper. I don't know how they can earn enough, but prices in Poland are much lower than in Germany.

After supper I make my way to the Saturday evening Mass (the Mass for Sunday) a few blocks away. I get a feeling of gloom as the interior of the church is dark with decorations on every surface. My knees slide off the slanted kneelers till I realize other worshippers rest their bums on the edge of the pew seats while kneeling. The Mass seems to be a shortened version with only two readings (instead of the usual three) and no sermon.

As was our ritual half a century ago before the Second Vatican Council, we kneel in a row on the marble sanctuary ledge to receive communion. When I try to stand and return to my pew, my legs won't let me. There is no communion rail to give me support and I shuffle awkwardly, trying to rise up on one foot and then the other. A woman of about my age gets up easily, notices my dilemma and lifts me with her hand under my upper arm. I appreciate her helpfulness, and we exchange the glimmer of a smile – mine, one of embarrassed appreciation. It's as though my hiking muscles have taken over all others, and I have no problem in walking back to my pew. However, in needing this support, I suddenly feel old.

The 40-minute Mass is followed by a 20-minute Exposition of the Blessed Sacrament and Benediction: this seems an odd mix of celebration followed by adoration. In fact, the Mass itself is not celebratory though the organ music is beautiful. There are no young people or families in attendance, and the only people taking an active part are the priest and an elderly man acting as altar server. The ritual is sombre: once again, I prefer the Sunday Eucharistic Celebration back home; it has a sense of community.

Back at the hotel, the dining room has been converted into a dance floor and a three-piece band is in full swing. In their cowboy hats, they do a great job of polkas and a strain of Polish country and western music. A woman is sitting alone, and I need to polka, so I ask her, "Do you want to dance?" We have three dances till the band takes their break. Twirling in sandals proves tricky, but my hiking boots would have looked out of place. My ease in asking this woman for a dance reminds me of past struggles. When I left the seminary and its path to the priesthood, I was not alone. At 20 years of age, my companions were my reclusive personality, an incomplete adolescence and social awkwardness. Asking someone to dance was torture.

Now I'm comfortable with who I've become as I make my way to the deserted patio area with a last glass of Old Krupnik before bed. The agony I felt in social situations as a young adult who had just left the seminary is well in the past. Instead of worrying needlessly, I can now relax. I feel more comfortable, too, with the duvets that have grown slightly longer since I entered old East Germany, and I have started wearing my sock liners to bed. Now I can make it through chunks of the night without waking up with cold feet (and I can ask someone to dance without getting "cold feet"!).

I hope to have lunch in the town of Barwice, located halfway through my day's 43-kilometre walk. It is Sunday, many businesses are closed and Polish towns have few restaurants in any case. In the middle of streets of grey stucco housing, I find a modern pizza joint with a wood-burning oven. While I have my pizza, four young teen boys at the next table can't take their eyes off me. I must look like something from outer space. They speak neither English nor German, but – with a few words and lots of gestures – I explain that I'm walking from Portugal to Estonia. I tell them, "I'm from Canada," stressing the second syllable of "Canada" as they do here, and I give them each a maple leaf lapel pin.

They leave while I'm finishing my last slice, and I meet them as they wait for me outside the restaurant door. They had hurried home to find gifts for this Canadian stranger and proudly present me with a flag and bracelet for the Polish World Cup of Soccer. After this touching moment, they tag along behind on my way out of town, and I turn for a final wave. Then they and I are left as only memories.

**Surprises**

Both at home and abroad, we like consistency: it feels right when things follow a pattern. Suddenly patterns are being broken at every turn, starting with bugs on the road.

My disposable camera is a simple device that has no close-up feature, but I have tried to get a picture of a green-gold bug attacking and eating another. They looked to be of the June bug family, and this may have been a protein-sparing strategy between mates in the animal world. Over a few days, I noticed more and more dead bugs at the side of the road. This morning I wondered how many there would be, and I find not a single one. I must have reached the end of their habitat, but it's eerie: it seems as though someone swept the road overnight.

During this Sunday morning hike from Połczyn-Zdrój to Szczecinek, I drop in at a church and arrive during the priest's homily. In this bright church, I see an assembly of all ages (including many families) rapt in attention as the priest speaks from the front of the centre aisle. In many respects this is the opposite of last evening's sombre Mass. I had guessed that cheerless Masses were the standard here; instead, I find another pattern broken, and it's refreshing.

A few kilometres before the city of Szczecinek I run out of drinking water and stop at a village house. The man is interested in my story and adds: "I have a cousin who went to study in the Netherlands but started travelling instead." His family wishes the young man would stop his search and come home, but he wants to walk through as many countries as he can. I'm always pleased to hear that I have rebellious compatriots everywhere.

Entering Szczecinek, I expect to see humdrum grey apartments or small factories. Instead, I pass well-appointed houses in the country that become neat homes in the city, each with a pretty lawn and garden. After the residential areas I have seen in Poland – old, new, fancy and plain – this one feels familiar: it reminds me of my former tidy neighbourhood in north central London, Ontario. In addition, these residents share a view of a lake that stretches a kilometre or two along the edge of town and makes their homes even more attractive. After a few kilometres of houses, lawns and gardens, I suddenly arrive in a downtown with rows of stores sporting dozens of signs. Here the residential area is so pastoral; the downtown so urban.

The street number for the hostel confuses me: it seems to be missing from the series of house numbers I pass. A local person suggests it might be in a lane off the street, so I head down an alley, but it leads to a construction site. An elderly gentleman is raking around some shrubbery. When I ask him where the hostel is located, he gets out a key, walks a few steps and unlocks its front door. I am taken aback: renovations on the outside of the building mean scaffolding and debris; the inside is spotless. He understands no English, so I hold up my wallet as the way of asking if I pay now or later. This action is always understood as is miming the need for sleep by leaning my head against my folded hands as a gesture that asks: "Is there lodging nearby?"

A young man from Gdańsk, Poland is the only other guest at this hostel, and we have an interesting conversation. He had worked in a nursing home in England, so we communicate easily. I ask him about Lech Wałęsa, the anti-communism shipyard leader who also came from Gdańsk, and he tells me opinions are mixed – not everyone agreed with Lech Wałęsa's approach. The young man himself had grown tired of life in the big city of Gdańsk: "I took agricultural courses and bought fields not far from here so I could grow crops. I'm living in the hostel till I can build a house on my property." I'm pleased to come across yet another adventurous person.

It may be my lack of Polish, but this country seems to have a lot of billboards. In the monotony of walking, I appreciate the distraction of figuring out what all those words mean. They are starting to come together: *"sprzedam"* means "for sale," *"toalety"* means "toilets" (the "y" indicating the plural form) and *"meblowy"* means "furniture." Variety stores are everywhere, so the word *"sklep"* ("store") shows up often.

On this trip I have taken a "day off" once a week. This allows me to rest up, do my laundry, check my e-mail and write my blog entry. The Szczecinek library proves to be welcoming and helpful, as have libraries throughout my six trips (except for Madrid's as one needed to be a resident to use its services). I simply walk in and ask the person at the desk: "Internet?" Then I'm directed to the row of tables that are usually busy with customers – young people playing games or doing homework; older people looking things up or sending e-mail messages.

An indoor-outdoor bar, located near the hostel, seems a good place to go for supper. I tell the waitress I'd like a draft beer and something to eat. She brings me the beer and a dinner plate of what must be the chef's special. It consists of a tasty mound of shredded carrot-cabbage salad snuggled beside three potato shaped lumps of starchy grease or greasy starch – I'm not sure which of the two.

Early in Portugal I had enjoyed a plate of fried pork bits floating in oil as they reminded me of the Dutch *kaantjes* (cracklings) of my youth. Since then I have emptied my plate after many unusual meals, but these three lumps are truly nauseating. I dig through one to find a treasure of grey fragments of hamburger tucked inside. I can stomach only half a lump. The waitress frowns, but there is only so much I can do for the sake of good international relations.

The next morning I can leave early: since Polish hostels do not provide breakfast, I do not need to wait for the appointed time. (I now see a pattern in Poland: hostels offer no breakfast; hotels serve extensive ones.) Yesterday I bought an iced roll with jam inside (all of it too sweet) and a yoghurt drink to start me on my way this morning. Up at five-thirty, I find my way down the road shortly after six in the morning. It is May 22nd and, for the first time on this trip, I'm wearing shorts on what proves to be the hottest day so far. On each of my journeys, I have slathered face, arms and legs with sunscreen and used a hat – today those are essential once again.

Eager for a cup of coffee on the way out of Szczecinek, I stop at a café and ask the woman who is tidying and preparing for the day whether they are open yet. She says they are not. I'm disappointed till I realize I have posed the wrong question and ask if I could have a cup of coffee. That arrives immediately. One needs to know the special language of travel. Asking if they are open yet means: "Is your kitchen staff in so you can provide me with a meal?" For just a coffee, my question is rather silly. Of course, they are open: otherwise, no one would be there, and the door would still be locked.

As I finish my coffee, a man comes in and says, "Hello." As he starts working at his laptop, I wonder about his English greeting and ask where he is from. He is from Norway and with an agency concerned about destruction to the Baltic Sea.

"Shipping? Overfishing?" I ask.

"No, agricultural runoff – mainly nitrogen and phosphates. There's already a dead area on the Baltic Sea floor that's the size of Denmark." Reversing this trend will take years.

My walk takes me through an area reminiscent of home in New Brunswick – wooded hills, curving roads and logging trucks. Five minutes later I mount a hill and delight in a scene that looks like Canada's Prairies spreading out as grain and canola fields undulate to the horizon.

I planned for a 53-kilometre hike to a hotel in Człuchów (pronounced "too-hoov"). Thankfully, I come across a highway motel at the 40-kilometre point in Barkowo. The dining room is full of a wedding anniversary celebration. When they leave, I have lunch alone. After soup and the tastiest ice cream sundae I have ever had (berry and chocolate sauces, peaches, whipping cream), I go out to the restaurant patio and enjoy the family interaction.

The place is run by the middle two generations while granddaughter plays with her toys and great-grandmother struggles with a garden hose among the flower beds. I am intrigued by the mother of the family as she uses a sprinkling of English words but has trouble forming them into sentences. She eases my curiosity when she says, "I spent 15 years in Chicago, a long time ago."

On my European journey, whenever a pilgrim trail or a bike path has not been available, I have studied my map to choose from among the coloured lines. I have avoided the white lines that are small country roads with no conveniences, loud dogs and suspicious looks. I have also avoided the red lines that are major highways in favour of the secondary roads that are the yellow lines. This has worked elsewhere, but it hasn't worked in Poland. Here the secondary roads are used as racetracks for speed demons and as trucking shortcuts, leaving me no room on the shoulder as the big rigs fly by.

Now I discover that the red lines, the highways, are preferable: traffic moves more slowly, and there are fewer trucks. I appreciate being given a bit of pavement to share with the few bikes as well as some comfortable pea gravel and a flat grass shoulder. I'm still not sure why the traffic is slower or lighter on the highways: it may have to do with police presence although I see little evidence of that.

At a roadside pond, I admire the overlapping croaking of a dozen frogs sitting between the duckweed. Of all the travellers, whether the few by bike or the many by car, I am free to stop, explore and enjoy.

As I pass through Człuchów, I am astonished at the commotion: in public areas hundreds of people are painting, cleaning and trimming (with more loud string trimmers). Then outside of town, I come across roadsides abuzz with similar activity. I am guessing all of this is in connection with the hordes of tourists expected in the coming World Cup of Soccer activities, co-hosted by Poland and Ukraine. It's just a guess; since it involves the king that is soccer, it's probably true.

Many countries on my journey have used the word *"centrum"* for the city centre. Arriving in the *centrum* in Chojnice I am surprised to find a massive, bricked gathering place like those in Spain. Restaurant umbrellas and quaint shops are spread throughout this tourist haven.

Later, stopping for a pee in the woods, I feel under attack by half a dozen mosquitoes biting my arms and legs, two wasps trying to land on my face and a giant fly taking a bite of the dime-sized scab left of the loony-sized piece of skin I lost to that hotel floor. As the act of urinating makes one defenceless, scientists tell us all animals take only 20 seconds to do so, whether the dribble of a mouse or the torrent of an elephant. Then they can go back to protecting themselves. Here that doesn't work for me: I am under attack from the first second to the 20th! This is my first experience with northern Europe's famous mosquitoes, and I move along quickly.

I try to control an old compulsion of looking at every license plate: with so many cars passing, that can become irritating. Yet these plates provide their own lessons in geography. Going eastward through Poland, I am starting to see cars from Lithuania (displaying "LT"), so my next country is getting closer. In France I met a couple who were traveling through the country and had stopped for a picnic. When I asked where they were from, the man pointed to their license plate: in France these show the two-digit number indicating the *département* (administrative district) in which the car is registered. When I didn't understand, he explained but seemed surprised since those codes are common knowledge – or so he thought.

In Germany the first few letters on license plates indicate the part of the country where the car resides. In Oldenburg those letters were "BRA" followed by a space and other letters and numbers, so the word "bra" appeared thousands of times in traffic. You'd think that a minor government official somewhere would have noticed and suggested, "Let's try a different letter combination," but likely no one listened.

I thought this would be a good day to follow the suggestion of my family physician: "You could find church rectories to stay in overnight." Usually I arrive in a place exhausted from the trek and in no mood to start negotiating with a Polish-speaking priest. I have arrived in Czersk in good time, the church is right in front of me and another building looks like the priest's house. I am about to go to this rectory when I notice the church doors are open and there is activity inside. It is a confirmation class practicing for the visit of the bishop at their upcoming ceremony. The priest is busy getting everything just right. I'm relieved he's not available and sprint to the nearest hotel.

Hotels are certainly more reasonable in price than they were in Germany. Here I might pay less for a hotel room than I did for a bed in a German youth hostel – and I don't even have to make my own bed or share the room with others. Not only is the Hotel Roal in Czersk inexpensive, but I am struck by its modern decor. One wall of the glassed-in elevator is a mirror, so things go by in symmetrical form. The restaurant wall features four poster-size photos of classical car grills, and designer touches are found throughout.

Here the young people are sharply dressed, and light blue seems to be a favourite colour for mens' shirts, pants or sneakers. A young man wears light blue trousers with half a dozen brass zippers running up and down and back and forth on the legs. A young woman wears a dainty black business suit covered by a flowing fuscia sweater. Such fashions highlight the differences with the drab work shirts and pants of their fathers or the housedresses of their mothers.

As I look for the street out of town in the early morn, a young man is walking to work: he has a briefcase in one hand and a vase of flowers in the other. He detours into the cemetery gates and walks among the mass of flowers decorating the gravesites. Then he sets the bouquet beside a gravestone, and the tradition of care for the dead continues.

I overnight at a hotel in the industrial area of Starogard Gdański and gallantly offer to carry the suitcase of a woman struggling to get it up the stairs. I'm astonished that I have trouble lifting it and exclaim, "What have you got in here – gold?" She smiles as though that might, in fact, be true.

Up in my room, I watch a bit of television. Much of the programming is not originally Polish, and a male voice provides commentary about the action on screen. This is similar to our Described Video for visually impaired viewers. This sounds unusual at first but must be much more practical than expensive – and tricky – voice dubbing. On my way through Germany, the television system was changing from analog to digital, and many televisions provided spotty service. In Poland TV reception is consistent, but I still watch little of it.

Here each radio advertisement starts and ends with the word *"reklama"* ("commercial"). I don't know the history of this, but it's kind of neat the way it differentiates the enjoyment of programs from the sale of products.

Every 10 kilometres or so, I take in a shrine to road accident victims. I am struck by the senseless loss of life. I also pass war memorials highlighting other pointless deaths. One marks the death of 6,000 Polish people – most of them intellectuals and Jews – killed between September 1939 and January 1941 in the Szpęgawsk Forest while fleeing the Nazis. As I pass this dense wooded area, it seems so peaceful and utters not a whisper of the horrors it has seen.

A bumpy section of highway consists of small square rocks, and the speed limit is 50 kilometres per hour. At roadside people are sitting in lawn chairs hoping for the slow traffic to stop and purchase their strawberries. If they had been cherries, I would have bought a handful: they are less messy than strawberries and tastier. Then the raised approach to a bridge starts and – half a kilometre later – the crossing over the Wisła River. I hold down my hat brim to prevent losing it in the stiff breeze and to block the nauseating view of the swirling water below. I discover it's a long, long bridge.

In Malbork I appreciate viewing the much gentler Nogat River from a low bridge, and I treat myself to a "European Burger" at McDonald's. I am no connoisseur of burgers, but it looks like all others with meat patty between the two halves of a bun as well as lettuce, tomato, relish, ketchup and mustard. The name must be a sales gimmick.

Malbork is another city of incongruities: ancient towers stand guard over modern elements. In the downtown area, I discover a fluorescent fountain at street level spraying pulsating formations upward as people watch from park benches and patio bars. I feel bad for the hostel management because only two of us are spending the night. My fellow guest has a motorcycle as his "baby" and has even had it shipped to North America for a tour of that continent. He mentions, "I wanted to stay for two nights, but a large group of students is coming tomorrow, so there's no room." I'm glad to hear it: hostels are a great service.

On the way out of town the next morning, I stop at McDonald's for breakfast. Back home I occasionally have their pancakes with sausage, and I enjoy those. I order that now, but sausage is not available here. The pancakes arrive, but I'm dismayed that they come in the form of two lonely muffins and a package of honey to drizzle on top. It's the small stuff that can be the greatest disappointment.

During the day's hike, I come across a bike path of a few kilometres, the first I have seen in a while. I'm discouraged when it abruptly finishes. On this narrow road with no shoulder and heavy traffic, I need to continue behind an unending guardrail, inching through tall grass and past fat trees on a slanted hillside. It is slow going for someone trying to get to Estonia.

A family is celebrating a boy's First Communion in a café while I sit on the patio for a cup of *herbata* (herbal tea). As family members come out for their smoke breaks, I feel welcome as they talk all around me – so unlike the isolation I feel in meeting people as they bike past. In other countries local cyclists would nod, wave or greet me; here I might as well be a tree they are passing. I still can't stop the habit of saying hello or nodding and then, when they've ignored me as they passed, saying: "Sorry. Forgot."

I feel at peace on a quiet road taking me past flat land and channels of water – decorated with lily pads and yellow irises that give it the appearance of a Dutch landscape – and to the city of Elbląg. Upon entering the city, I remember to buy a street map at a service station to avoid having to ask my way around. Then I miss a turn toward a bridge and end up walking an extra kilometre along the Elbląg River to reach the next crossing into the downtown. A map doesn't do much good if you don't keep checking it.

As I round a corner, I'm surprised to see two cars up on a lawn. Police are gathering information, and a crowd has collected. One car has a dented front end; the other is up behind a tree. I'm sure we're all thinking: "That must have been quite a collision."

I continue my search for the local hostel and find the street address, but it is that of a school. The attendant at a nearby gas station tells me I found the right building: the school is used as a hostel in summer when students are on vacation. As I look for other lodging, I'm surprised to meet a priest, in cassock and Roman collar, who is going into an old church building that is now used by a social agency. I ask about staying in a church rectory, and he looks uncomfortable, shakes his head and mumbles: "No. Hotel." I didn't have time to get out my crucifix and place it around my neck as my doctor had suggested. It is secure in my hip pack – next to my panic alarm – where I think it will stay.

I find the tourism section of the city in its *centrum*: within a block or two, I see four hotels and pick one at random. At its front desk, I ask about the price for the night, and it seems steep, so I suggest: "I'll check at one of the other hotels."

The receptionist replies: "That's not necessary. I can give you a better rate." I thought she said the decrease was 50% but, no, it is 15%. I am usually not one to bargain – it feels too much like begging – but her wish to have me stay becomes a challenge. She says she'll phone her boss to see what he might offer. He can't be reached, so I go to the hotel restaurant for an *herbata*. When she's able to contact him, she asks what I'm willing to pay. I had already decided on a figure, and they agree to it. After all that, it goes from 480 złoty for 2 nights to 300 złoty – as with all hotels here, that's including breakfast – or about $45 dollars Canadian per night. It is one of those luxury hotels that is due for a few upgrades but is comfortable, nonetheless.

Hours later I am amused to experience another strange moment in my trek. I think, "Here I am, sitting in a hotel room in Poland soaking my feet at 4:30 in the morning," and I recount how that came to be. Having been greeted in Elbląg with a closed hostel that wouldn't open till summer and a priest who had no bed for me, I bargained for this hotel room. With some difficult walking behind me, I took a shower, had supper and fell asleep on the bed at 6:30 in the evening. I woke up at 10:30 to send Joanne a text message, went to bed and was wide-awake at 4:30 in the morning.

Two years ago I had bought a universal plug in Mirambeau, southern France and now used it to cover the drain hole in the shower. I filled the bottom few inches with warm water, pulled the desk chair up to the shower and dangled my feet in the soothing spa. My toes are bruised, and corns are threatening while a row of old blisters decorates the back of each heel. The balls of my feet are thickened and tender, and the ligaments and tendons within my feet often beg me to stop and go home. And that's why I'm soaking my feet. In a hotel room in Poland. At 4:30 in the morning.

## People

The following day my map of Elbląg helps find my way to a laundry service and a hair stylist. The woman at the laundry seems to say that my clothes will be ready tomorrow morning. I'm concerned about getting back to my walking, so – through a series of gestures – we agree to three o'clock this afternoon. Again, I feel vulnerable in getting a foreign haircut and beard trim. As on previous occasions, the stylist seems hesitant but becomes more comfortable with me and eventually relaxes. This has become a pattern throughout my European journey.

My search for a note booklet, dental floss and contact lens solution becomes an adventure. In my hometown of Sackville, I simply go to the drug store where all three items are available; here none are available at such a shop. The *apoteka* doesn't sell contact lens solution; an optometry service does so. Nor does it sell dental floss; that's done at a place that sells shampoo and soap. A bookstore would sell the booklet, but – at 6:00 p.m. – it is closed for the day. (A roadside *sklep* happens to have a few little books in stock the next day.) It all leaves me confused.

My map indicates the Elbląg cathedral, and there I feel overwhelmed by the artwork covering walls and ceilings as in so many Polish churches. Half a dozen sisters in two types of habits (so, probably from two different orders) are scattered throughout the pews. One of these habits is "old fashioned," revealing only the centre of their faces and having a headdress that looks like a tent. I haven't seen that in a while, and I'm reminded of the nuns' habits of the past. As Catholic immigrants, we were familiar with religious sisters: they taught my siblings in elementary school in the Netherlands, and they instructed Bill and me in our Saturday afternoon religion classes in Forest, Ontario.

I respect the nuns' decision to serve God in such a special way, but I am disheartened by the image of subservience these sisters represent in our Church. I would not seek employment in an organization that treats its women staff as second rate. Yet this is expected of me as a Catholic where the hierarchy is no place for a woman.

A first communion class of boys and girls in white gowns attends the cathedral's benediction service. The priest hands them the microphone in turn so they can announce what they have been taught about the faith. I cannot understand the language, but the procedure seems lengthy. I've read somewhere: "Jesus taught adults and listened to children; now we're doing it the other way around." I think that writer had a point. After exploring a walkway along the Elbląg River and viewing sightseeing boats, I drop by the church out of curiousity two hours later. Group pictures are being taken around the priest, and the children are finally returning to their parents and walking home in their gowns.

I go to an outdoor café for the Polish equivalent of a Turkish coffee, and the waitress speaks English with a British accent. I ask if she is from England, and she replies, "No, I'm from here, but I listened to a lot of BBC as a child." That's neat, that someone can learn a language and even develop its accent through a fascination with its radio programming. During my brief chat with the waitress, I realize how I miss an easy rambling conversation in English (or Dutch or French, for that matter). This gives me a renewed appreciation of our parents' choice to emigrate despite a future of being challenged by the English language.

On the way out of Elbląg, I pass an installation of several dozen kennels, each built of chicken wire and covered with a roof. This must be the local animal shelter at feeding time as the barking is more than I can stand. I won't be applying for a job there anytime soon! Each of this area's small farms has half a dozen milk or beef cattle chewing their cud as they eye me distractedly. I want to go up and cuddle each one and turn all of Europe's dogs into cows.

In Poland I have rarely seen people from Western Europe, but now a vehicle approaches me slowly, and I notice the French license plate of this *"camping car"* (French for "camper van"). I'm surprised as there seem to be so few French tourists outside of their home country, let alone this far into Poland. The van turns in a driveway behind me and then stops across the roadway from me.

I have surmised that they are lost and looking for directions, and a woman gets out and crosses toward me clutching a map. I call to her: *"Malheureusement, je ne suis pas d'ici."* ("Unfortunately, I'm not from here.") Now it's her turn to be surprised – and relieved – at my greeting her in French. They are looking for a vacation farm located near a town in the area. We decide that their destination lies ahead as we have not yet seen signs for that town. She is pleased with my information and waves as they drive on.

My hike leads me up toward Frombork, a tourist town on the Vistula Lagoon that leads to the Baltic Sea. In the last kilometre or two, a fog bank approaches, the wind comes up and I put on my jacket. Lupines line the ditches, and I long for home. The feel, smell and taste of this salt-water wind are identical to those I experience at home on Shepody Bay, part of the Bay of Fundy. In our Dorchester Cape, we are familiar with fog banks rolling in and ditches ablaze with lupines.

However, ours is a quiet gravel road, travelled at low speeds and with wide ditches. Here a stretch of road has me increase my recent statistics about traffic accidents. I come across three memorials to fatalities in a half-kilometre stretch – one with several victims. These narrow roads, with mature trees about a metre from the pavement's edge, are not meant for speeds of 140 kilometres an hour. I am beginning to think a solid line before a hill does not mean, "Do not pass;" it means, "Pass twice as fast."

I imagine a movie of a car that will blow up if it goes below 100 kilometres per hour. It could star the Canadian actor Keanu Reeves and use Polish stunt drivers. Or maybe something like that has already been done. (Okay, it has been done – but using a bus at a meagre 50 miles per hour – in the 1994 movie "Speed.") I've seen police cars but have not seen them stop a vehicle, and I'm told that photo radar is in use, but I question whether it is making a difference. I spend a lot of time making my way through ditches and marvel at the bravery of the few people riding bikes on the travelled portion of the road. They pedal in the direction of traffic, so they don't even see the cars coming up behind them.

My walking world continues to fascinate. A shallow creek with sandy bed follows along close to the road. I stop to enjoy its trickling water and realize I'm going so slowly it doesn't make much difference if I stop. I ponder, "That's not true of bikes and cars, or they would stop and enjoy nature more often." A plane above me is tugging a glider and releases the fledgling to a mix of air currents. And I finally see a substantial freight train pulling 22 cars piled high with logs. The odd field now features rows of potatoes or sugar beets.

In Braniewo my hotel key fits a door that is tall and narrow – different from the other doors in the hallway. Mine opens to a curved staircase leading up to a loft in the hotel's attic. This is a cozy space, and I picture myself as a struggling, starving writer looking down through the skylights at the city below. I envision the dark underbelly of this beast of a city with its death, doom and destruction. Instead, all I see through the bird droppings are two apartment buildings planted on a lawn and a solar panel being fitted to the hotel roof below me. I guess I'm not the American beat poet Allen Ginsberg after all. He attacked society's materialism; I enjoy a quiet break from my hike.

I keep meeting a German family of seven here in Braniewo – at a local café where I have a delicious plate of spaghetti, at the hotel restaurant for my evening cup of tea and now at breakfast. They are a friendly bunch of older parents and grown sons, daughters and in-laws, and their conversation exposes me to more German vocabulary. In the red-brick vaulted cavern that is the hotel restaurant, they greet me with a cheery, *"Guten Morgen,"* as they plan a side trip to visit an old family friend. The father uses his *Handy* (cellphone) as they make arrangements to meet just off the *Autobahn* (love that word!). I suppose they may need to stop for fuel at a *Tankstelle* (another new favourite word). All seven say, *"Tschüss"* ("Goodbye"), in my direction, and they are on their way.

Starting my hike out of town in the morning, I stop in at the basilica. As the organist practices a sonorous piece, I am enthralled and look up expecting to see a series of organ pipes. Instead, the loft wall is an array of speakers that provide the voice for this new electronic instrument. They seem out of place when the church walls feature scenes from the Middle Ages. I am disappointed with the exodus of those grand organ pipes, but the performance is moving, nonetheless.

From Braniewo I go eastward for another 250 kilometres through Poland instead of heading northeast toward Estonia's Baltic coast. This detour takes me around the region of Kaliningrad, a part of the Russian Federation for which I do not have a visa. Months ago I looked at getting that document, but the application form required a list of the places I would be passing each day of my hike. That was impossible to predict. Instead, I'm trudging an extra couple of hundred kilometres by staying south of this Russian enclave till I arrive in northeastern Poland where I shall turn north to Lithuania, Latvia and Estonia.

I had asked the hotel staff in Braniewo to check on their computer for a place where I could stay the next night and was told the Internet mentioned a hotel in Pieniężno. However, when I arrive in that town, several people tell me there is no hotel there. (I never did learn where it had gone!) A friendly young woman in the butcher shop suggests: "Ask the husband of the woman who owns the flower shop. He sometimes rents out a room." At 80 *złoty* for the night, I have an apartment above their store. I assume the family lives there and that I get to use one of the bedrooms, but at closing time they leave the shop downstairs, and I am alone. Later they show up with items for my breakfast – doughnuts and the things I need to make myself coffee or tea. The husband's shirt is streaked with plaster drippings, and they mention he builds houses for a living. While their teen son Laurence translates their questions and my answers about my hike, I go from being a tenant to being a guest. They are heartfelt people, and I feel an immediate bond. However, Laurence's interpretation services fall short of my old standards. I notice gaps in his commentary, which I avoided when I was a child, acting as my parent's translator – for Dad at the feed mill, for Mom at the hairdresser. I was persistent in translating every idea and doing so word for word.

Those early days have now become so immediate. I am a child once again, concerned only with meeting my body's needs, being polite and staying safe. I cannot understand the language of the adults around me, and written signs are a mystery. My old adult life seems so distant, whether starting an intravenous in the hospital's Intensive Care Unit or making a decision at the school board table or commenting on the implications for the Atlantic Region of a new prison health services policy from National Headquarters in Ottawa. All of that was another lifetime, surely someone else's lifetime.

Having left the key under the mat outside the back door as instructed (how universal!), I enjoy the early morning quiet of a pleasant road. This one looks like a wide bicycle path and has few cars – all travelling at moderate speed – and a gravel shoulder.

My day's hike provides a variety of experiences. Storks inhabit platforms on cement utility poles, and I pass a farm with massive storage silos while further along the woods are full of the sound of chainsaws. In a village a man waves from his yard and calls, "Compostela," as I nod in response. Crucifixes and shrines to the Blessed Virgin Mary are located at intersections and feature fresh or plastic flowers and a set of glass lamps with candles inside. I pass a farm where a tractor is pulling a hay baler making small rectangular bales and enter the town of Bartoszyce.

Some hotels in this northern part of Europe provide a sauna for their guests, but the Bartis Hotel goes further with its swimming pool, sauna and steam room. It prides itself on the extras that take it a step or two above the Polish hotel standard.

**Dampness**

On the following day, the month of June starts with a rainstorm and reminds me my poncho is still water resistant but no longer waterproof. It cannot withstand the downpour, and I feel the start of dampness on my shoulders.

I stop at a *sklep* for a bottle of yoghurt and tell the man I'm from Canada. He asks about someone he knows who moved to Canada while his wife tut-tuts his question because Canada is such a big country and how could I possibly know that person. In fact, I welcome the interest, and I'm surprised more people haven't asked such questions. Given the few Canadian visitors here and the influx of Polish people into Canada, there should be frequent recognition of me as representing that new Canadian homeland, but there is not.

The wetness and my soggy boots toughen me even further against the elements. I'm so determined to persevere that any concerns about discomfort become secondary, and nature's challenges reinforce my resolve to finish this crazy pursuit before I return to my family. Yet, my hiking world absorbs me so completely that I begin to think, "If I return home," rather than, "When I return home."

I am well past the 1,000 kilometres of this trip and am starting to feel it. As I tell Joanne by phone, "I wouldn't want to make a living doing this." Yet it seems strangely attractive. For her part, Joanne senses my fatigue, worries about my getting rundown and suggests two rest days a week. I know I'm tired, but taking more days off would prevent me from finishing before my scheduled return to Canada and would necessitate another trip to Europe. My solution is to simply keep trudging.

In a bus shelter, I remove a stone from my boot and wonder how they find their way there. I don a warmer shirt and wrap the waterproof cover around my backpack, which hasn't kept dry under my poncho. Each rainfall brings on a six-step procedure – take off my knapsack, remove the rainwear pouch from a compartment, unzip that pouch and remove the poncho, put the cover around the knapsack, place the pack on my back and put on the poncho. This process becomes irritating, especially in the middle of a downpour.

On this trip half a dozen drivers have stopped to ask me for directions. Imagine that: they are even more lost than I am! Now a car stops, but he is signalling that he can give me a ride. I want to tell him: "Yes, please. I understand there's a quaint little bistro just up ahead. It has a glowing fireplace, a bubbling pot of soup and a variety of herbal teas. Drop me off there." But, I don't. Instead, I wave him on and just keep going, remembering to call, "Thank you," when his car door has already closed. For me it really is the journey and not the destination – at least, until I reach the Baltic coast.

At some point I pass through Gierloza, a village that was the site of Adolf Hitler's headquarters from 1941 to 1944. I'm not sure what I'm missing. In the driving rain, I don't care.

I have now entered an area of long hills, lakes and tourism that includes many German and Dutch visitors. I'm surprised to come across three trees that have the yellow-on-blue stylized shell signs of the Camino pilgrimage path painted below the white-red-white bands marking this as a major European hiking trail. Again, I am the lone hiker, and I see no further evidence of this Camino route. It may have been a local person's wishful thinking.

Moments later, I see an unusual bug with wings folded and resting on a leaf. With its transparent appearance and blue tip, it looks like a miniature Bic ballpoint pen, of all things.

The few railroad tracks have stop signs that drivers obey faithfully. They might go 140 kilometres an hour and pass on blind hills, but they come to a standstill at railway tracks, which hardly ever see a train.

At the hotel in Ketrzyn that evening, I spread my clothes over every surface to dry and use the hair dryer on my boots. Then the bass boom starts to pound from the basement café up to my room. It is disco evening and, waking at midnight, I make my way down for an Old Krupnik. I'm not sure what to expect from the young crowd, but they are a respectable group of neatly dressed friends having a good time. With flashing lights and loud music, it is a fun time for all. But, unfortunately, no polkas.

The next morning I chat with two fellow guests who are cyclists from Manchester, England. In response to their questions about my hike, I tell them, "A British knight performed a misdeed, and he employed me to carry out his penance." I guess at their knowledge of such matters, and they understand: to gain the church's indulgence in the Middle Ages, rich people often paid others to go on a pilgrimage for them. I'm still waiting for my cheque.

We agree that Poland seems to be progressing and that its people work hard. We talk about the Queen's jubilee celebrations getting underway. When they mention that they just came through Kaliningrad, I tell them I avoided that part of the Russian Federation because of the difficulty getting a visa. The authorities need to know where you will be each day, and I did not have that information ahead of time. They comment: "That's not a problem. You just pay an agency to do that, and they do the lying for you." This is an interesting concept – one that hadn't occurred to me.

Before the town of Giżycko, I notice a poster advertising a campground hotel. I make my way to the lovely setting overlooking a lake. The room is simple with a space heater instead of central heating on this cool evening, and the bed is a pullout couch. The shower is – I'm sure – of Dutch design since the bathroom floor gets flooded.

While I enjoy the supper of pork, potatoes and salads, my hostess remarks: "There's a beautiful rainbow out there now." It is fading by the time I race back from my room with my camera, so I catch only the last vestiges. Back at my meal, a song comes on the radio. It sounds familiar, but I've heard it sung differently. How can that be? Then I recognize it from the dance in Połczyn-Zdrój. I've now been in Poland long enough that I can compare versions of a song.

After supper I enjoy a relaxed conversation with the English-speaking owner and her husband. Our discussions range around recent economic concerns that are reflected in their decreased number of guests. She mentions that the majority of Polish products once went to Russia; now they go to Germany. We talk about the European Union, challenges facing Poland and our own local situations.

Her husband is looking after other guests when I ask the woman why there are so few trains in Poland. She responds with a rant, the last word of which shocks me: "It's the big oil companies trying to sell their product. They want cars, cars, cars. Old tracks can be re-built, but they would blow up the trains if they were used. It's all the work of the Jews."

I am stunned and burble something about it being the big oil companies, maybe, but not the Jewish people. She looks over my left shoulder distractedly and says nothing ("Like a passing cyclist," I muse). Then the conversation continues, but the bond between us has broken. We are suddenly far apart. I have glimpsed the dark underbelly of the beast that is Old Europe, and I feel violated.

The next day is a feat of endurance as I experience one hurdle after the other. Breakfast isn't served till 8:00 a.m., so I'm late getting away. I get stuck in the old Giżycko battlements, in what I hoped would be a shortcut, till I'm forced to backtrack for a kilometre or two. On the way through town, I have to wait for a worker to close a swing bridge. As he walks round and round, pushing an angle iron stuck into a mechanism in the bridge surface, it creeps shut.

After a 40-kilometre hike, I couldn't find the hotels that I had been told serve tourists in this area. I worry about having no bed for the night and, in the late afternoon, stop at a house in the country to ask a Polish man about local accommodation. He speaks neither English nor German, he says, but he does speak Dutch. That takes me by surprise, and I switch into our shared broken Dutch. He farmed in the Netherlands and must be one of the few Dutch-speaking Polish people in the world. He directs me to a few hotels and rooming houses in the area, and I waste valuable time searching for each one and asking people for directions. As it turns out, they are all temporarily closed or no longer in business.

Night is setting in and I decide to hoof it to Olecko following a quiet country road. I am concerned that I might spook dogs and they will chase me, but the constant barking stays distant. A few cars pass, and I hide from their headlights in the roadside bushes: my safety stays a priority. I reach the city of Olecko well after midnight and tread down deserted streets where I chance upon two downtown hotels, but both are locked and not staffed at night.

I may have more luck along the main road that heads toward Suwałki and try to discern how to get to that part of the city. I have become expert at sensing which city streets lead to a major thoroughfare that will take me toward a highway and on to the next town. Those with stop signs are not going to lead anywhere whereas through streets are more hopeful. The ones widening to four lanes or opening to far-off businesses are also more promising. Of course, the noise of traffic could provide a hint, but I hear no sound of cars in this silent night.

That knowledge is now vital since there is no one to ask for directions: everyone is asleep. I hike through eerie neighbourhoods and find a highway hotel that has a dim light in its reception area though the door is locked. I knock and awaken the clerk bundled under a blanket behind the desk. I'm exhausted after a 60-kilometre trek – my "record" to date.

I tell the clerk I'll be leaving early, and she kindly says: "No. You sleep." I feel worn out, and my face must be drooping. After a few hours of sleep, I'm wide awake and trudge a wearying 37 kilometres to arrive at Suwałki's seven-storey hotel for a rest day as I prepare to cross the border into Lithuania.

If you're trying to come up with names of fictional characters, I suggest the map of Poland. It is a delightful mix of words that sound like evil geniuses or interplanetary beings – Stargard Szczecinski, Drawsko Pomorskie, Szczecinek, Czersk, Starogard Gdański, Malbork, Elbląg, Frombork and now Suwałki. You can't go wrong. The guys on television's "Big Bang Theory" would be impressed.

## Suwałki

In Suwałki, Poland I find a heartless hotel within a heartless city. Oh, the people are very nice, but neither the hotel nor the city has a "heart" – a centre of activity.

On entering Suwałki, I'm astonished when it takes me 15 minutes to pass the cemetery. It stretches over a kilometre, making it the biggest graveyard I have ever seen. As with all Polish cemeteries, it's a florists' dream: each grave has a flat ornate slab of marble with an upright marker, and even the graves of those long gone are decorated with blossoming plants or fresh flowers.

Each block in downtown Suwałki consists of a series of attached buildings with the occasional alley running under an archway beside the street. The width of the streets and length of the blocks is remarkable: each is as long as three or four regular city blocks. If you plan to go a few streets away for an item, you'd better pack a lunch. It takes that long.

I traipse all over in search of new hiking boots as the heels on mine are getting worn. In the whole city, I find only two pairs and they are not my size, so I conclude there must not be a walking culture in this area. I decide to keep wearing my present boots as they are definitely broken in and still serve the purpose. If worst comes to worst, I can buy sneakers for the last part of the journey. I visit the tourism centre that proves to be a great source of information for the next part of my trek. They also provide an Internet service, and I'm grateful for a

301

few hours of typing my weekly blog entry on their visitors' computer.

The Hańcza Hotel looks like the tall Holiday Inns of old, but worn and tired. I was amused at being greeted by buckled asbestos sheeting at the edge of the awning and a trek of 22 steps up to the reception area. As another guest mentions, "It was built in the 1970's, and they haven't done anything to it since." Pictures are hung inches from the ceiling, and the elevator is one step up from the caged contraptions of old. I suggest a facelift, both inside and out, costing millions of Euros. The few guests are middle-aged men on business trips or, in the case of some Russian visitors, members of a sports organization. No families are to be seen.

Breakfast is simple but tasty. For supper we are given a choice from a few types of soup, salad, main course and drink. There we sit at our individual tables in silence while, in the distance, the television blares the news (including mention of the Queen's jubilee), features about soccer (of course), ads that seem more artistic than ours and lots of hip hop music. It feels like a cruise ship without any fun or a monastery without any prayer. But the price is reasonable – just over $30 Canadian for the room, breakfast and supper.

With no bar or gathering space of any kind in this hotel, the reception desk becomes the source of contact with another human being. Just like her friend, Basia (Barbara in English) at the tourist information centre, the receptionist is welcoming. Upon my arrival at the end of a long march, she insisted on helping me with a 10-minute class in Polish spelling and pronunciation even though I wanted nothing more than to get to my room and crash.

My room is, in fact, a suite with bedroom and sitting room. This feels like luxury in a building that is anything but luxurious. As usual, my things get spread around. When travelling with a suitcase, it is possible – though challenging – to open the lid, access your items and replace them. When using a backpack, that is not possible. Invariably, you need something from the bottom of a stuff sack, and in no time contents are spread everywhere. I have learned to empty my knapsack in a systematic way so I know where I have placed items and can easily return them to their homes in the early dawn.

In this hotel room, I am pleased with the space: I can cover the sofa with my stuff and leave the armchair as a place to sit and unwind. After a long hike both body and mind need a time of numbness. I don't usually drink alone (oh, except when cooking or baking), but I buy a glass of red wine and a dark chocolate bar downstairs, sit in my armchair and doze – at one point waking up to a mouthful of melted chocolate. All part of my strange life on the trail.

On my second evening, I leave the business district, take a walk into residential area and discover one of the most delightful scenes of my six trips. Within a minute's walk of the hotel is a lake surrounded by a brick walkway on which people are strolling hand in hand, cycling or power walking. A few ducks rise up from an island and are silhouetted against the greys of sunset reflected in the calm surface. To admire this spontaneous scene in such a structured city, I take a seat on a café patio with a cup of Turkish-style coffee. The recipe for this popular beverage is simple – put the special grind of coffee in a cup and add boiling water – and the trick lies in taking sips so you don't get a mouthful of grounds: as with life, take it a little at a time.

**Worries**

Leaving Suwałki, I stop for a cup of *herbata* at the café of an inn, the Gościniec in Krzywe. I am struck by this example of the use of natural wood in interior design. Tables, benches, doors, flooring inlays, pillars and ceiling – all look perfect. Joanne and I will need to find our way here someday.

I've enjoyed the nature lesson the trail provides: I discover the same things over and over but in the next stage of development. So, it is with storks. I have seen them hovering around their nests on platforms atop utility poles – posts of concrete, not wood as at home. Then I saw one use its beak to clean out its nest, throwing droppings up and out to the ground. Now I pass a nest where the mother is kept busy tending her two stork chicks.

I planned to hike north from Suwałki into Lithuania, staying in the town of Kalvarija the first night. However, there are two problems: the highway is a busy trucking route between the two countries, and there are said to be no hotels in Kalvarija. Instead, I feel confident in finding accommodation about 30 kilometres east of here in the small, but touristy, Sejny.

After one of my first trips, our son Trevor asked if I didn't ever get the urge to start running with my backpack since hiking seemed so slow. I can't say I have, but it comes close on this part of the journey. I receive a text message from Joanne: "Haven't been able to get through. You okay?" (I find out later that, when she tried texting and phoning, she was told there was no such number.)

I text back: "I'm fine. Try again." But I hear nothing. Then it's my turn to worry because she'd be worried, and I need to take action so far from home. I recall a *sklep* half a kilometre back, and that's when the running starts. I don't actually run, but it becomes a brisk walk. A salesman who is visiting the store lends me his cellphone and waves off the 20-*złoty* bill I hold out to cover the cost. But I can't get through to our home phone or Joanne's cellphone. (I assume there may have been a systems problem in Poland.) I am 17 kilometres from Sejny and take off. If I walk fast enough, I can be there in less than three hours and find a way to contact Joanne.

A kilometre or two down the road, I reach the village of Krasnopol. This place is bigger than I expected, and I'm hopeful it has a library. Sure enough, it does, and I use one of their half dozen computers to contact all five of our children, asking them to let Joanne know I am fine. Contacting all of them is a sure way to reach at least one of them, and I get a few replies immediately. The librarian may wonder about my loud sigh, but I don't care: the pressure is off.

I may have had a look of desperation as I entered that village and asked a man who was coming out of the *sklep*, "Where do I find the library?" He could simply have pointed to the doors in the distance, but he walked me there to make sure I went to the right entrance. I have now revised my opinion of the remoteness that Polish adults show publicly. (Interestingly, children and young teens are demonstrative in their greetings and waves; that changes in the mid-teen years.)

The appearance of distance may actually be a circle of safety as adults feel secure and comfortable in not having to react to everyone they meet. Yet, my circle and theirs intersect easily and quickly. If I ask for help, they go out of their way to make sure I get what I need. I have had more people in Poland walk with me to help me find the way than anywhere else on my trips.

In the village of Sejny, I stay at the Skarpa Hotel, which is of an impressive size. It looks as though it started small and had several wings added. I've been surprised that a sizable town may have no hotel whereas a small village may have several. It's all a matter of tourism demand. I see no lake or other attraction nearby; people just seem to want to spend time here and arrive by the busload. For breakfast I can choose from the restaurant's Polish menu. The waitress doesn't speak English, and I would like an egg, so I say, "Cluck, cluck," as I flap pretend wings. She smiles, and I'm grateful chickens have a universal language. Why can't we all be like that?

About to leave Poland, I am still the only person walking the roads with a serious knapsack. I haven't made a difference but have learned a number of lessons. I've found that my backpack makes dogs bark all the louder. In the evenings, when not carrying it, I get a less vicious reception.

I remain puzzled by the ridges at the side of the pavement that run for a few metres. These may be melted pavement or a design, but the gathered water must be a source of hydroplaning in a rainstorm.

For the importance of religion in Polish life, I've seen little evidence of towns or streets having saints' names. On the other hand, in France I had even taken a photo of a sign "Rue Jesus Christ" ("Jesus Christ Street"), which seemed an unusual street name, even for France.

I have enjoyed the pretty streams from atop Poland's many bridges but was prevented from coming closer to some of these streams by the irritating nettles that grow in the long grass. In contrast to nature's orderliness, I have witnessed an array of discarded items and hundreds of hubcaps as well as a menagerie of animals, mostly dead at roadside – birds, bats, snakes, mice, moles, caterpillars, a lizard and a badger.

Riddle: How do I know of a McDonald's outlet in the next town before their signs appear? Answer: By the McDonald's cups and containers in the ditch. A company that can sell so many billions of hamburgers that they've stopped counting must be able to manage its mess better than that.

In the hamlet of Poćkuny, I reach an intersection and watch my compass needle as I turn a corner while it turns from east to north. I have travelled eastward for more than 1700 kilometres, since crossing the Afsluitdijk and entering the province of Friesland in the Netherlands. Now, finally, I continue northward, facing a stiff breeze but pleased with my progress.

## Lithuania

Within eight kilometres I reach the border and make my way into Lithuania. The crossing features a tourism office, restaurant with souvenir shop and banking machine. On this apparatus I pick the middle number of the amounts that can be withdrawn as cash since that seems reasonable and I know nothing about the local currency. I'm content as I come away from the border with a full stomach, a list of hotels into the distance and a wallet of Lithuanian currency that is the *litas* (symbolized as "Lt" and called the "lit"). The university student providing tourist information is welcoming, interested and knowledgeable. He ensures I have the required details as I wander through the deserted customs plaza and into Lithuania.

The reception desk at the downtown hotel in Lazdijai will not open till 8:00 p.m., which means I am stuck with my backpack till then. On a town map display, I notice a second hotel in the nearby residential area. I ask a woman with shopping bags the way, and she follows me, but – before turning in to her home – she has mentioned to another woman following me to help me find the hotel. When I walk right by it, not realizing *"viešbutis"* is Lithuanian for "hotel," the second woman calls me to turn back. I'm touched by such helpfulness.

It proves to be another inexpensive place – on the way to my room, I'm given sheets so I can make my bed – but the food is great (including "white beet borscht"). I ask the woman who manages the *viešbutis*: "Can you help me put my new Lithuanian SIM card in my phone and top up my cellphone minutes?" I discover that replacing the SIM card and topping up the minutes take long fingernails and a mastery of the Lithuanian language respectively. I have neither of these attributes; she has both.

This hotel, the size of a large house, provides no breakfast, which is advantageous for me as I can find my way down the road early. Before setting out, I consume the items I bought the previous day – sardines on crackers (better than it sounds) and a bottle of yoghurt. The sardines come in a can and are dripping oil, so I eat them over the bathroom sink, and I think: "It's come to this. It would look as though I've lost all refinement."

I'm the only guest and had been instructed, "Just leave by the back door," and I'm in my glory, hiking down a sleepy road by six in the morning. Along the way I stop for a cup of coffee and supplies. The variety stores at four gas stations in turn have spotless shelves with items lined up perfectly – gotta love that! At one of these, I'm surprised to see a woman my age use an abacus to tally sales. She smirks at the calculator used by the younger clerks. Years ago our BP (British Petroleum) gas stations became Petro-Canada. In Lithuania I'm surprised to see BP service stations till I realize it stands for "Baltic Petroleum."

Over a few days, I amuse myself by listing those things that I find different in Lithuania from my experience in Poland. The money is now the *litas*, valued just above the Polish *złoty*. The language on signs looks different with fewer symbols. Polish is a Slavic language; Lithuanian is in the Baltic group. In spoken Polish the words ran into each other; Lithuanian words sound more distinct.

Barns are of a wood plank design, with the boards running horizontally, vertically or diagonally. Houses are of wood siding painted in the yellow-brown range of colours (never, for example, red, green or blue). Other houses, of stone, are larger than I had seen previously, some even featuring a third floor.

I notice how things have changed as I pass through the Lithuanian hiking environment. Farm equipment seems older than that of Poland, where it had been less shiny and new than that of Germany. In the latter part of Poland and now here, the only enclosures have been electric fences – not barbed wire fences as I have seen elsewhere. Cattle and horses are often tethered to a stake in the ground, each creating its own crop circle. In the case of stallions and bulls, their front legs are attached to each other with a leather strap so they can't breed the mares and cows sharing the field.

As a gesture of kindness to this sole hiker, the roadsides are designed to meet my needs with gravel shoulders continuing behind guardrails allowing me to walk comfortably. The border means nothing to the flies buzzing around my face and arms: from one country into the other, they continue to annoy but don't land if I walk briskly enough. A rare Lithuanian intersection has a crucifix or a shrine to the Blessed Virgin, and cemeteries are less elaborate with few horizontal slabs and with green plants instead of the masses of flowers I saw in Poland. The coolness of passing cyclists continues into Lithuania.

I send Joanne a text: "Wheat fields, hay bales and Holstein cows with distant lake as a background. Lithuania is nice too." Moments later I delight in a children's storybook scene of a rooster with his hens and a few sheep behind a fence of thin logs.

I feel welcomed as a four-kilometre bicycle path leads me into Marijampolė. It becomes the sidewalk running past the downtown Europa Royale Hotel, so I pick that as my home for the night. If you're going to stay at a four-star hotel, choose this one as it is less expensive than the standard hotel in a Canadian city. However, the four stars do not mean I have to like it: the extravagance, loudness and formality leave me cold.

The lobby is all glass and polish, and my room comes with half a dozen packages of soap and shampoo. In the evening the hotel's restaurant Pizza Jazz hosts a disc jockey complete with scratchy turntable. This is an open-concept area so the sound carries throughout the ground floor forcing older folk to search out alcoves away from the hubbub. At breakfast the volume continues with speakers set at bass boost to squeeze the most out of the American music.

The lobby clock indicates my watch is off by an hour. I'm confused about the time and ask the receptionist: "Is there a one-hour difference in time between Poland and Lithuania?" She says it's the same time there, and something must be wrong with my watch. Later I find out there is, in fact, this difference in time, and I attribute her answer to a lack of experience with time zones in such a small country. The Canadian expanse across east and west means we are aware of time zones: in Canada they are part of our lives.

The receptionist is pleasant and helpful: she says she has given me a room overlooking the square. As it turns out, the square is just an empty square. At one point, a young couple sit on a park bench for a moment before moving on in the breezy evening. One week into June, days are pleasant but nights are cool, so that is the extent of the action in the square.

I don't really care that, "Your room was cleaned by chambermaid Moringa." Here the bottom sheet is not tucked in, just draped over the mattress: with any tossing and turning, it is a mess by morning. This is the kind of journey where I make my own bed one night and experience luxury the next – and where I prefer the former to the latter.

As I continue down the road, I am pleased to stop and chat with a German traveller. He is cycling from Berlin through Poland and into the Baltic countries and explains: "This is the second half of the circle I started biking last summer." He is full of information about local cultural groups and how they can be identified, "You can tell which areas had a German population because they planted trees next to the roadway."

I want to say, "Perhaps not a bad idea back in the day of horse-based travel, but they tend to get in the way of cars now," but I stay quiet as he continues.

"It's the traditional Baltic communities that have the yellow wooden houses." He speaks of entering and leaving "East Prussia," which I thought had been added to Middle Ages history courses just to give us something else to memorize. Before its bombing during the war, Kaliningrad had been the beautiful German city of Königsberg, and he is disappointed with the way the Russians have re-built it. As he bikes away, I ponder the centuries of history Europeans carry in their hearts. In comparison, we Canadians are beginners.

The city of Kaunas is still some distance away, and I'm hoping for a bed a little closer. I approach a father and his adult son relaxed on lawn chairs in their yard. The son suggests, "I know the people at a motel about 20 kilometres from here," and he gives me the address. It is too late in the day to reach that point, I think, but I thank him for the information.

The son is interested in my hike, and I casually ask if he wants to come with me. No one ever does, but he is excited by the idea, though – on second thought – I don't really want this stranger as a companion. He may later have gone to the motel he suggested in order to join me in my trek, but I'll never know as I was relieved to find one closer, the Motelis Armènija just before the city of Garliava. There I have the Armenian dish "pork sashlik," and it is delicious. In Poland, you were brought your napkin and silverware on a plate; here that has become a basket, so things keep changing.

In Lithuania I have seen two lengthy freight trains, which could replace a convoy of trucks. For the first time since Germany, I have heard police sirens and seen their flashing lights. I am drawn to outdated farming practices: in Poland I saw a man use a dump rake pulled by a horse; now a farmer is using a horse-drawn machine to fluff up the hay, which jumps up behind him – a piece of equipment that is new to me.

On Sunday morning I happen to come across a Catholic church at 7:45 when Mass is starting in 15 minutes. Again, I am disappointed with the lack of celebration I feel. The people are certainly reverent: each person kneels and says a short prayer on entering the church before silently proceeding to a pew. During the Mass I am surprised to see a second priest put on an alb and stole to take up the collection. In my experience that has always been a layperson's role. I support my own parish financially and, as a guest, feel it unnecessary to put money in the basket at a church I visit. This time it seems interesting enough that I have my money ready, but the priest passes me by.

Entering Kaunas, I make my way to the avant-garde structure that is the Akropolis Mall to buy a disposable camera. The façade of the building is glass and red brick with two-metre-high letters on a tubular steel cobweb announcing the name of the shopping centre. Here I experience another side of Lithuanian life. I see those cute crocheted hats that cling tightly to the children's heads and emphasize their plump faces. Many young men are wearing three-quarter length pants and sporting a handbag. The men's handbag is of leather with a thin strap over the shoulder and looks like a flat camera case. In Lithuania I continue to see that men are as partial to light blue clothing as they were in Poland.

Now here I am, sitting at a café in the Akropolis Mall and having chicken soup with dumplings. Meat Loaf is singing "Total Eclipse of the Heart" on the sound system. A tot dressed in pink and with wisps of blonde hair is playing with her dad's wallet as coins scatter to the floor. People are going up and down escalators and ramps, and the colours dazzle. I feel homesick as I ponder: "How did I get here? How did I get so far from a quiet Sunday afternoon at home in Dorchester Cape, New Brunswick?"

I purchase a disposable camera at the mall's Fuji Film shop, adding to my list of experiences in buying cameras. Before leaving Canada, I visited Jean Coutu Pharmacy in our nearby town of Sackville and could choose from a shelving unit of disposable cameras. I bought two although I know by now that I end up taking about five cameras worth of pictures (totalling about 150 photos) on every trip.

Now the further eastward I travel through Europe, the more difficult it is to buy a disposable camera. I have asked, unsuccessfully, in many shops and take the only one this store in Kaunas has in stock. I could buy a digital camera but do not want to tempt fate following the theft of my last one – and most of my possessions – in Aljustrel, Portugal. Besides, I don't want to expend energy on getting just the right pictures. I didn't commit myself to producing a documentary, only to walking and writing.

The writing consists of frequent stops by the wayside to note a word or two in my booklet. I have discovered that it is easiest to fill the right-side pages till I get to the end of the book. Then I turn it over and complete the other pages, allowing me always to scribble my notes on the right side, which is simpler when walking.

On previous trips I sent myself an e-mail message with the start of my notes and added to them at later stops several times a week. Now the length of my walking day gives me limited time to hunt for a computer. Instead, I take a "day off" once a week, find a computer (usually at a library) and sift through my notes. Then I might not remember why I wrote, "Yellow flowers," for example, and would exclude that from my narrative. About half my notes make it into print.

The pressure of time (as others wait their turn at the computer) and unusual keyboard layouts has forced me to ignore refinement in spelling and grammar. Then my left brain gives up on the logic of proper writing, and that encourages my right brain to be more creative. At the end of each of these "days off," I have trouble falling asleep: my body doesn't like breaks in its tough routine.

On the way out of the Akropolis mall, I am uncertain of the direction I need to go and ask the information people a question: "I'm walking to Jonava. Do I turn right or left out the front doors of the mall?" This is obviously not in their area of expertise. The four women turn toward the male employee (a common occurrence when I ask for directions), and they discuss things further.

Then the young man points over his right shoulder and says: "It's that way." My compass has already confirmed that, but I thank them very much though they have been of little help. I choose a right turn out the door, walk an extra few blocks and find the street that will take me to the highway out of town. The street begins to rise and rise and rise over several kilometres. This is the longest hill I've had to scale since the Pyrenees.

**Wall**

Halfway up this climb, I hit the wall. This is the wall that long distance runners are said to hit far into a race. As a long-distance hiker, I lose my spirit. My legs can't keep their rhythm, my backpack has gained weight and I have nothing left to talk to myself about. Imagine that happening to me.

Since childhood I have mused on language or relationships or interesting facts, but these thoughts have now dried up. My mind had been locked into the rhythm of walking, which pushed my brain to constant activity, so that much of my life on the trail was inside my head. Now all that has come to an end: I'd like nothing better than to sit down and just call it quits. It's a struggle, but my perseverance wins, and the top of the hill finally arrives.

I want to share my feelings with Joanne without alarming her and, in an e-mail message, I write: "I'm still walking and doing well, I think. Sometimes it feels a bit wearing (and wearying), and I wish I could just get on a bus for the next stretch. But I'll keep on and be home soon."

I have resigned myself to the fact that it would be hard work: if it weren't hard work, it couldn't have been a dream. However, the feeling I now have is one of annoyance: "Why do I have to do everything?" It's interesting that we spend our childhoods seeking independence and our adult years trying to get others to do things for us. In the end I simply have to work through the negatives and keep going. Using my Baltic States map that shows the Baltic coast at the top of the page helps put a spring back into my step – it now looks so close.

In a phone text note, Joanne relays a message from one of our daughters who said a sign at her work reads: "Best dad ever!" Shanna thinks they must mean me, and I notice that those things help push me on.

Halfway to Jonava I cross the road to enjoy an early supper of herring pieces and mashed potato covered in a mushroom sauce – a tasty combination. This *kavinė-baras* (outdoor café) consists of two dozen picnic tables under canvas awnings. Families and young people are enjoying the pleasant sunshine of a Sunday afternoon, and spirits are high. The only dark spots are my melancholy and the eagerness with which two men attack their *kartaczes*, those awful potato-shaped things that nauseated me back in Poland.

Other than the *kartaczes*, I miss the foods that were new to me in Poland. The fermented rye soup was tasty, "Like a nourishing vegetable soup with a spoonful of vinegar added," I thought. I learned to enjoy the soured grain drink and the potato pancakes with various side dishes. Each plate in Poland came with a sizable pat of butter, maybe two tablespoons worth, and most of mine would return to the kitchen. I'm not sure what kefir is, but it tasted like a cross between yoghurt and buttermilk. The strawberry-flavoured kefir was the tastiest.

Before heading out again, I check my map. This trip, more than any other, has seen me pore over maps to work out the best routes. This wasn't necessary in Spain or France as I followed pilgrimage paths. Nor was it required in Belgium, the Netherlands or western Germany where I followed bicycle trails. Now I puzzle over my maps and could use more detail. I cut out the unused parts to simplify my load, and I mark the completed route with a yellow highlighter to encourage myself. Lithuanian cities are distant from each other and do not form a neat row, so I study how to hopscotch back and forth in order to have a bed every night. The cities in Latvia are in a line going north, so the walking there will be more straightforward.

My long days add to my irritation, and the arrival in Jonava caps a three-day total of 140 kilometres. I also have a new blister, this one on the side of my foot where I've never had one before. I seem to be getting more blisters on my left foot than my right, perhaps because my left foot is slightly smaller than my right. I start to wear an extra sock on my left foot, making the boots fit my feet uniformly, and hope that works.

Jonava strikes me as a drab city. Two teen girls shouting at passing cars from a park bench and two men drunk on the lawn of a bar add to my dislike for the place. I approach several people before finding someone who knows the location of my home for the night, and its only indication is a tiny sign beside the front door. This apartment building, within a group of similar structures, has been renovated to become a luxurious guest house.

Upon my arrival, the receptionist needs to copy information from my passport and struggles to get all the syllables of "Josephus Everardus Koot" in the right order while I wait patiently to be assigned a room. My "room" is actually a suite with modern kitchen, dining room and sitting area. In the oversized bedroom, two beds cower against the wall. Again, I find that the higher the price for lodging, the less the contact with others and the more lonely it seems, and this place is lovely but impersonal.

I find a grocery store near my lodging and store a few items in my fridge since no restaurant services are available in this guest house. On the next day, my day off, I appreciate being indoors as I watch the teeming rain through the public library windows while typing my blog entry. This town, too, has its share of off-white brick apartment buildings. These forlorn dwellings tell me Karl Marx didn't have a sense of humour and thought the proletariat shouldn't either. In each window is a pair of sheer curtains that make me think the apartments are probably homey and well tended.

A few blocks from the guest house is a restaurant named "Arma." I'm surprised that the American music is so loud in such a classy bistro, and I search out the seat farthest from the speaker system. The chef must have had advanced training: my perch dinner takes an hour to prepare and is spectacular. The receptionist at the hotel had recommended Arma and mentioned that it closed at 9:00 p.m.

By the time I get my perch dinner, it is 9:15. The staff don't seem concerned about my late arrival, but it bothers me, and I rush through my meal while still trying to enjoy every morsel. Upon paying the bill – now it's about 9:30 – I say something like: "Sorry to keep you past closing time." But the waitress casually replies that they don't close till 10:00 p.m. Grrr!

I leave Jonava and hike into the country, crossing two long bridges over the Neris River as it winds back and forth. A bicycle path hugs the highway, and I follow it. After a kilometre the path strays from the road, but I keep going, in hopes that it will rejoin the highway a little further on. It does not, and I veer away from my intended route as the path curves south when I'm supposed to be headed north. I backtrack, and an extra kilometre or two brings me back to the highway that I now follow faithfully.

I'm feeling comfortable with the countryside pattern that continues as it has for hundreds of kilometres – stretches of woods alternating with small farms near the road and with big fields (now of wheat and potatoes) running into the distance. The crops do not seem as lush or to take up as large an area as they did in the Netherlands, Germany or Poland. One crop has me baffled – fields of tall grass with no sign of crop heads or of a timothy, clover or alfalfa mix. It is a seeded crop and looks like grass, but I wonder whether it is cattle feed or serves some other purpose. ("Perhaps it's a source of biofuel," I muse.) It remains a mystery yet to be solved. Meanwhile the stork chicks are now being fed from the parents' beaks, so life goes on.

The receptionist at the hotel in Ukmergė is a great help in using the Internet to locate hotels where I can stay for the rest of my walk through Lithuania. In this hotel I am pleased to meet Michael, a retiree with a New Zealand accent who has lived in many places, including Norway. He had one of those jobs that makes sense while the person is talking but is hard to recall afterwards. I think he said: "I made sure that international laws were followed when companies started mining or drilling for natural resources" – something like that. Many of his fellow workers in Norway hailed from this part of Lithuania, so this is where he settled. Now he is living in this hotel for a few months every year and learning the Lithuanian language.

Michael is full of tidbits about the history of the area. Not far away are buried some of Napoleon's tattered troops who died while trudging home from the disastrous campaign against Russia. Part of this city was a Jewish community of leatherworks, schools and a wooden synagogue – one of the oldest places of worship in Europe and now in a state of decay – and, in a local town of 2700 Jewish residents, only one person survived Hitler's murderous rampage. During the "Cold War" (mainly between the USA and the USSR – Union of Soviet Socialist Republics), local silos held ballistic missiles ready to be fired at strategic spots throughout Europe. Even an out-of-the-way city like Ukmergė can provide a collection of historical facts.

In the village of Kavarskas, I seek out a gas station for a cup of coffee. Here cars use liquefied natural gas (LNG) in addition to gasoline or diesel fuel, so the attendant pumps the LNG while the customer pumps the other. I have my coffee (from a machine but tasty) at a round picnic table under the trees where the owner of the station and a neighbour have bet 20 Lt on their chess game.

The son – who has finished school and is not sure of a career choice – translates, but the father's knowledge of Canada surprises me. I say I am from the eastern part of Canada, and he asks, "Montreal?" When I say it is further east, he responds, "Newfoundland?" I talk of joining my wife in retirement and sitting at home drinking tea, and he says: "And Scotch whisky. Oh no, Canadian whisky." He is astute.

Down the block two women are selling strawberries and insist I try one. It is tasty, but I was more impressed with the product of a young lad at the roadside a few days earlier. He had litre jars of wild strawberries – those tiny buds that smell and taste so yummy – which must have taken forever to pick. I held out my cupped hand and asked: "Can I have this many?" But he wanted his jars to stay full, so on I went.

Here in Kavarskas I also stop at a store for supplies. With all those different people having contact with me, I am amused that this could be the start of a legend "The Day that Canadian Stranger Came to Town."

Suddenly a shot rings out, but it is only one of those cannons scaring birds away from a fruit crop. I appreciate this change in scenery as I hike past a few kilometres of apple orchards and berry bushes.

I arrive in Anykščiai just as the hotel receptionist is locking the front door. She is filling in for the regular staff and must have thought (perhaps hoped) that no one else would arrive. I get there just in time to be assigned a room for the night, and later Vita and Linus come back from their project. They and their seven workers are living at this hotel.

These two archeologists started a business, "We restore old buildings, and it can be tricky work," says Vita. She speaks English well and translates for Linus from time to time, as he is left out of the conversation. They are now working on an ancient monastery in the area and struggling with the process of injecting material into its crumbling walls so they remain intact. They are interesting people and have been sampling a bottle of Slovenian wine from a friend. I enjoy a glass of wine and their gift of a box of marzipan filled chocolates (which I've consumed by morning), and they each get a Canada pin – the best I could do since I didn't come bearing gifts.

Twice in the last few weeks, people have not wanted to fill my water bottle. They may be concerned that their water is not safe for me to consume. Then I buy bottled water and think of David Suzuki's rule, "Use the water local people drink." However, this close to the end, I don't want to chance it.

The stomach discomfort I experienced in Spain and France has come back to be a challenge. Coca Cola and a few burps – in travel writing one needs to be descriptive – seem to help.

This is a good point to talk about my body and losing the soap in the shower. I was using a hotel's bar of soap that I thought I must have dropped. Then I found it in my armpit. That sounds silly, but it's been years since I had anything that you might describe as armpits. The use of hiking poles has caused my shoulder capsules to thicken. The fat pads in my armpits have decreased to the point where I have caves there.

On previous hikes I would be concerned that my hands were often swollen by the end of the day. This may have been caused by pressure of the backpack straps against the lymphatic ducts in my shoulders. Using the poles has prevented this swelling from recurring.

Though I'm eating well, my ribs are showing a bit more. Never having been much of an athlete, I hardly knew I had thigh muscles. Now they work overtime, and my calves are firming up. In Poland men had tight slacks that fit them well, and I realized they had no bums to speak of. This must be a Slavic trait, not like our rounded Dutch features. Anyway, I'm firming up and becoming more and more Polish! (Enough of that.)

My stop in Kupiškis turns out to be a simple motel, but one with a great feature. It has a zigzag tubular unit that is meant to warm the towel before your shower. Instead it serves to dry my handwashed t-shirt, socks and underwear by morning. In other hotels such units have been linked to the central heating system that is off for the summer. This is an electric plug-in type, and I'm pleased with its efficiency.

The next day marks the middle of June, and now the rain starts, and truckers move away from me so they won't splash. Sometimes they succeed. Arriving in Rokiškis, I find a hotel near the highway while a map display shows a second hotel at the far end of town. The Viešbutis Angelė seems deserted, and I consider the walk through town to the other hotel.

However, the back door is open, and a sign gives two phone numbers, so I use my cellphone to ask about a bed for the night. A woman answers, says something in Lithuanian about not speaking English (I guess) and hangs up. I try the other number and get the same response about *"angliškai"* ("English") from the same person. Then I hear activity in the building, so I knock, and there is the same voice at the top of the stairs!

My persistence must have won her over as I can get a bed. Then this pleasant-looking woman sees my Canadian credit card, and she says, "No," she can't accept foreign charge cards and will need cash. I'm flustered in being short of Lithuanian cash because I'll be entering Latvia tomorrow. So, I gather a last bit of energy to trudge through puddles left by stubborn storm drains to a Maxima supermarket to extract cash from a machine. I also get a ready-to-eat chicken leg and some salad for supper as well as supplies for the next day.

As I arrive back at the hotel, I see a couple in a car with Lithuanian plates eyeing the building while I head upstairs to be signed in. The receptionist sees the car pull up to the wrong parking area, opens the window and starts yelling at them. Her string of words includes, *"Policija"* ("Police"), so the authorities must have complained about people parking in the wrong place. I think they find a parking spot – at the other hotel in town – as I do not see them again. I'm astounded that this middle-aged woman with a relaxed face within waves of auburn hair can be so stern. I end up giving her a Canada pin just to show her. Actually, I'm not sure what I'm trying to show her, but it seems the right thing to do.

Despite the mood the hotel is tidy, and I'm impressed with the tasteful sheer curtains. My room is on the chilly side, so I wear my "Riverview Winterlude 2010" toque with its embarrassing earflaps. A heavy blanket is provided, and I sleep soundly: once more I make it through the night without awakening once. At about $16 Canadian, this may be the least expensive hotel – and the best sleep – on my European adventure.

Here are a few more thoughts on language before leaving Lithuania. In parts of the country, Russian is the second language. People must struggle with choices around learning a second language: "Should it be English, German or Russian?" Or, in the impressive European tradition, "Should it be all three?"

If a menu does not include English translation, I often guess and just point to an entry. Then I'm not sure what I'll get, but it usually works out since I'm not a fussy eater and I'm always hungry. Most restaurants have English menus that are meant for all foreign guests, not just those whose first language is English. Dutch people visiting Lithuania, for example, would ask for the English menu.

My attempts to learn a language are often foiled. In Germany I asked a woman where the *Jugendherberge* was located, but she didn't understand till I explained, and she said they always called it the "youth hostel." In Poland a clerk in a *sklep*, couldn't grasp my request, "*Ziemne solone* (salted peanuts)," because he was taken aback that I would know that term. In Lithuania I met some boys walking through town and asked whether they were not supposed to be in school. They said they were going to the store, and I asked if they were buying ice cream. Then I added: "What's the Lithuanian word for 'ice cream'? It's *'lody'* in Polish. You have a word like that."

They shrugged and responded: "We call it 'ice cream.'" The word is actually *"ledai,"* but how can I learn a language that way?

In Poland I found that the spelling of words and their pronunciation were poorly linked, like the "ough" of some English words – through, though and trough. Lithuanian seems more like the Dutch arrangement, where you can learn some basic rules of pronunciation and have 90% of it right.

I now realize the public distance here can serve me well. No one needs to know I'm a foreigner. If I don't need to talk, I just keep walking although the walking continues to provide challenges, including that of cars passing other cars beside me. During my hike in Portugal, cars coming up from behind would overtake and pass each other when right beside me. It can be disconcerting to have a car pass at 140 kilometres an hour at your elbow.

I tried attaching a mirror to my hat to see those cars coming, but concentrating on the mirror made me vulnerable to an accident. I have tried listening for the harmonics between the two cars coming up behind me – the one in the driving lane and the one picking up speed in preparing to pass. Now I simply move toward the ditch when a vehicle approaches, whether from in front or behind. In Portugal and Poland this often meant going right into the ditch as the shoulder was so narrow.

Despite the pleasantness of Lithuanian drivers and their lower speeds, this passing of cars beside me occurred 19 times in Lithuania, out of 55 in my whole European journey. (Yes, I count these things!) I'm convinced no one passes in the clear section ahead of me. It's as though there's a rule: "Challenge pedestrians wherever you find them." And there are so few of us to be challenged.

I went 10 kilometres out of my way to find a significant highway crossing over the border into Latvia. I wanted to visit the information centre, get a wallet full of local currency (which will now be *"lats"*) and find something to eat – all of which I had done when crossing into Lithuania from Poland. However near Subate, a border village off the highway, I am disappointed to find there are none of the above. They do have the plaza of wide pavement I saw on entering Poland and Lithuania. It would have been teeming with customs officers in communist days. People may have been cowering in their cars in the act of smuggling Russian vodka or western cigarettes. Now the centre of the plaza is the area cars and trucks zoom through, and the rest is weeds and memories.

## Latvia

If you're planning my type of hike across Europe, start at the northeastern end. Get the most difficult part out of the way first and leave the bicycle trails and pilgrimage routes of western Europe till later: they are so much easier. And so, I start my sojourn in Latvia with frustration over finding a place to sleep.

As I enter this rural part of Latvia, I am apprehensive since I have only rough information on where to stay for the night. A few hotels back, a receptionist checked the Internet for me and found that a small village just inside the Latvian border had both a hotel and a guest house. I stop at a farmhouse to ask where this village is located, but the woman and her daughter have never heard of it. So much for the Internet's usefulness.

I also have the name of "Juris" as someone who has a room for visitors in the town of Aknīste. Since the first few numbers in the European phone system remain a mystery for me, I ask these people to punch in the numbers for Juris on my phone. He answers immediately and suggests: "We'll meet at the Kalniņā kafejnīca at 8:00 p.m." I picture Juris as an older man who goes to that café for supper and will meet me there.

This paved stretch of road has been quiet when I'm surprised to see six transport trucks approach. Local comments have led me to believe a grudge exists against the Russian people for imposing communism and all the misery it brought.

These trucks have Russian plates and may be travelling in convoy to find safety in numbers.

A bit further on, I stop at a farmhouse as my water supply is running low. A young woman named Agnise comes out to fill my litre bottle. I comment on their beautiful flower gardens, and she responds: "The women do that work. My father looks after the farm." She has taken Baltic philology (study of the Baltic languages) at university. I ask if she might not consider teaching that subject, and she says, "I've had some offers to teach, but I think I'll stay here on the farm."

As I pick my jaw off the ground, her mother comes out to eye me suspiciously. I think: "Honest. I was only stopping for some water, not to spirit your daughter away to a lucrative job in the big city."

A rivulet gurgles below me over three kilometres as I approach Aknīste and look for the café where I am to meet Juris. To my surprise, the place is closed, and I wonder what to do next. I'm relieved to find a bank machine next door so I can get Latvian currency as I'd been concerned about not having any. Two young men pull their new cars side by side so they can converse through their open windows. ("Like a drive-thru conversation," I muse.)

"We're just chillin'," one says. When I ask him to contact Juris for me, he asks: "You mean the one who owns the café?" This will be a totally different Juris than the elderly gentleman I've been expecting.

On the phone Juris says he'll be here in 20 minutes, and he soon drives up in the company van with a few staff and family members. Juris greets me, "We closed the café because we had to cater banquets, banquets, banquets. Are you hungry?"

I respond, "I'm starved," and become Juris' project. With a full glass of Chilean wine, a bowl of white beetroot soup and a plate with slabs of pork, potatoes and salads, I'm in my glory. I feel bad about not finishing the pile of potatoes when Juris returns from driving his family home. He refuses my money: "The meal is a gift to you from my family."

Juris talks about a guest house in the neighbourhood, loads me into his van and drops me off there. This place is three kilometres outside of town, and I noticed it earlier on my way in. I would have gone there for the night if Juris hadn't been waiting for me. Whether he had a room for visitors and where it was located remains a mystery. His name may have been on an outdated list, and Juris didn't want to miss out on meeting this Canadian hiker.

Window screens are not a European tradition, and I awaken as the mosquitoes' breakfast. The guest house owners are away, and the person filling in for them cannot provide breakfast. So, in the stillness of morning, I leave the guest house and locate a store for supplies to cover breakfast and lunch on the long gravel road ahead – herring roll-mops to go on my leftover crackers, rolls of poppy seed and apple, chocolate milk, kefir and fresh cherries. The road is being rebuilt, and the dark blue sign with its circle of yellow stars shows this to be another of many European Union infrastructure projects.

I approach a peat bog and find its size overwhelming: I estimate that a thousand acres of birch trees have been clear-cut, leaving a wall of birch as the edge of this expanse. Hundreds of peat bricks lie sliced on the ground and in piles awaiting shipment. These bogs must be a breeding ground for a variety of biting insects as I am constantly under attack. In most of my journey since Portugal, bugs have stayed away if I walked quickly enough. However, these have not been taught that rule, and they cling to me. I stop in the rare *veikals* (store) on a hunt for insect repellant, but none seems to be available here – here, where it is most needed.

I have seen no wind turbines since early in Poland, but I am reminded of that country by a hamlet featuring another of those white brick communist-style apartment buildings. I feel saddened as it looks out with dead eyes through broken windows and, no doubt, awaits demolition. Buildings contrast with nature as Latvia shows its pretty side. I admire a host of butterflies – small blue ones, big black ones with white dots in a row on each wing and medium-sized green ones with yellow dots. Then I watch a heron with a white neck wing its way upward from a swamp.

A series of logging trucks pass fields of wheat and canola as I enter the city of Jēkabpils. I notice a park that turns out to be a graveyard with trees and shrubs, as well as benches by the tombs that are indicated by small markers – quite a change from Poland's extravagant cemeteries. I walk on the edge of an overpass above the railway track, but it is so disintegrated that through the rebar I can see the rail line far below – another project to be completed.

This is a Baltic city where I find hope for the future: sidewalks throughout Jēkabpils have turned into excavated trenches as they are rebuilt, and I wonder how they could have gotten to the point of needing so much reconstruction. How could communism have ignored the obvious, the need to spend money on infrastructure? I pass furrows of gravel and a fleet of wheelbarrows as I turn into a cozy sushi bar with a brick interior, order a serving and receive 38 pieces – meant to be shared but enjoyed all by myself. A few doors down, a pleasant librarian provides the computer for typing my blog entry.

I stay at the Luiize Hotel and notice a fan kept on the bar stage, so I borrow it to dry my wash. When you are continuously hiking, you have to make do. Also staying here are a couple my age who have travelled from Switzerland by motorcycle. Two other guests are young men from Denmark who are installing timber-sawing equipment in a converted cement factory. One of them, an electrician, says: "You've probably seen more of Europe than most Europeans." I'm intrigued by this comment: he may well be right.

I feel as though I've taken a step back in history during a visit to Holy Spirit Orthodox Church, built from 1886 to 1888 and topped with five cupolas. An elderly woman in flowered kerchief is polishing ornate candlesticks. A man in black, whom I assume to be the priest, stands behind the gift shop counter. With his stern look, scraggly grey beard and long sideburns forming tufts reaching past the end of his beard, he could have come off the set of Dr. Zhivago.

Despite my degree in psychology and my work as a nurse, I'm not sure what is most therapeutic for me. However, this walk seems to have been therapeutic: I have found a renewed sense of calm. Then I go for supper in the hotel's restaurant, and the clerk-waiter-receptionist has the television's volume turned up but the picture off while he is toying with his computer. So, I have to listen to a television show with a "beep" every 10 seconds or so. I would rather hear the vulgar words being replaced with those beeps. I fume and exclaim: "Can you turn that off?" He does, and I am left to muse over my inner calm that evaporates so quickly in the face of irritation.

The next morning I bring this fellow my room key. I don't understand their shifts: it's often the same staff in the late evening as early the next morning. He asks if he should call a taxi because rain is threatening. How I wish!

Much of the 54 kilometres to Madona takes me along gravel road. A tandem truck of logs approaches in the distance. I visualize bygone days with an old couple shuffling to town for supplies. I fantasize the smell of an ox cart piled high with manure swaying on its way to the next field. I imagine the giggling of children as fistfuls of wildflowers are carried to a neighbouring aunt for her birthday. Then, from within a cloud of dust, I wonder: "Could that driver not have slowed down for me?" and "When did we surrender the space between our ditches to flying hunks of metal, rubber and glass?" and "What can we do to get it back?"

Main Street in downtown Moncton, New Brunswick (our home city) has numerous pedestrian crossings. As a driver, I've experienced the frustration of repeated stops to let people pass in front of my car. You'd think the people were more important than the vehicles. Now I'm eager to get back to Moncton and to stop as someone ambles across. Meanwhile, here in Latvia a deer saunters onto the road, eyes me intently and crosses into scrubland while the flies continue to annoy.

Sitting on a roadside stump eating blue cheese on crackers, I start texting Joanne and realize I'm out of phone credits. I hike through the village of Laudonia where I buy more minutes and ask the store clerk to enter them for me. I still can't get through to Joanne and realize I need a SIM card for Latvia although I'd been assured that Lithuania's card could be used here. Again, I'm concerned that Joanne can't hear from me, and I detour to the village library to contact her by e-mail, but the library is closed. Joanne will have to wait.

I arrive at a hotel in Madona where supper is served buffet style. The cook is surprised to see me choose hunks of pork that are 50% fat, a dish I would normally find repulsive. However, with the need to ease my hunger and to consume a large number of calories, it becomes delectable.

The hotel features a bathtub (the first I've seen in ages), so I luxuriate. Then I have a fitful sleep as I try to send Joanne a telepathic message: "Phone me!" Though I can't phone or text out, she would be able to phone me. Later she says my telepathic message must not have been able to cross the Atlantic Ocean as she did not receive it.

When the mall in Madona opens at ten in the morning, I am eager to get to the Bite phone desk to buy a Latvian SIM card and to fill it with minutes. This delays my departure, so I decide to walk only the 22 kilometres to Cesvaine today. On the way I text Joanne: "You asked about Latvia – women in kerchiefs, lovely woods, road construction." That sums it up.

When I arrive in the tourist town of Cesvaine, I am hopeful as it seems to have several places to stay overnight. Before searching for lodging, I decide to have some lunch, so I stop at the Post Office to ask about the café that is supposed to be next door. I'm told the eatery has gone out of business, but two of the post office customers – Astra and her teen daughter Emma – greet me in English and are pleased to meet a fellow Canadian. Astra says her husband Karl would probably like to have a chat in English for a change and gives me his phone number.

I find another café for some lunch and later visit tourism information in the town's castle for help in locating a bed for the night. They phone a youth hostel as well as someone named Karl who once had a bed and breakfast. I'm all set to go to the youth hostel when Astra phones back to say I can stay at their place. (It's a small town, so it turns out to be the same Karl.)

I enjoy an evening of conversation with these people. Astra graduated from my alma mater, the University of Western Ontario in London, and Karl was brought up on a farm near Abbotsford, British Columbia. They are of Latvian background and were part of Canada's intensive Latvian culture. As children, they attended Latvian language school on Saturdays, Latvian church on Sundays and Latvian festivities throughout the year. The couple chose to return to this land of their roots, and we explore details on the country's history, communist ruthlessness and the Latvian diaspora.

They tell me: "The projects of the European Union are not always those that are the priority for the local people." They feel the people themselves need to rebuild their shattered communities and change their way of doing business. "The mindset of only working 9 to 5 is not helpful when a busload of British tourists arrives ready to spend their money but it's 5:15 so they are sent on their way."

Astra comes in with a delicious deep-dish pizza fresh from the oven. With that and a cup of coffee, the discussion continues. This country was the last in Europe to practice serfdom, and the ownership of farmers by a lord persisted into the 17th century.

The 1939 Treaty of Non-Aggression between the Soviet Union and Germany divided their world in two: Joseph Stalin got the Baltic States and some of Poland; Adolph Hitler got the rest. The communists removed community leaders (mayors, school principals) and sent them to Siberia. Labour unrest was resolved by shooting a representative group of workers; in this horrible way, Karl's grandfather was killed.

Apparently, the Lutheran Church here was not as successful in protecting the people as was the Catholic Church in Poland.

Before I set out the next morning, Karl takes me for a tour of the "castle" (actually a manor) that is the centre of tourism for the town. The building was devastated by fire a dozen years ago and is in a state of constant renovation. The tower's 107 steps lead to a dizzying climb as I clutch the railing and Karl notices: "Is the height bothering you?" I am rewarded for my endurance with views of the distant road to Gulbene and the nest on a nearby chimney. The mother stork and her young pose for a close-up.

On the quiet highway to Gulbene, I mull over what I've heard. I see a mix of older and modern tractors working the fields, signifying hope for the future as farming becomes more cost-effective. A few logging trucks pass as they come from both north and south. They are heading in opposite directions but carry the same kind of wood, and I wonder: "Could they not switch and deliver closer to home?"

Until now the driving schools in all countries have displayed a big white letter "L" with a blue background on the roofs of their cars: this has been visible at a distance. A few countries back, one of these vehicles was bright red with yellow and lime green circles all over it. You could recognize it a kilometre away – I guess that was the idea. Now in Latvia a glass pyramid (like that on a taxi), displaying the letter "M," has become the indicator of a student driver. And so, the little things continue to interest me on this long trek.

I pass an intersection with a carved cross that is twice my height. It holds a corpus not much longer than my hand. The difference in size between the structure and Christ's body seems odd, and I have noticed this representation a few times now. I appreciate the use of natural products: at the ends of laneways are a variety of burls, branches and rocks formed into interesting features or holding a sign with the family name.

Speeds are more moderate than in Poland, where every driver wanted to win the Indianapolis 500 or – since this is Europe – the Grand Prix. Now I have come to another conclusion: the driving culture is newer in Europe than in Canada, so the age of drivers is generally younger. This gives hope that speeds will decrease as people become older and wiser. I can't help but reflect on the tiny effort of drivers to push down on a gas pedal: a child could do that. In comparison, my hiking is a Herculean task.

I estimate that over 100,000 people have now seen me – from cars, in stores, at hostels. I wonder: "What kind of memory does that leave, the fleeting image of a figure walking the roads of Europe?" I think of the contact I've had as I looked for items – the easy to find (contact lens solution, writing booklets, barbershops) and the difficult (disposable cameras, laundromats, sunscreen). I muse over future hikers and their use of a smart phone with GPS: however, without the need to ask for directions, they would miss out on contact with the local people.

A meadow bordered by Queen Anne's lace displays a profusion of mauve, yellow and white flowers against a blue, blue sky. I'm impressed with nature's beauty and stop to take a picture. On a bridge I catch a rehearsal: over the water, darkened by overhanging branches, two insects seem to be preparing for the evening's performance of the Blue Butterfly Ballet.

Gulbene proves to be another of those Latvian centres with a downtown of fat two-storey pastel buildings. A park with water fountain makes this *centrum* feel welcoming and relaxed. The other guest in its hotel is a young man, expert in lasers, who travels throughout the country. It sounds like interesting work, but he adds, "I'm tired of being in a different hotel four nights a week, so I'm looking for another job." I'm intrigued that such fascinating work can come with conditions as dull as staying in a series of hotels.

In one of Gulbene's shops I find a chocolate bar that will be a tasty snack on the way to Alūksne. Dark chocolate is a favourite, and this one contains hazelnuts and quince seeds. As I chew the hazelnut, one of the quince seeds catches between my upper and lower front teeth and a filling pops out.

As with my last trip, this one includes a new irritation that will be followed with a visit to my dentist's office upon my return home.

Approaching Alūksne, I see signs to the Jolanta Hotel and find it at the south end as I enter the town. Although the hotel is adjacent to an industrial park, I discover that it is a wonderful home for the night. A dozen people at three or four tables are having supper when I arrive. The food is tasty, the service friendly and the decorating perfect. Its great windowpanes give the space a sense of the outdoors.

My room is on two levels: a few steps lead up to the bedroom. Besides the standard television set, I am provided with a stereo for relaxed listening. I notice I am the only overnight guest and feel bad. To all travellers: "Latvia is welcoming, its nature is beautiful and its prices are reasonable. Don't count on the European Union to build up this small land that has been kicked around once too often. Take your money and come spend it here. They need you."

Only three times on my European trek – in Signy-L'Abbaye, France; in Buxtehude, Germany; in Rokiškis, Lithuania – have I slept through the night. Sleeping all night long may not be unusual for others; it is for me. Now in Alūksne I awaken even more often than usual since I have to appreciate the night sky. I have gone so far north that the sun sets late and rises early. We had a similar experience living in Iqaluit, Nunavut Territory, but were nearer the Arctic Circle there, so the summer night was even shorter. In Alūksne dusk stretches to midnight, when the sky is finally dark. Then dawn begins at about two in the morning.

Ligo, the celebration of the summer solstice, is held on June 23rd and 24th and involves a lot of drinking, "But only beer," I'm told. A half dozen young people celebrate a night early in the gazebo behind the hotel, and my rest is disrupted by shouts from the courtyard and by my viewing the sky. At three in the morning, I close my window to the noise and resolve to ignore nature's wonders so I can get a few hours of sleep before my day's hike.

My breakfast table is provided with an appliance I have not seen through a number of countries – a toaster. Tomato wedges have been a common breakfast food, and I scrape off the decorative bits of onion to enjoy the tomato on bread sprinkled with sugar, an old family favourite. This morning I'm served white bread, another item I haven't seen in a while. Toasting a few slices, piling them with tomato wedges and sprinkling the package of sugar meant for my coffee, I'm in my glory.

When I begin the day's walk, I pass under a row of oak trees with the sign "Oak Alley," followed by the Latvian and Estonian equivalents. Why the English words come first, I may never know – another mystery as I near Estonia and the end of my journey.

## Estonia

A gravel road directs me north to the highway that crosses the border into Estonia. I make it over the border, text Joanne that I have crossed it and turn to take a picture of the deserted border post. As I resume walking, a camper van comes toward me, and I wave frantically as my trained eye has caught its license plate. "NL" it reads, and Dad's voice rings in my ears, *"Die mo 'k hebbe"* ("That's the one I need"), as I think of a break with Dutch coffee and a chat. I give the hiker's automatic salute of raising my right pole toward them and then wave toward their rearview mirror. As the van veers left on the border plaza to turn back toward me, I hear Dad again, *"Ze doen 't nog ok"* ("They're doing it too").

After I introduce myself, Jos gets out on the passenger side, and she takes a picture of me at both the Latvian and Estonian border signs. I pile in and Jan drives us back to the border plaza out of the way of traffic. With two cups of coffee and a Dutch cookie, I feel refreshed. They come from North Brabant, and we chat about a range of things – my hiking, the Netherlands and Dutch emigration. On this last point, our opinions differ.

I feel that a Dutch immigrant who worked hard was able to make a living in the new country. They are less positive: "We know a man who went to the United States and worked for a dairy farmer. He was at the job from early morning to late evening, and after many years he still had nothing. The priests made promises but didn't help." I do not see this as the role of the priests – to help someone financially. They were there for moral support and to do some networking, helping immigrants to help each other. In any case, we have a good talk that ends with an exchange of e-mail addresses so Jos can send me the pictures (which she does).

Now in Estonia I turn off the highway onto a winding road. In Latvia this would have been a gravel road, but here – in more affluent Estonia – it is paved though little more than a wide bicycle path. Through rounded hills I head for Ruusmäe and my home for the night. The Rogosi Manor is part of an L-shaped complex. It holds the local school, a hall for weddings and a dozen rooms for travellers (each with a heated bathroom floor!).

It reminds me of the Memramcook Resort not far from our home in New Brunswick, though this place has less of an institutional feel. You enter through a dining area displaying artwork, wines and jams – all locally produced – and feel like you're in the middle of the region's culture. The Memramcook people could learn from this. As all Estonians are home celebrating summer solstice with their families, I am alone in enjoying the homemade rhubarb wine and a dessert of cake smothered in berry juice and whipping cream. Then in the early morning hours, someone arrives to cook my breakfast – thick oatmeal on a plate and fried medallions of meat that look like sliced wieners.

During the day's hike, I'm amused that Estonia smells like smoke as it wafts from a wood fire in front of each house. This continues throughout the day and is the summer solstice custom. I'm told, "It is our tradition that people jump through the bonfires." I don't see any jumping, but I do see Estonian blue, black and white flags everywhere as well as drunken young men at a gas station where I stop for directions. I imagine that the drinking and fire jumping don't mix well.

I'm relieved when the young woman in tourism information in Võru provides me with a list of places to stay as I trek through Estonia. She mentions, "They say that our country is the most atheistic in the European Union." It is also one of the most successful economically although I assume that is not related to their lack of church attendance.

The Randuri Guesthouse in Võru provides me with a comfortable home for my two-day break. It is another I would recommend – except for its breakfasts. One day the scrambled eggs have that grey, watery appearance that is so unappetizing. The next day I have bacon and eggs, but I gag on the rind left on the bacon slices. Other than that, full marks for the Randuri Guesthouse.

I have an interesting chat with Chris. He is of Estonian background and grew up in the state of Virginia. He moved to Tallinn, the capital of Estonia, where he has a company that translates documents from Estonian to English. As there is no high-speed service at their summer home just north of Võru, he has made his way to this guest house to use its WiFi network in preparing his income tax documents.

I ask him about his laptop that I take to be a MacBook Air but is in fact the smallest version of the MacBook Pro. He advises: "Anyone looking to buy a Mac should review the Internet discussion about the Air. One concern is that the battery in the Air is not replaceable. If the battery fails, the whole unit needs to be returned." Good information, I think. Thanks, Chris.

I find a library where I can type my blog entry, but the keyboard is even more ornery than usual. To allow for Estonian accents, some keys have up to four functions, and some do not match what they type. The question mark, for example, is found by using the "shift" and "equals" keys. At times I feel as though the typing is more challenging than the walking.

Getting my haircut has been simple: I find a shop somewhere and they cut it. Here two places are fully booked, another only does women's hair and one is closed when I arrive there at 4:00 p.m. It is open on my way out of town the next day, so I drop in. As always, I say I want it short. This woman takes me at my word. She shows me a clipper attachment as they sometimes do to ask if that's how short the sides and back should be cut. However, she zooms the thing right over the top of my head.

By then I'm committed and end up with the summer brush cut of my youth on the farm. With enough Brylcreem my brother Bill could train his hair into the brush effect; mine just lay there. Actually, I like my hair this short for a change. Besides, it doesn't really matter what frames such a handsome face!

For about 50 kilometres, I shall be following the old Postitee (Post Road), the road that was travelled in delivering mail by horse and carriage between Tartu and Võru over several centuries. It comes with displays about former stabling and lodging, as well as a tourist centre and dining area halfway along. I am surprised that much of the information is transferable to Dorchester, New Brunswick since my home village served as a stopping point for mail delivered by stagecoach in the 1800's.

I note a stork's nest high on a pole: the chicks are left alone while the parents are out for groceries. Then I pass fields of potatoes, wheat, barley and sugar beets, each of which is hundreds of acres in area.

I am suspicious of the grass crop I described earlier and saunter down to a field near the road. This sure looks like quack grass, also known as twitch grass. I have heard that this crop is a source of bio-fuel but hadn't thought half the arable land would be growing this stuff. It's also a source for my next anti-automobile rant since it looks as though we are feeding cars instead of people. This stuff should be grown in an area where farming is on the decline and the soil is not rich – some non-productive areas of New Brunswick, for example. But the crops in this vibrant countryside should feed people, not cars.

Thunder leads to rain, and I get soaked. I dig through my knapsack for the information on my home for the night and can't find it anywhere. (Later I locate it among pamphlets I planned to review. It's surprising how you can lose things in a backpack.) I know that the bed and breakfast, or whatever, is just beyond a village in the distance. The tourism woman in Võru phoned there to arrange my night's stay, and now I'm desperate to know where that lodging is located. I'm hopeful for an answer as I walk through the village, but there is no one to ask: everyone is inside because of the rain.

I wave down a van coming out of a side road. The man driving and the two women passengers do not speak English but motion for me to get in. With rain streaming down my face, I try to explain that I'm looking for the place I have to stay and that I have lost my piece of paper. They convince me to get in, and I think this feels a bit like being kidnapped. We turn right onto the main road, then right again into a lane through woods that open to reveal a set of houses.

Two young men greet us at the door, and they speak a smattering of English. I ask them to contact their neighbour who has the bed and breakfast where I am to stay for the night. They reply: "This is the place you're staying. The tourism woman phoned our father, and he drove you here." Meeting their father as he drove up was a coincidence that's hard to explain but leads to a pleasant sleep and a great breakfast at the "Mesikamäe B and B." On my way out the door in the morning – now dry and refreshed – I am told to turn left at a fork in the laneway as that takes me back to the point where they picked me up. They understand walking every step through Europe.

In some areas 90% of barn and house roofs are corrugated asbestos sheeting. There must have been a sale on this material and on white bricks during communist times. Some of the barns have walls of an adobe material covered in boards. Should the boards deteriorate, the whole structure begins to collapse as the adobe cannot withstand the ravages of weather. I appreciate the tidiness of the firewood beside many homes: it is thinly sliced and neatly piled in cribs out of the rain.

Again, I endure a day with buckets of rain, this time with both thunder and lightning. I find a bus shelter, wait for a lull in traffic and change to a dry shirt. Hundreds of cars can go by when there's a pause with no vehicles for a minute or so. Then I think the Middle East has run out of oil, but suddenly they start right up again.

While I'm eager for this downpour to settle, I think of the series of bus shelters I have passed on this trip. With few trains in eastern Europe, buses are the means of mass transit. Each community is served, and many of them provide a haven for passengers to wait out of the elements.

Away from the built-up areas, there is no standard design and that makes bus shelters all the more interesting. Some are made of stuccoed concrete blocks; others are of brick. A structure in Lithuania looked like a giant's chair made of logs. Some are decorated with painted flowers in bright colours; others are provided with only a garbage container. A number of them have seen vandalism and graffiti. Bus shelters of all types have provided me with breaks out of the sun and rain. They would make a great book of photos.

As I trudge through sheets of rain, an Armenian restaurant appears, and I order soup and a meal. "But it has to be hot," I say, and the waitress smiles. Then I disappear into the bathroom to change my socks. You know your boots are wet when you empty them in the bathroom sink and you hear the water gurgling down the drain.

This brings me to the university city of Tartu and a chance to buy an Estonian card for my phone. Since purchasing the phone in Amsterdam, I've been told several times that SIM cards can be used in adjacent countries. No matter what they say, each country needs its own card. Meanwhile, my cellphone is fast becoming part of the story.

In Tartu I hike through smartly dressed groups attending a function in one of the greystone university buildings. Well into a residential area, I reach the hostel, but – in a touch of Robert Louis Stevenson's "Kidnapped" – from an upstairs window, a scowling man with a droning voice tells me: "There's no room for you. We're full."

I hike back to the downtown area of fancy hotels, and I'm relieved when the second one I try has a vacancy. The room comes with a hair dryer for my soggy boots and a fan to dry my laundry by morning. An outdoor concert of local singing groups is taking place in the courtyard of a neighbouring hotel where I order a glass of red wine and soon get bored with covers of old American tunes of the "If I Had a Hammer" variety.

From old East Germany to Latvia had been a gradual shift: there were small differences, but the regions continued to have a lot in common. I'm astonished at the extent to which Estonia is different. Cars are newer and bigger here, and those that break down are taken to a garage by tow truck. In the previous countries, disabled cars were pulled at the end of a rope as they sped down the highway.

Poland's breakfast salads have been left behind; now I see oatmeal porridge, cottage cheese and short wieners, as well as square white slices of bread for toasting. Having tasted drinking water in thousands of communities, I've become a connoisseur, and here I notice a hint of sulphur.

Considering the quality landscaping and home renovations in the countryside, the city of Tartu looks shoddy. For heritage reasons the wooden buildings must be saved, but I feel as though I want to pitch in on reattaching trim and painting faded siding.

The distances I hike require fuel, and I consume my fair share of food. The Aleksandri Hotel displays an extensive breakfast, and I take full advantage of it. I have a glass of orange juice, a glass of berry juice, two cups of coffee, oatmeal drizzled with honey, a boiled egg, cottage cheese, a few pieces of herring, a sausage, two meatballs, three slices of cheese, a slice of ham, three slices of sausage meat, two slices of brown bread, two slices of white bread (toasted, with tomato and sugar!) and yoghurt. A 40-kilometre hike burns this up quickly. A sign reads 175 kilometres to Narva and tells me it is possible. I just might finish this thing. However, excitement over nearing the end will use up the energy I need for walking. I have to stay in control. The whole journey has been one of staying in control – talking myself into starting out in Portugal; reacting to being assaulted; continuing for thousands of kilometres; scribbling notes in my booklets; dealing with people, beds, water, food, cultures, languages and dogs. I've had to be in charge of my little world, to stay on top of things and to persevere. But I'll tell you: "On the flight home, the pressure will be off, and I'll be the giddiest person on the plane!"

On my first day in Estonia, I heard a few distant barks and had been hopeful. I am proven wrong when a dog barks once every 10 seconds or so till I'm a kilometre into the distance. I don't understand how the owners can handle the noise. Then a St. Bernard type with black jowls follows me. Later a black dog with evil eyes sneaks up and yelps at my heels giving me a start. There may be fewer dogs here than elsewhere, but they seem noisier and freer to roam.

In the tourist town of Alatskivi, I stop at a restaurant for a cup of coffee and directions to a nearby guest house. The waitress takes me to a window by the kitchen and points to a red roof among a far group of houses: "That's the place you're looking for." I become disoriented in having to take several turns in leaving the restaurant, and I can't find the red roof anywhere. I walk back and forth among the collection of houses, but it has disappeared behind a building. I go back into the restaurant, find the same window and line up the red roof with my compass. Outside once again, I finally find my way to my home for the night. The smallest things can be the most frustrating.

At this bed and breakfast, I enjoy a chat with two couples on a bike tour of the area. They speak Swiss German, but one is originally from the Netherlands, her husband is from the Italian-speaking part of Switzerland, the other man is from the Romansh-speaking section of Switzerland and his wife is from Germany. Talk about a United Nations of languages and backgrounds!

At four in the morning, I grab my phone to see what time it is. As I push a button, the phone dances and sings in my hand with six text messages from Joanne. I have not been able to send messages and guessed that dampness was the problem. Suddenly the system becomes unplugged, and I'm happy to be back in business.

Nature again provides me with panorama and music. Purple wildflowers with four yellow flowerets growing from their stems delight me. Above them white birch trees reach arms heavenward and a silver willow sparkles in the breeze. Hidden in a hayfield, an animal sounds like the winding of an alarm clock, and I assume it's a cricket.

A friend of mine in Sackville has mentioned that you should never trust a green country: it means a lot of rain. This is true of Estonia. I was told it seems to rain at every summer solstice, and I thought, "It's no wonder: it always rains here!" One fifth of the country consists of marshes and bogs, and I pass an area with trees knee-deep in water. I tell them: "I know how that feels. It's not pleasant."

A bit further along, a dozen cars are parked beside an overgrown field, and gleaners are picking something from the ground. Then a man comes out of the field with a little pail of wild strawberries and gives me a few. They are as refreshing as those we would find in the roadside ditch on the way home from school so many years ago. Later I pass people selling pickles – your choice of fresh or in brine – and using weigh scales to ensure a fair deal.

Then a tour bus passes: it is one of many I have seen over the course of my journey. I imagine that the tour guide at the microphone might be telling this vehicle full of visitors: "Here we have a hiker with knapsack. This is a beautiful country for such long overnight ventures." (In fact, I am still all alone in my hiking.)

I come to Peipsi järv (Lake Peipus, in English), and for 80 kilometres I'll follow the road running near its edge. I climb a gate to go down to the shore; the water feels warm and looks a bright blue.

In the last few kilometres before the town of Mustvee, many houses look poorly managed and have cast-off items in their yards. This changes as I enter the town itself, which appears well tended. I stay in a tidy house advertised as a hostel. The couple who own the place live next door with their aging mother, and I assume the hostel was their former home. I'm alone for the night and take this quiet time to list the distance to remaining towns as I head to the coast. It's getting close now.

My education in Europe has included lessons on how to make a hostel bed. There are dozens of varieties of bedding linen. In this hostel the cover for the duvet comes with a slit in each of the four corners. You insert the duvet through a short open seam and hold its four corners to straighten it within its case. This is neat and is another of the design items that will make me rich – the others being improvements in backpacks and showers. With all my experiences, I can't help but become an expert.

The woman who owns this hostel says, "I'm Estonian, but my husband is Russian," and I see a great deal of Russian influence here. From this neighbourhood I take a path that crosses a short suspension bridge over a stream and arrive in the commercial area for supplies. On some store signs, the Cyrillic alphabet takes precedence over the Roman. It must be a continuous balance between the two nations – the huge and the tiny – as their shared history has been a troubled one. I wonder whether Russia has offered to help remove the old abandoned structures built during Communist times.

I see a parallel between Christianity and Communism in the way both began with fervent ideals to help people. They followed a prescribed text – the Christian Scriptures (New Testament) and the Communist Manifesto. They centralized power among male figures. They built the haunted churches of

Southern France and the haunted apartment complexes of the Baltics. I wonder if the building zeal could have been controlled had authority been shared with women. I question whether the initial ideals could not have been implemented without the systems that weigh them down. I'm a "child of the '60's" and need to ask these things.

By six o'clock on this Saturday morning, a neighbour is using a power mower, and I think: "Oh, that happens here too!" I munch on the breakfast items I bought the previous evening and go on my way with the sound of surf drifting through the trees. Cars with boats on trailers speed by. Fishing and camping areas are advertised. With all this tourist activity, I'm surprised at the small number of restaurants – these can be 20 kilometres apart. Roadside stands sell *suitsukala* (smoked sprat), and the black smoking stoves billow as they are fed old hay. Customers also stop for fresh fish that are gutted while they wait. I buy three dried *meritint* (smelt): they are chewy and no McDonald's.

I recognize a change in my behaviour: on this island of isolation, I'm beginning to talk to myself out loud. I address my equipment as to where it should go in my backpack. I talk to a car that comes up from behind and passes another car right next to me: "You sneak! You thought I wouldn't notice, but I did, and you're being counted too." Sometimes I feel as though I'm walking on a rotating ball instead of a horizontal surface. Yes, it's time to finish, but I should be okay as long as I stay aware and avoid danger.

This walk has been all about time and distance. Having to hike 20 kilometres is impossible; knowing it takes about four hours makes it feasible. Checking my watch to see how far I've gone has become automatic. The journey has also been about obstacles and overcoming them. As long as I can do that, I'll succeed. But, leaving philosophy aside, the walk has been all about food and showers.

On the first leg of this journey, I started in Portugal as a retired nurse manager; now I'm arriving in Estonia's northeast as a writer. Actually, the story is busy writing itself as it opens up to me. I just need to arrange the words, to pick parts and make them interesting. Then, as a set of experiences appears on the page, I am freed to leave it behind and go on to a fresh one. I'd like a boring few days to relax in writing my notes. Instead, typing the blog entry from those notes continues to be a challenge – so much to say in so few words. The story is a tough taskmaster.

Making my way around Lake Peipus, I feel like an intruder as I pass through a swarm of translucent moths. Between the trees I see simple cottages and elaborate houses, but no place for me to call my home for the night. A sign to a campground looks promising until I'm told all it's A-frame cabins are taken: now, at the end of June, the summer vacation period is well under way. While reviewing my options, I have a meal at their bar. This is not a family campground: it has music blaring over loudspeakers and people hanging over bottles of beer. No vacancy is perhaps to my benefit. Someone mentions a hotel in Alajõe; though 10 kilometres out of my way, I aim for it.

Villa Marika is not a posh hotel but a family hostel with shared rooms, lots of socializing and the message to relax. I am overwhelmed by a heartfelt greeting from the owner, Taavi Vogt, and he is overwhelmed by my tale: "You don't have to pay for anything. What do you need? Some supper? A drink?" Over a bowl of white beetroot soup and a full glass of red wine, I tell Taavi and his teen daughter the story of my journey. His wife, who speaks no English, works quietly in the background while I keep wishing she could join in.

Taavi has overcome serious injury incurred during the struggle for Estonian independence. Now he is trying to find meaning in life from the writings of Mahatma Gandhi. His daughter tells me: "I find your story inspiring."

And I ask: "Where did you learn your English?"

"I watched a lot of Saturday morning cartoons on TV." And so, Europe's use of languages and its cultural complexities continue to astound me.

EUROPE, ONE STEP AT A TIME

A photo of Taavi and me is taken in front of their building, and I am to send them a note for their Web site when I get home. (I send it but don't see it on the site.) After a 44-kilometre day, I go to bed tired but fulfilled. In my note booklet, I write: "Another hostel – less luxury, more fun."

Taavi had promised a great breakfast the next morning, and I had understood he would be up to wish me well in my wanderings, but he doesn't make an appearance. Early on this quiet Sunday, his staff provide something to eat, and I walk away from Lake Peipus and back into farm country.

I muse over my status as a hiker. I have to continue to be careful: a twisted ankle would be as devastating now as at anytime on the journey. I can't afford to be self-satisfied despite a creeping sense of accomplishment. This, in turn, is kept in check by my backpack. It should feel lighter as I become stronger; in fact, it feels heavier now than anywhere else on the journey.

Once again I tell myself the old joke about my Portuguese starting point, "I think I forgot something in Cabo de São Vicente, and I'd better go back to get it," and it's still not funny. I muse over my blog entries and the need to edit, check and correct details when I get home. These will become a book, and I play with possible titles, like "Looking for Europe, Finding Myself," which I then reject as I continue on past farms of grain crops and beef cattle.

Stopping at an Olerex service station for a coffee, I am given a card that will entitle me to a fifth coffee for free. I don't ever get beyond this one cup of coffee at that chain of stations, so the card joins my hospital information in Portugal and my name in Lithuania's library system as footprints of my travels.

A young man is gassing up his car and tells me, "I saw you hiking yesterday." I've enjoyed the few times this has happened: it makes the walk more real. He knows the area well and advises me that the hotel I am headed for in Mäetaguse is probably my best bet. I have wondered about aiming for a hikers' lodging in the woods that would take me farther and shorten the following day's walk. But he says the building is hard to find in the forested area and will not save me any time. I appreciate his grasp of these details; he is knowledgeable about hiking.

Then he continues with a suggestion that makes me realize he has not hiked across Europe. He mentions: "You'll soon be passing a fire tower. You should climb it so you can see the whole area from up there." What's wrong with this idea? The structure is a kilometre off the road; it means climbing 200 steps; it has height – height is not my friend. I let the tower slide by in the distance.

A few kilometres further, I stop at a bar for some lunch. As this is a bar, there is only one employee. You place your order at the counter and take your dirty dishes to a shelf by the kitchen. If it were a restaurant, the waitress would take the order at your table and remove the dishes. Bars and restaurants look alike, so you need to check the sign on the building to know what service is provided and how to do your part.

That night's bed is located in a historical mansion in Mäetaguse that has become the Meintack Manor Hotel, complete with spa, and my spirits are lifted. I soak up renewal in the lap pool and whirlpools and then find the broccoli with blue cheese soup and wild boar entrée delicious. My map indicates only 90 kilometres left to go, and I am comfortable with my progress: I should be able to get to my destination at Narva-Jõesuu before my scheduled return home. Then shouts from several hotel rooms remind me that this time of year in Europe is still all about soccer.

During my hike through Estonia, it rains once per day; that usually occurs during the nighttime, but it starts again now at midday. A field of cut hay looks soaked and needs to dry before it can be stored for winter so it doesn't mould, and I recognize the challenge of the weather in the livelihood of farmers. In comparison, mine is just a game.

In a woodsy area, the bugs zigzag around my face, find their way into my ears and bite me mercilessly. Another of Estonia's roadside parks has become a garbage dump with bags of household waste. To my dismay, I have to announce that this country wins my award for the messiest woods.

My 42-kilometre walk gets lengthened by an hour (five kilometres) because of overpass construction in the town of Jõhvi. Cars are directed in one lane over the bridge, but pedestrians are sent around it and through side streets till I'm lost. I stop at a car dealership – of all places – for directions. I'm told, "At the next corner, you'll need to turn left to join the road to Sillamäe," so I need to go northwestward to reach the highway that will take me northeastward to Sillamäe. There I am, going west when I need to be going east. Sometimes this hike makes no sense.

In Sillamäe I arrive at a series of fat pastel buildings that date from Joseph Stalin's time. One of these has become the Hotel Krunk and is a mix of old building style with new décor and cuisine. As I step out of the shower, my feet cling to the towel on the floor. So, I briskly lift my left foot, then my right, bashing my knee on the corner of the metal door jamb. I think: "Is this how it ends – breaking my kneecap on a doorframe?" And I think of American astronaut John Glenn spinning around Earth in a space capsule only to suffer a concussion when he falls in a bathtub. I check my knees: they seem symmetrical. A slight indentation and some pain, but I should be okay. Phew!

I'm beginning to feel a sense of loss. This project has been so absorbing over six years, it has become part of who I am. Perhaps I'll need to follow it with new challenges.

So close to the end of my journey, I'm surprised that a hotel breakfast is scheduled for 6:00 a.m. That's perfect: it will let me reach Narva in time to visit the tourist information office for a map directing me toward Narva-Jõesuu, the seaside resort that is the end point of my hike. The tourism people can also provide details on bus routes to Tallinn, the capital of Estonia and location of the airport through which I'll return home.

I see my first wind turbines since Poland. I wonder about three-metre-high hills with metal doors in concrete entrances. They appear in farm fields along the road, and I question what they would be storing – perhaps root vegetables. I see a driver stopped by the police – that's been twice in Estonia and not once in the previous three countries. And, as a reminder not to do this again, I have a new blister.

In Narva a billboard advertises the café in a casino, so I stop for lunch. Not being "signed in," I can't eat there after all, and I make my way through an elaborate buffet in the adjacent mall. I am hopeful in looking for shoes to wear in place of my worn hiking boots, but – to my surprise – my size is not available.

The Hotel Narva has few vacant rooms thanks to a seniors' bus tour and a horde of employees from a major construction project. The receptionist manages to find room for me in the crowd, and I spend a pleasant two days at the final lodging of my hiking journey. Near the hotel is the official-looking border crossing into Russia. It appears intimidating, and I'm glad to be staying on this side of it.

In the hotel's dining area, the TV soap opera and the piped-in radio music are at equal volume. I have no idea why they do that. I've asked; no one can tell me. Then a radio song sneaks by the television noise, and I find myself enthralled by a tune I have heard over and over during this trip. It's a catchy melody – an earnest tale of youth and love – and I discover later that it's the American band "Fun" singing the hit "We Are Young." With its frequent radio play, the song has become another companion on this trip.

On the way back to my room, I insert two Euros in the hotel's massaging chair to help me relax. That's as close to ritual as I can get – a ritual that verifies it's almost over. It's difficult to celebrate alone.

I look forward to sitting at home in the sunroom with stimulation from surroundings that I understand, in which I feel comfortable. I don't want to be a senior taking bus tours. So, what can I do next? At this point I'm not excited about finishing; I'm just tired. Finally, I'm free to understand what I've done and to let it affect me, but it continues to be a mystery. Ultimately, it's been only one human body moving through space and time.

While I'm philosophizing and writing a few notes, I hear cars gather on the paved area behind the hotel. Young men are gunning their engines and doing "doughnuts." I get out the last of my package of crackers and sit in the windowsill munching, watching and musing: "If I had been part of such a group, how would that have changed my life? Instead, I liked quiet. I enjoyed being alone. I walked across Europe."

**Narva-Jõesuu**

The next day, July 4, 2012, is the one I've anticipated over the 6,000 kilometres. I leave my knapsack in the hotel to hike the 15 kilometres to my end point of Narva-Jõesuu, the most northeasterly point in Estonia and in the European Union. The journey ends the way it began when I hiked from Cabo de São Vicente to Sagres, Portugal without my backpack. From behind me a car passes another, coming within inches of my elbow. That's car number 73 to have done so on my journey and, hopefully, the last.

I'm excited about arriving in Narva-Jõesuu, a beach town of cottages and hotels. My compass leads me to the most northeasterly spot on the beach. Here the Narva River meets the Gulf of Finland; a few hundred metres away – on the opposing sandy shore with its backdrop of woods – lies Russia.

I pass children playing, adults sunbathing and a few people fishing as I near a set of rocks that are my finish line. No one is there to take my picture, so I take a few shots of my face (a disposable-camera selfie!), my boots and the point of land. To get to the northeasternmost tip, I step onto one rock after the other and unto a final partially submerged one.

Three things: I may have been over-enthusiastic; walking 15 kilometres can make you less coordinated; rocks are slippery when wet. Whatever the reason, I slide of the rock and splash into the water. Both boots fill with seawater, but my camera stays dry, so no harm is done. This marks the other end of the journey that began with dipping my feet into the Atlantic

Ocean at Cabo de São Vicente five years ago. It also serves as the exclamation point at the end of my journey and a reminder to stay home and keep my feet dry.

A man is leading his family along the beach and agrees to take my picture. I think: "I'm here. Now what?" With my dislike of team sports, I didn't learn what athletic success or acclamation felt like. It was not part of my past, but now I feel successful. I can appreciate myself and be admired by others. On this journey people have connected with my sociable side and identified with the adventure I represent.

I muse on the extent to which I have now become my late brother Bill: I am no longer the defensive dreamer; I have become the active athlete. My childhood ramblings have now brought results. I can ramble through Europe and ramble in my blog entries. And it's all okay since, without a story, the hike does not exist.

Starting in southeast Portugal, I developed as a walker, from initial ignorance to increasing knowledge and adaptation. My need to hike changed from having to get started, to having to keep going, to having to be finished. I realize the joy of completing the journey is slow to set in and may not arrive till I see my family at Moncton Airport. I'm excited to text Joanne that I have reached my end point after 6,000 kilometres. She writes: "Here is an electronic hug for you!!!!!" And so, it ends.

I have finally reached the point of not having to walk another step, so I'm happy to catch the bus back to the hotel in Narva. But, mainly, I'm happy that I do not have to plan anymore. My drive to do things right is double-edged: it leads to great accomplishments but at the price of constant doubts. Now I can return to a more routine life with fewer uncertainties. Now there will be no more counting kilometres, no more getting drenched in the rain, no more tending to blisters, no more handwashing my clothing, no more learning how things are done in all those countries, no more SIM cards, no more foreign money, no more finding beds or water or food. I'll miss it.

**Return**

The next day I take the bus 200 kilometres to Tallinn to catch the flight home through Frankfurt. From the bus windows, I can see farther but in less detail and with nature's sounds turned off. I am more tired watching the roadside pass so quickly than I felt when I was tackling it. And I have a twinge of grief for the loss of my walking days.

The bus arrives at the Tallinn depot, which is under renovation, and I walk to the nearby hostel, which is also under renovation. In my notebook I am disappointed: "No services at all at hostel. It might as well be a hotel!" A French family of husband and wife, daughter and father are enthusiastic about my walk, but mostly about my being Canadian. The elderly man worked for the French railway and took a train trip from Toronto to Vancouver at some point. He keeps following me to hear more about Canada as his family heads in the other direction and then comes back to round him up.

I enjoy sharing a room and trying to communicate with a pleasant young man from Russia who speaks no English (and my Russian is non-existent). In the middle of the night, another Russian man arrives in our room. Hostels need to be welcoming and adaptable, but the late arrivals are annoying – not so much for us, we just go back to sleep, but for the people arriving. In the dark they need to find their way, make the bed and arrange their belongings while trying to stay quiet. By then we are all fully awake, and the new arrival enters the land of slumber before the rest of us can find our way back there.

Tallinn is another city of crumbling doorsills and gleaming malls: the old looks so old, the new looks so new. The architecture and arcades of Tallinn's old town "Vanalinn" prove to be worth a visit – as is Vana Tallinn, the Estonian liqueur and a new favourite. I delight in an hour or two of gawking at old buildings, quaint shops and tourist activity, as well as a lunch of wild boar at an outdoor café.

I stop to buy Joanne a salmon-coloured scarf as a souvenir, and the shop owner gives me a final history lesson on Estonia. I ask about the state of disrepair of some buildings, and she explains that during communist times the buildings were taken from their owners. They were returned to them after the break-up of the Soviet Union, "But these people are poor and have no money to fix up their homes." She adds that over the years Russian people have moved into Estonia so that 50% of the country's population is now Russian. I sense a longing for the old days, but which old days?

The next morning I walk the 40 minutes to the airport at the edge of town. The plane ride gives me another view of the Baltic terrain. Now I am at the top of the travel hierarchy but cheated out of contact with the earth below.

We circle Germany's Frankfurt Airport waiting to land as its radar-computer system had been out of order for two and a half hours. This leads to thousands of people being stranded overnight as flights are rescheduled. My night in Frankfurt was planned so I could catch the next morning's flight to Montreal and then home to Moncton. But now I become part of this anthill of stranded passengers.

On Spain's Camino I had been an impostor – not a real pilgrim going to Santiago de Compostela but a long-distance walker using the services of the Camino for selfish reasons. Now I'm an intruder once again as I'm not really stranded, and the Star Alliance people even provide me with a "Male Overnight Kit" of t-shirt and toiletries. A van takes us to Frankfurt's Holiday Inn Airport North, which provides the final bed of my journey. I find a lawn chair on the patio and watch planes fly over and trains shuffle by as I enjoy a final glass of red wine.

The next morning my phone still shows Estonian time, so I'm up an hour early, at five o'clock, to take a healing bath and walk the trails that surround the hotel's park-like setting. The airport shuttle delivers us back to Frankfurt Airport where the standing and sitting make my calves cramp and tell me they want to go back to hiking.

As we cross the Atlantic, I think: "I did it. No one on this plane knows I did it. I'll have really done it when I see my family at Moncton Airport." I look back on those 2,300 kilometres through Germany, Poland and the Baltic countries, and I shudder. Did this really happen? What does it mean to me now? And I muse on the thousands of experiences in the trek I have just completed.

Overnight facilities were farther apart than on previous trips, but hotel receptionists continued to be helpful in finding distant lodging. I puzzled over my regional maps to decrease the length of hikes to those faraway cities: "If I angle over to that city today will that allow for a shorter walk tomorrow?" My ballpoint pen became a measuring device, and I learned how many kilometres I'd have to walk from nib to clip. I would lay it across the next day's route and know exactly how far I'd need to go.

A tough part of the trek were the surprises – long construction detours, short bicycle paths and sudden rainstorms. If I could have predicted how each day would go, it might have caused less anxiety, or it might have convinced me to stop the madness right then and there. My ignorance let me continue to the end.

Though I found high bridges overwhelming, low ones continued to comfort me. Way back in Portugal, I would look down from a bridge and see a dried creek bed. Here in northeastern Europe, the water was plentiful. I would cross the road to compare the slow-moving upstream side with the turbulent downstream side. The gurgling and sparkling delighted me.

It was remarkable how many people I would see limping or using canes or crutches. I felt fortunate simply to walk; others had such difficulty. Did these people stand out because I was so mobile? We would look at each other knowingly till we both realized my situation was quite different from theirs.

The length and intensity of this hike taught me about leg muscle memory. I became more adept at walking and less secure in climbing stairs. The walking was automatic, the climbing awkward. Even standing still to admire a scene required effort.

A road might become a major highway where walking was prohibited. Then I would hike through the woods beside that stretch, thinking the police wouldn't mind my treading so far from the travelled portion. I wasn't concerned that they might put me in jail; that was hardly likely. However, they might drive me back to the last built-up area and suggest I take a smaller road, which could mean an extra day's walk. Luckily, this didn't happen: the police likely had more serious issues to handle.

I was often confused by arrows indicating a hotel or restaurant. A sign might give the name of a restaurant, a distance of 500 metres and an arrow to the right. The arrow could indicate that the business was up ahead on the right or that it was on a nearby side street to the right. The European Union is all about standards. They could have standardized this signage and saved me some needless trudging.

People in service industries were eager to break through the language barrier. In a store I might ask the clerks: "Do you speak English?"

Then I would receive one of two replies: "One moment," meant they would find someone to serve me; "Of course," meant they would help me. The exchange – Do you speak English? Of course – sounded odd till I realized their response was a shortcut to saying, "Of course, I am interested in helping you in the English language." I appreciated their success with a tongue they had learned at school and through the media.

I was surprised at how a word was impossible to understand when I placed the accent on the wrong syllable. If I asked the way to a hotel, people would give me puzzled looks. Then I would stress the first syllable when repeating, "Hotel," and they would understand.

Restaurants and stores seemed to have a shortage of change. If I paid for a 7 Lt item with a 20 Lt bill, for example, the clerk would be peering into my wallet to see if I didn't have a 10 Lt bill. If I followed their wishes, I could use up all my small bills and be left to pay for a small item with a 100 Lt bill. In comparison to our Canadian freedom with change, this was hard to understand and became annoying.

Older people were more likely farmers or blue-collar workers while employees in service industries were well under middle age. These young people were often the children of the hotel or restaurant owners. In some cases, this worked well; in others, I found the service lacking. It would seem easier to tell a stranger what you want done than to tell your own children.

For all the members of visible minorities in France, Belgium and the Netherlands, I saw few as I went from eastern Germany through to northeast Estonia. Roaring economies need foreign workers to provide additional labour, particularly those jobs local people prefer not to do. Beyond Hamburg there were struggling economies and local labour willing to provide menial service. This seemed to make those areas less attractive to immigrants.

In each country, I watched for the word, "store" as it appeared in large letters on its façade – the Polish *sklep*, Lithuanian *parduotuvė*, Latvian *veikals* and Estonian *pood*. I am grateful to these variety stores for meeting many of my needs, including lunch foods, drinks and SIM cards. I am also thankful to the people who helped me top up my phone minutes in the various languages.

Public buildings did not follow our strict codes. Adults and children entered the Narva public library up a set of steps to a platform that was one and a half metres off the ground, yet was lacking a railing. Such dangerous construction shortcomings were a constant distraction. Even the sparkling Saturn electronics store in Hamburg had each of its displays raised off the floor with angled boards. I saw several people trip over these planks while searching for a new TV or computer. In my vigilance against injury, I felt like a herd of gazelles living next to a pride of lions. I sensed every change in my environment.

I leave daydreams behind as we start our descent toward Montreal airport. Again I need to face the irritations that come with air travel. The mechanism for removing our bags from the plane isn't working, and I wait for my backpack to appear so I can take it through customs. An hour later our things arrive on the conveyor system, and I am on my way.

Despite stormy conditions, our flight arrives at Moncton Airport 10 minutes early while Joanne and family members sit chatting in the airport café. They suddenly realize the plane has landed while I see no sign of them. They rush in and set up my end point with a "Welcome Home, Opa" notice, checkered flags and balloons. I walk through a streamer as my finish line to complete my hike in the Moncton Airport arrivals lounge. The moment is perfect. It's good to be home!

# Home

The people of Europe assumed I was from a modern, urban area of Canada with everything at my disposal. On the contrary, at the end of the journey, our two cars are a 6-year-old and a 13-year-old Jetta. (I was excited to see a twin to our 13-year-old in Poland – the same model and colour – like a touch of home.) We don't have broadband Internet coverage and our two small television sets date from the 1980's. We live on a gravel road, have few neighbours and enjoy an ocean view. But we are only 40 minutes from Moncton International Airport through which I returned home with a heart full of memories after each European adventure.

After reaching my goal in northeast Estonia, I settled back into retirement in Dorchester Cape. I took the time to reflect on my trek – starting in Portugal and continuing across Europe to Estonia – and was amazed at the variety of experiences.

Language was a challenge, particularly during the first and last parts of the walk. My French and Dutch were manageable. Portuguese, Spanish, German, Polish and the Baltic languages were foreign to me. With many people so hard to understand, I appreciated the story of the Tower of Babel in the Hebrew Scriptures (Old Testament). The story goes that construction of that monument stopped: its builders understood each other less and less as it rose higher and higher. Problems in communicating made my hike much more complex, and people kindly helped out by writing the numerals

357

to do with time or money on a scrap of paper when I couldn't understand the spoken words.

I was surprised at how everyday words differed, even within language families. As I crossed from Portugal through to Estonia, "Thank you" became *obrigado, gracias, merci, bedankt, vielen dank, dziękujemy, ačiū, paldies* and *aitäh*. And that was only one expression. Imagine tackling thousands of words in nine languages.

Late in the journey, I realized that sporting a sign "Portugal to Estonia" might have helped people connect with my project. Of course, I would have had to change the words as I went through the nine language communities. The word for Estonia would become Estônia, Estonia, Estonie, Estland (in Dutch), Estland (in German), Estonia, Estija, Igaunija and Eesti. In the Netherlands and Germany, I had learned to say I was headed for Estland. Then at the first hostel in Poland, a staff member corrected me: suddenly the word had gone from Estland to Estonia. And in Estonia itself it was Eesti – different again from the other languages. It was all quite confusing.

People were sometimes disappointed with my inability to speak their language. I wished I were fluent, but spending only a week in a small country like Latvia made that unlikely. On the other hand, they had a great deal of exposure to English media – radio songs and television programs – providing a continuous lesson. Some of the residents might tell me, "We should have less English and more of our own language," but they seemed to enjoy the influence of English in their lives.

I am dismayed with my lack of exposure to foreign culture, other than the architecture of public buildings. The soul of a people lives in its language, art and music. The subtleties of language were usually beyond my grasp. I saw some local art, but it was often limited to great works in great museums.

That leaves music, the cultural expression that should be everywhere. Instead, I was over-exposed to American pop. Only rarely did I hear local music. It is available for tourists to seek out – flamenco dancers in Madrid nightclubs, lounge singers in Paris cafés or classical music in Riga concert halls. I was not a tourist but a wanderer. In my wanderings I encountered little in the way of local culture.

Travelling through Europe, I must have been a spectacle. I walked long distances, wore hiking boots, sported a backpack, struggled with local languages and hailed from Canada where I had worked as a nurse in a prison, of all things. The size of my home country left people dazzled: they couldn't fathom the fact that Paris is 1000 kilometres closer to Moncton than is Vancouver.

Besides, I couldn't be considered a real Canadian as I was born in the Netherlands. Everything about me was odd, including the fact that I came from New Brunswick. No one had heard of our province or the city of Moncton let alone the hamlet of Dorchester Cape. Perhaps, I should have said I was from Toronto. That was a word people understood.

My arrival in a restaurant was often greeted by annoyance on the part of the staff: "Don't sit at those tables" or "No English menu here" or "I'm busy right now." Once they realized I was trying to fit in, they became more gracious. The exception – the place practicing consistent hospitality – was McDonald's. Their staff was trained to put the customer first, making it my retreat.

When you finish your main course at a Canadian restaurant, the waiter might ask if you would like dessert. This was not the case overseas. The decision on dessert needed to be made when ordering the meal and not later. It seemed that the kitchen staff set the rules.

The walls between local people and me broke down quickly. I practiced skills as a "good traveller" in not keeping staff from their jobs while giving them a bit of information on my project. I was comfortable with my interactions as an unusual customer – interactions that were brief and relaxed. I was often handed off to an English-speaking employee, but others would soon be milling around fascinated by my tale.

"Did you feel threatened by wild animals," someone asked. It didn't occur to me to be afraid of wild boars or foxes, though dogs were another story. In the Netherlands I had heard the comment that it must be a nuisance for Canadians to keep clapping when they go into the woods. Apparently, it's commonly thought that's what we do to keep the bears away. There are lots of stories about Canada over there.

Rarely were people unpleasant, though this did occur when I arrived in the village of Sejny and searched for the Skarpa Hotel. A man was walking his dog and said, "I'll take you there," but he became overly familiar, stroking my hand while expressing a great love for Canadians. I felt uncomfortable and escaped by stopping to buy supplies in a nearby store.

And so, this man joined my list of half a dozen unsavoury people since the assault in Portugal. Twice men were pushy in demanding I have a drink with them instead of giving me the directions I had requested. As related in this narrative, at two campgrounds in southern France, campers spoke aggressively: one group jeered me about my hike; another said I was not allowed to stay in their campground.

At the edge of town on a gravel road in Latvia, a young man shouted at me from among a group of rowdy people in front of a dilapidated house and ran across the lawn in my direction. I felt threatened, kept walking and shouted back, "Canada." The weight of my backpack made it difficult to run, causing me to feel like a target, so I walked faster as I assumed bad people move more slowly than good people. By the time someone decided to do me harm, I would be half a kilometre down the road. But 99.9% of the people were wonderful, and I gave out several hundred Canada lapel pins in appreciation.

It's often a little thing that becomes the greatest joy or the greatest irritant. The latter – something I haven't yet mentioned in my ramblings – is the pouch holding my passport and credit card. This item, worn next to my body, came with a plastic catch that caused me no end of annoyance. My sensitivity to plastic led to an itchy red area on my right hip. In Europe I bought another one of these with a different design, but the problem continued. The issue was resolved by wearing the pouch over my t-shirt inside my shorts. Eventually the itching stopped.

In well over 200 days of walking, not once did I need to take a day off because of illness. That alone seems an accomplishment. At home I visit a chiropractor to reduce backaches, but on the trail my body felt content with the pressure of continuous exercise. I would worry over the damage the constant grind – with the added weight of the knapsack – might cause my hips and knees. I pictured those structures as staying healthy as long as the surrounding muscles were supportive, and I would think, "So far, so good."

Other than the irritation of blisters, my feet would be comfortable in their boots while I walked. However, when I stopped, they would beg to be taken out of the crush of that footwear. Way back on the Via de la Plata, Peter and I had met a hiker who was employed in an apothecary in Germany. She had professional knowledge about blisters and had found her own way of controlling them. With each stop, at a café for example, she would remove boots and socks, hang the socks to dry and put her bare feet on a chair to regain their blood flow. I followed her example, aiming for a table where my feet would be hidden from the view of other customers. And my feet would say, "Thank you."

My hike was a sport as it required physical exertion, mental stamina and a defined goal. It could be the perfect sport – perhaps an Olympic event – as it entailed no competition, no rules and, therefore, no need to cheat. Admittedly, a participant might be tempted to accept a driver's offer of a ride. I had a dozen such offers over the course of my journey and they would have shortened my hike and given me another opportunity to meet local people. However, my rule of walking every step forced me to decline, and my contact with drivers consisted solely of their honks and my waves. Frequently a vehicle would honk at me, and I would ponder: "What did that mean?" Short honks seemed friendly; long honks were annoying. I wouldn't be sure of the message but would respond with a friendly wave.

I estimated that a hike through the city took twice as long as a similar distance in the country, and I felt more tired at the end of such a stretch. Traffic, stoplights and distractions slowed my pace, and the search through cobwebs of side streets could be frustrating. In the town of Bourg, France, my guidebook sent me to "Rue Nationale" ("National Street"), which I assumed was a major highway. After a lengthy search and seeking direction from the tourism centre, I found this street, which was little more than an alley and just a few blocks long!

Walking in the city was troublesome; walking in the country, invigorating. I felt a sense of loss when a busy highway or approaching buildings disturbed the peaceful countryside, and I would wonder: "What will I experience this time? How irritating will I find the vehicles and sidewalks?"

Yet, rush hour traffic often gave me a feeling of self-satisfaction. While cars were creeping through traffic tie-ups, I would keep moving. I seemed to walk my fastest early in the morning and late in the afternoon, and during rush hour I would be zipping along at over five kilometres per hour, leaving the tail end of the line of cars far behind. In those line-ups the exhaust of European cars smelled different from Canadian exhaust. I wondered how their diet of biogas or liquefied natural gas affected their breath.

I must have put on my backpack 1,000 times during the course of my journey. I would check that all zippers were closed, swing it up behind me while putting my arms through the loops and adjust various snaps and straps. This should have become so automatic. Yet any distraction caused me to stop later and make the required adjustments: it took my full attention to get everything right.

By the time I reached Narva-Jõesuu, the heels of the fourth pair of hiking boots of my journey were worn to the seams; my orange and black knapsack looked faded; my dark blue jacket and trouser set appeared worn. My two t-shirts, a red and a blue, were showing their age. Wearing my simple outfit every day – t-shirt with black or navy blue shorts or with trousers – had required little pondering over choice of work clothes. Those items, and all the others, had become dear to me as if to say, "We've been through a lot together." I miss them.

Adapting to about 200 different beds was easier than I would have thought; somehow, I could put my fussiness aside in accepting the rigours of the trail. Then, upon my return home, I would have trouble sleeping in my own bed, and the first few nights would be filled with images of Europe. I might marvel at a beautiful Portuguese tile floor when I realized it was the floor in our own bathroom. This was another side effect of my long-distance hiking mania.

On its surface the process of sliding back into a routine life in Dorchester Cape was simple – our children were to be visited, groceries needed to be bought, kitchen garbage had to be emptied. I appreciated the comfort of routine; I welcomed not having to check my compass at every turn – a compass that was no longer in my pocket in any case since my European search was now over. Then, walking through a store or along a sidewalk or on the beach, the giddiness would drift in. I would remind myself, "I really did it," and life continued as before, but now with a hint of grieving the end of my journey – a journey that taught me about my dreams, my hopes, my fears, myself.

Joanne joined me in retirement, and we continued with our urge to travel by visiting eight countries in a trip of three and a half months. Then we settled into a quiet life at home while keeping busy with Tantramar Seniors' College courses. Together we have taken a ballroom dancing course (including polkas!), gone on colourful fall hikes and learned to make hypertufa garden pots. I have taken introductory Spanish (a bit late for my hike on the Camino!), learned to play the penny whistle and dabbled in little theatre. And, of course, our children and grandchildren are a constant source of delight.

I have published the story of my childhood, "Looking for Bill, Finding Myself," which is distributed through Tidewater Books in Sackville, New Brunswick. The writing of that book and my hike occurred over the same six-year period, with each activity dependent on the other. My reveries on the 6,000-kilometre journey and the writing of that memoir helped resolve 50 years of turmoil around my late brother Bill. Now I can turn my attention to the less intense pursuit of publishing "Bemusings," my book of rambling thoughts.

In fulfilling my dream of hiking across Europe from southwest Portugal to northeast Estonia, I came to terms with my past. The anxieties of childhood are resolved, and I feel comfortable with myself as I settle into retirement. And yet, my dreams continue. Now I imagine a follow-up journey – a trek from Denmark southward to Greece – as another adventure in crossing Europe, one step at a time.

www.ingramcontent.com/pod-product-compliance
Lightning Source LLC
Chambersburg PA
CBHW071204090426
42736CB00014B/2711